FAIRY TAIL
100 YEARS QUEST
10 CONTENTS

FAIRY TAIL
100 YEARS QUEST
10

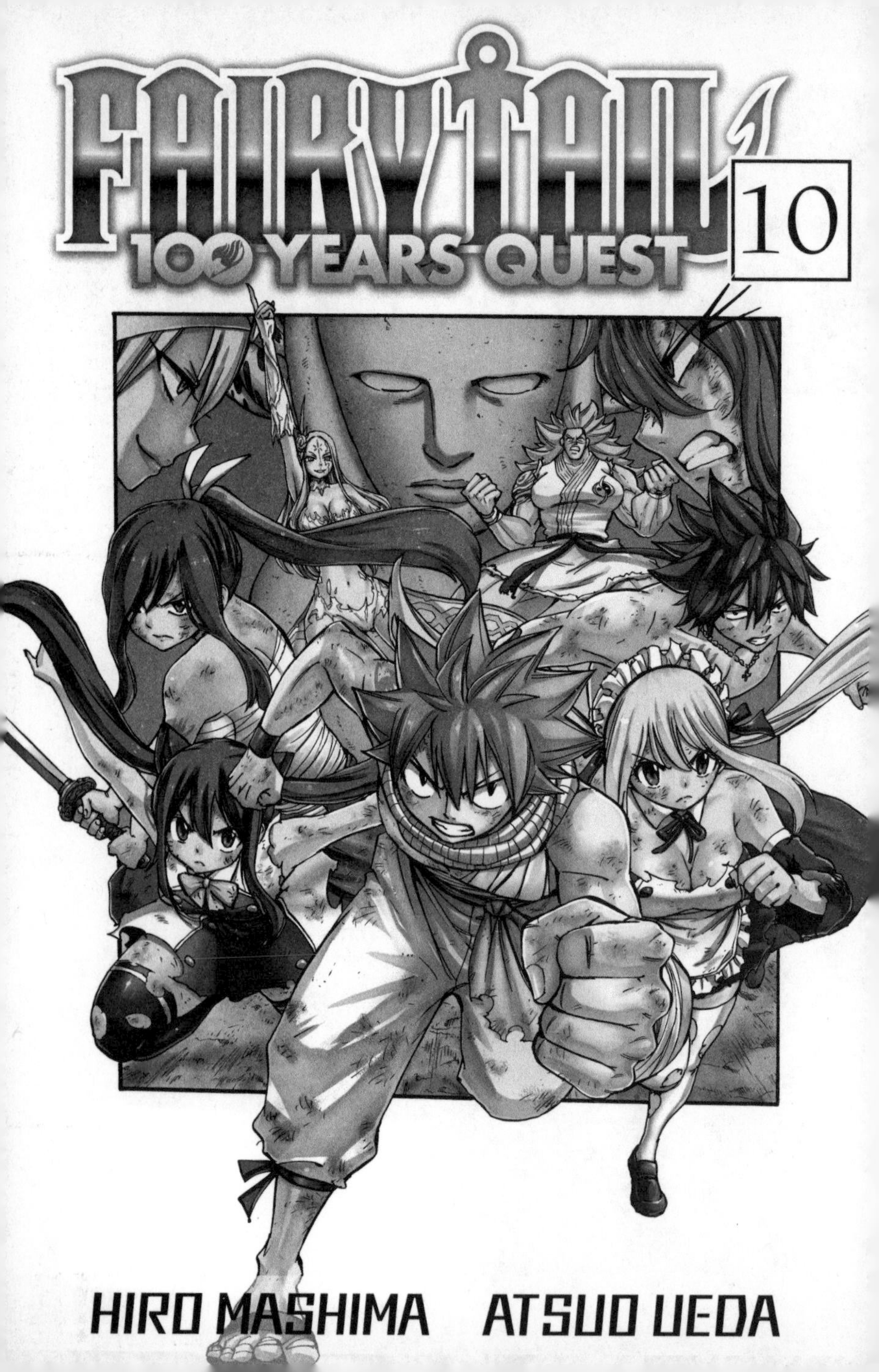

HIRO MASHIMA ATSUO UEDA

FAIRY TAIL 100 YEARS QUEST

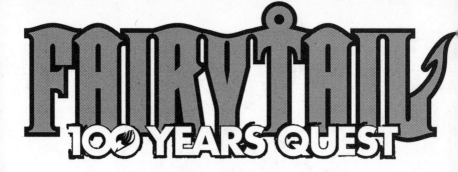

Chapter 82: Rematch

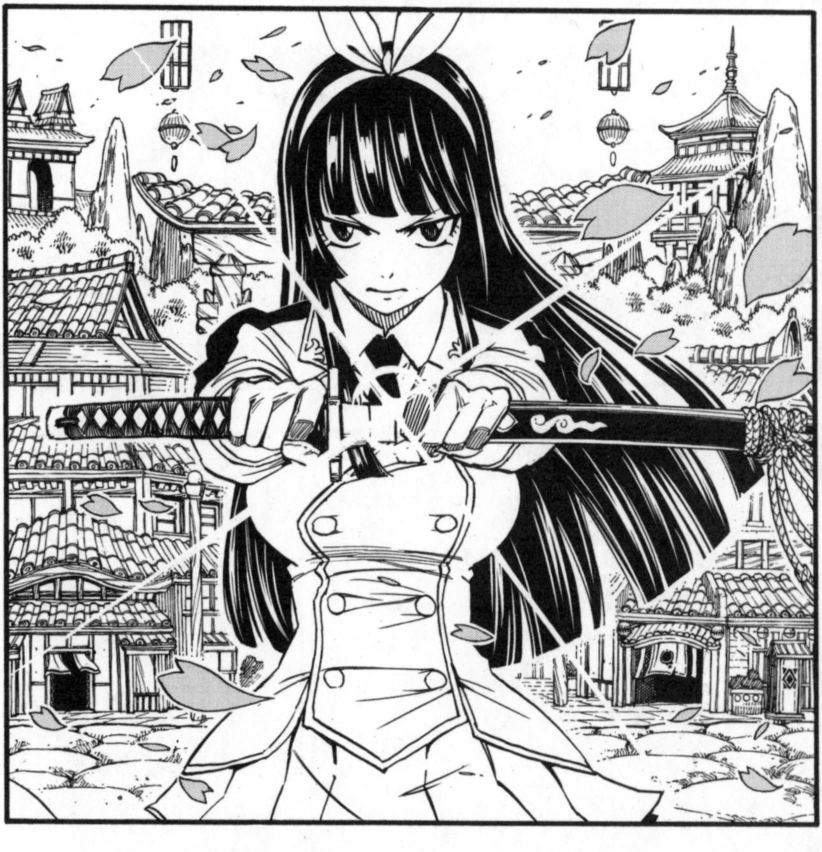

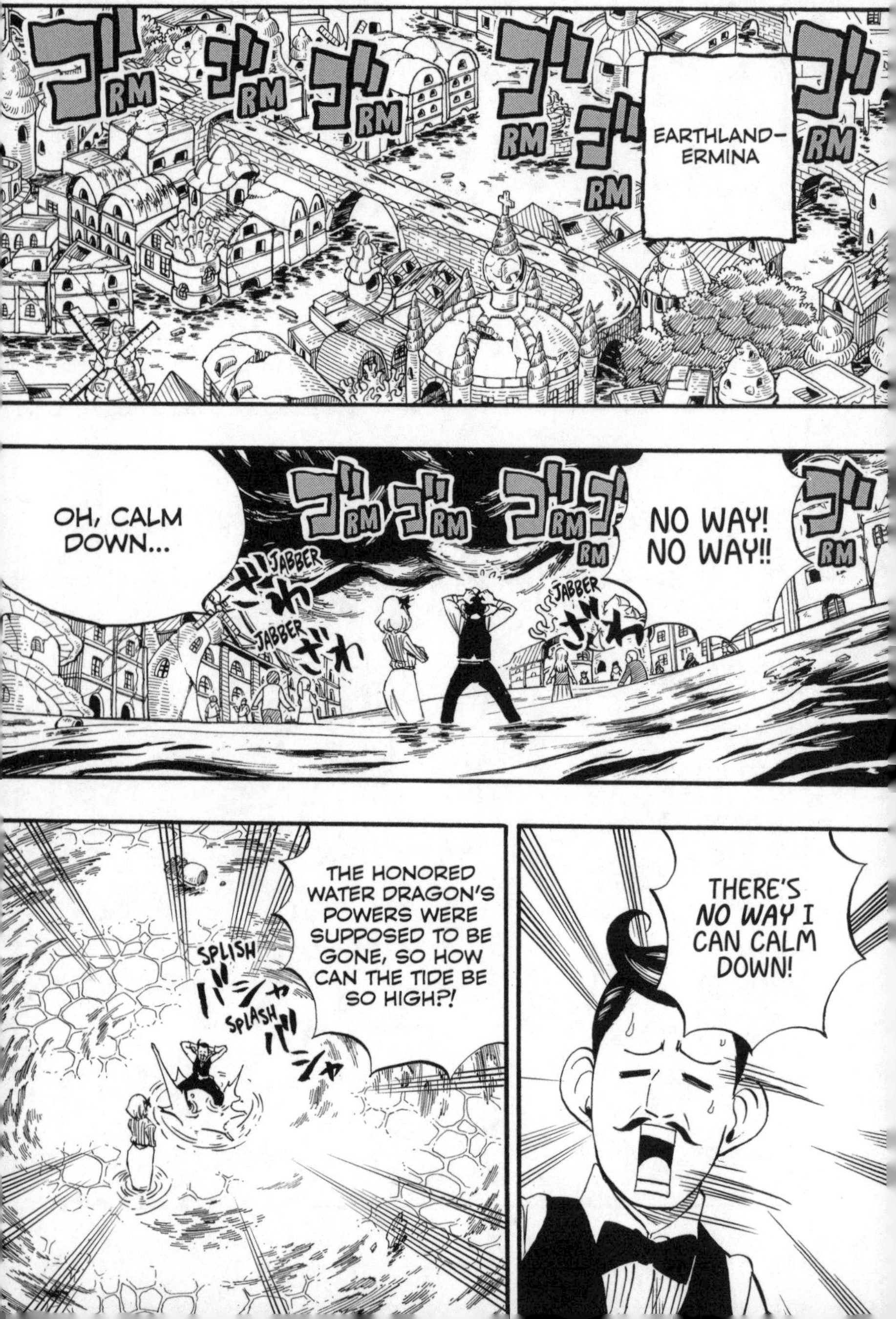
RM
EARTHLAND—ERMINA
RM
RM
RM
RM
RM
RM
NO WAY! NO WAY!!
RM
RM
JABBER ざわ
RM
RM
RM
JABBER ざわ
JABBER ざわ
OH, CALM DOWN...
THERE'S *NO WAY* I CAN CALM DOWN!
THE HONORED WATER DRAGON'S POWERS WERE SUPPOSED TO BE GONE, SO HOW CAN THE TIDE BE SO HIGH?!
SPLISH バシャ
SPLASH バシャ

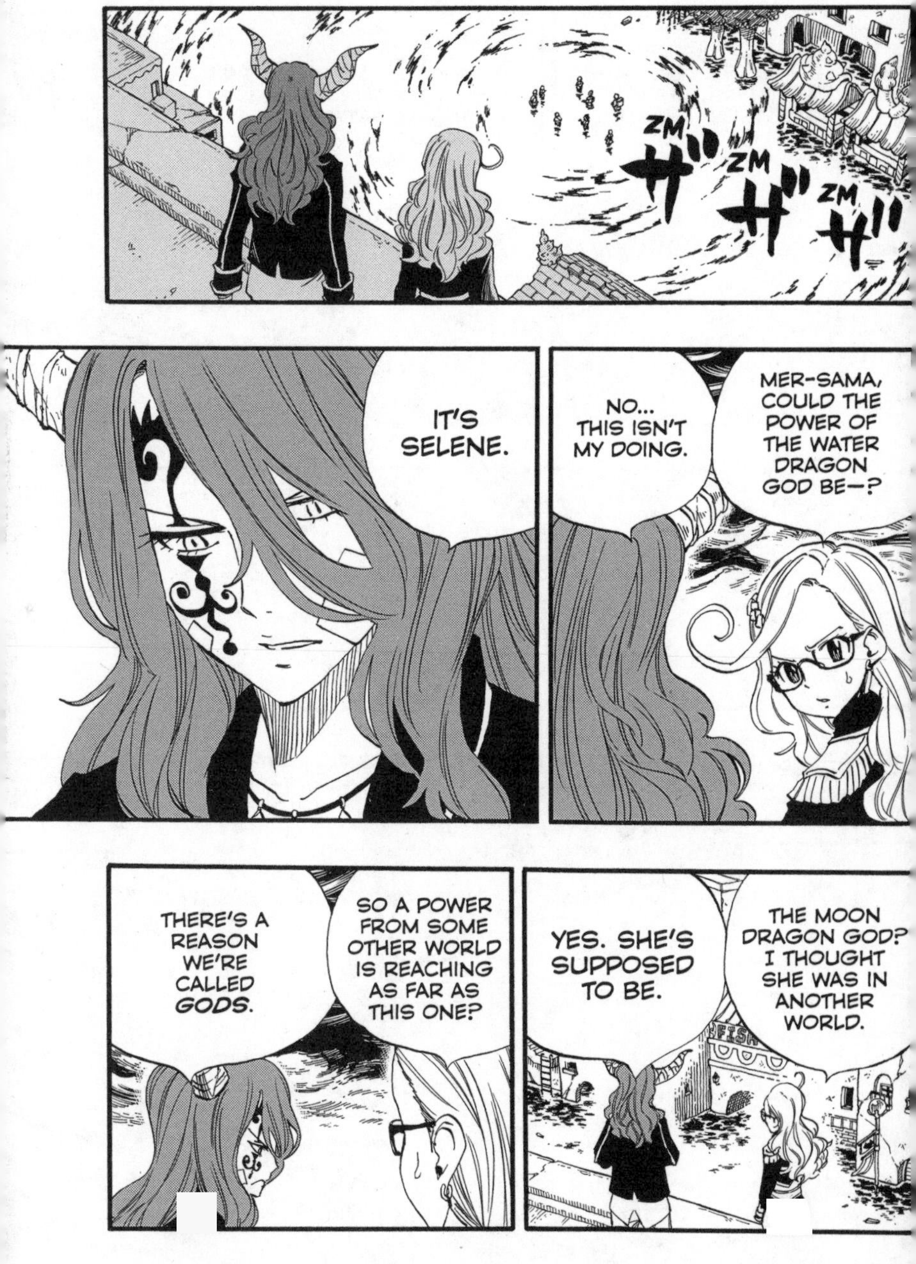
ZM
ZM
ZM
MER-SAMA, COULD THE POWER OF THE WATER DRAGON GOD BE—?
NO... THIS ISN'T MY DOING.
IT'S SELENE.
THE MOON DRAGON GOD? I THOUGHT SHE WAS IN ANOTHER WORLD.
FISH
YES. SHE'S SUPPOSED TO BE.
SO A POWER FROM SOME OTHER WORLD IS REACHING AS FAR AS THIS ONE?
THERE'S A REASON WE'RE CALLED *GODS*.

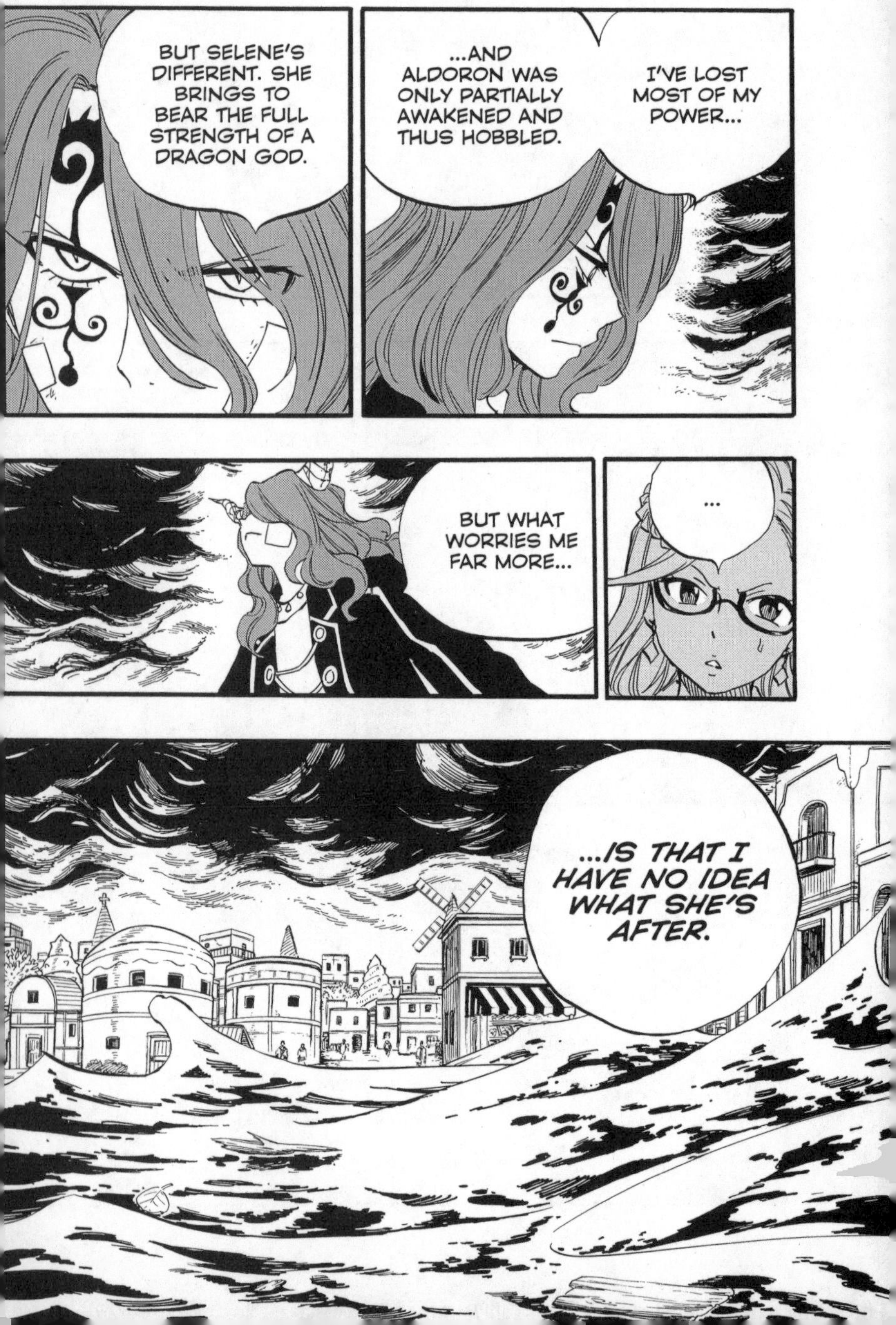
I'VE LOST MOST OF MY POWER...
...AND ALDORON WAS ONLY PARTIALLY AWAKENED AND THUS HOBBLED.
BUT SELENE'S DIFFERENT. SHE BRINGS TO BEAR THE FULL STRENGTH OF A DRAGON GOD.
...
BUT WHAT WORRIES ME FAR MORE...
...*IS THAT I HAVE NO IDEA WHAT SHE'S AFTER.*

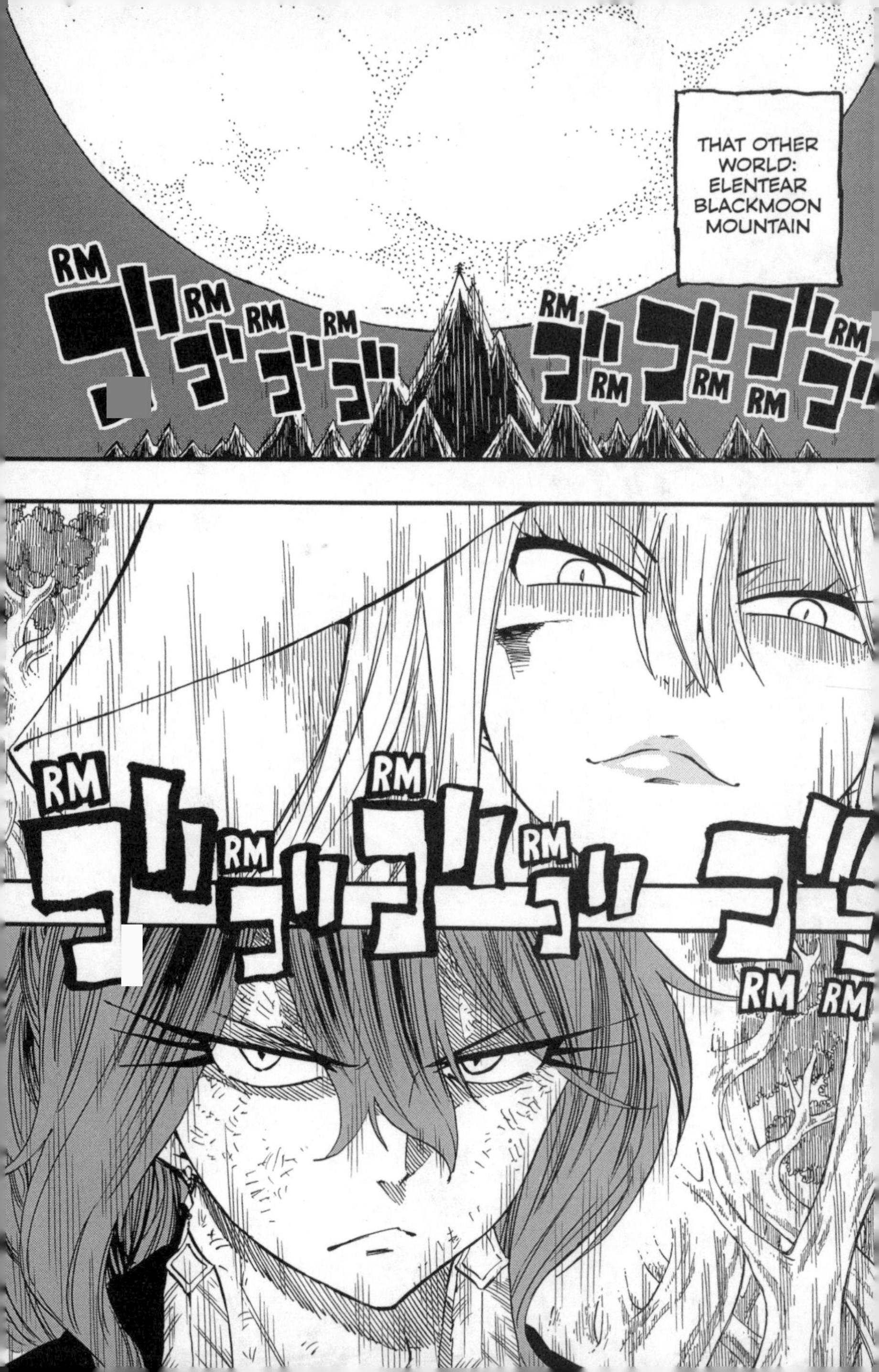
THAT OTHER WORLD: ELENTEAR BLACKMOON MOUNTAIN
RM
RM
RM
RM
RM
RM
RM
RM
RM
RM
RM
RM
RM
RM
RM
RM

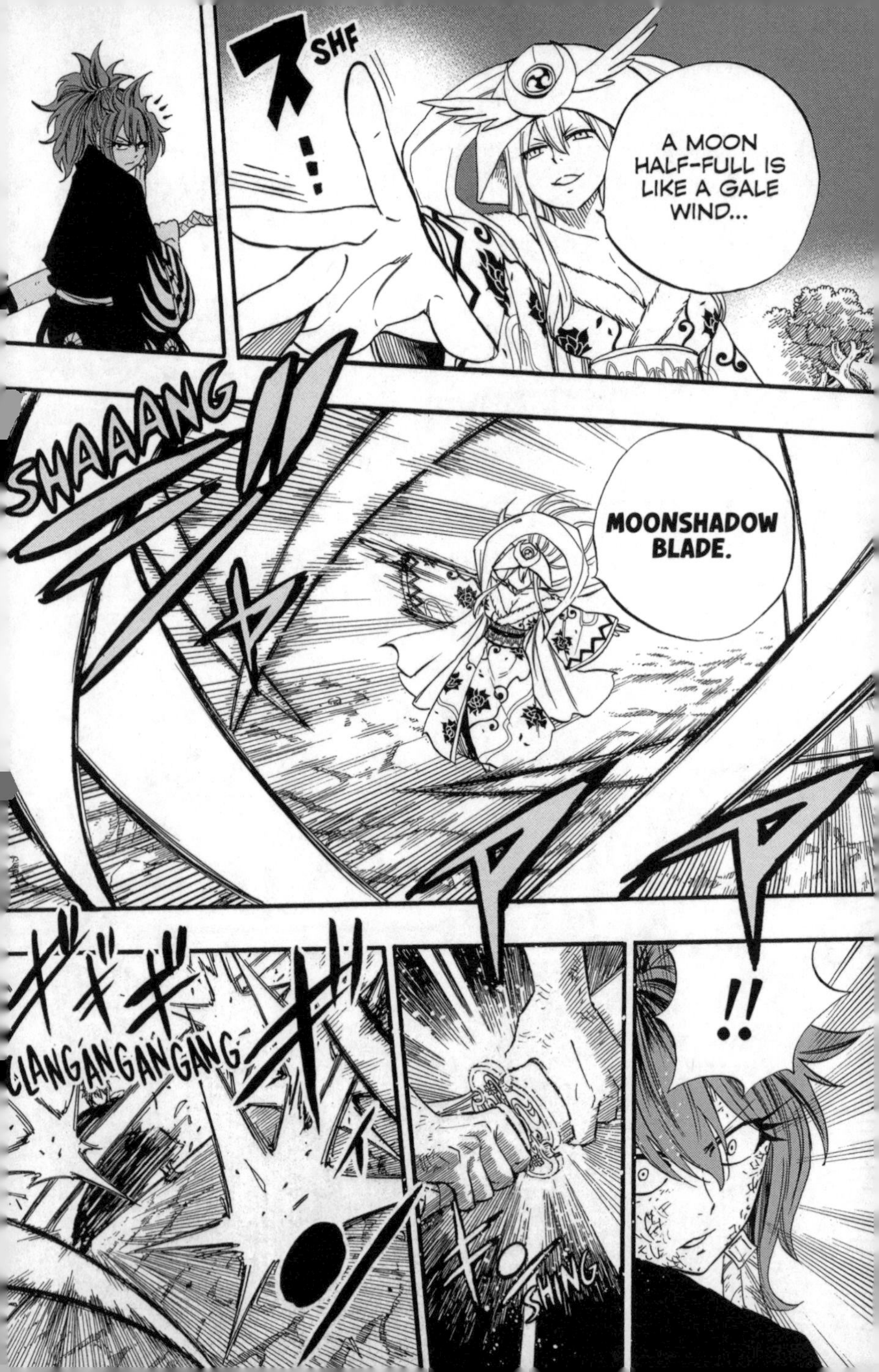
A MOON HALF-FULL IS LIKE A GALE WIND...
SHF
SHAAANG
MOONSHADOW BLADE.
!!
SHING
CLANGANGANGANG

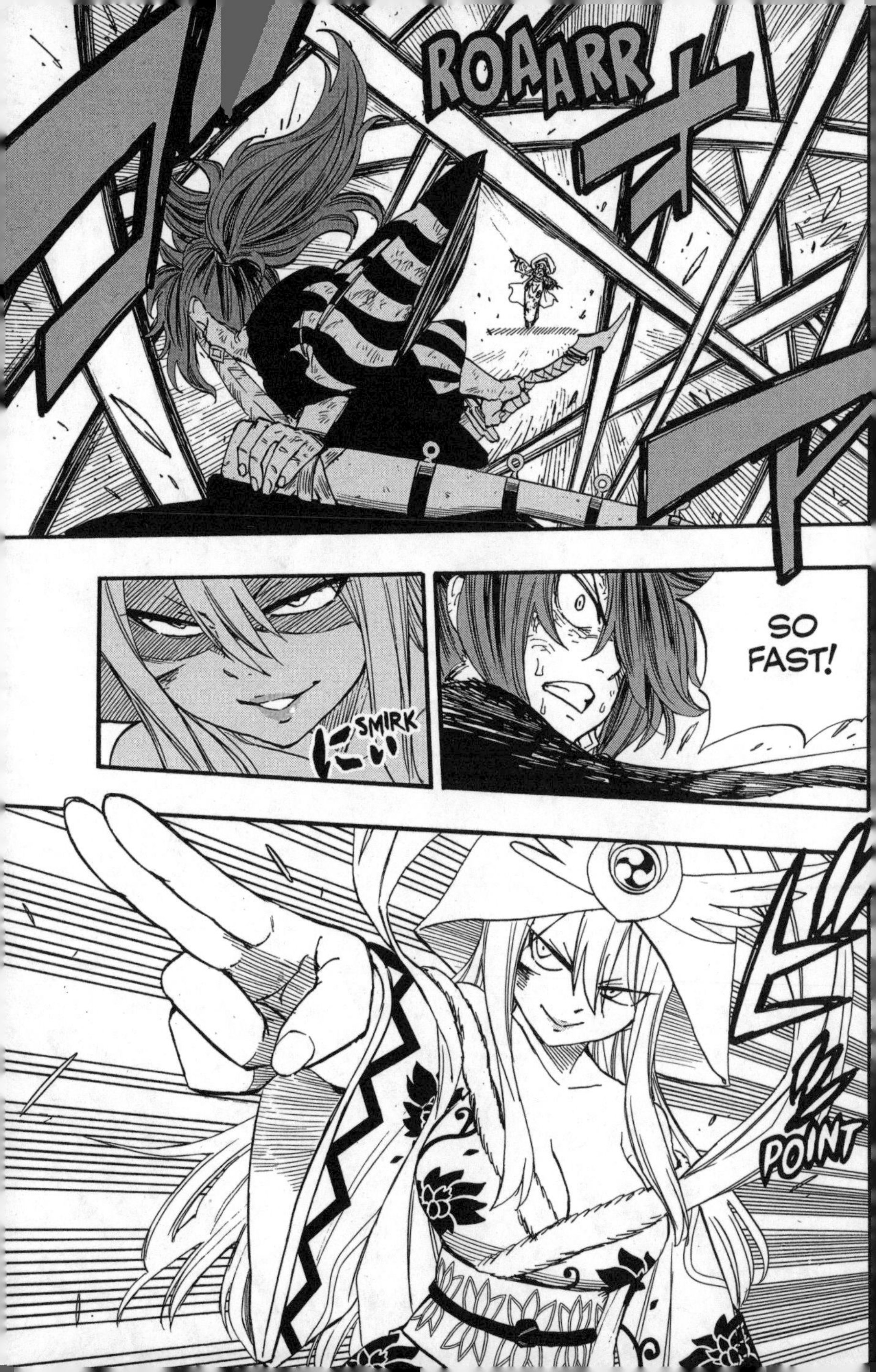
ROAARR
SO FAST!
SMIRK
POINT

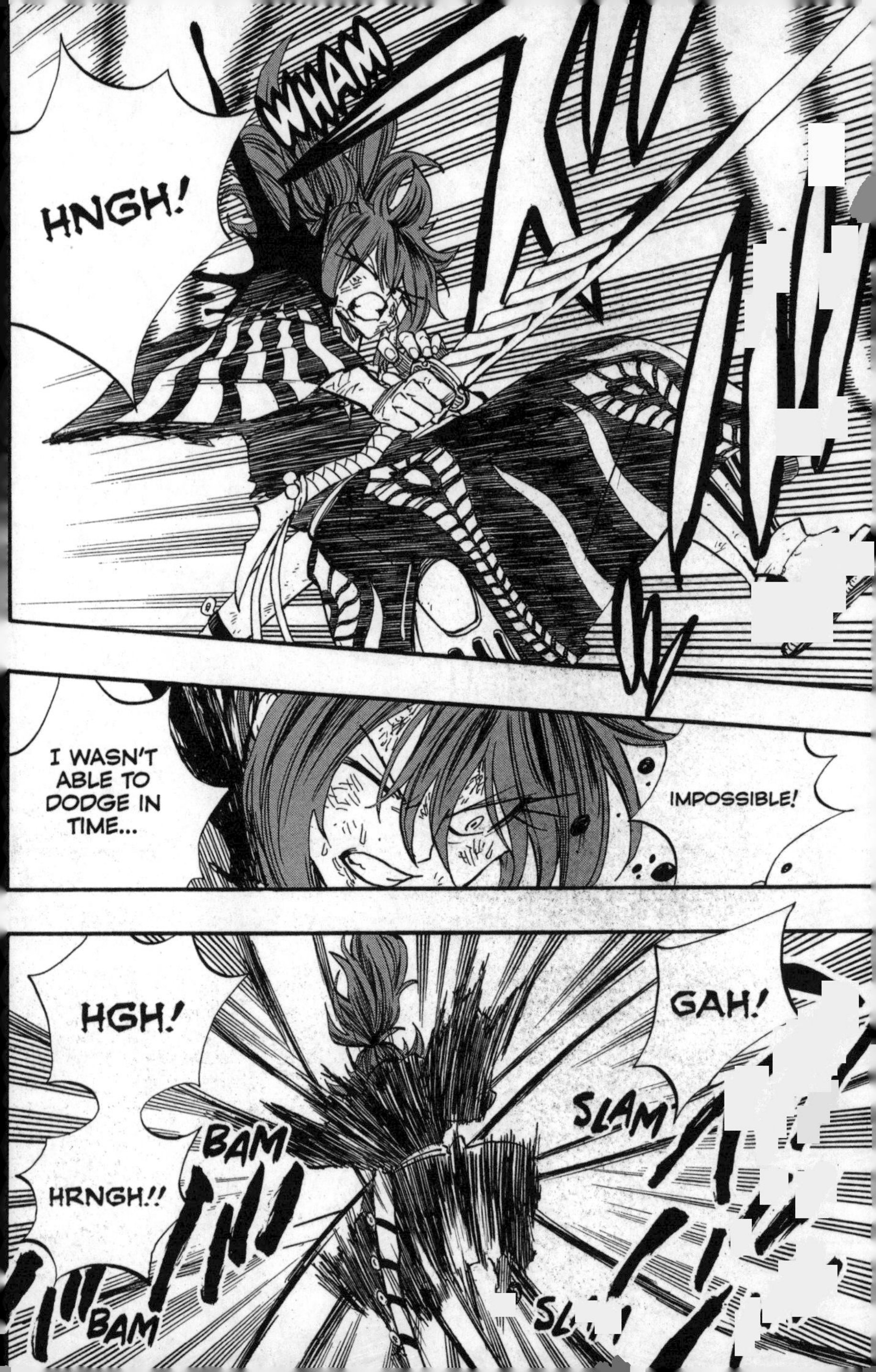
WHAM
HNGH!
IMPOSSIBLE!
I WASN'T ABLE TO DODGE IN TIME...
GAH!
SLAM
HGH!
BAM
HRNGH!!
BAM

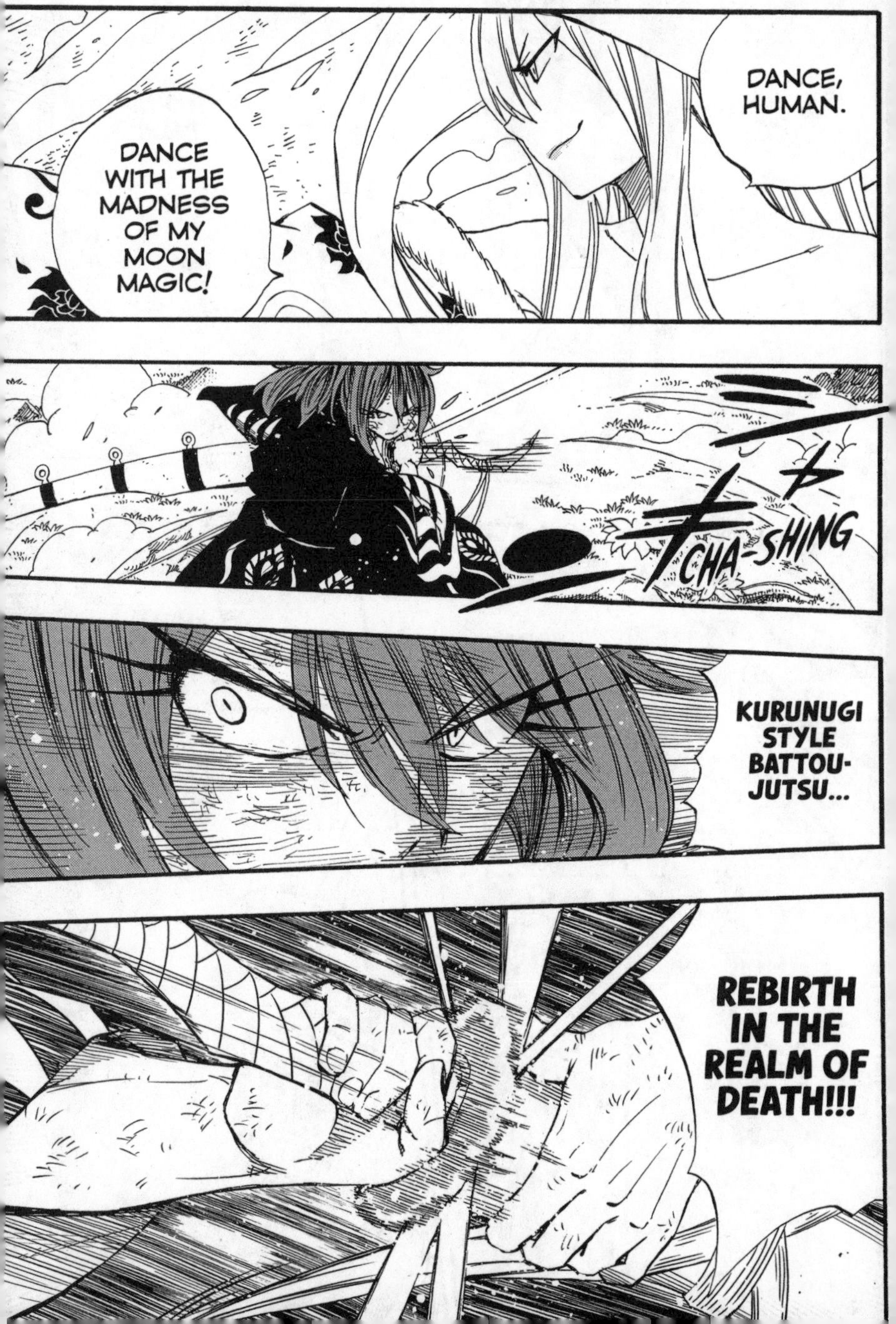
DANCE, HUMAN.
DANCE WITH THE MADNESS OF MY MOON MAGIC!
CHA-SHING
KURUNUGI STYLE BATTOU-JUTSU...
REBIRTH IN THE REALM OF DEATH!!!

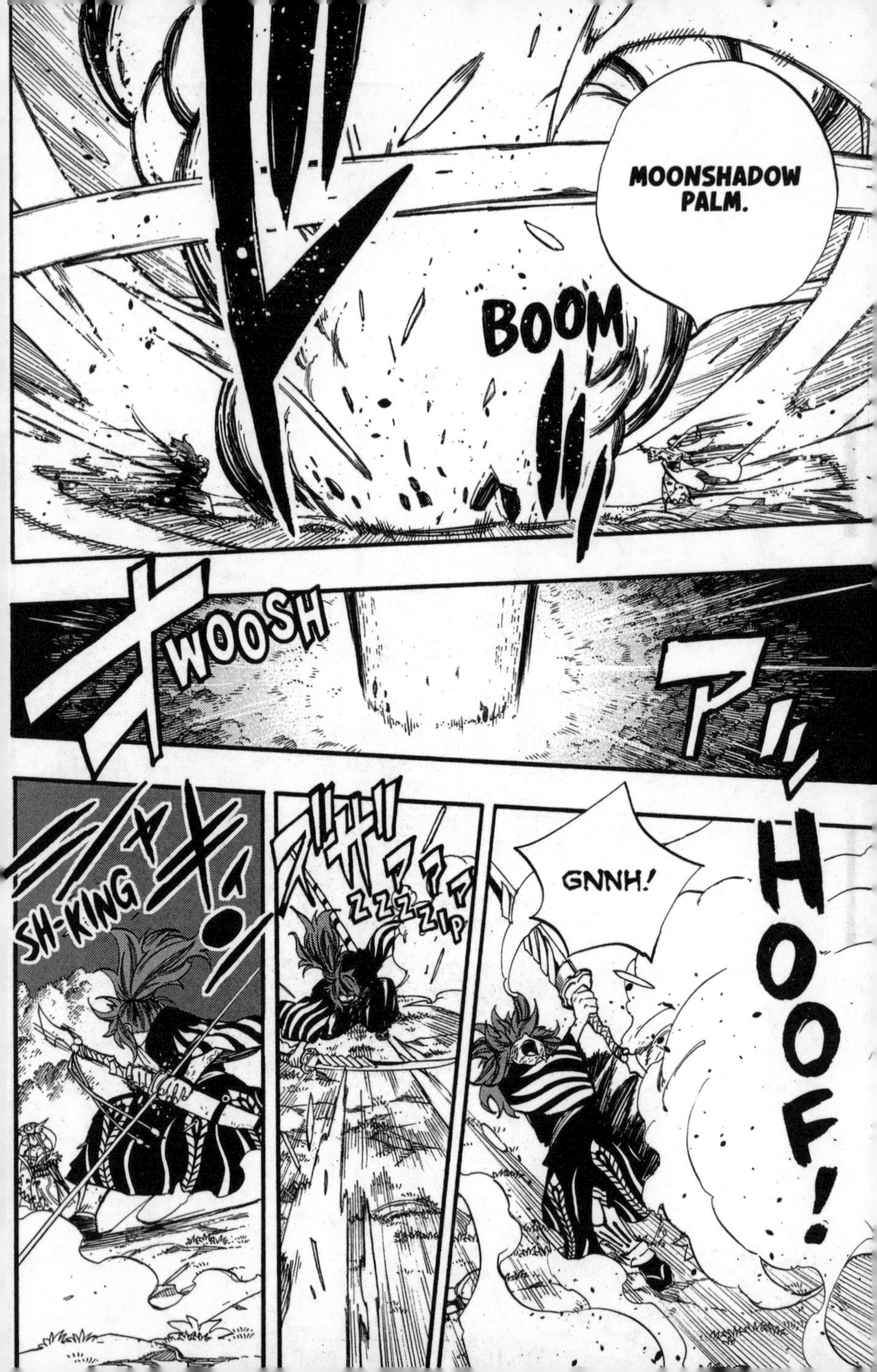
MOONSHADOW PALM.
BOOM
WOOSH
HOOF!
GNNH!
ZZZZZIP
SH-KING

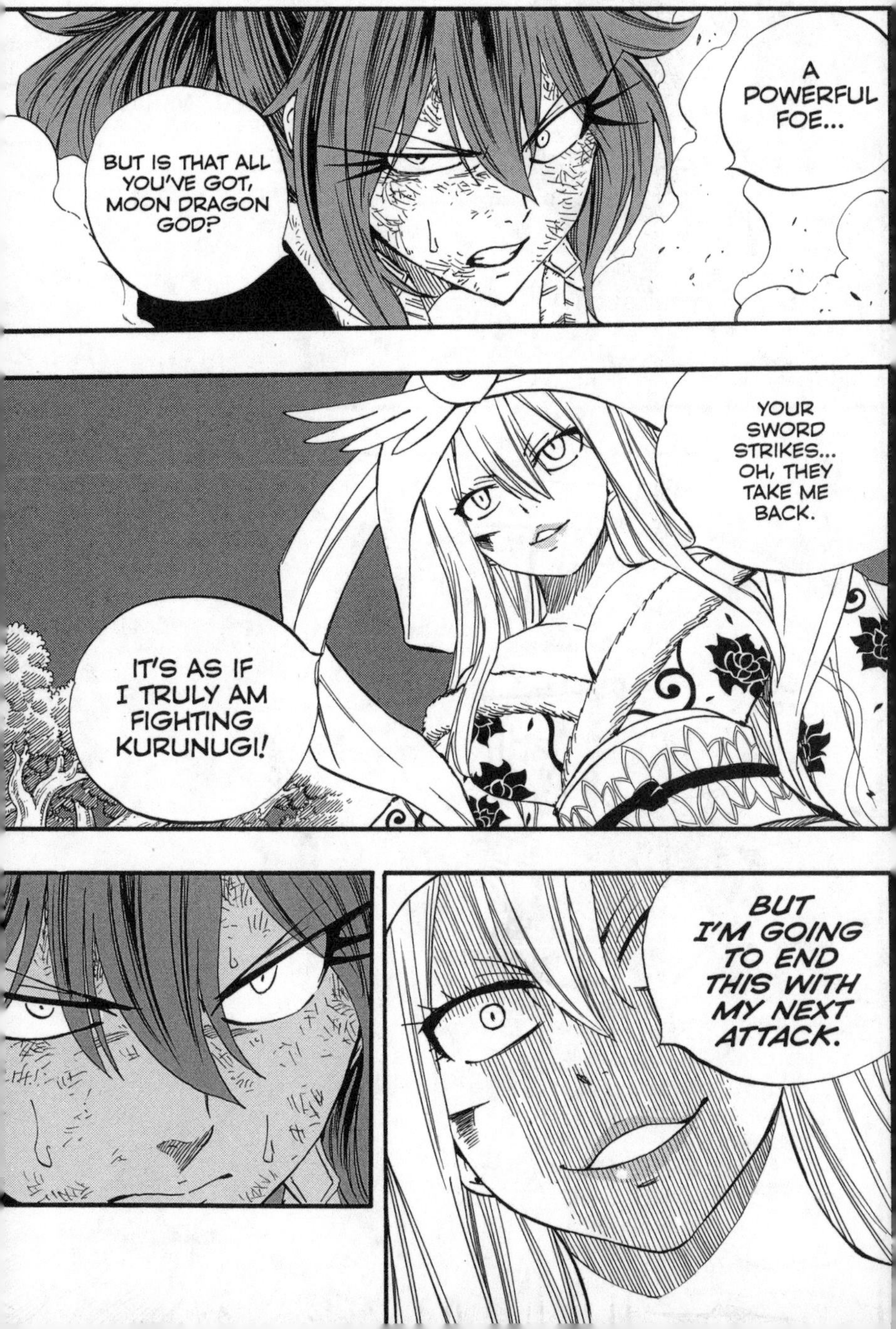
A POWERFUL FOE...
BUT IS THAT ALL YOU'VE GOT, MOON DRAGON GOD?
YOUR SWORD STRIKES... OH, THEY TAKE ME BACK.
IT'S AS IF I TRULY AM FIGHTING KURUNUGI!
BUT I'M GOING TO END THIS WITH MY NEXT ATTACK.

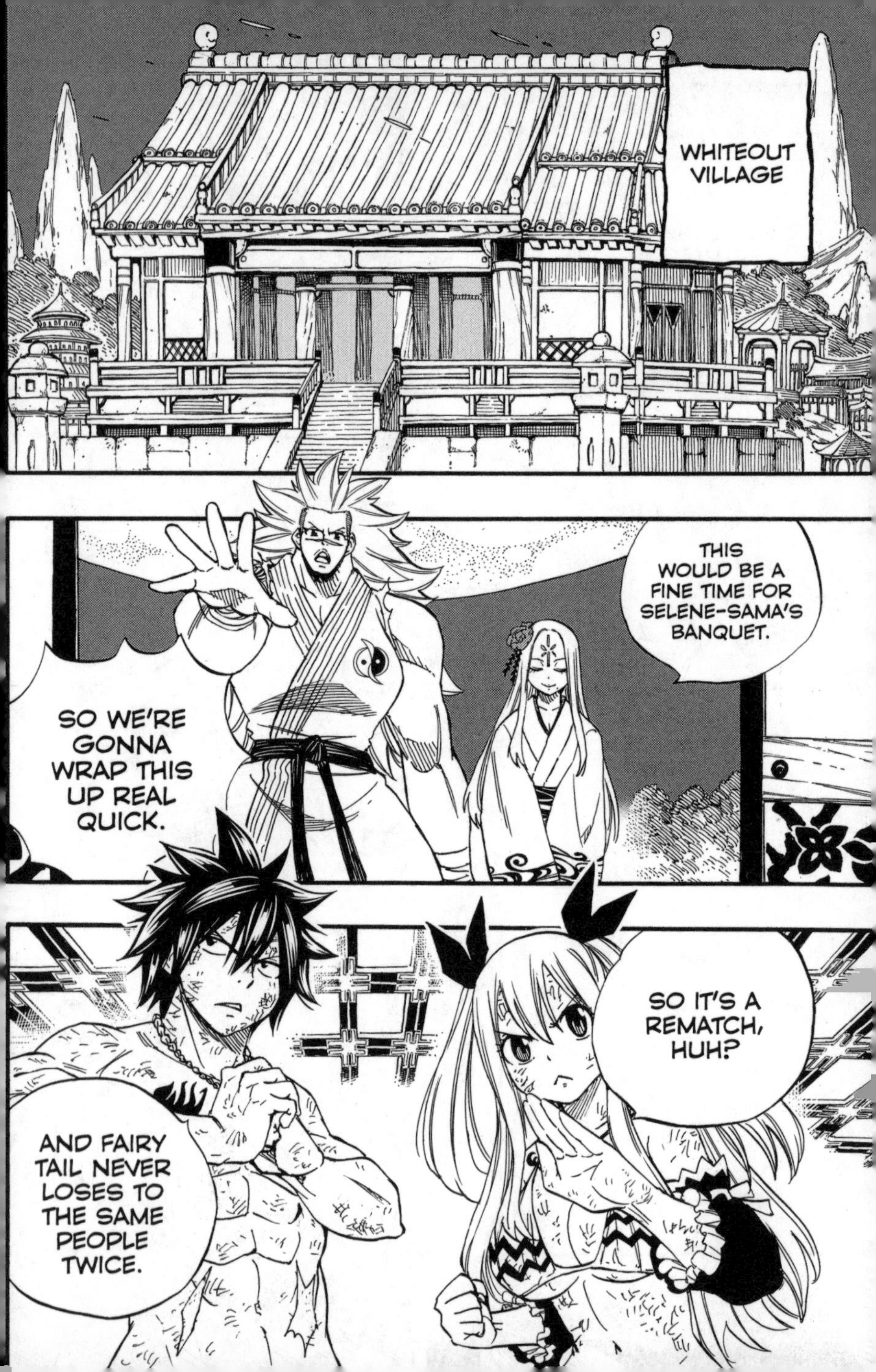
WHITEOUT VILLAGE
THIS WOULD BE A FINE TIME FOR SELENE-SAMA'S BANQUET.
SO WE'RE GONNA WRAP THIS UP REAL QUICK.
SO IT'S A REMATCH, HUH?
AND FAIRY TAIL NEVER LOSES TO THE SAME PEOPLE TWICE.

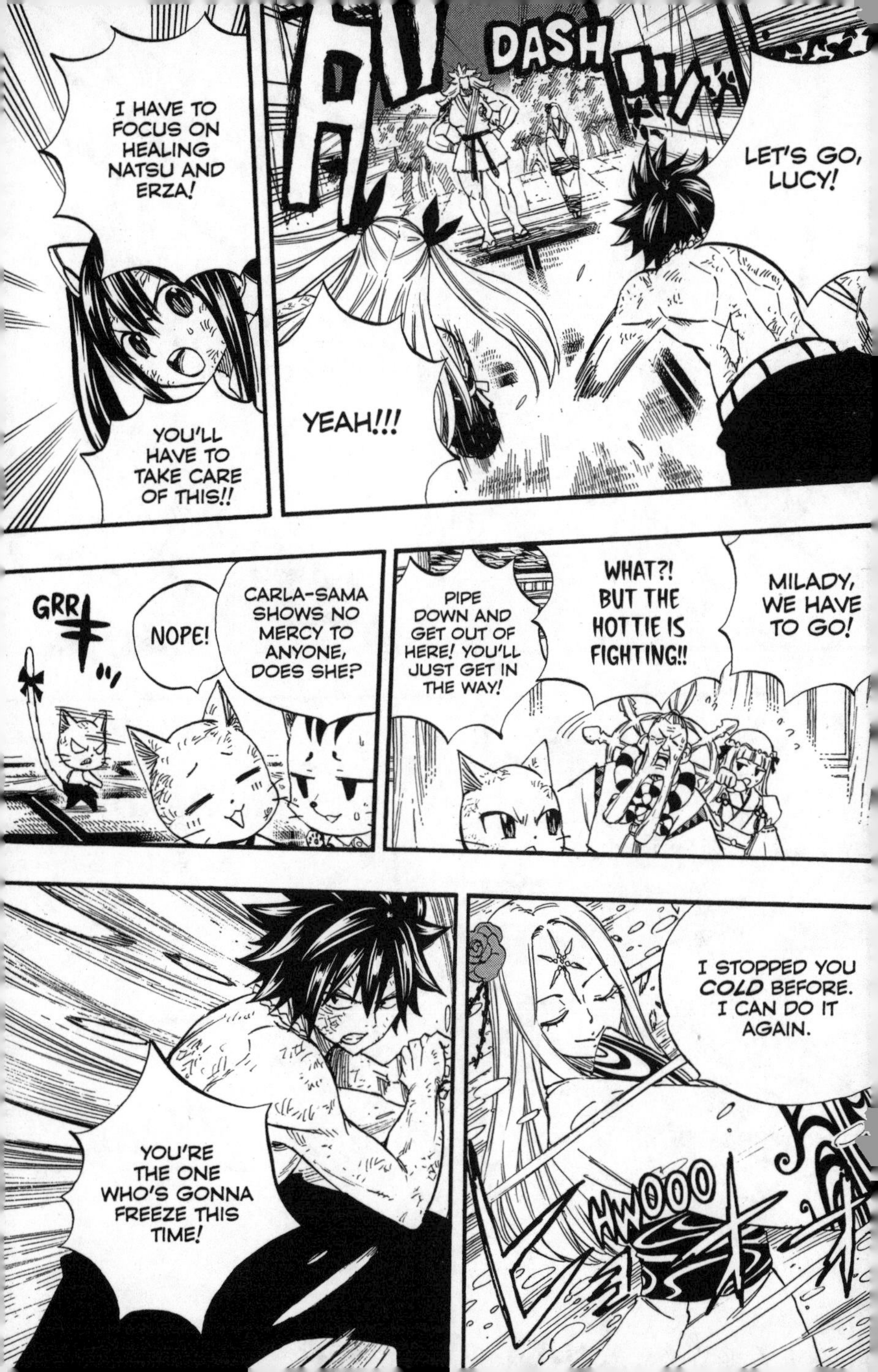
DASH
LET'S GO, LUCY!
YEAH!!!
I HAVE TO FOCUS ON HEALING NATSU AND ERZA!
YOU'LL HAVE TO TAKE CARE OF THIS!!
MILADY, WE HAVE TO GO!
WHAT?! BUT THE HOTTIE IS FIGHTING!!
PIPE DOWN AND GET OUT OF HERE! YOU'LL JUST GET IN THE WAY!
CARLA-SAMA SHOWS NO MERCY TO ANYONE, DOES SHE?
NOPE!
GRR
I STOPPED YOU *COLD* BEFORE. I CAN DO IT AGAIN.
HWOOO
YOU'RE THE ONE WHO'S GONNA FREEZE THIS TIME!

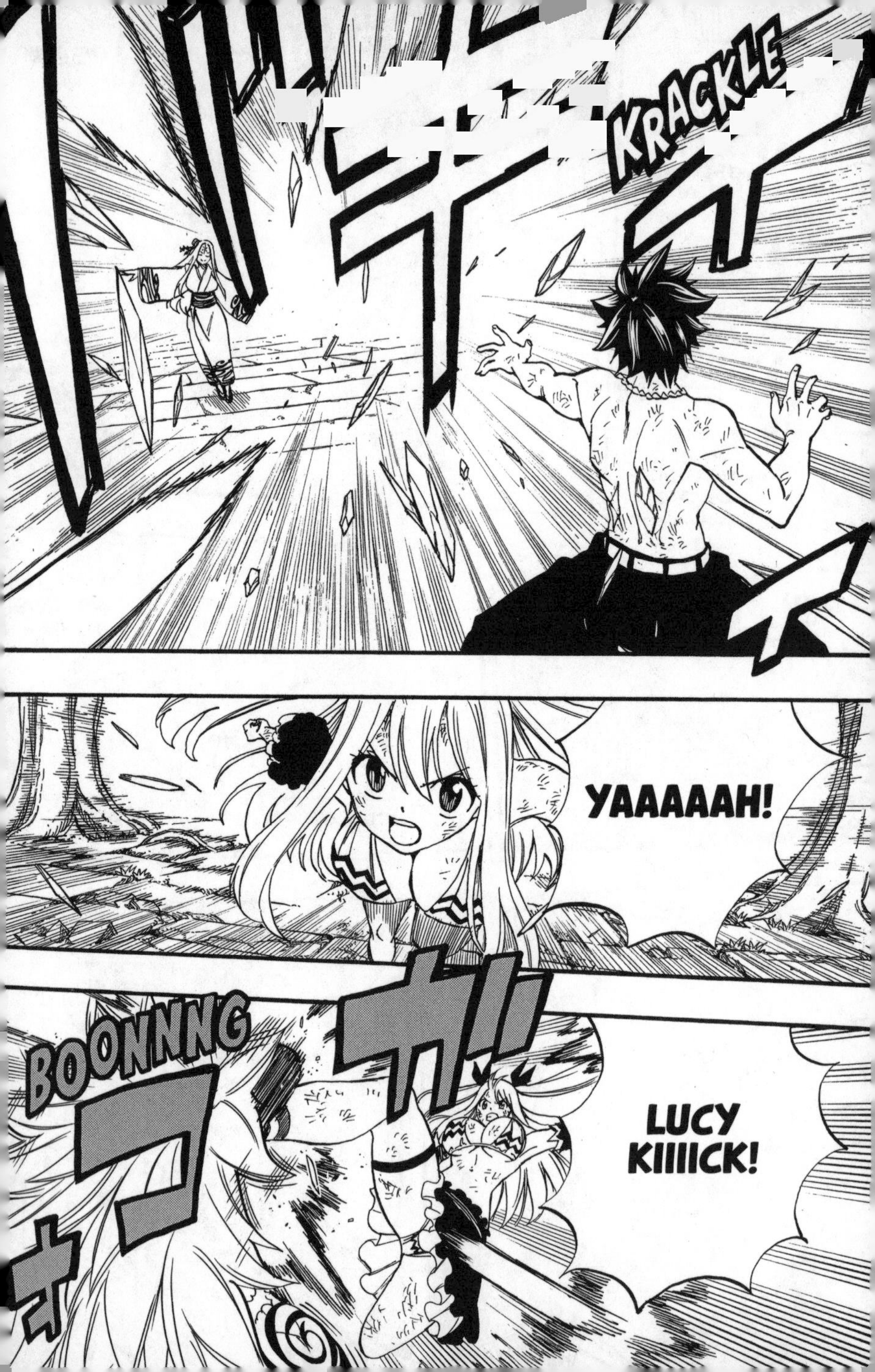
KRACKLE
YAAAAAH!
BOONNNG
LUCY KIIIICK!

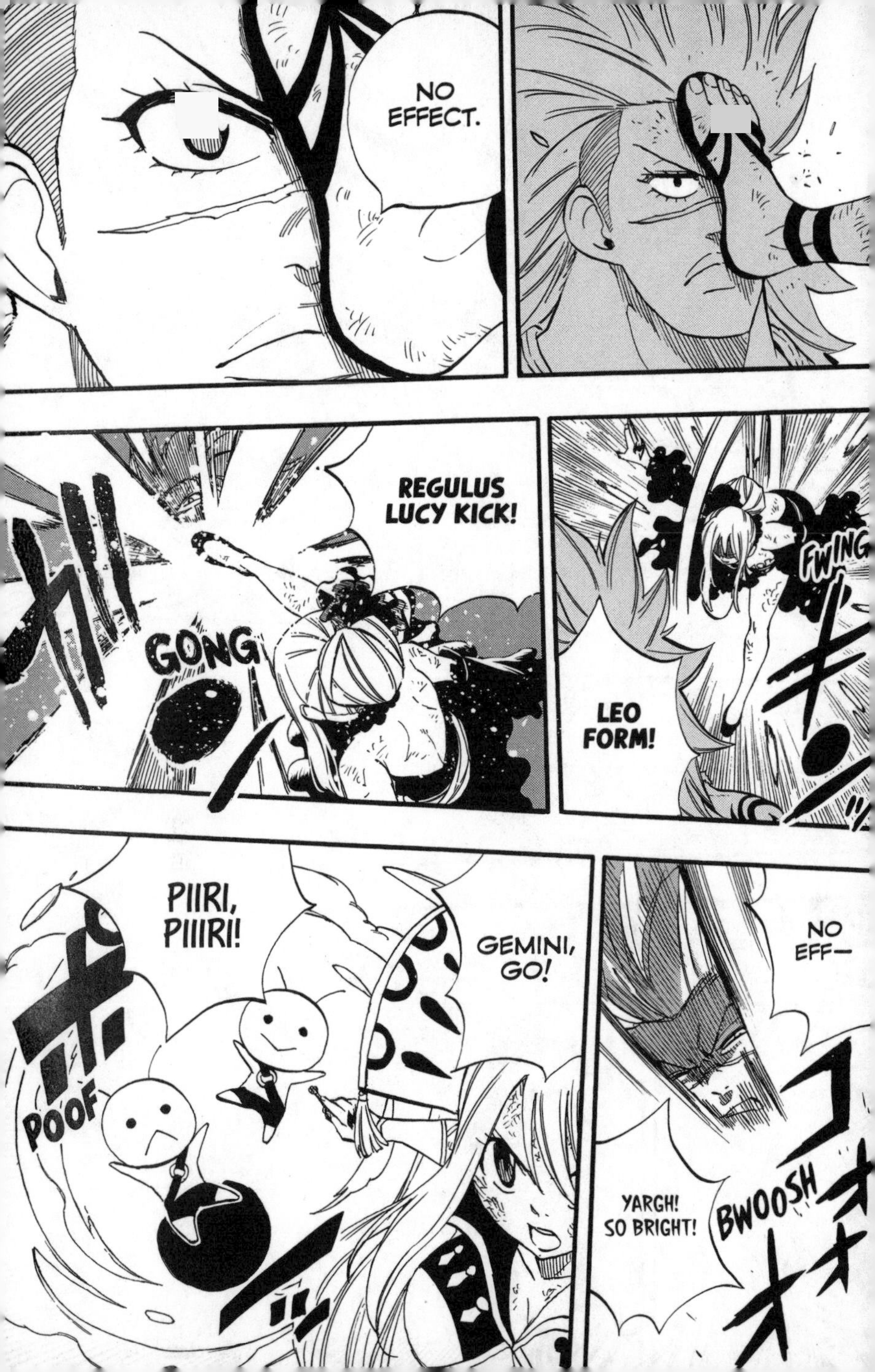
NO EFFECT.
FWING
LEO FORM!
REGULUS LUCY KICK!
GONG
NO EFF—
YARGH! SO BRIGHT!
BWOOSH
GEMINI, GO!
PIIRI, PIIIRI!
POOF

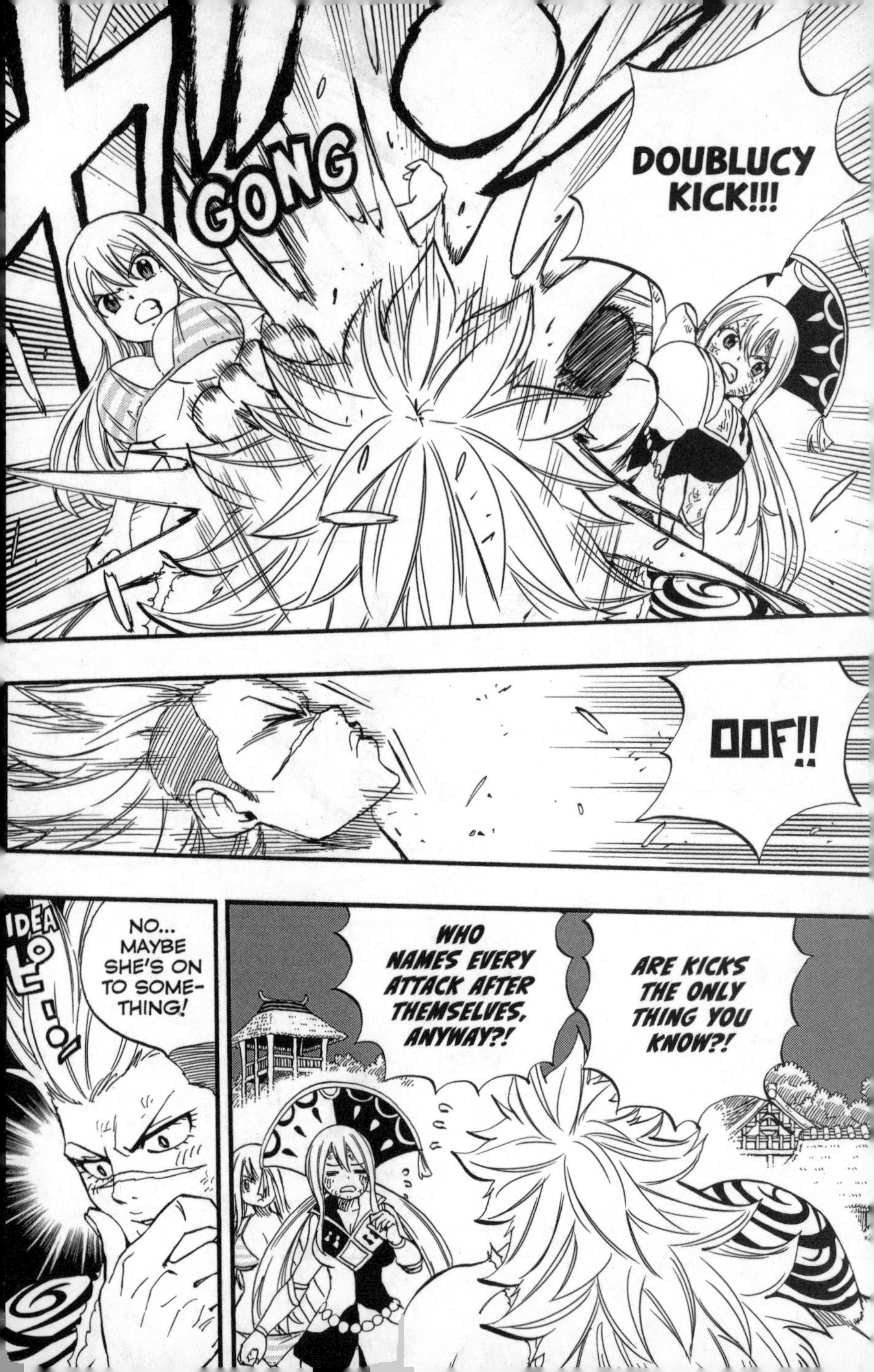
DOUBLUCY KICK!!!
GONG
OOF!!
ARE KICKS THE ONLY THING YOU KNOW?!
WHO NAMES EVERY ATTACK AFTER THEMSELVES, ANYWAY?!
NO... MAYBE SHE'S ON TO SOME-THING!
IDEA

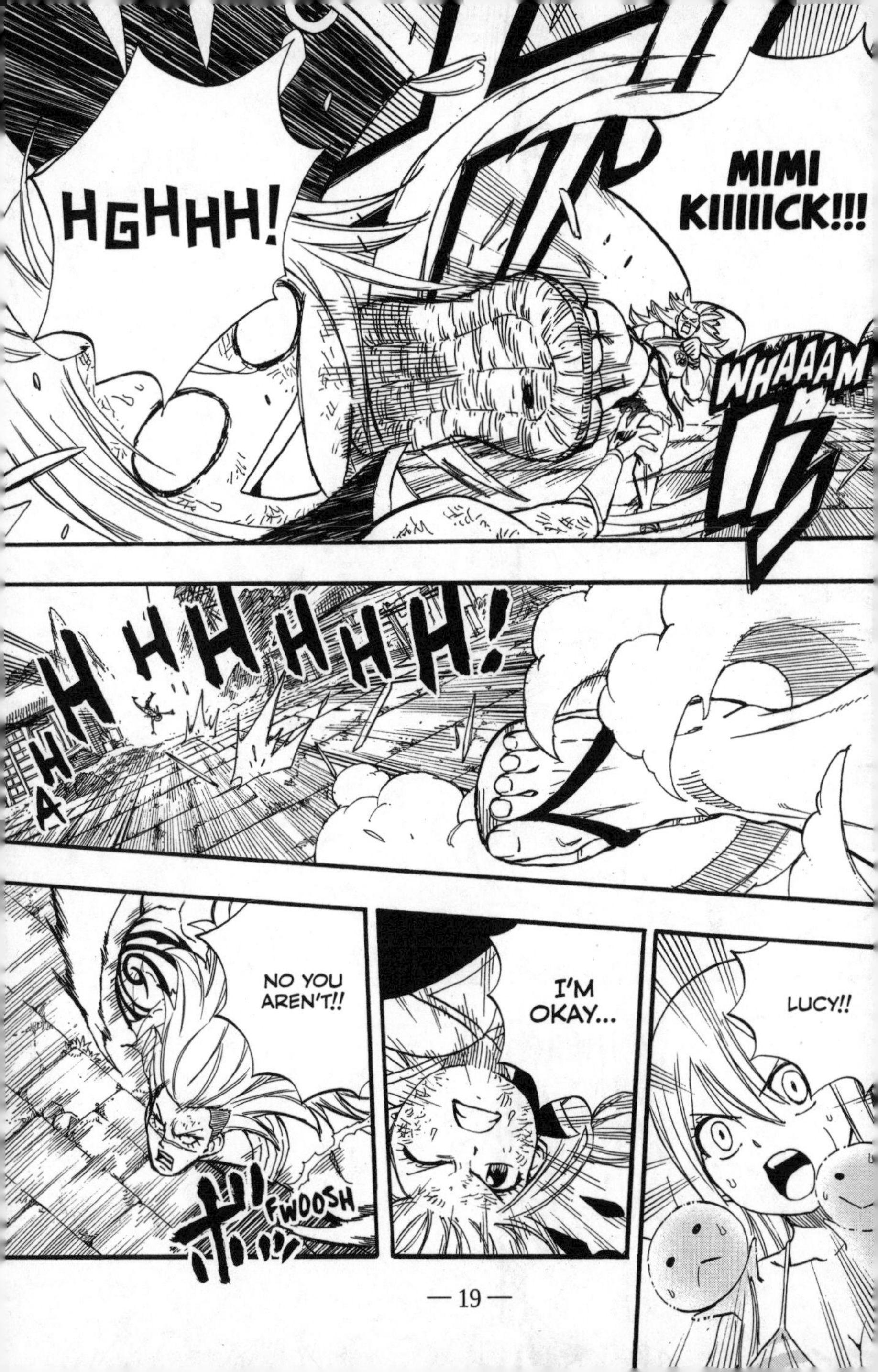
MIMI KIIIIICK!!!
HGHHH!
WHAAAM
AHHHHHHHH!
LUCY!!
I'M OKAY...
NO YOU AREN'T!!
FWOOSH

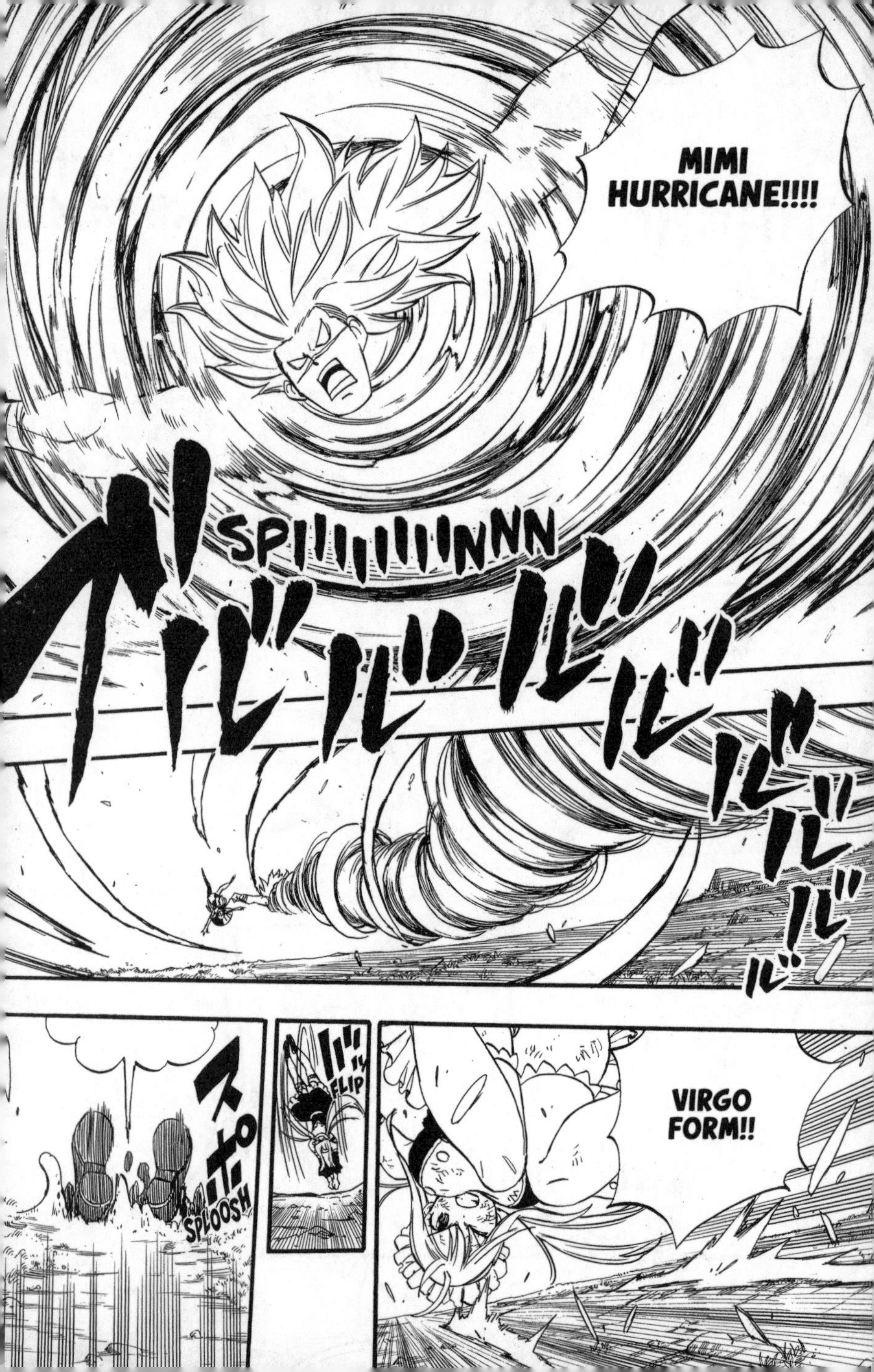
MIMI HURRICANE!!!!
SPIIIIIIINNN
VIRGO FORM!!
FLIP
SPLOOSH

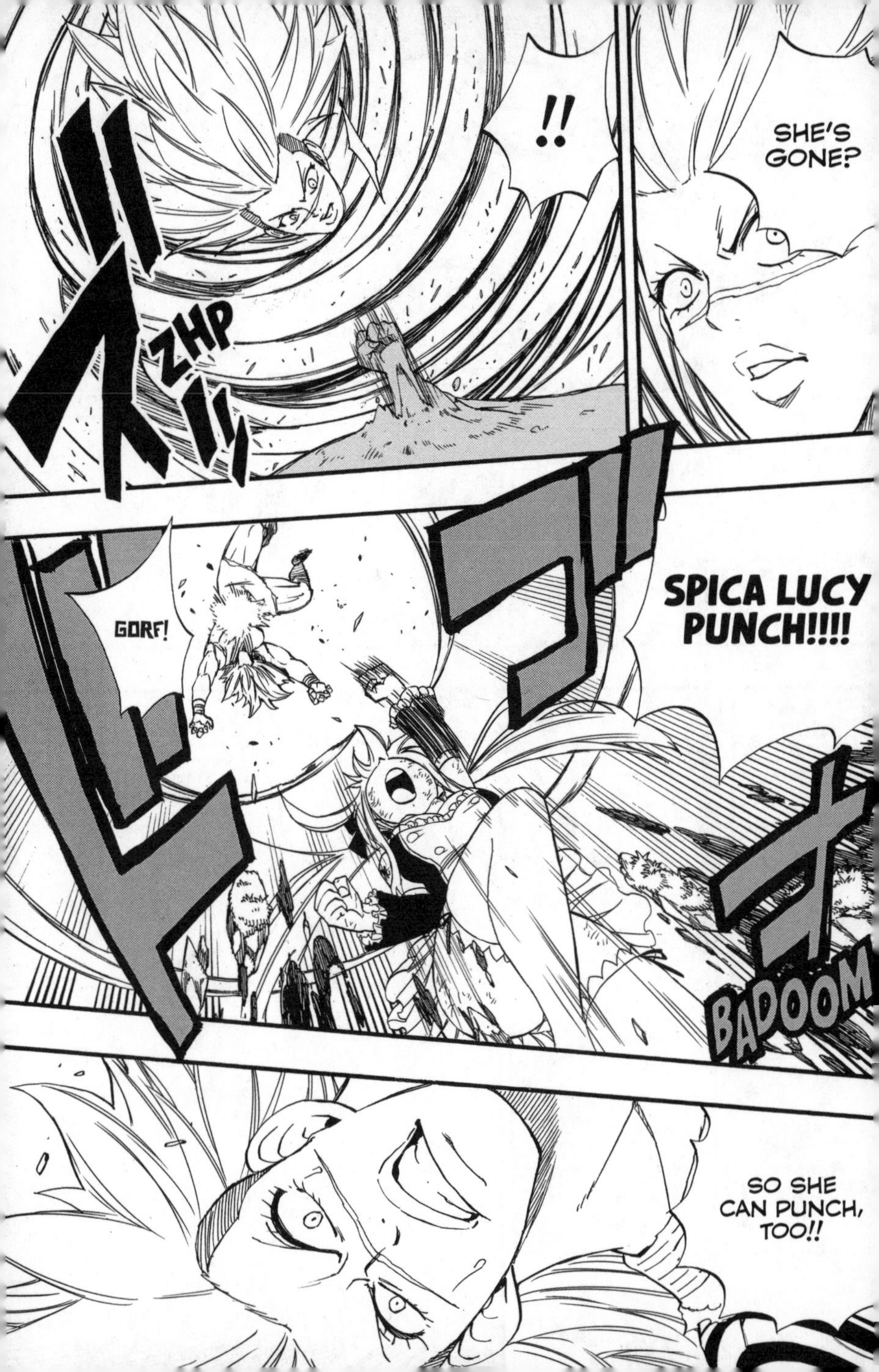
SHE'S GONE?
!!
ZHP
SPICA LUCY PUNCH!!!!
BADOOM
GORF!
SO SHE CAN PUNCH, TOO!!

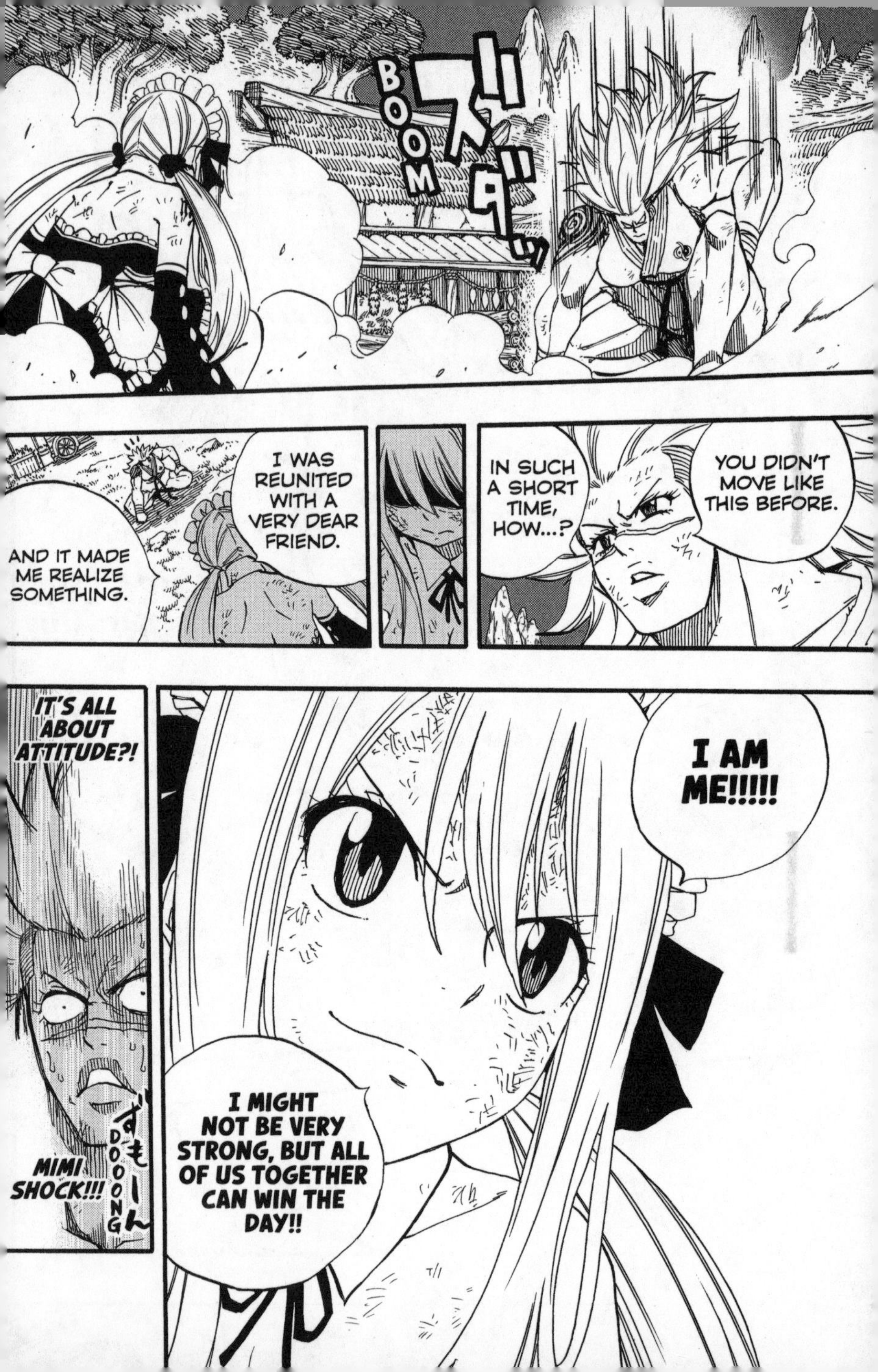

BOOM
YOU DIDN'T MOVE LIKE THIS BEFORE.
IN SUCH A SHORT TIME, HOW...?
I WAS REUNITED WITH A VERY DEAR FRIEND.
AND IT MADE ME REALIZE SOMETHING.
I AM ME!!!!!
I MIGHT NOT BE VERY STRONG, BUT ALL OF US TOGETHER CAN WIN THE DAY!!
IT'S ALL ABOUT ATTITUDE?!
DOOOONG
MIMI SHOCK!!!

FAIRY TAIL 100 YEARS QUEST

Chapter 83: Mimi the Immovable

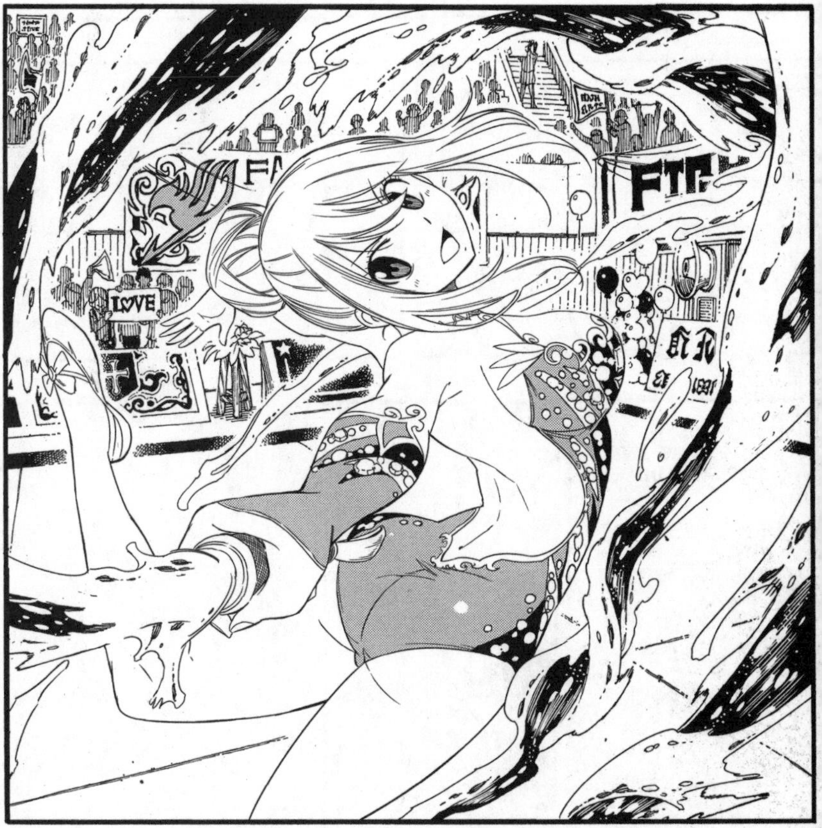
LOVE

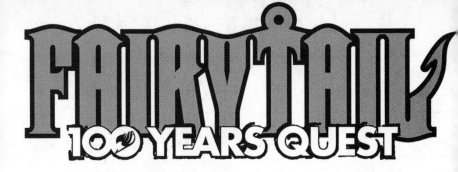

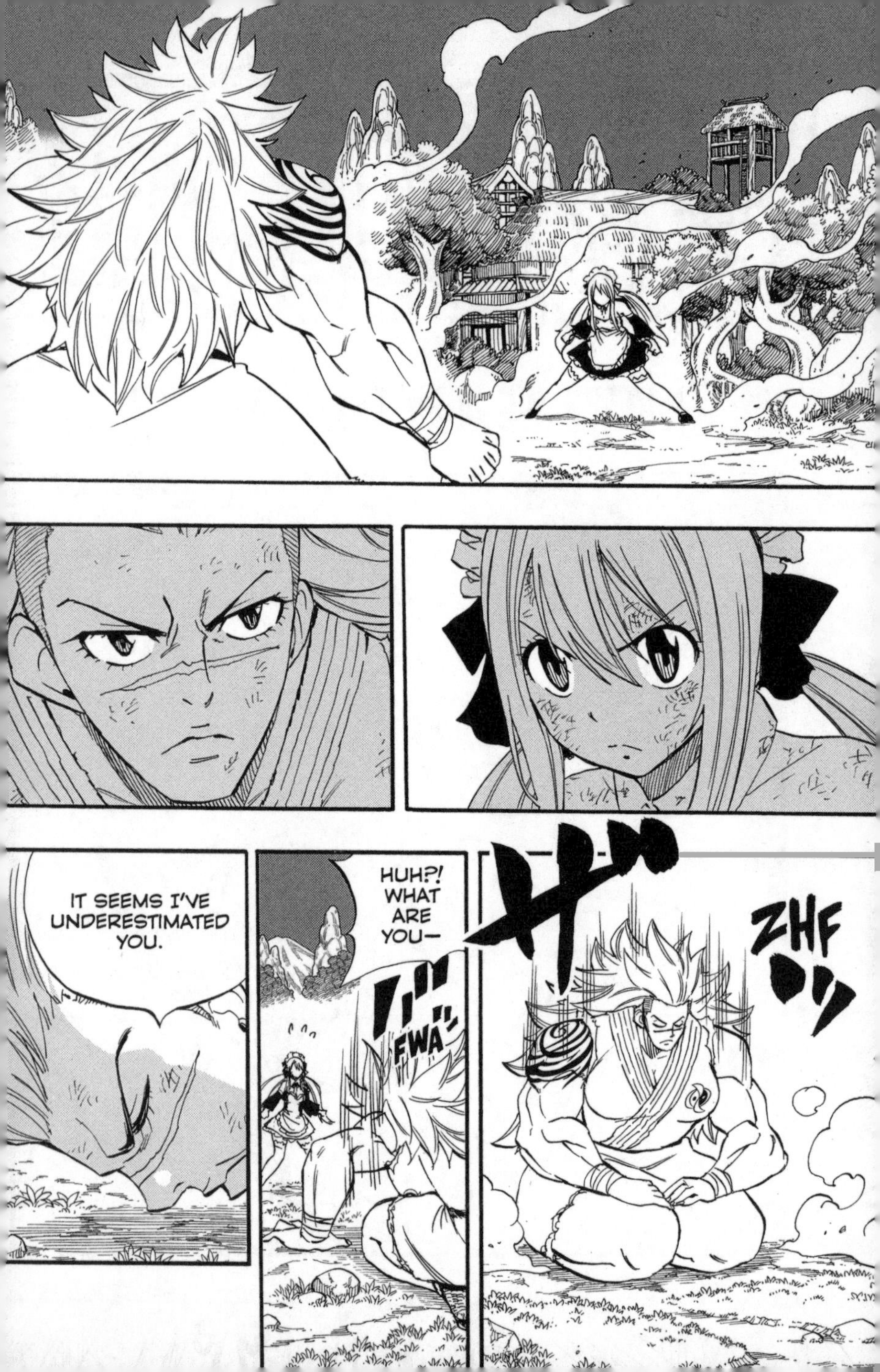
ZHF
HUH?! WHAT ARE YOU—
FWA
IT SEEMS I'VE UNDERESTIMATED YOU.

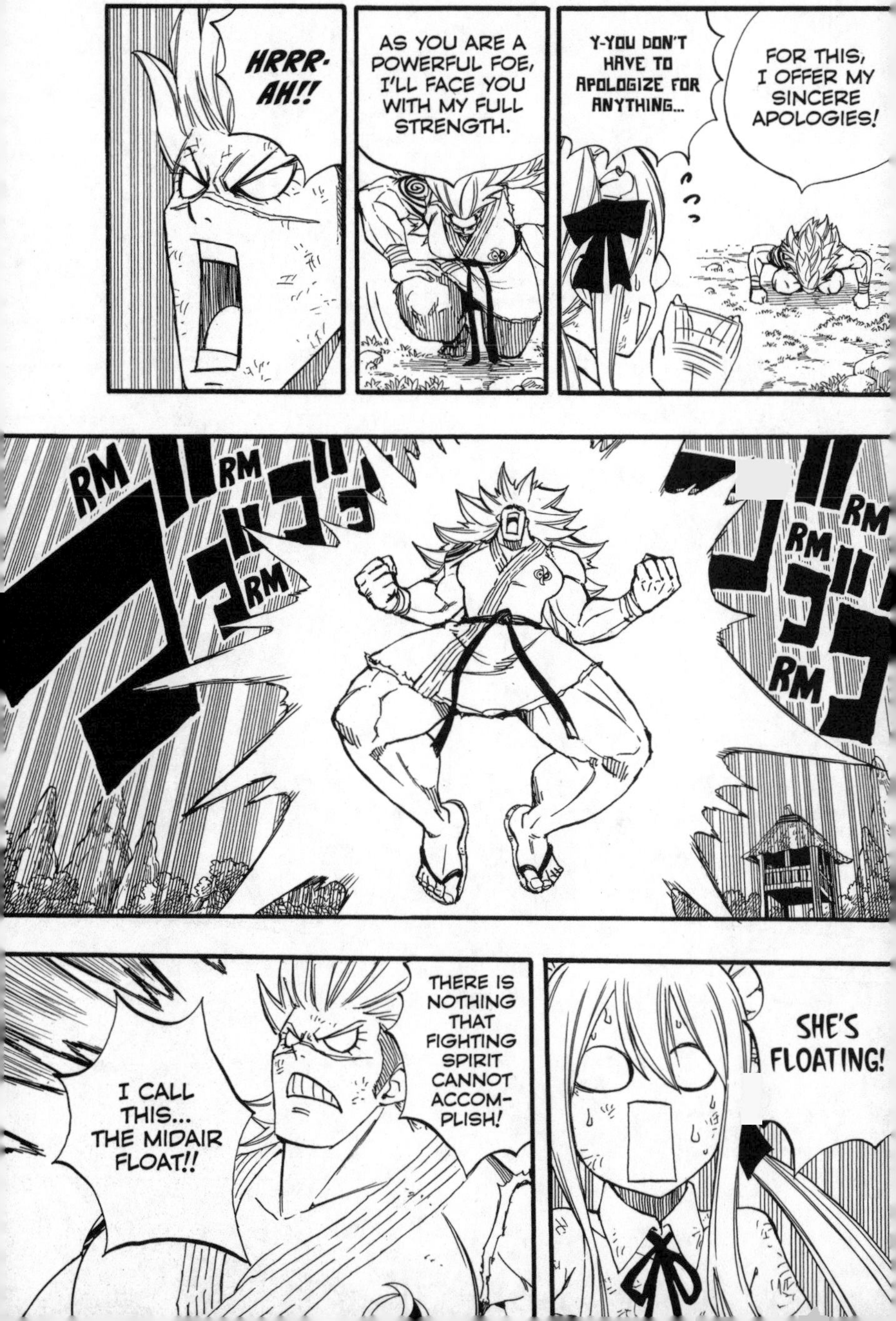
FOR THIS, I OFFER MY SINCERE APOLOGIES!
Y-YOU DON'T HAVE TO APOLOGIZE FOR ANYTHING...
AS YOU ARE A POWERFUL FOE, I'LL FACE YOU WITH MY FULL STRENGTH.
HRRR-AH!!
RM
RM
RM
RM
RM
RM
RM
SHE'S FLOATING!
THERE IS NOTHING THAT FIGHTING SPIRIT CANNOT ACCOM-PLISH!
I CALL THIS... THE MIDAIR FLOAT!!

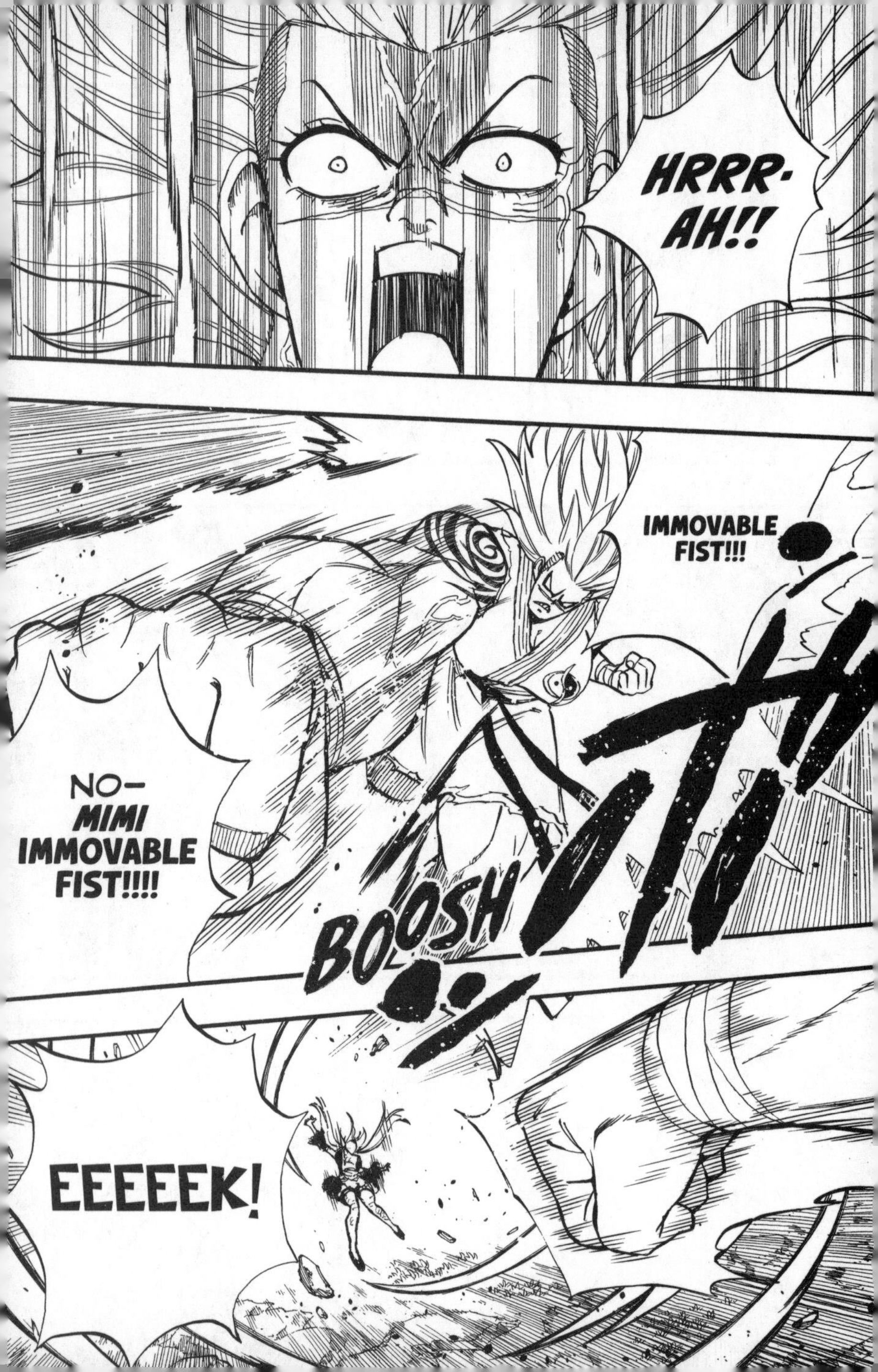
HRRR-AH!!
IMMOVABLE FIST!!!
BOOSH
NO-MIMI IMMOVABLE FIST!!!!!
EEEEEK!

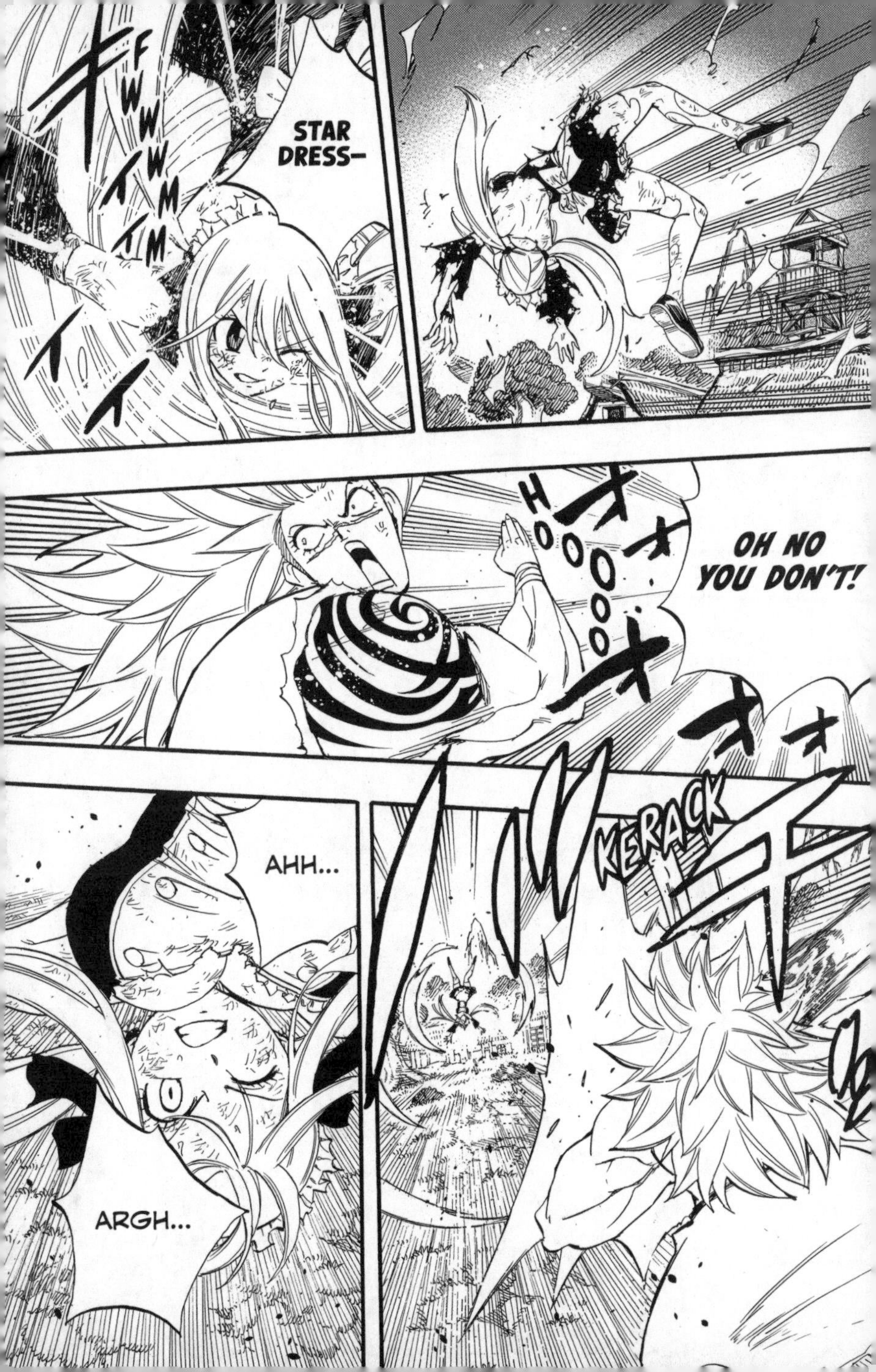
FWWWMM
STAR DRESS–
HOOOOO
OH NO YOU DON'T!
KERACK
AHH...
ARGH...

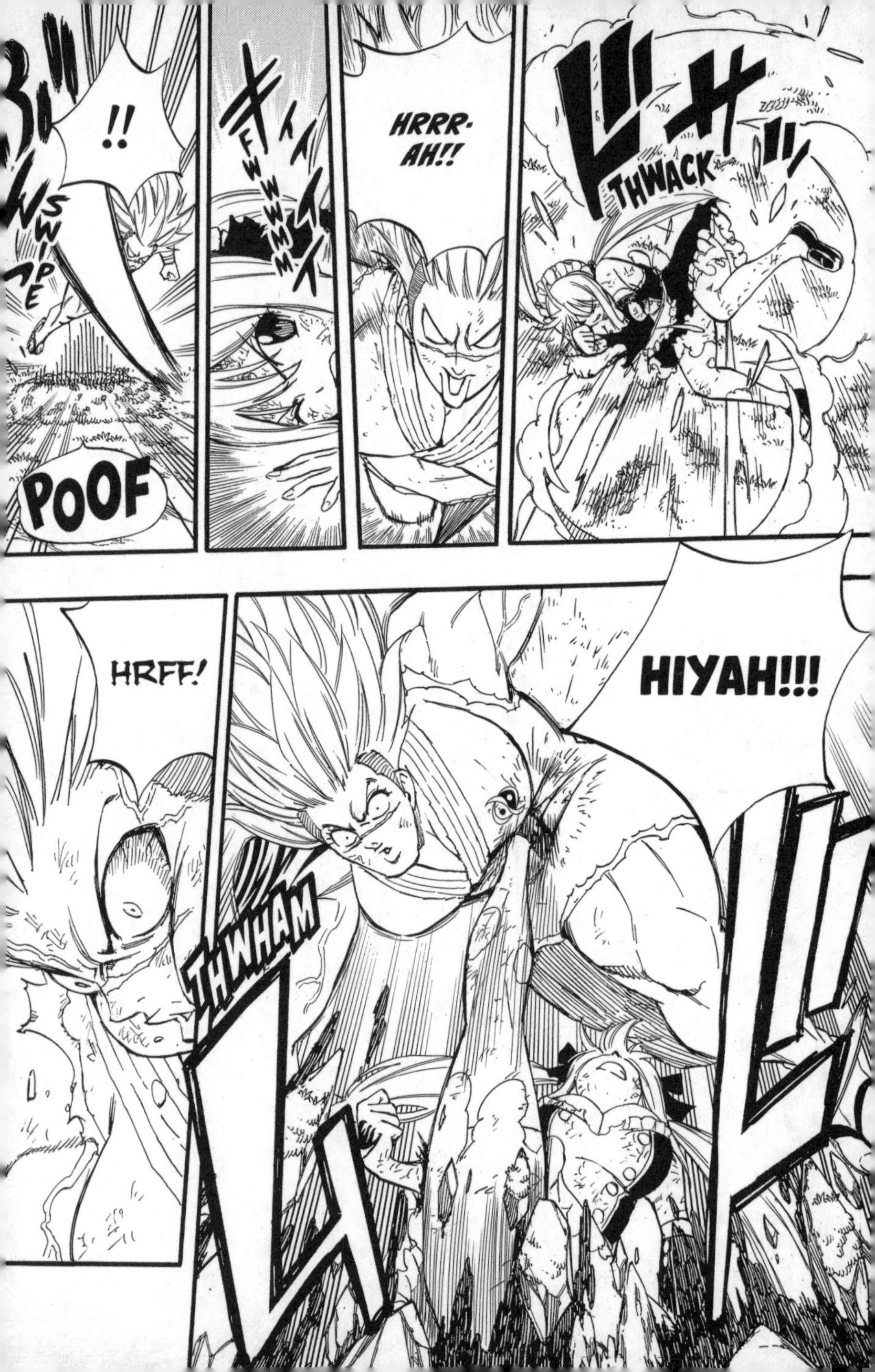
THWACK
HRRR-AH!!
FWWWWMMM
!!
SWIPE
POOF
HIYAH!!!
THWHAM
HRFF!

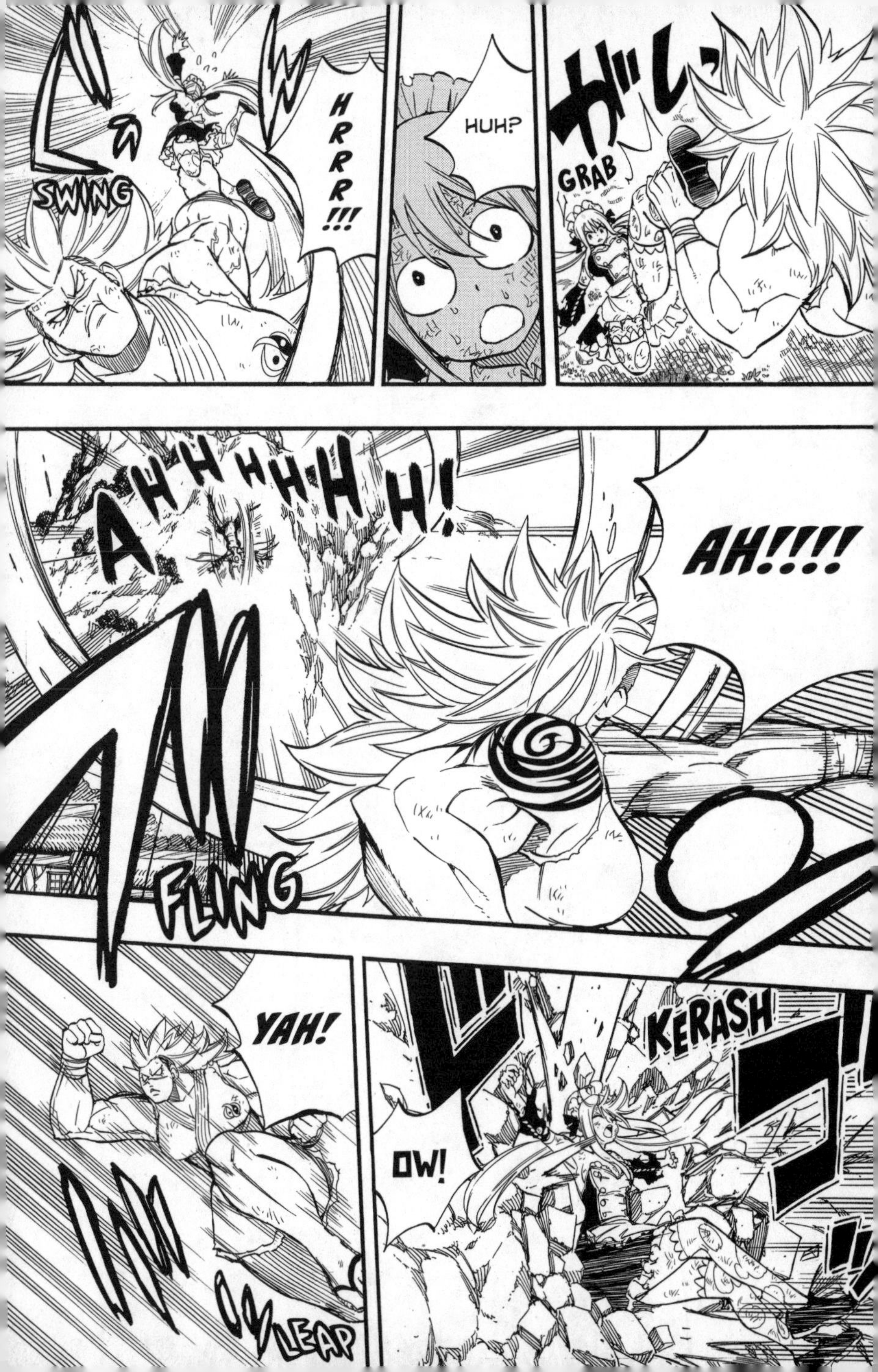
GRAB
HUH?
HRRR!!!
SWING
AH!!!!
AHHHHHH!
FLING
KERASH
OW!
YAH!
LEAP

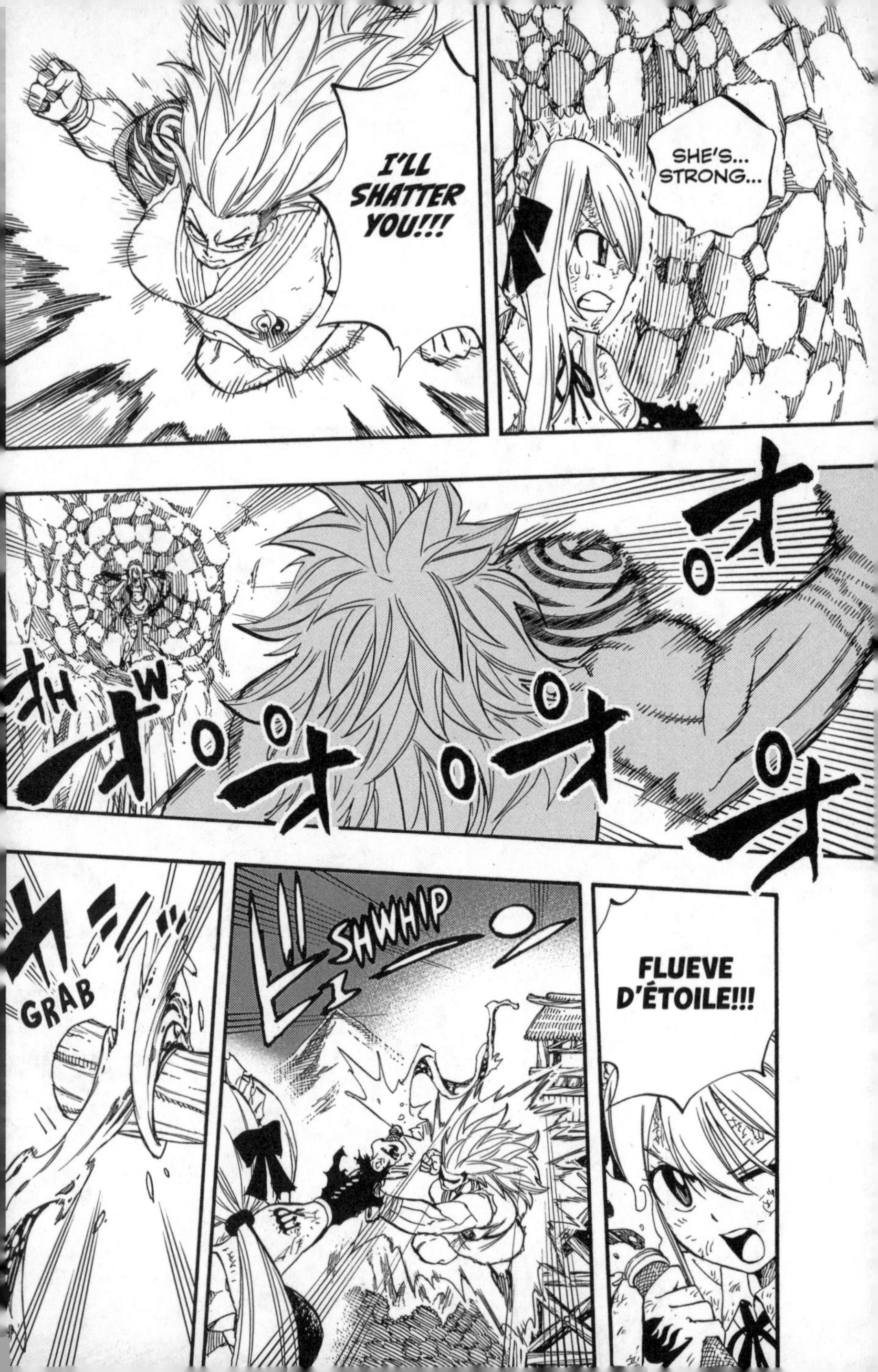
SHE'S... STRONG...
I'LL SHATTER YOU!!!
FLUEVE D'ÉTOILE!!!
SHWHIP
GRAB

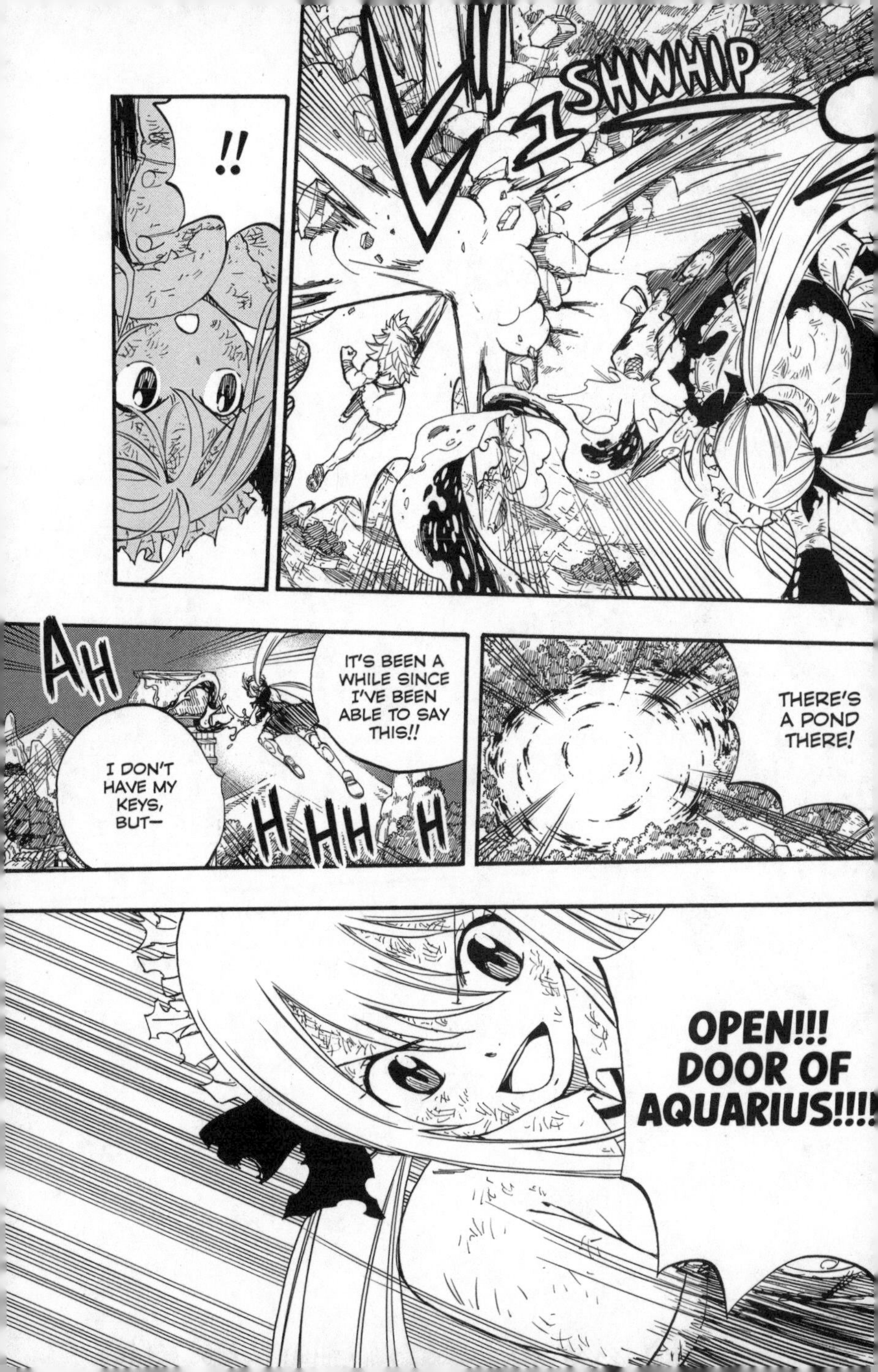
SHWHIP
!!
THERE'S A POND THERE!
IT'S BEEN A WHILE SINCE I'VE BEEN ABLE TO SAY THIS!!
AH
I DON'T HAVE MY KEYS, BUT—
HHHH
OPEN!!! DOOR OF AQUARIUS!!!!

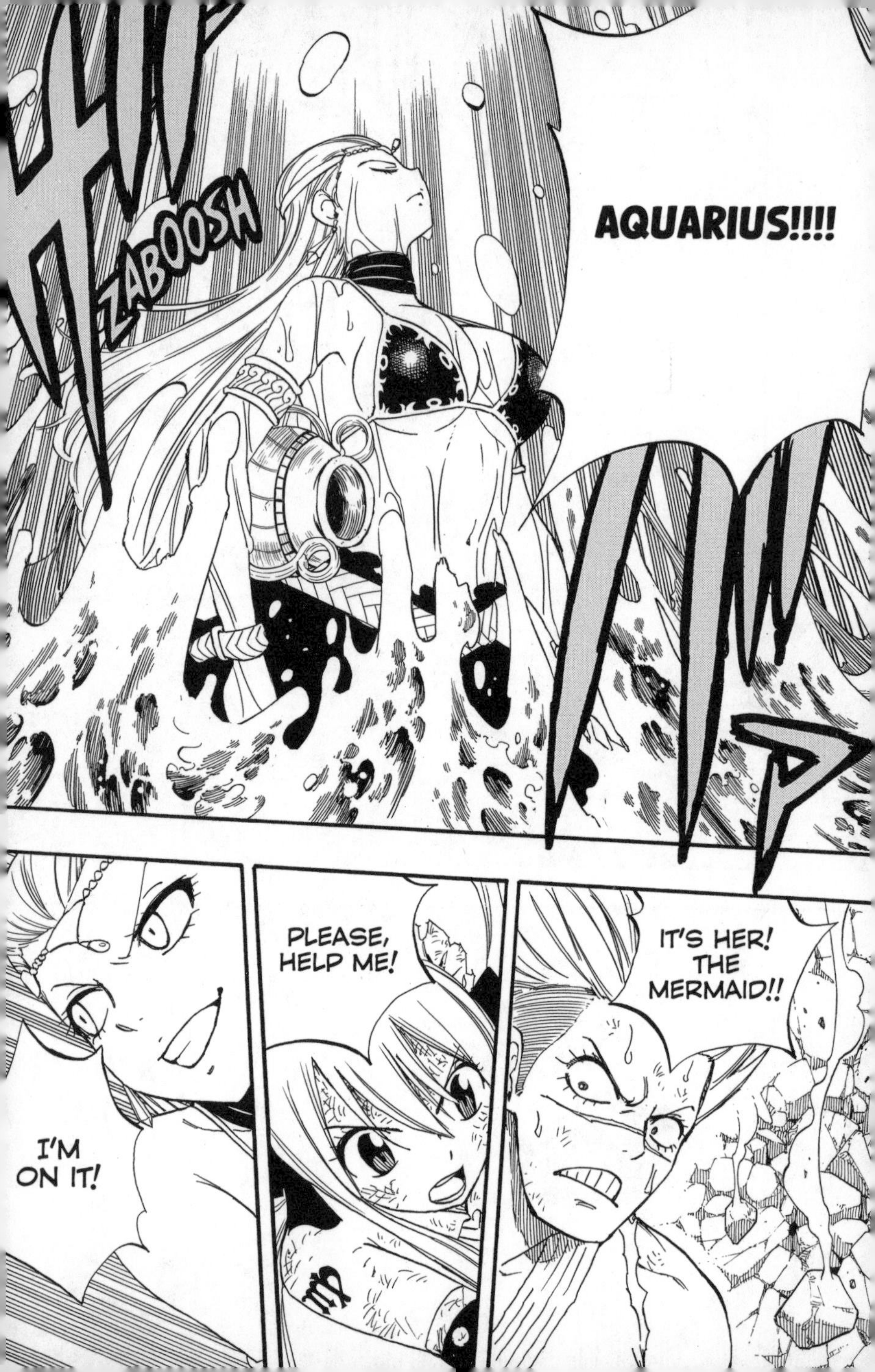
AQUARIUS!!!!
ZABOOSH
IT'S HER! THE MERMAID!!
PLEASE, HELP ME!
I'M ON IT!

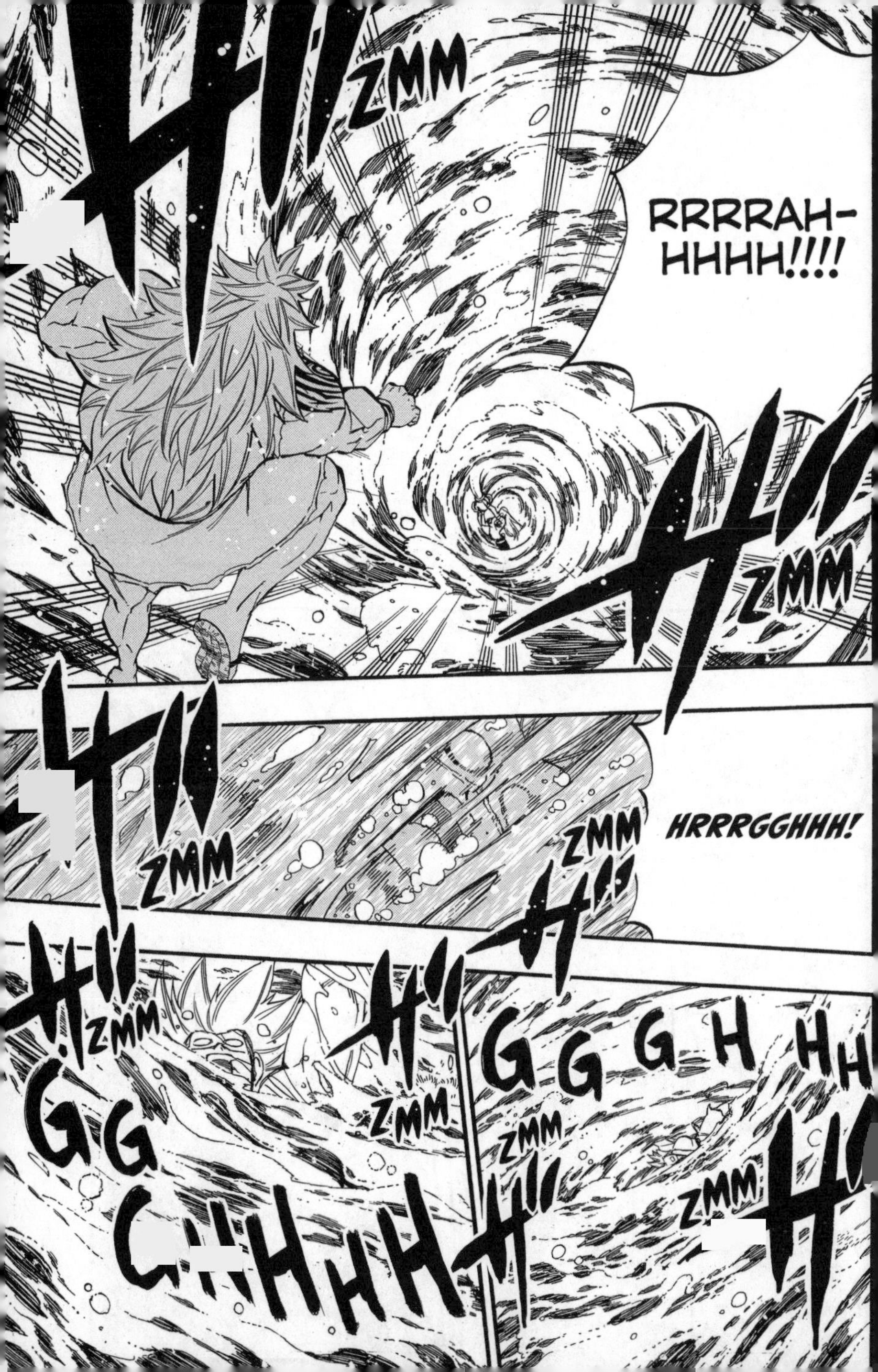

RRRRAH-HHHH!!!!
H!!
ZMM
ZMM
H!!
HRRRGGHHH!
ZMM
H!!
ZMM
H!!
GGGHHH
ZMM
H!!
ZMM
H!!
ZMM
H!!
GG
ZMM
H!!

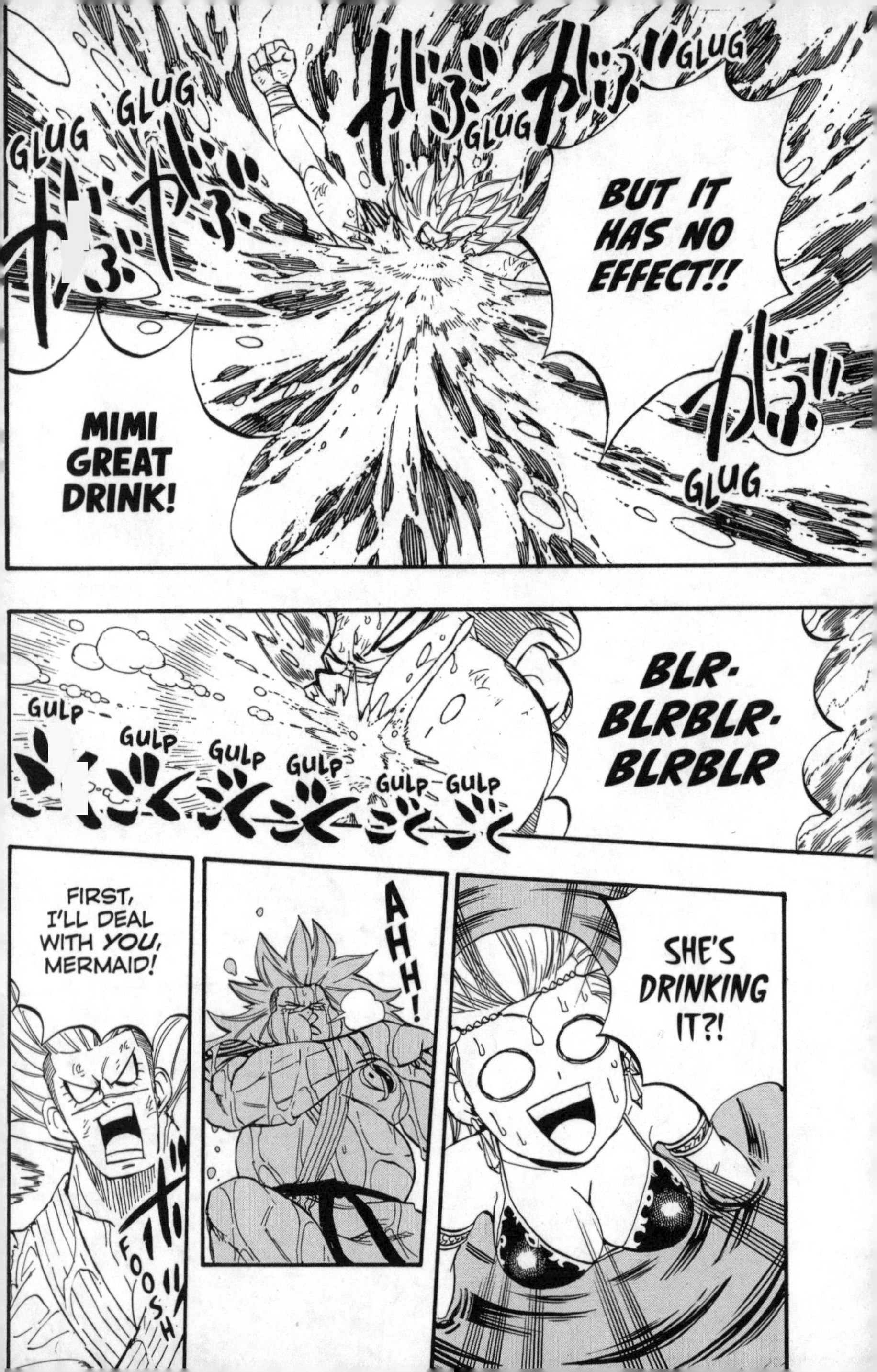
GLUG
BUT IT HAS NO EFFECT!!
GLUG
GLUG
GLUG
GLUG
GLUG
MIMI GREAT DRINK!
BLR-BLRBLR-BLRBLR
GULP
GULP
GULP
GULP
GULP
GULP
SHE'S DRINKING IT?!
AHH!
FIRST, I'LL DEAL WITH *YOU*, MERMAID!
FOOSH

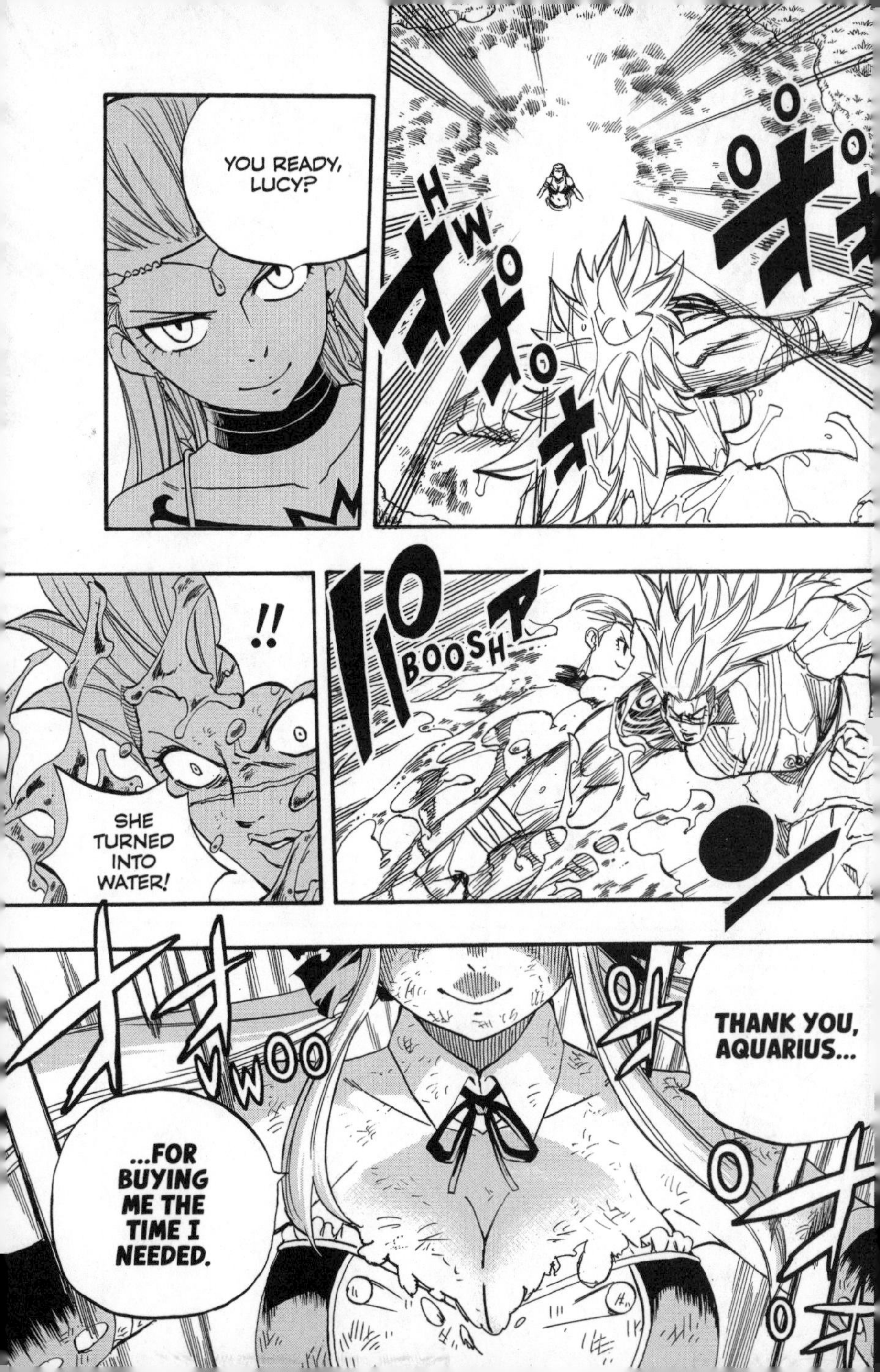

HWOO
YOU READY, LUCY?
BOOSH
!!
SHE TURNED INTO WATER!
THANK YOU, AQUARIUS...
VWOO
...FOR BUYING ME THE TIME I NEEDED.

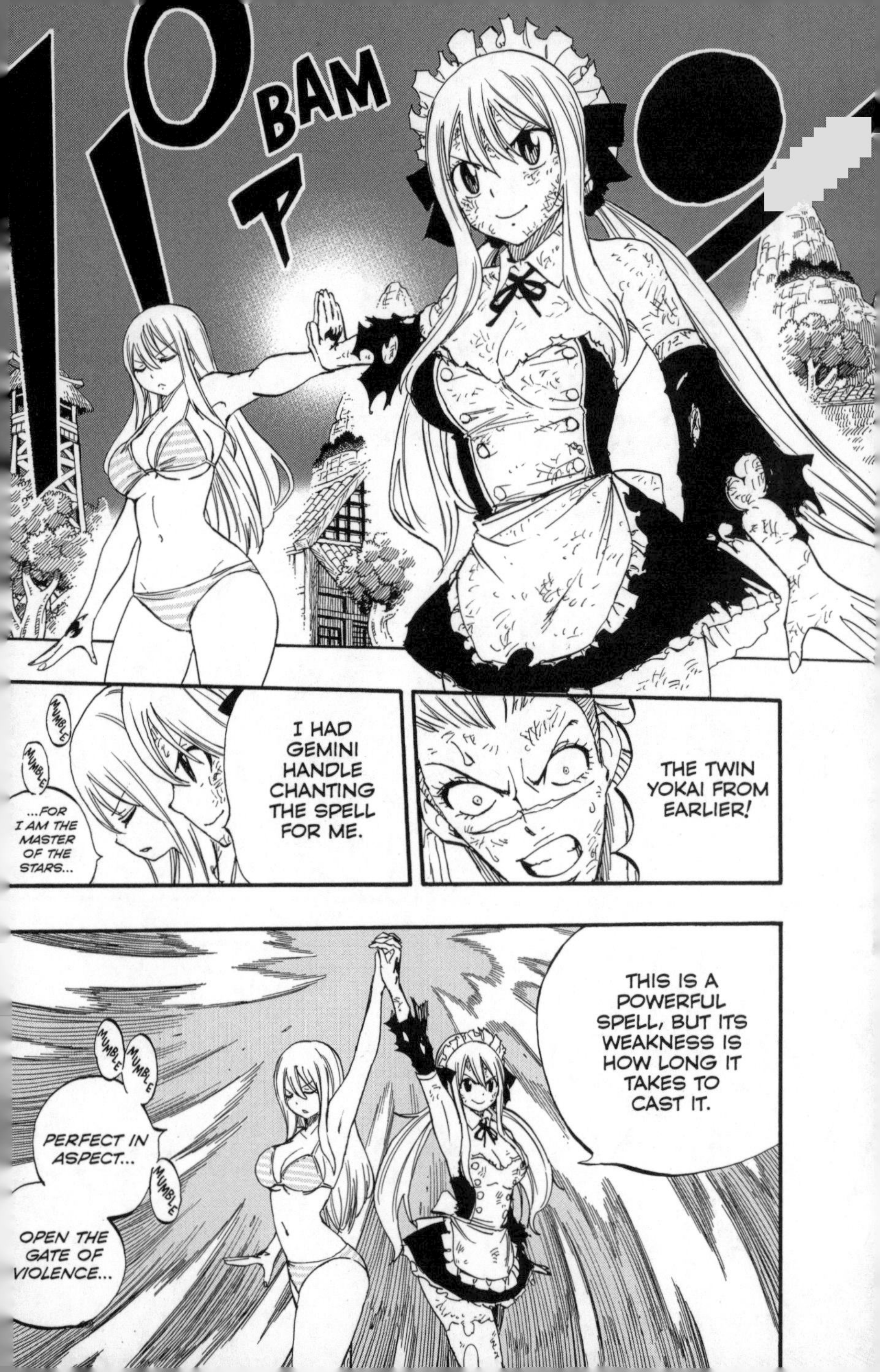
BAM
THE TWIN YOKAI FROM EARLIER!
I HAD GEMINI HANDLE CHANTING THE SPELL FOR ME.
MUMBLE
MUMBLE
...FOR I AM THE MASTER OF THE STARS...
THIS IS A POWERFUL SPELL, BUT ITS WEAKNESS IS HOW LONG IT TAKES TO CAST IT.
MUMBLE
MUMBLE
PERFECT IN ASPECT...
MUMBLE
OPEN THE GATE OF VIOLENCE...

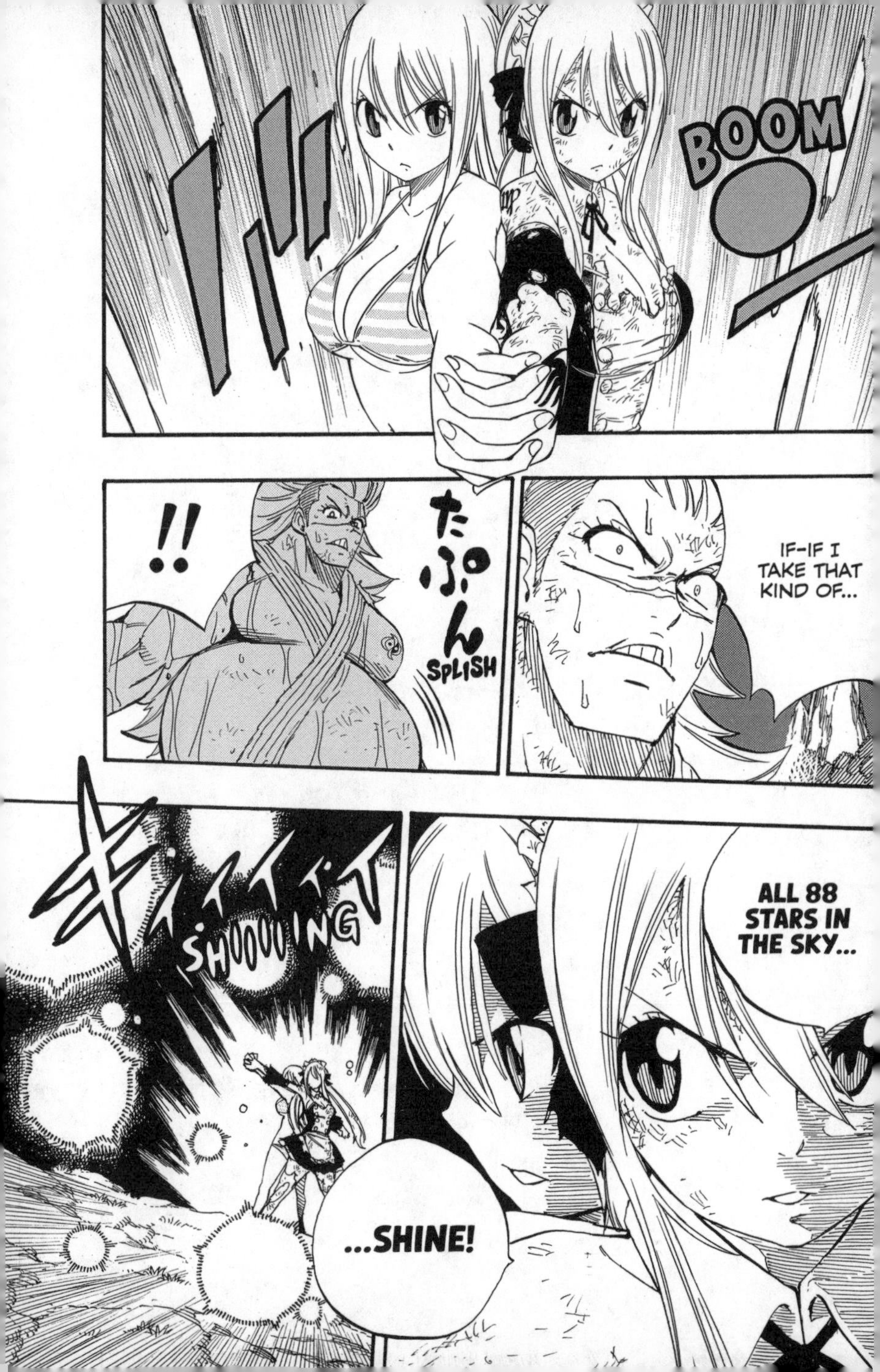
BOOM
IF-IF I TAKE THAT KIND OF...
!!
たぷん
SPLISH
ALL 88 STARS IN THE SKY...
SHOOOOING
...SHINE!

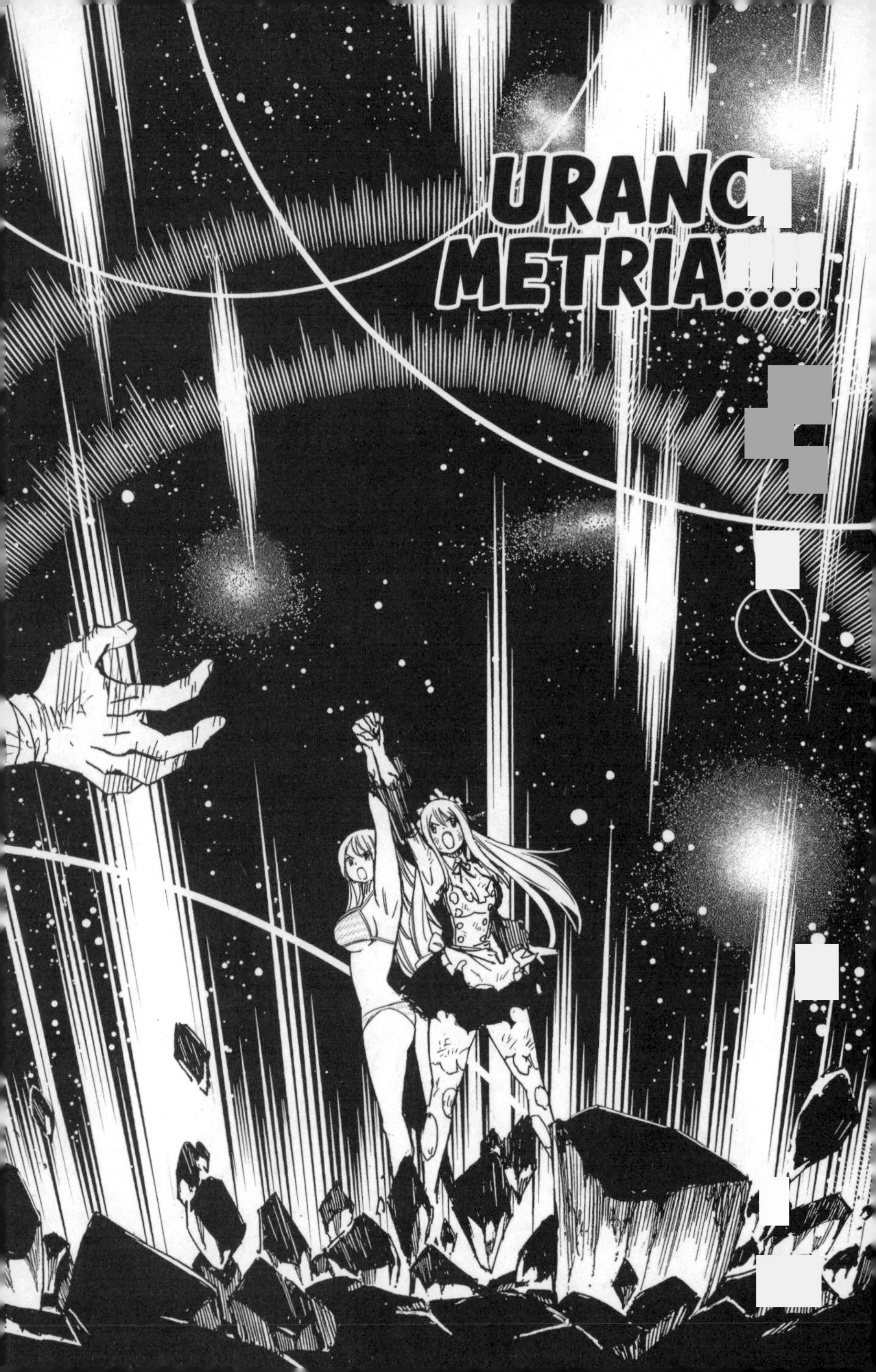
URANO METRIA....

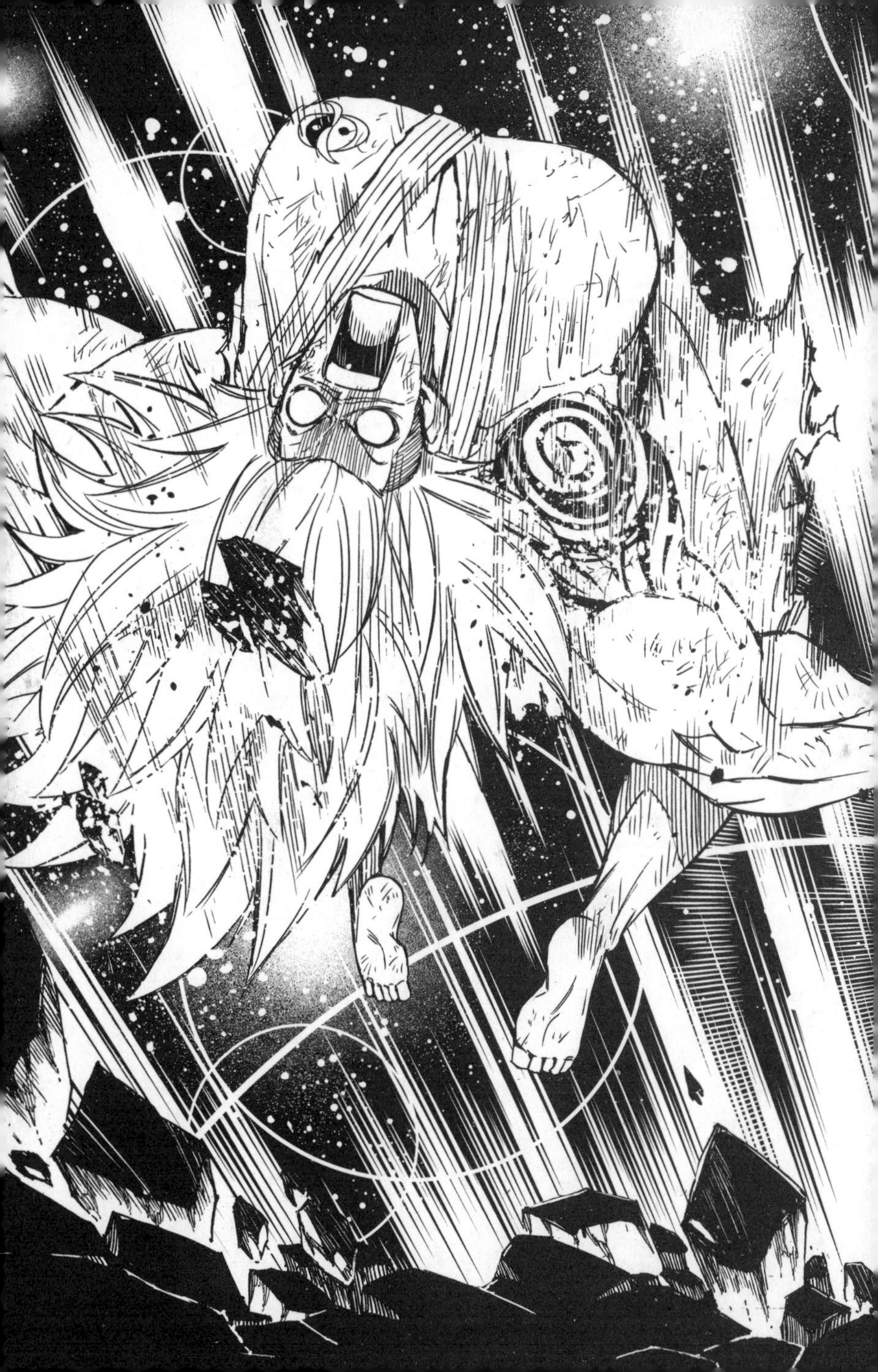

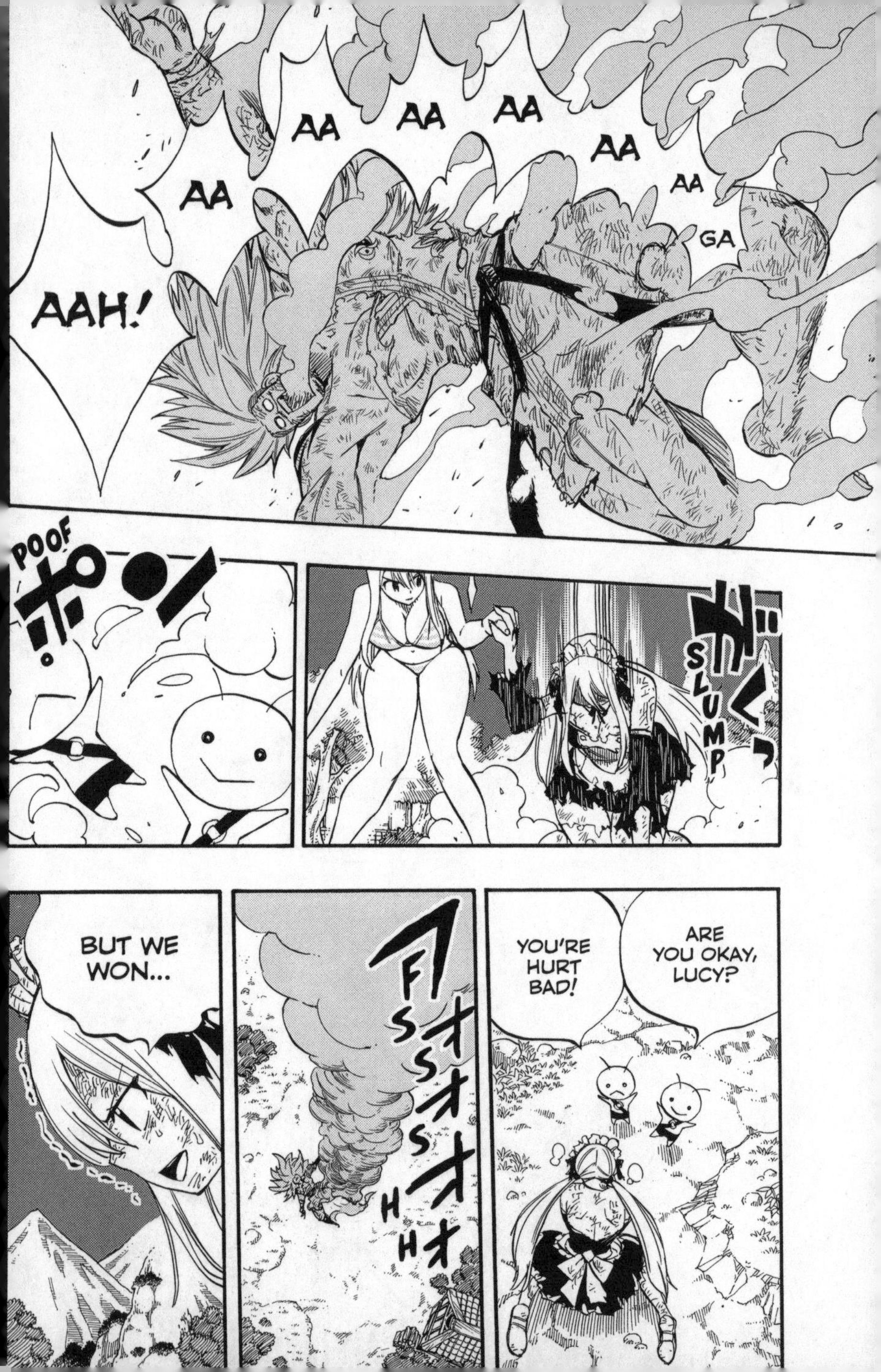

AAH!
AA
AA
AA
AA
AA
AA
GA
SLUMP
POOF
ARE YOU OKAY, LUCY?
YOU'RE HURT BAD!
FSSSHH
BUT WE WON...

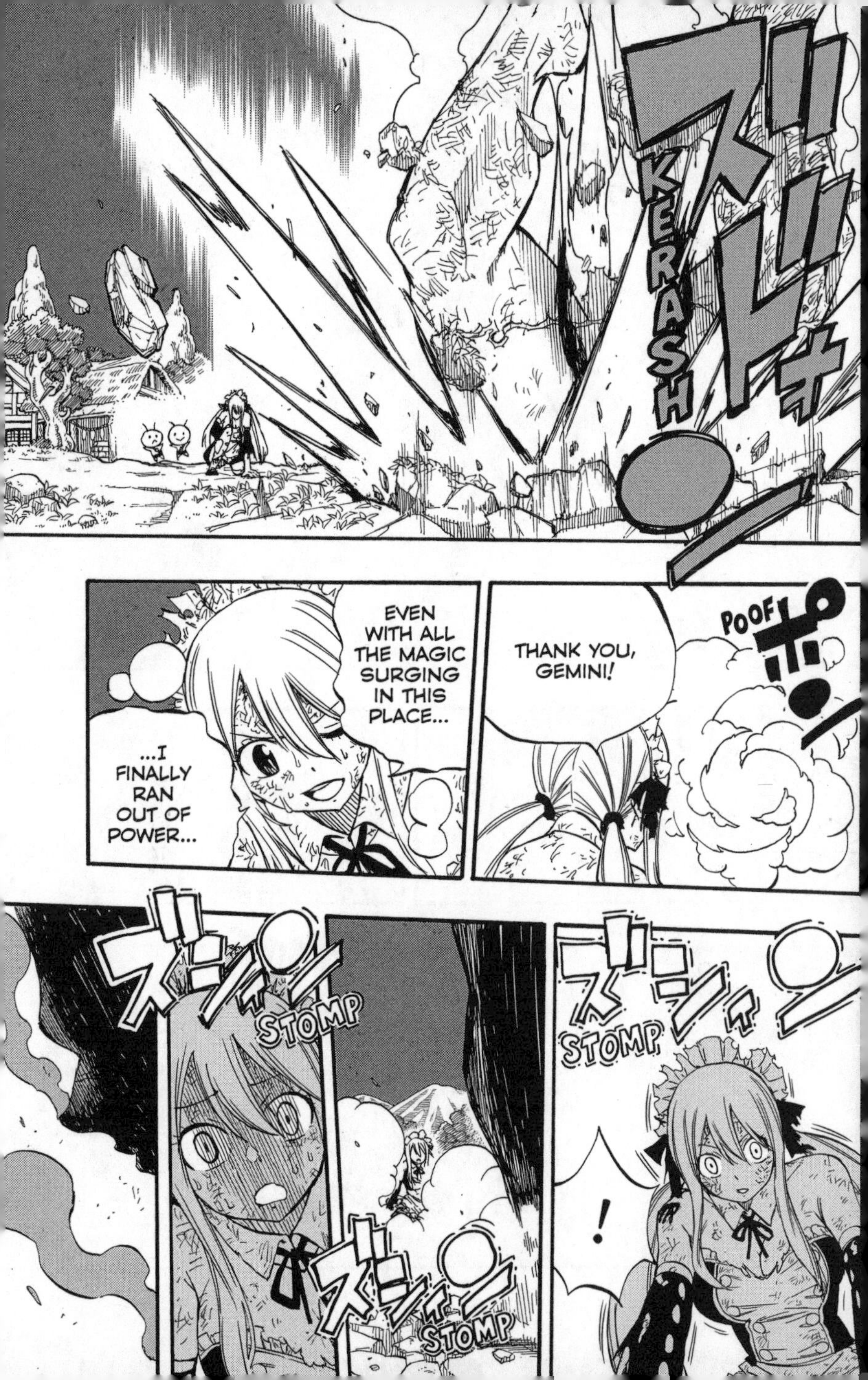
KERASH
POOF
THANK YOU, GEMINI!
EVEN WITH ALL THE MAGIC SURGING IN THIS PLACE...
...I FINALLY RAN OUT OF POWER...
STOMP
!
STOMP
STOMP

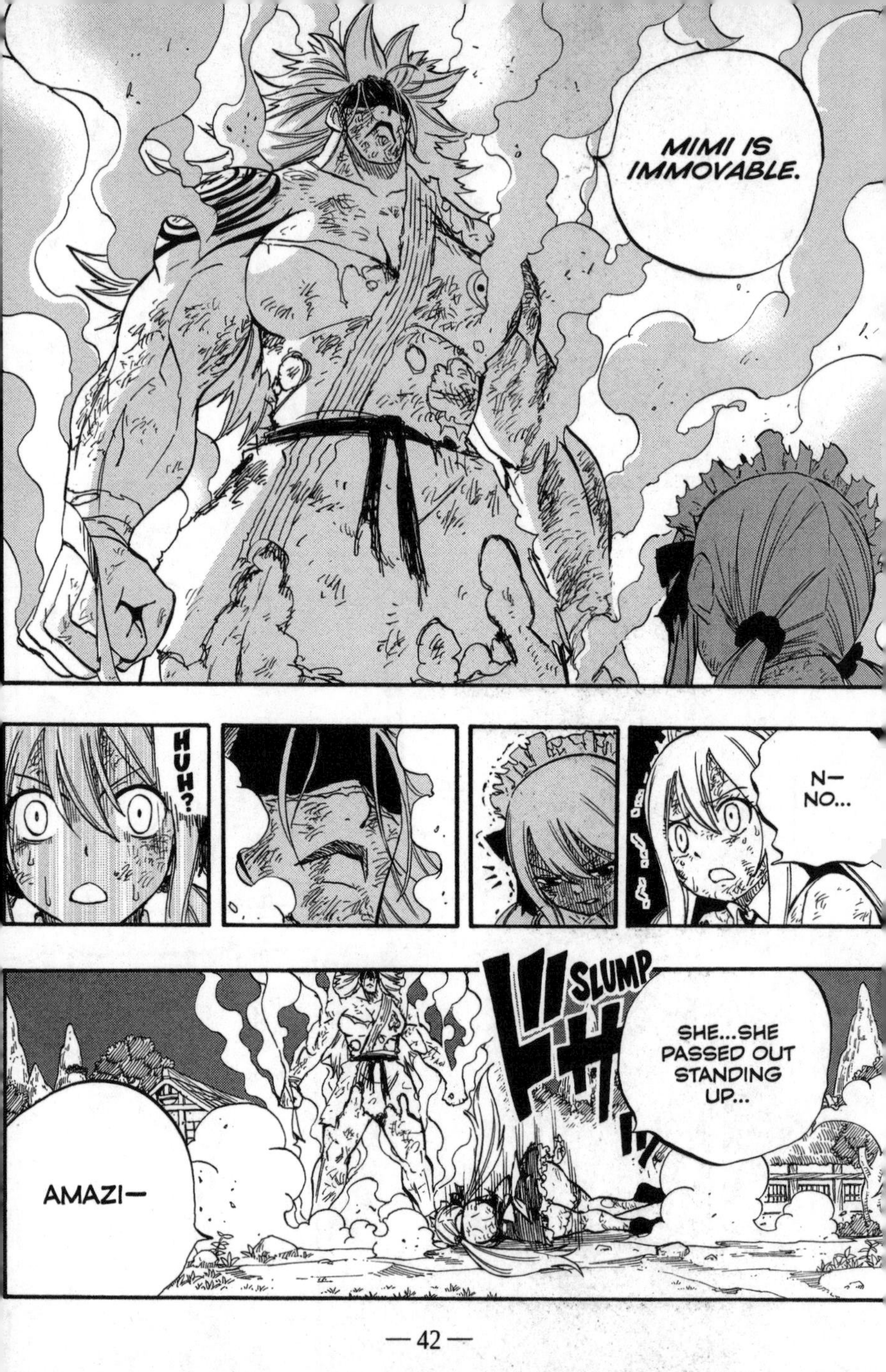
MIMI IS IMMOVABLE.
N— NO...
HUH?
SHE...SHE PASSED OUT STANDING UP...
SLUMP
AMAZI—

FAIRY TAIL
100 YEARS QUEST

CHAPTER 84: FROZEN FANTASY

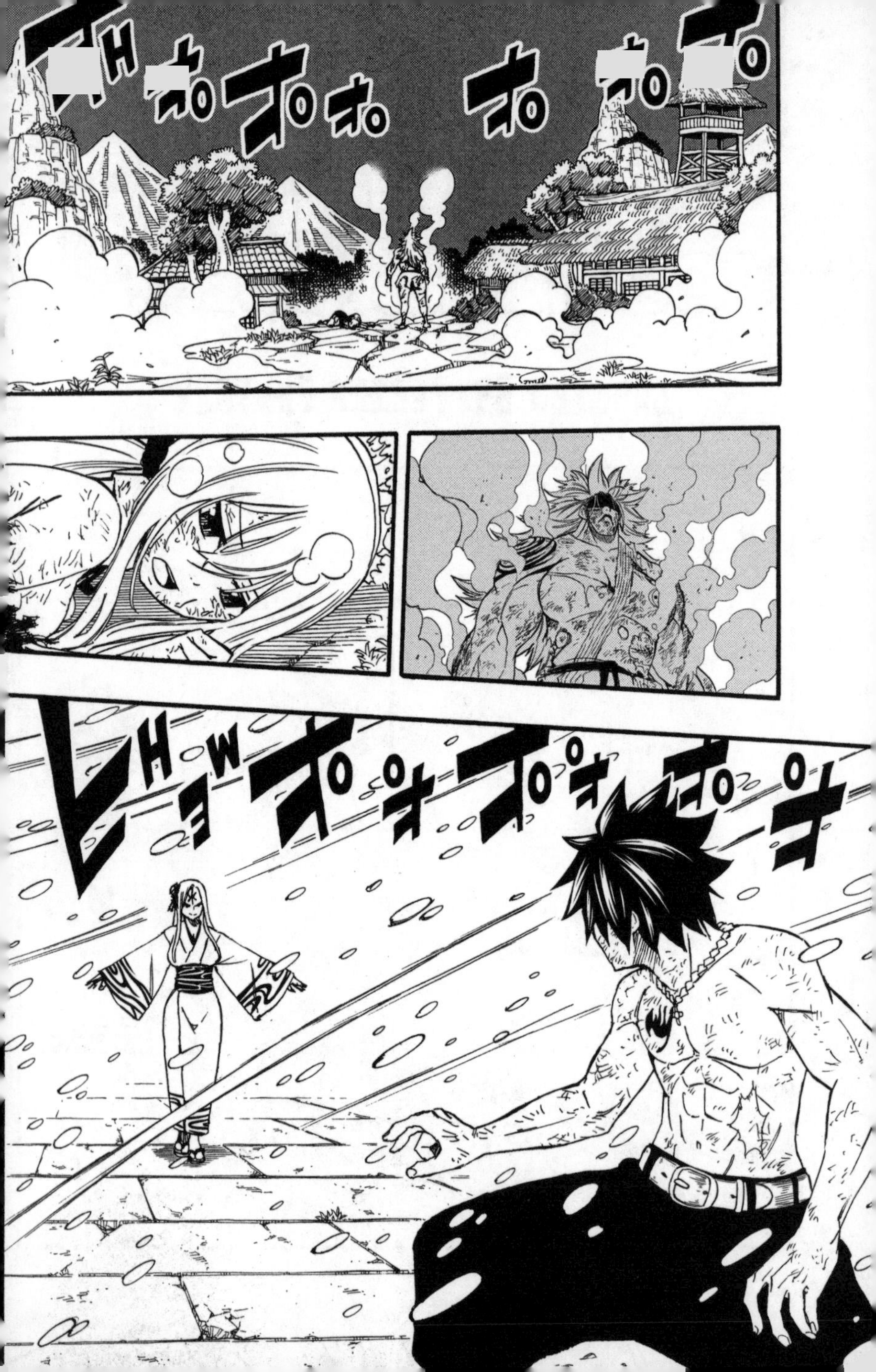

ヒョオォオォオォ

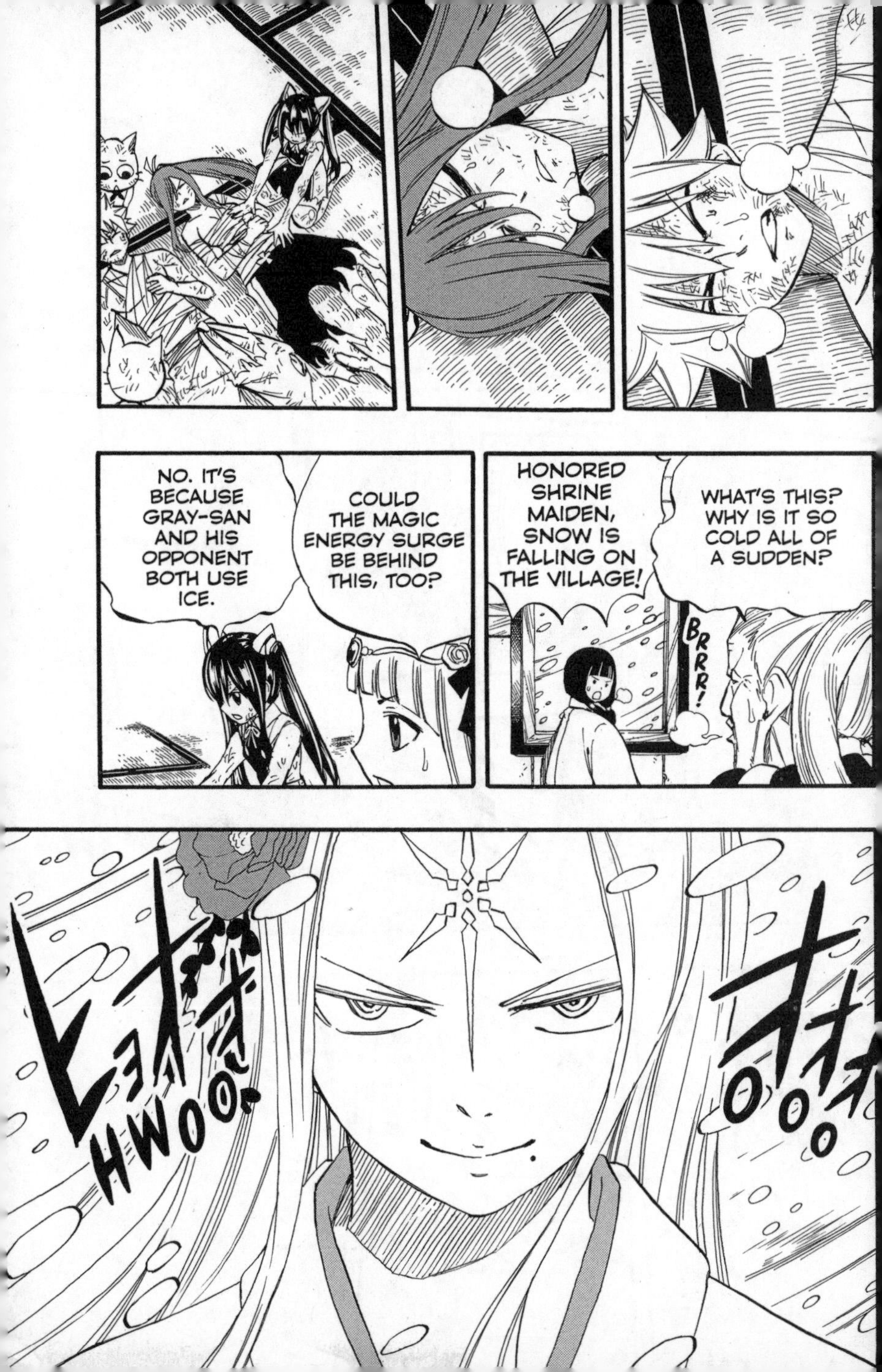
WHAT'S THIS? WHY IS IT SO COLD ALL OF A SUDDEN?
BRRR!
HONORED SHRINE MAIDEN, SNOW IS FALLING ON THE VILLAGE!
COULD THE MAGIC ENERGY SURGE BE BEHIND THIS, TOO?
NO. IT'S BECAUSE GRAY-SAN AND HIS OPPONENT BOTH USE ICE.
OOO
HWOOO

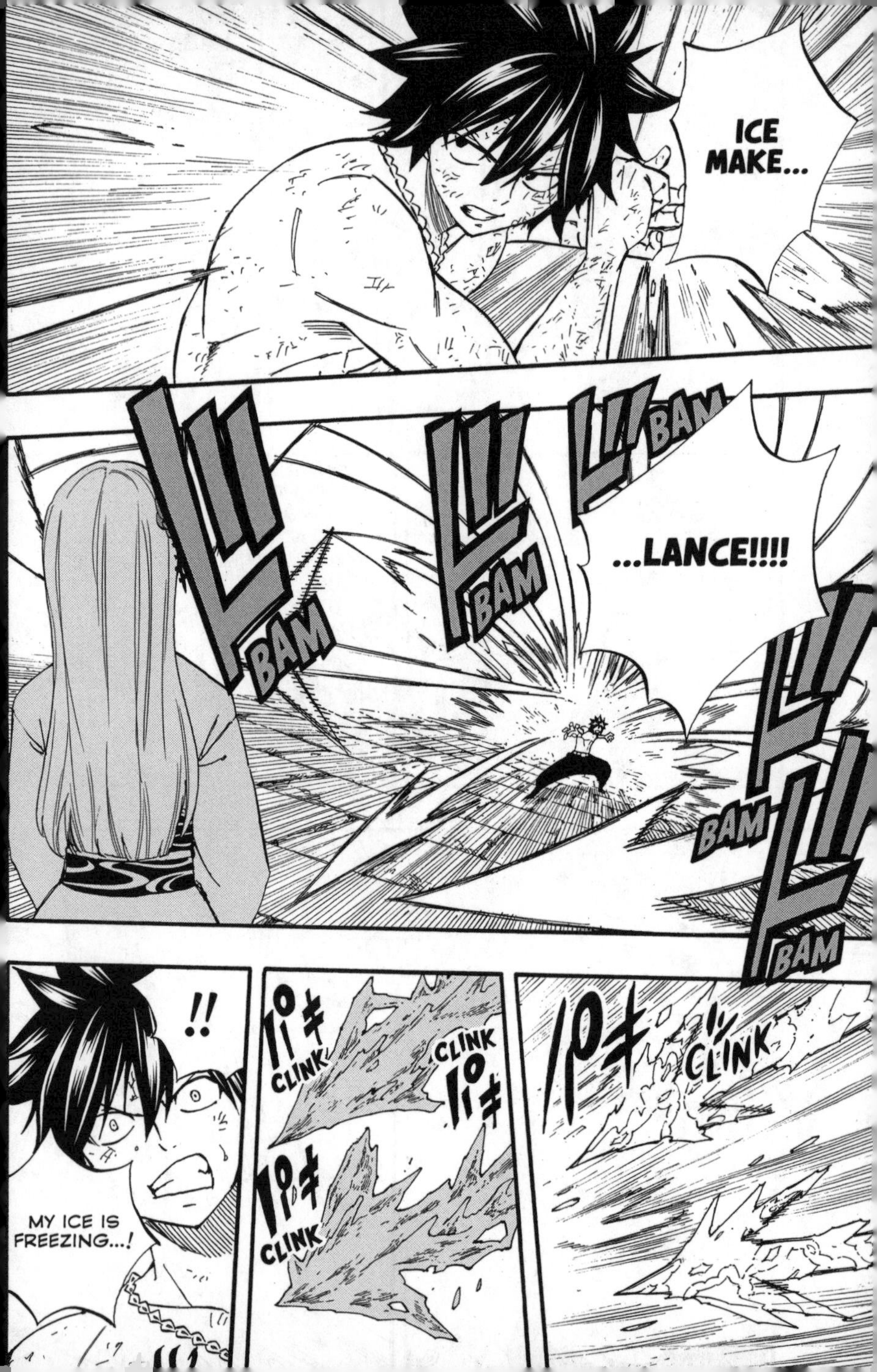

ICE MAKE...
...LANCE!!!!
BAM
BAM
BAM
BAM
BAM
BAM
パキ
CLINK
CLINK
パキ
パキ
CLINK
パキ
CLINK
!!
MY ICE IS FREEZING...!

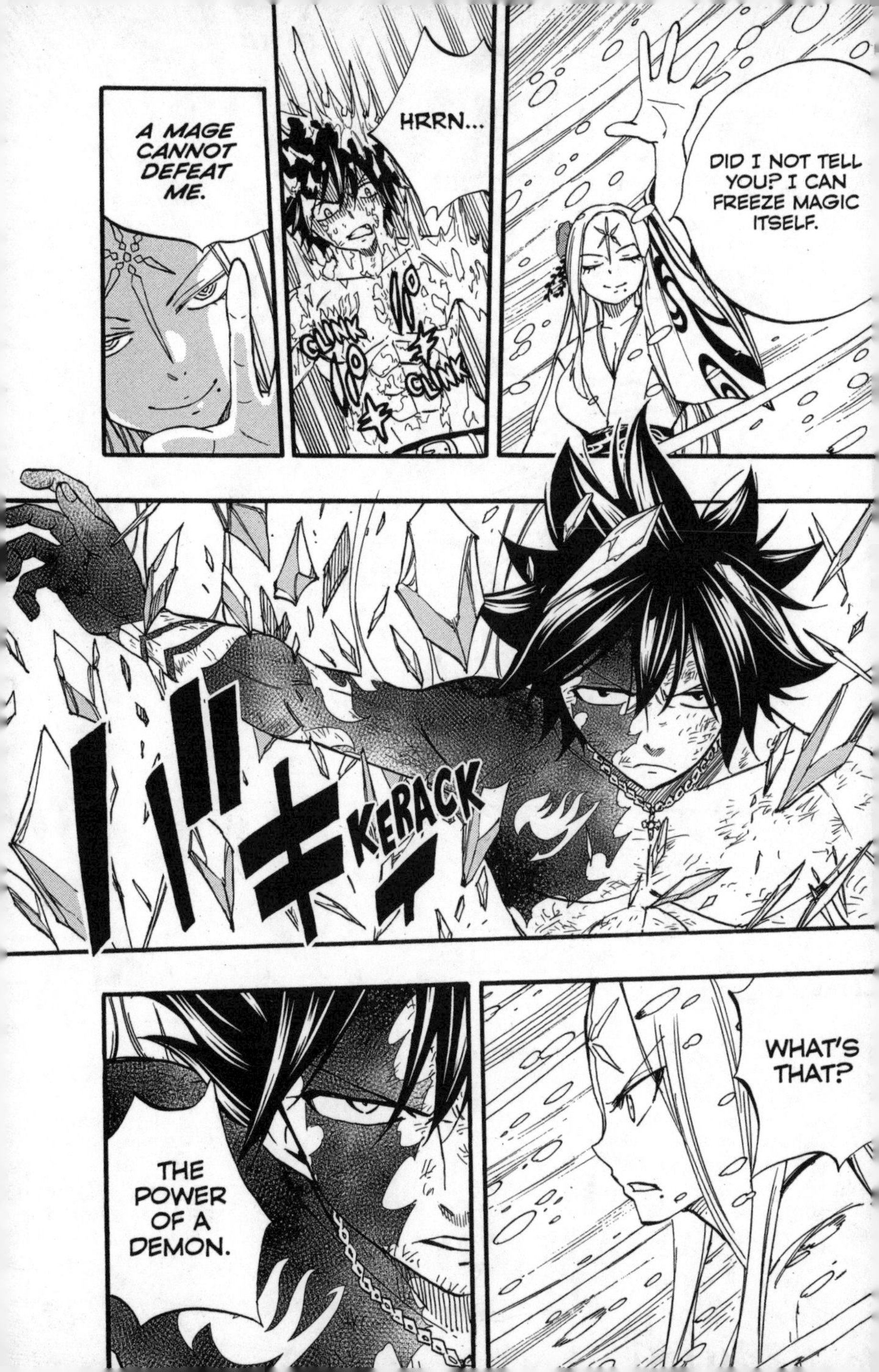
DID I NOT TELL YOU? I CAN FREEZE MAGIC ITSELF.
HRRN...
CLINK
CLINK
A MAGE CANNOT DEFEAT ME.
KERACK
WHAT'S THAT?
THE POWER OF A DEMON.

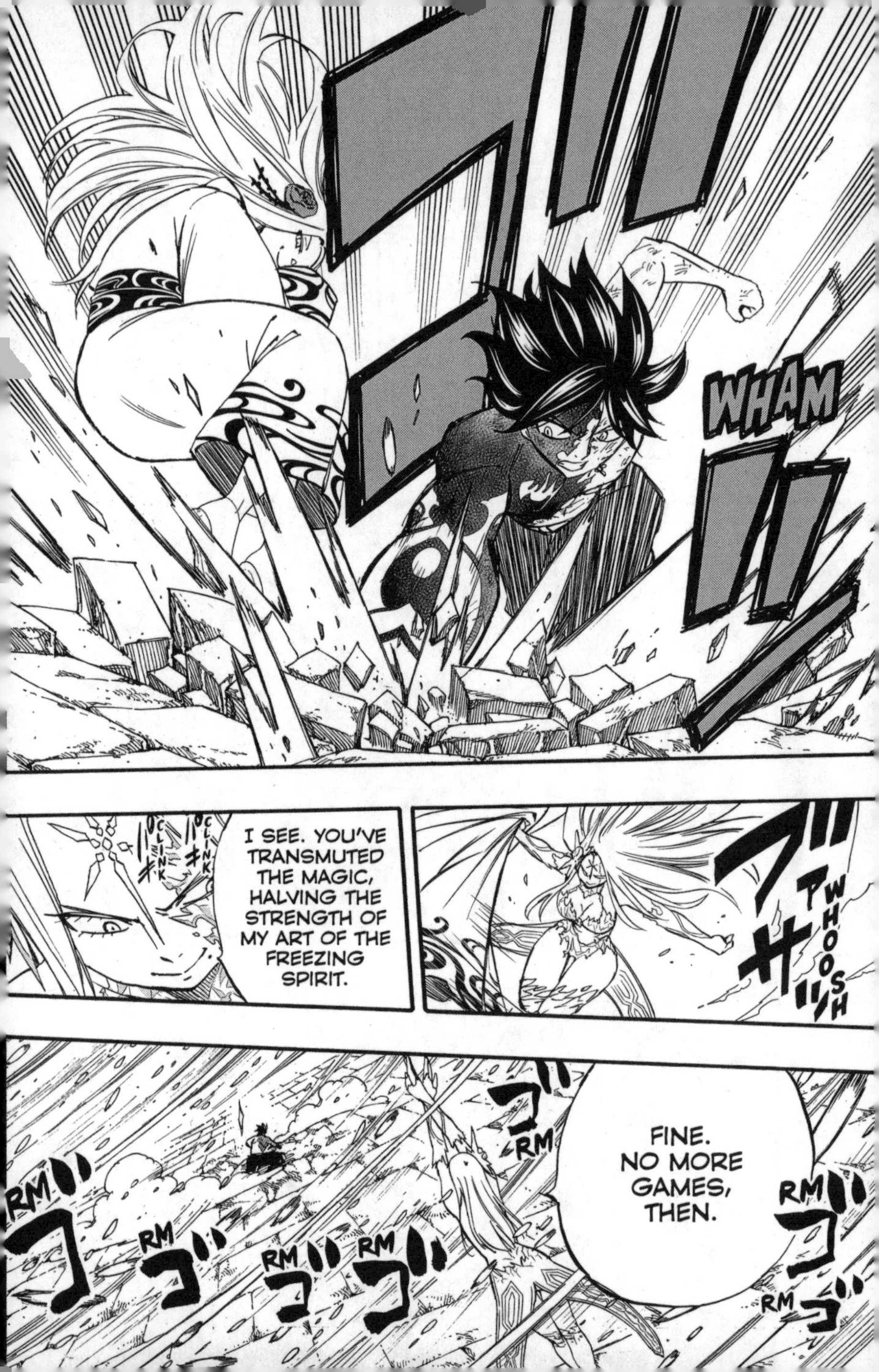
WHAM
WHOOSH
CLINK
CLINK
I SEE. YOU'VE TRANSMUTED THE MAGIC, HALVING THE STRENGTH OF MY ART OF THE FREEZING SPIRIT.
RM
RM
RM
FINE. NO MORE GAMES, THEN.
RM
RM
RM
RM

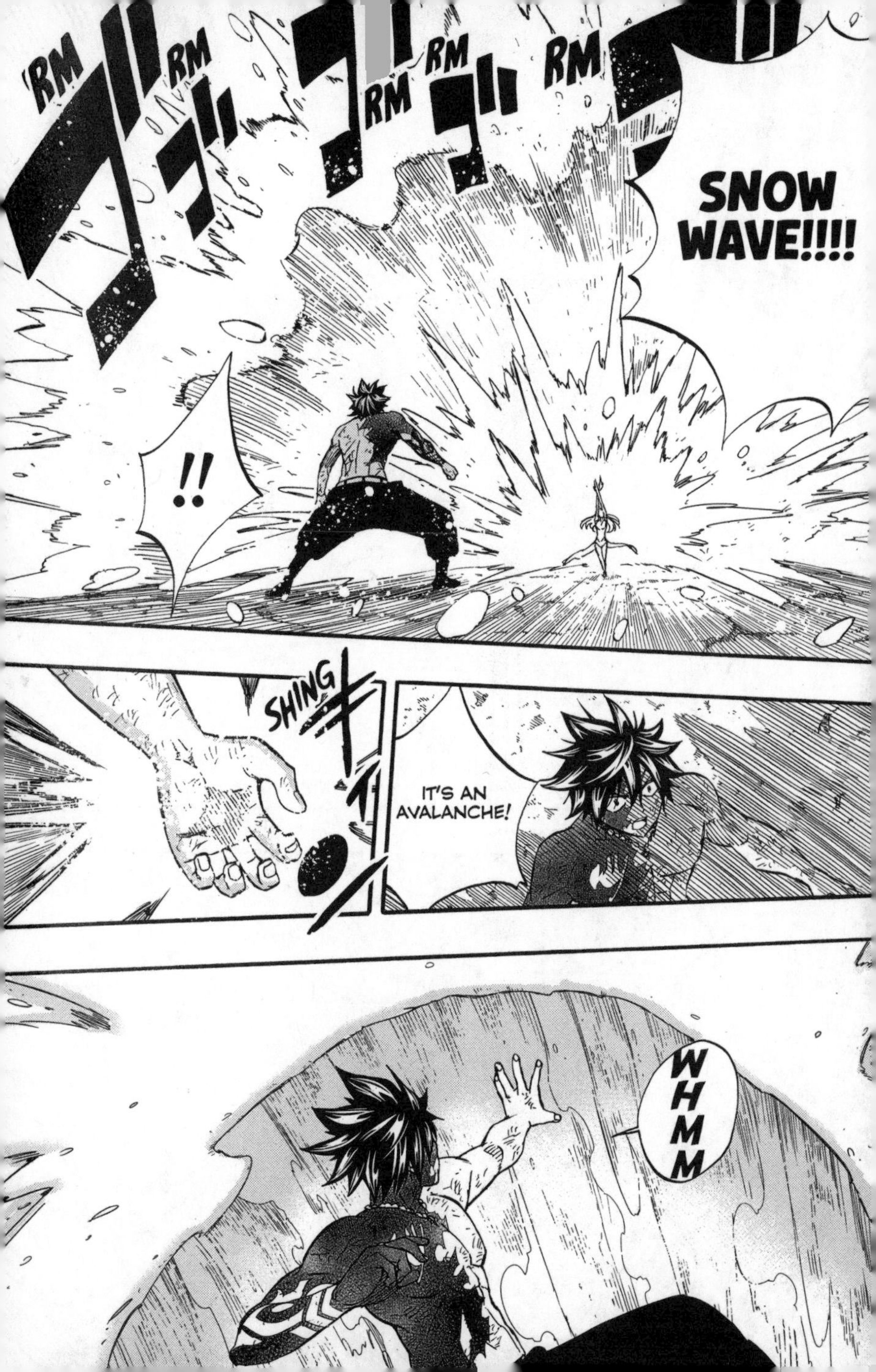

SNOW WAVE!!!!
RM RM RM RM RM RM
!!
SHING
IT'S AN AVALANCHE!
WHMM

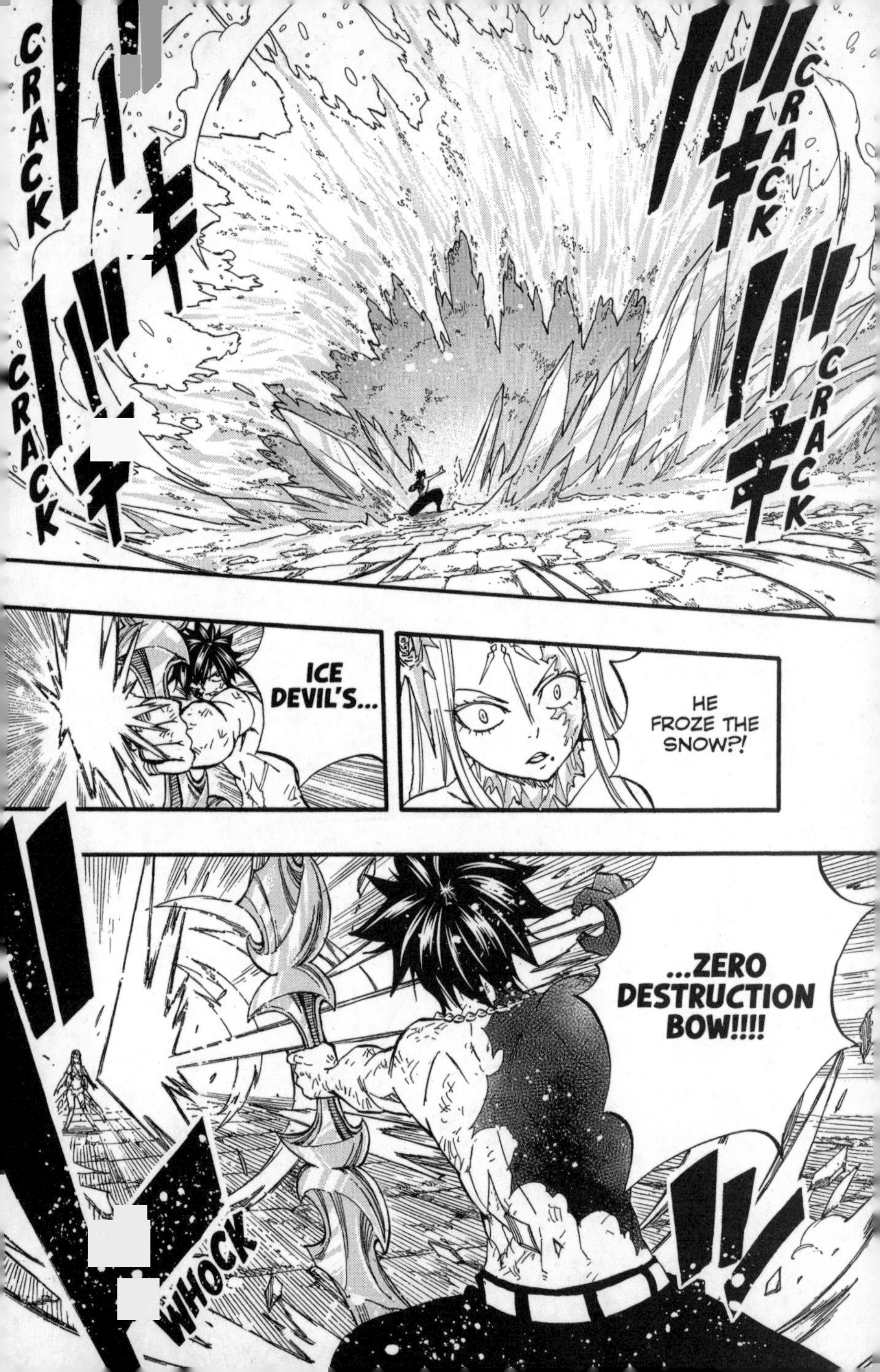
CRACK
CRACK
CRACK
CRACK
HE FROZE THE SNOW?!
ICE DEVIL'S...
...ZERO DESTRUCTION BOW!!!!
WHOCK

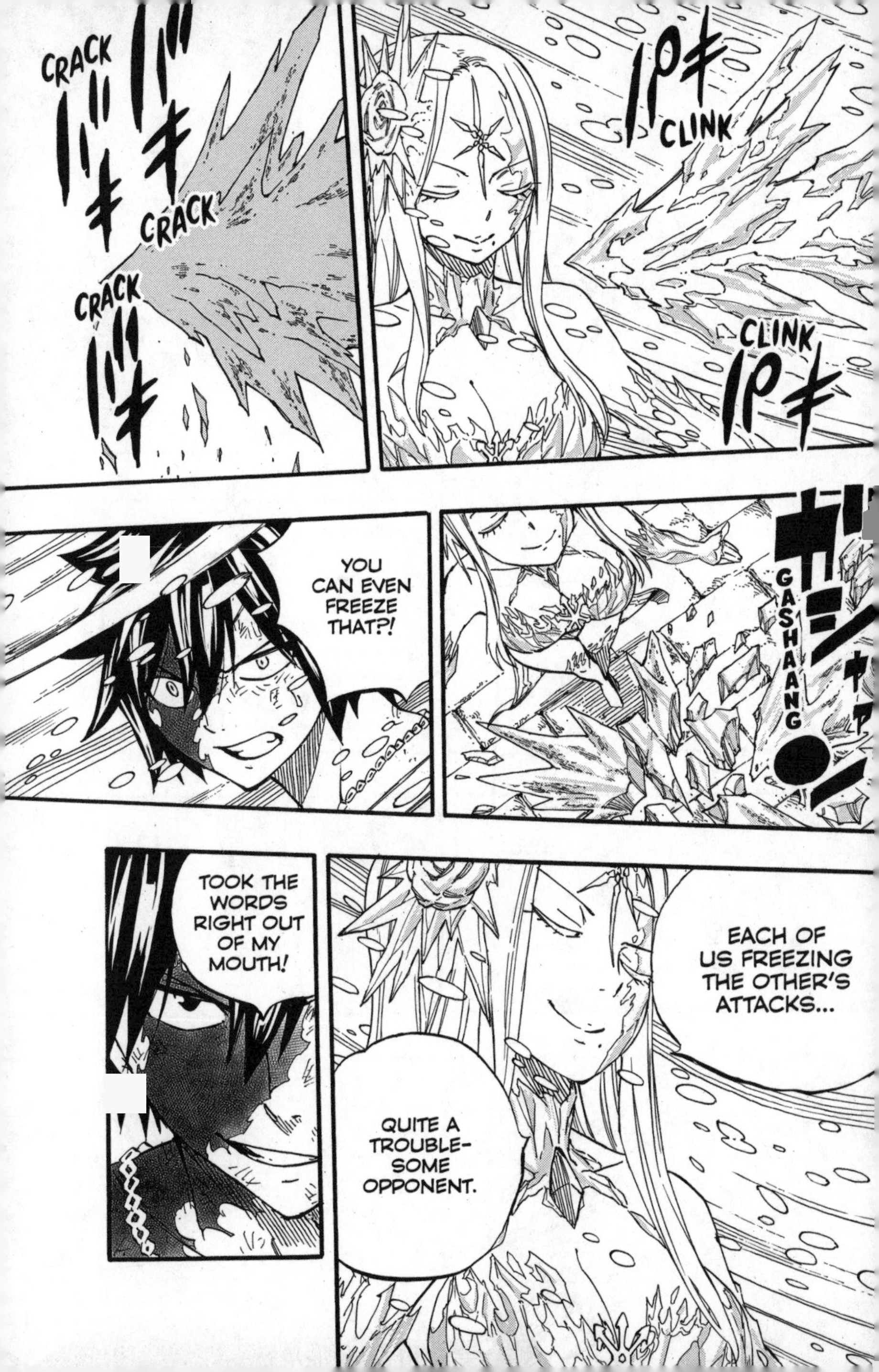
CLINK
CLINK
CRACK
CRACK
CRACK
GASHAANG
YOU CAN EVEN FREEZE THAT?!
EACH OF US FREEZING THE OTHER'S ATTACKS...
QUITE A TROUBLE-SOME OPPONENT.
TOOK THE WORDS RIGHT OUT OF MY MOUTH!

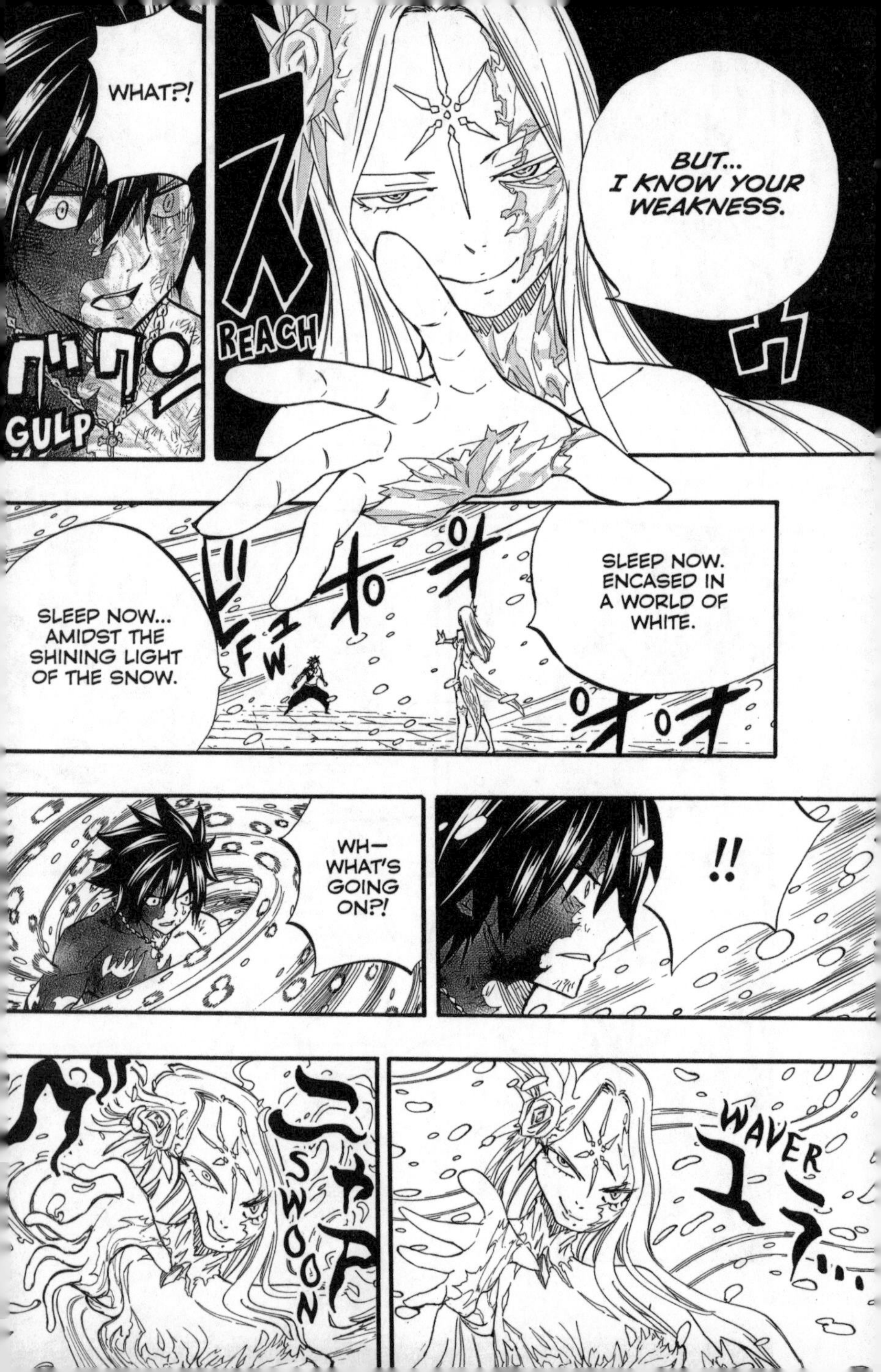
BUT... I KNOW YOUR WEAKNESS.
REACH
WHAT?!
GULP
SLEEP NOW. ENCASED IN A WORLD OF WHITE.
FW
SLEEP NOW... AMIDST THE SHINING LIGHT OF THE SNOW.
!!
WH— WHAT'S GOING ON?!
WAVER
SWOON

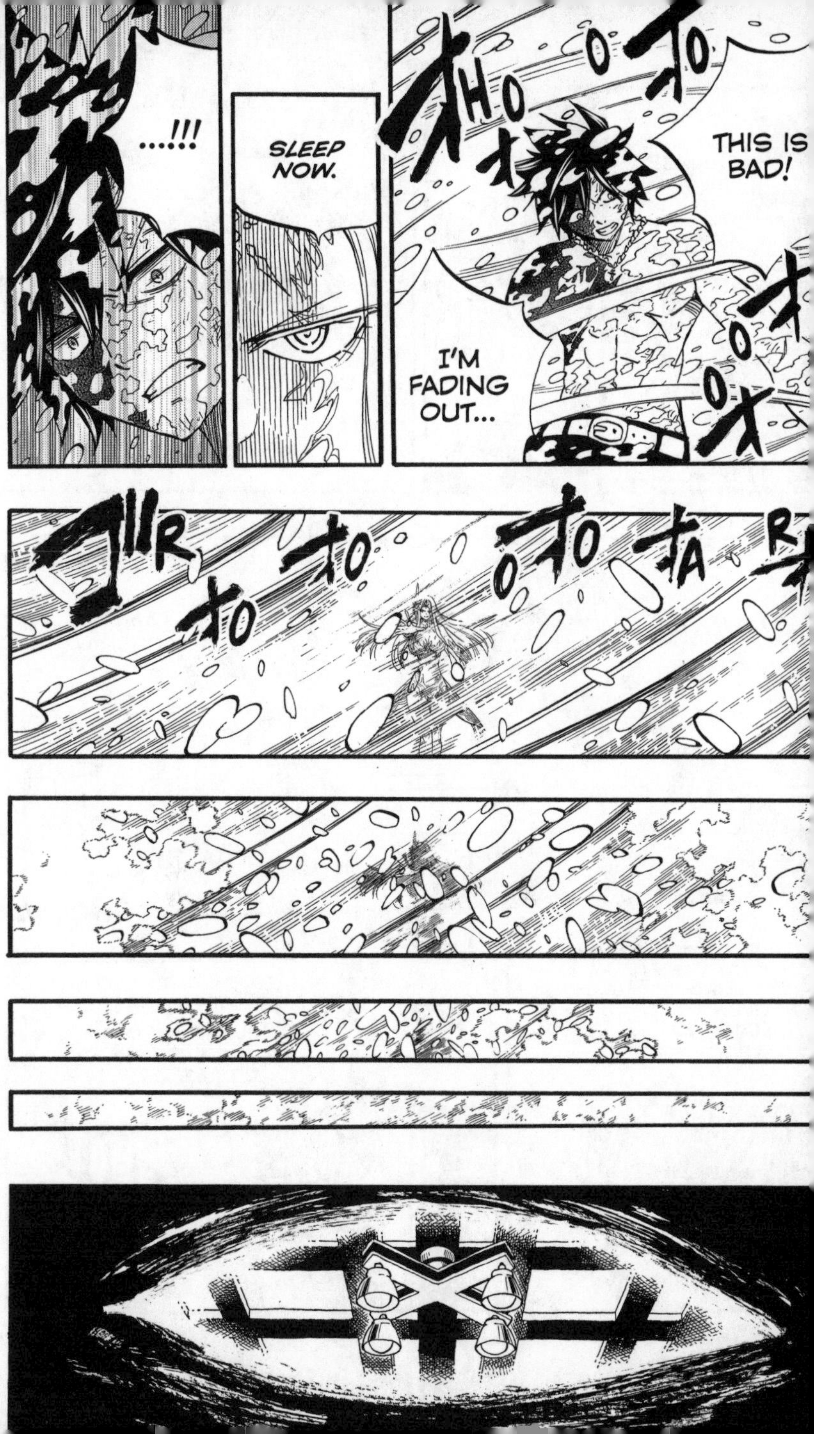
THIS IS BAD!
I'M FADING OUT...
SLEEP NOW.
...!!!

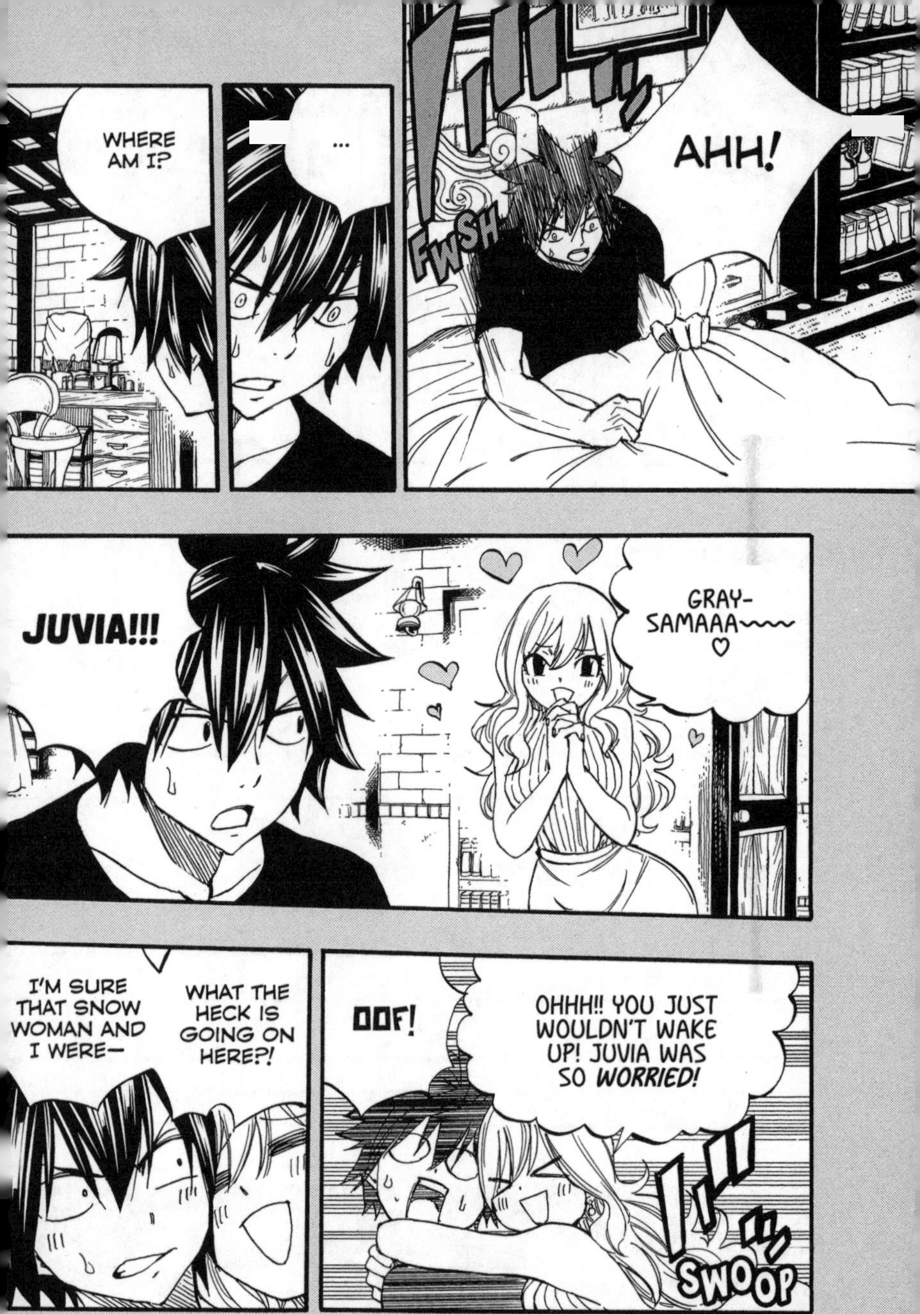
AHH!
FWSH
...
WHERE AM I?
GRAY-SAMAAA~~~ ♡
JUVIA!!!
OHHH!! YOU JUST WOULDN'T WAKE UP! JUVIA WAS SO *WORRIED!*
OOF!
SWOOP
WHAT THE HECK IS GOING ON HERE?!
I'M SURE THAT SNOW WOMAN AND I WERE—

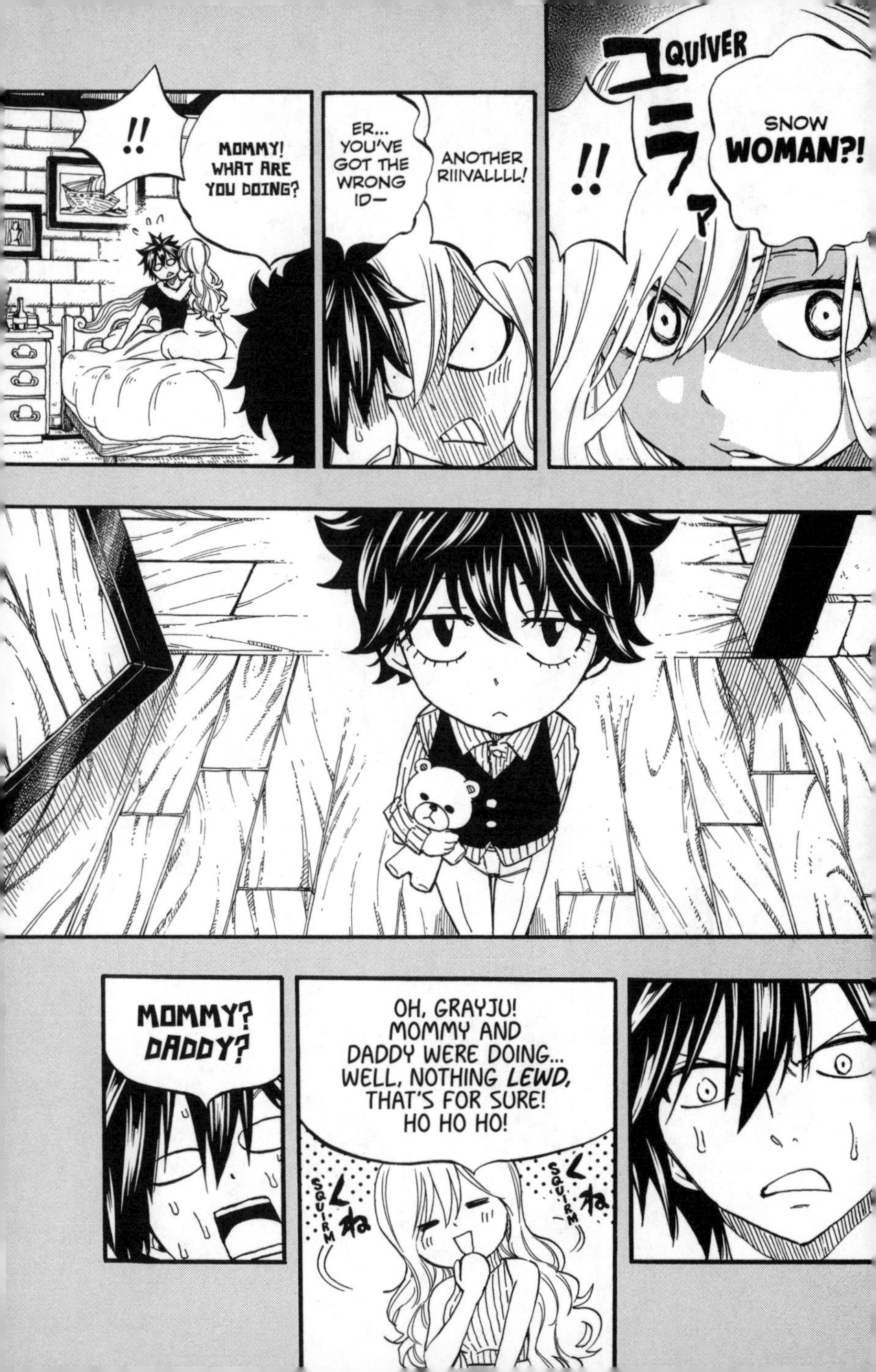
QUIVER
ユラァ
!!
SNOW WOMAN?!
ER... YOU'VE GOT THE WRONG ID—
ANOTHER RIIVALLLL!
!!
MOMMY! WHAT ARE YOU DOING?
OH, GRAYJU! MOMMY AND DADDY WERE DOING... WELL, NOTHING LEWD, THAT'S FOR SURE! HO HO HO!
SQUIRM
くね
SQUIRM
くね
MOMMY? DADDY?

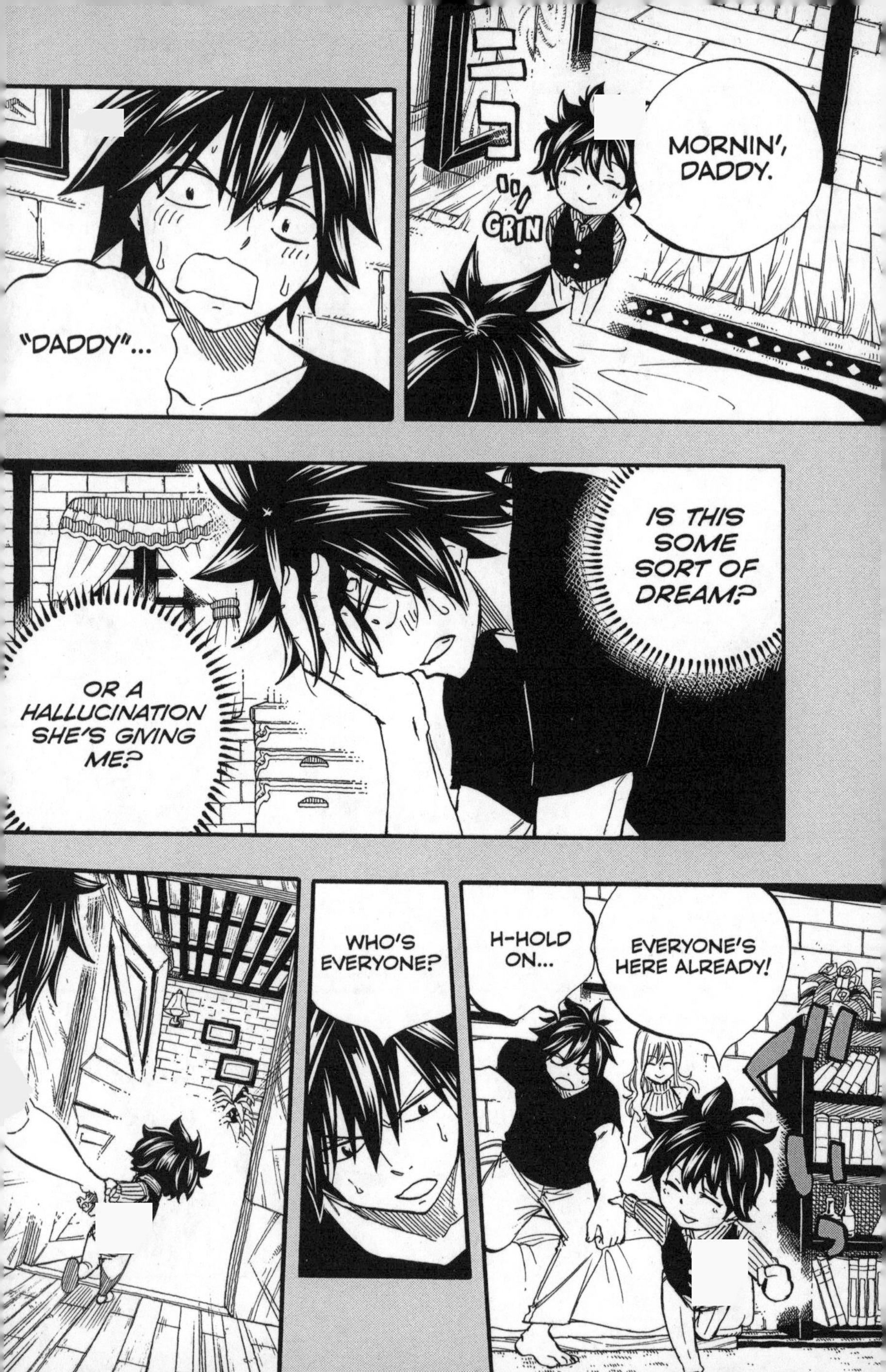
MORNIN', DADDY.
GRIN
"DADDY"...
IS THIS SOME SORT OF DREAM?
OR A HALLUCINATION SHE'S GIVING ME?
EVERYONE'S HERE ALREADY!
H-HOLD ON...
WHO'S EVERYONE?

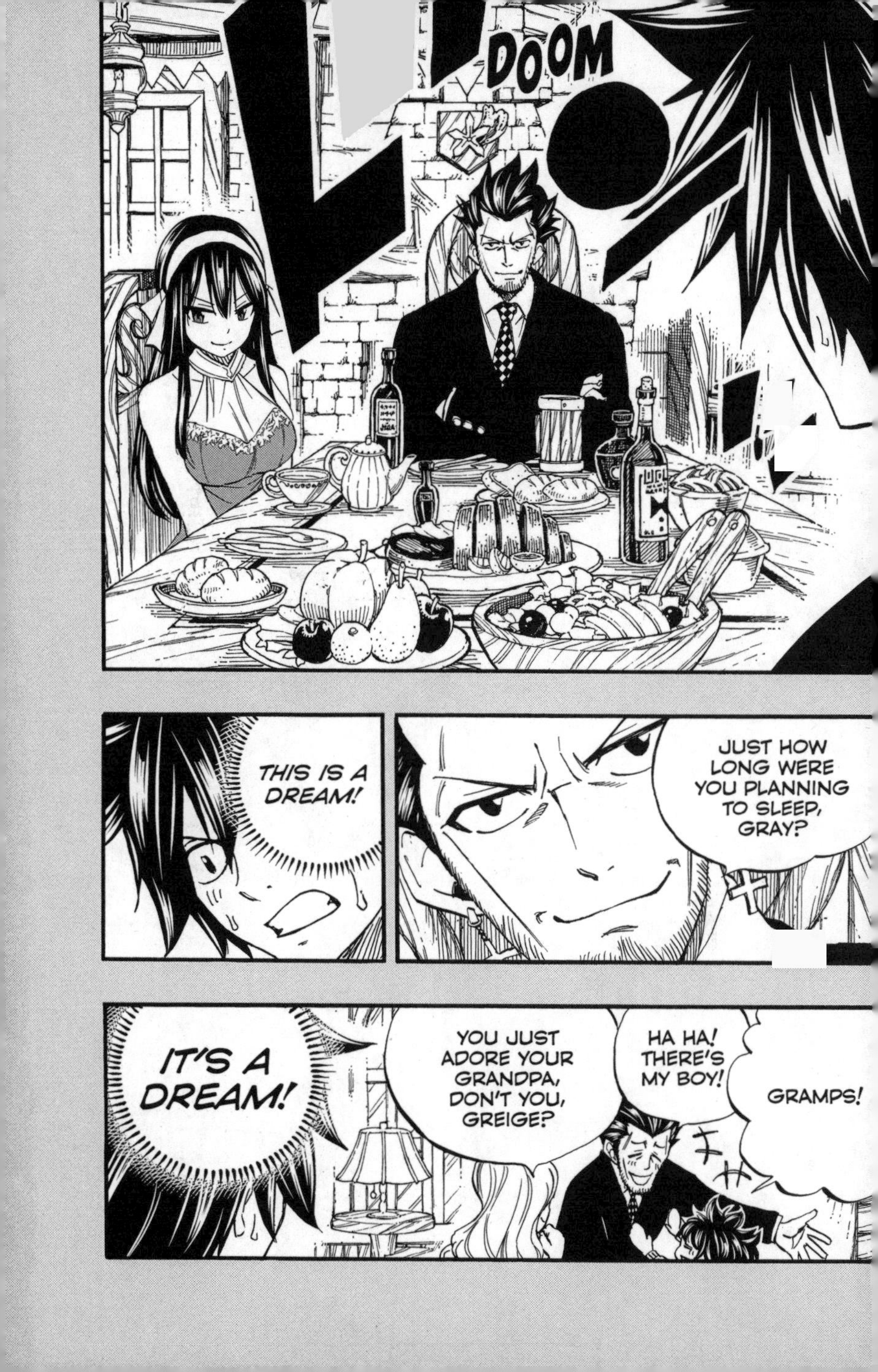
DOOM
JUST HOW LONG WERE YOU PLANNING TO SLEEP, GRAY?
THIS IS A DREAM!
GRAMPS!
HA HA! THERE'S MY BOY!
YOU JUST ADORE YOUR GRANDPA, DON'T YOU, GREIGE?
IT'S A DREAM!

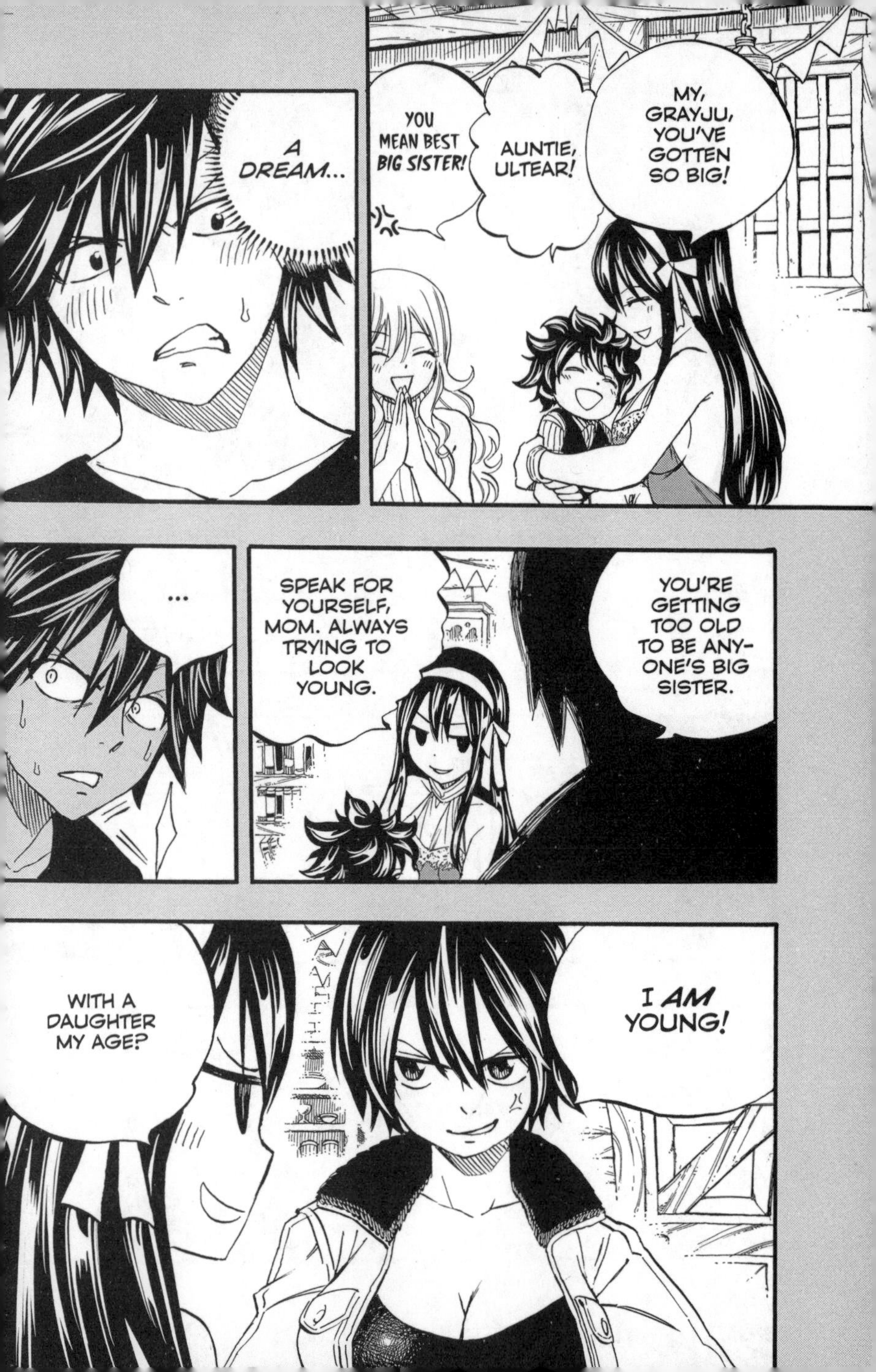
MY, GRAYJU, YOU'VE GOTTEN SO BIG!
AUNTIE, ULTEAR!
YOU MEAN BEST BIG SISTER!
A DREAM...
YOU'RE GETTING TOO OLD TO BE ANY-ONE'S BIG SISTER.
SPEAK FOR YOURSELF, MOM. ALWAYS TRYING TO LOOK YOUNG.
...
I *AM* YOUNG!
WITH A DAUGHTER MY AGE?

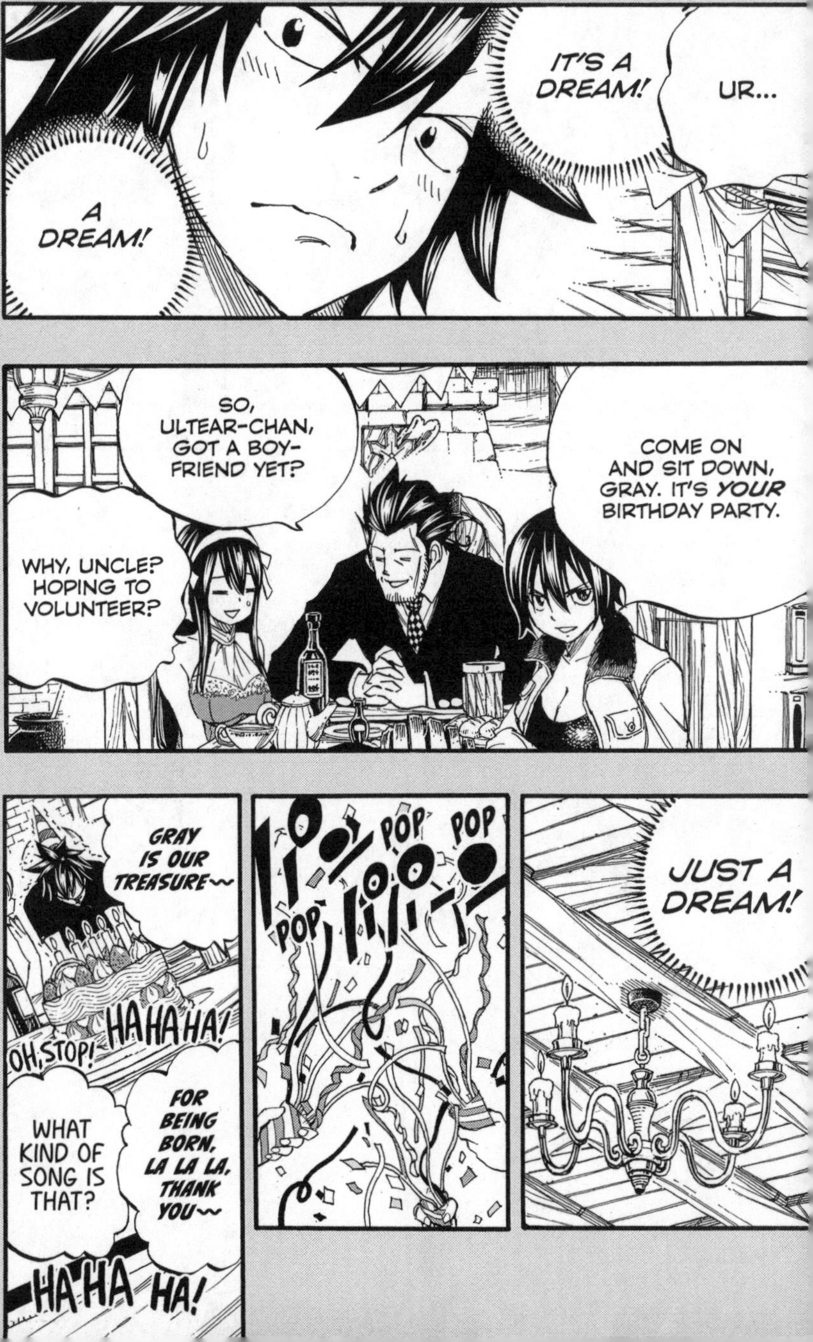
UR...
IT'S A DREAM!
A DREAM!
COME ON AND SIT DOWN, GRAY. IT'S *YOUR* BIRTHDAY PARTY.
SO, ULTEAR-CHAN, GOT A BOY-FRIEND YET?
WHY, UNCLE? HOPING TO VOLUNTEER?
JUST A DREAM!
POP
POP
POP
GRAY IS OUR TREASURE~~
HAHAHA!
OH, STOP!
FOR BEING BORN, LA LA LA, THANK YOU~~
WHAT KIND OF SONG IS THAT?
HA HA HA!

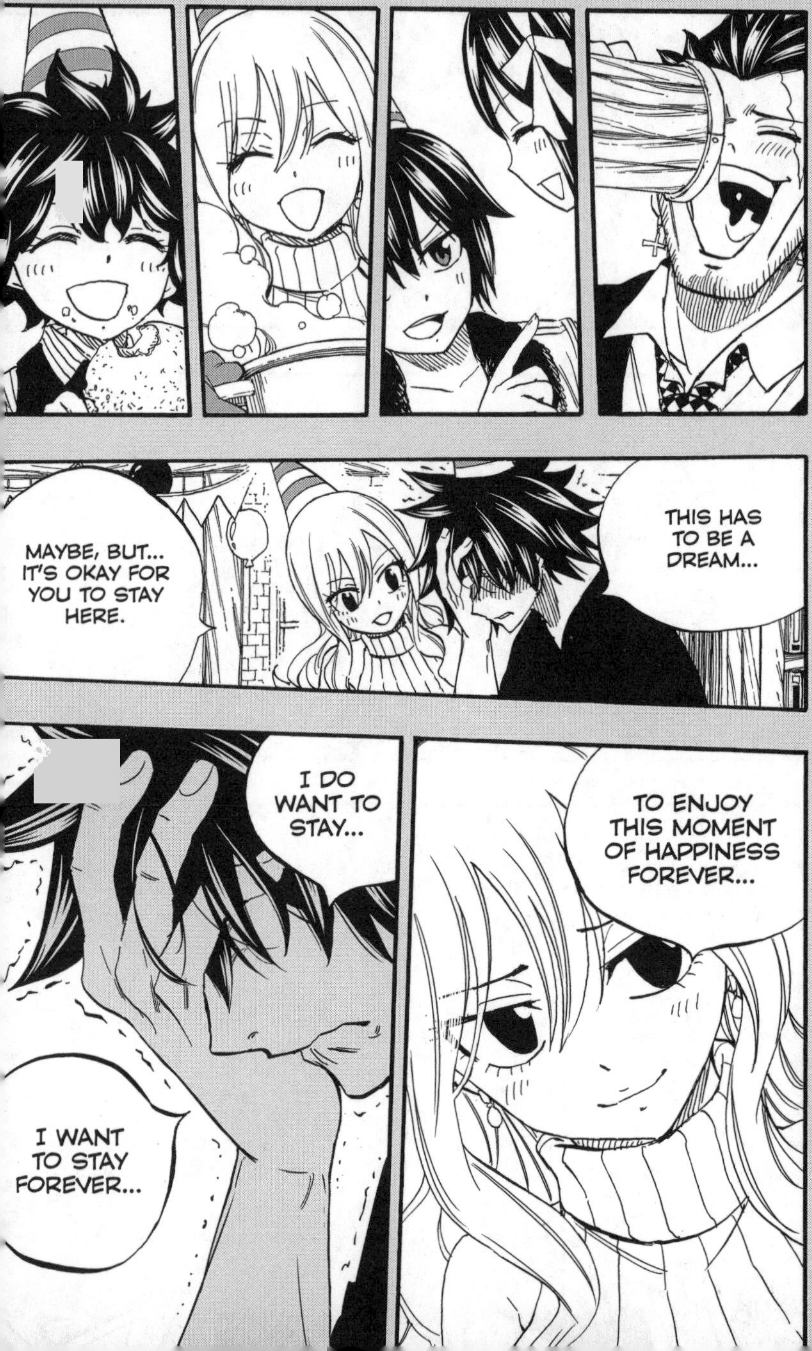
THIS HAS TO BE A DREAM...
MAYBE, BUT... IT'S OKAY FOR YOU TO STAY HERE.
TO ENJOY THIS MOMENT OF HAPPINESS FOREVER...
I DO WANT TO STAY...
I WANT TO STAY FOREVER...

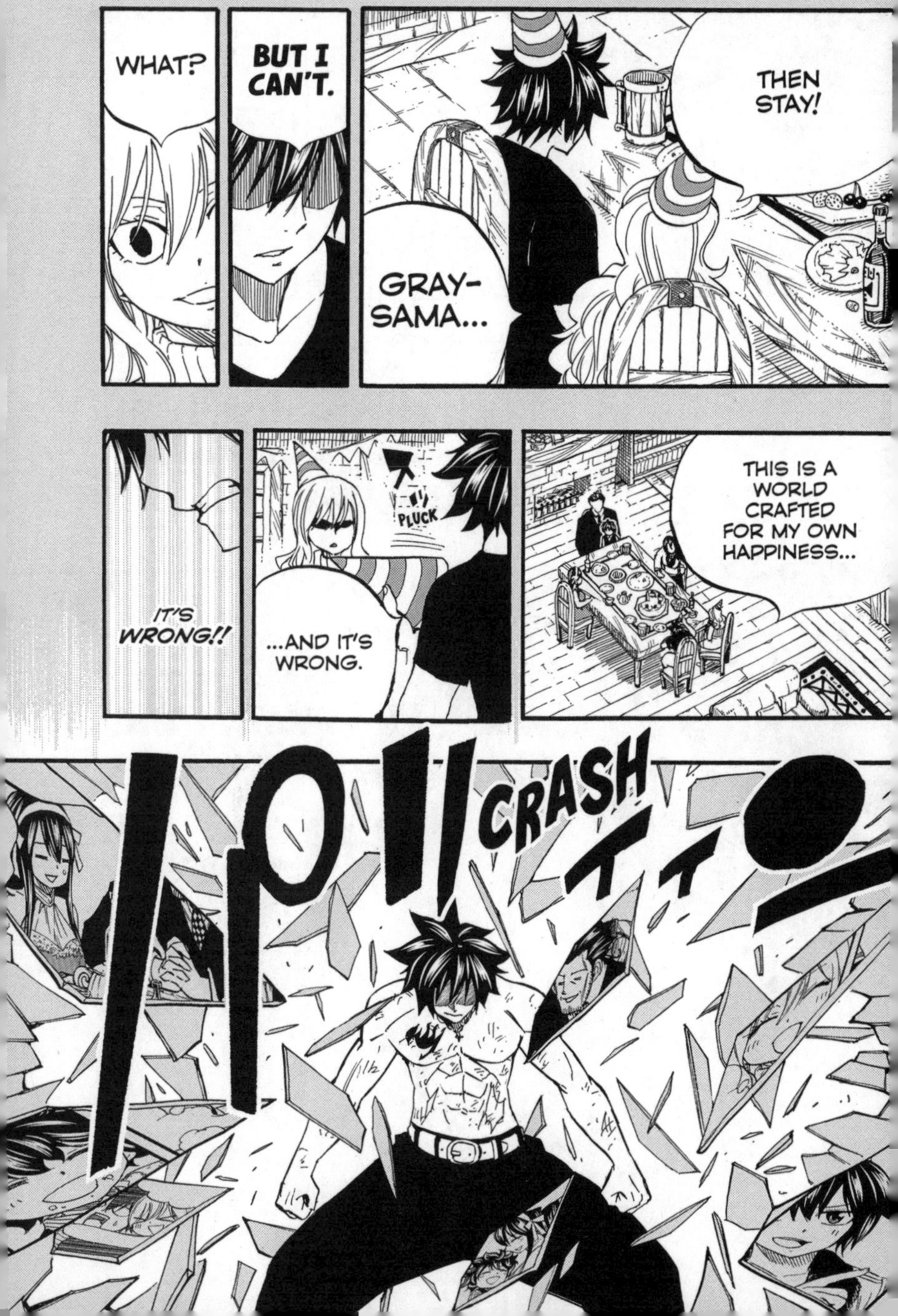
THEN STAY!
GRAY-SAMA...
BUT I CAN'T.
WHAT?
THIS IS A WORLD CRAFTED FOR MY OWN HAPPINESS...
PLUCK
...AND IT'S WRONG.
IT'S WRONG!!
CRASH

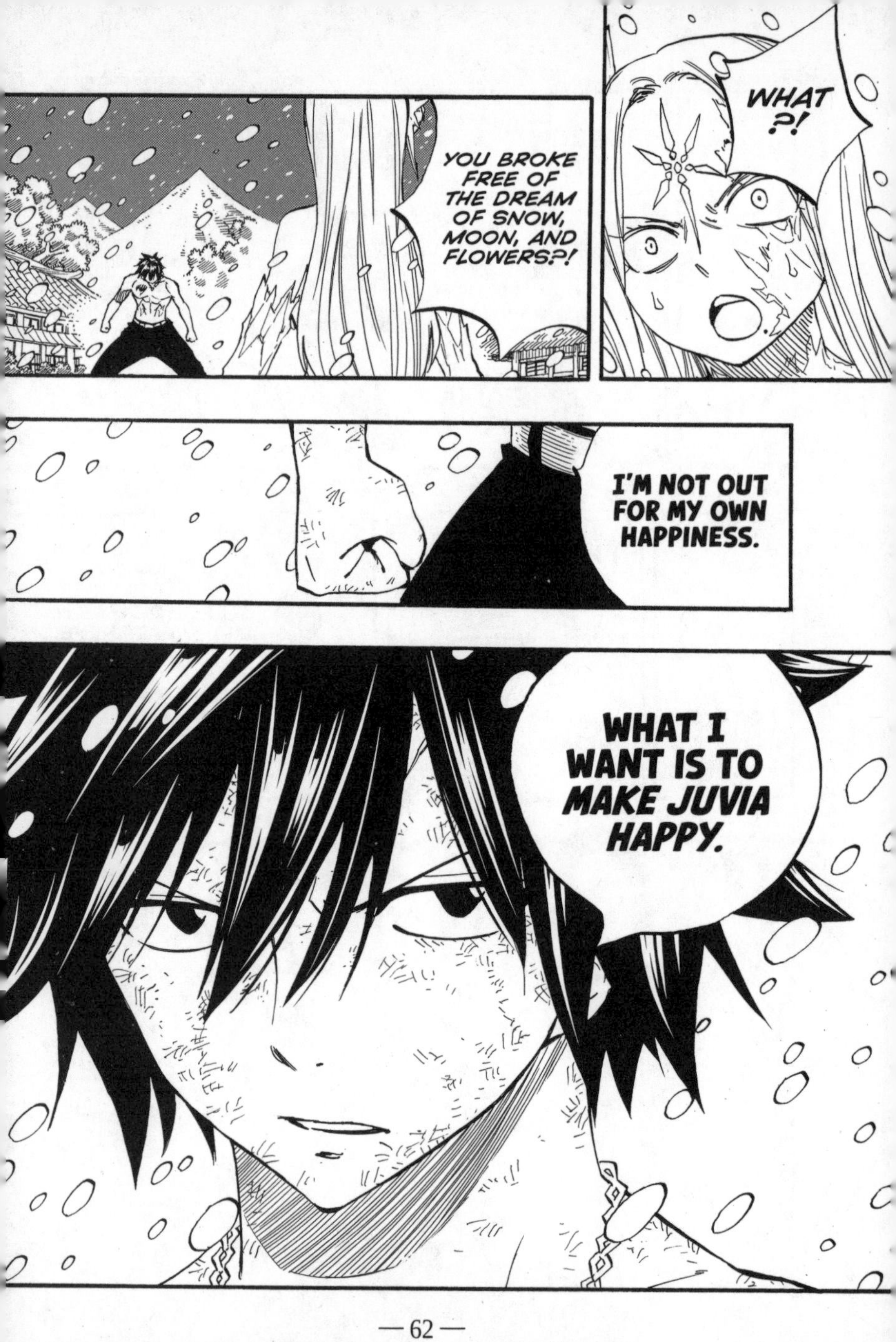
WHAT ?!
YOU BROKE FREE OF THE DREAM OF SNOW, MOON, AND FLOWERS?!
I'M NOT OUT FOR MY OWN HAPPINESS.
WHAT I WANT IS TO MAKE JUVIA HAPPY.

FAIRY TAIL 100 YEARS QUEST

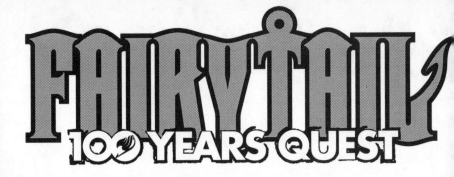

Chapter 85: Ice Giants

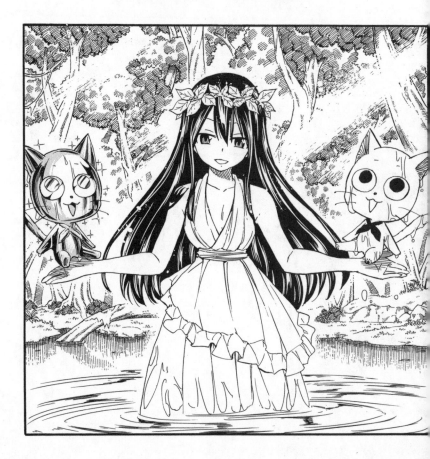

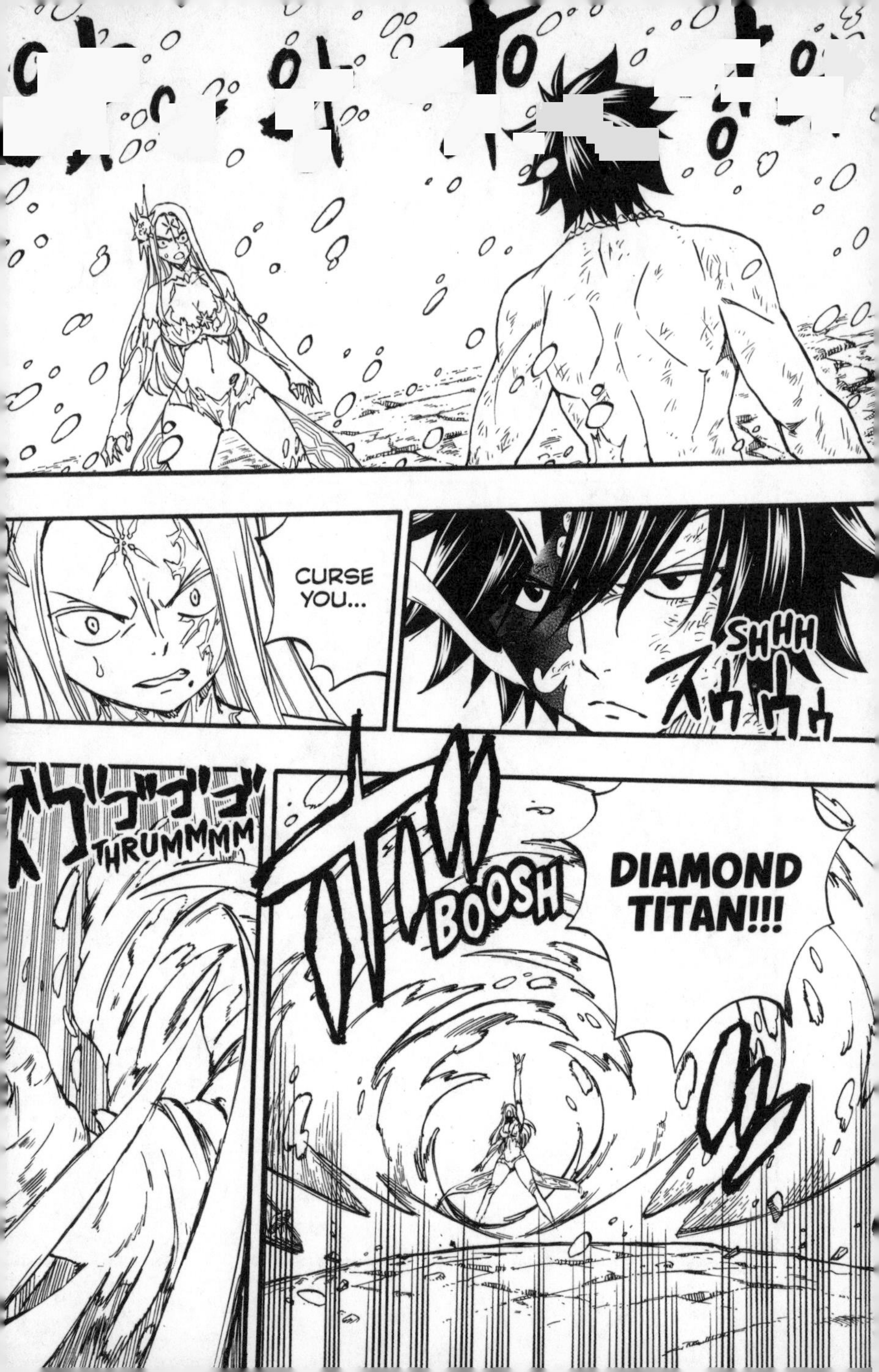
SHHH
CURSE YOU...
BOOSH
DIAMOND TITAN!!!
THRUMMMM

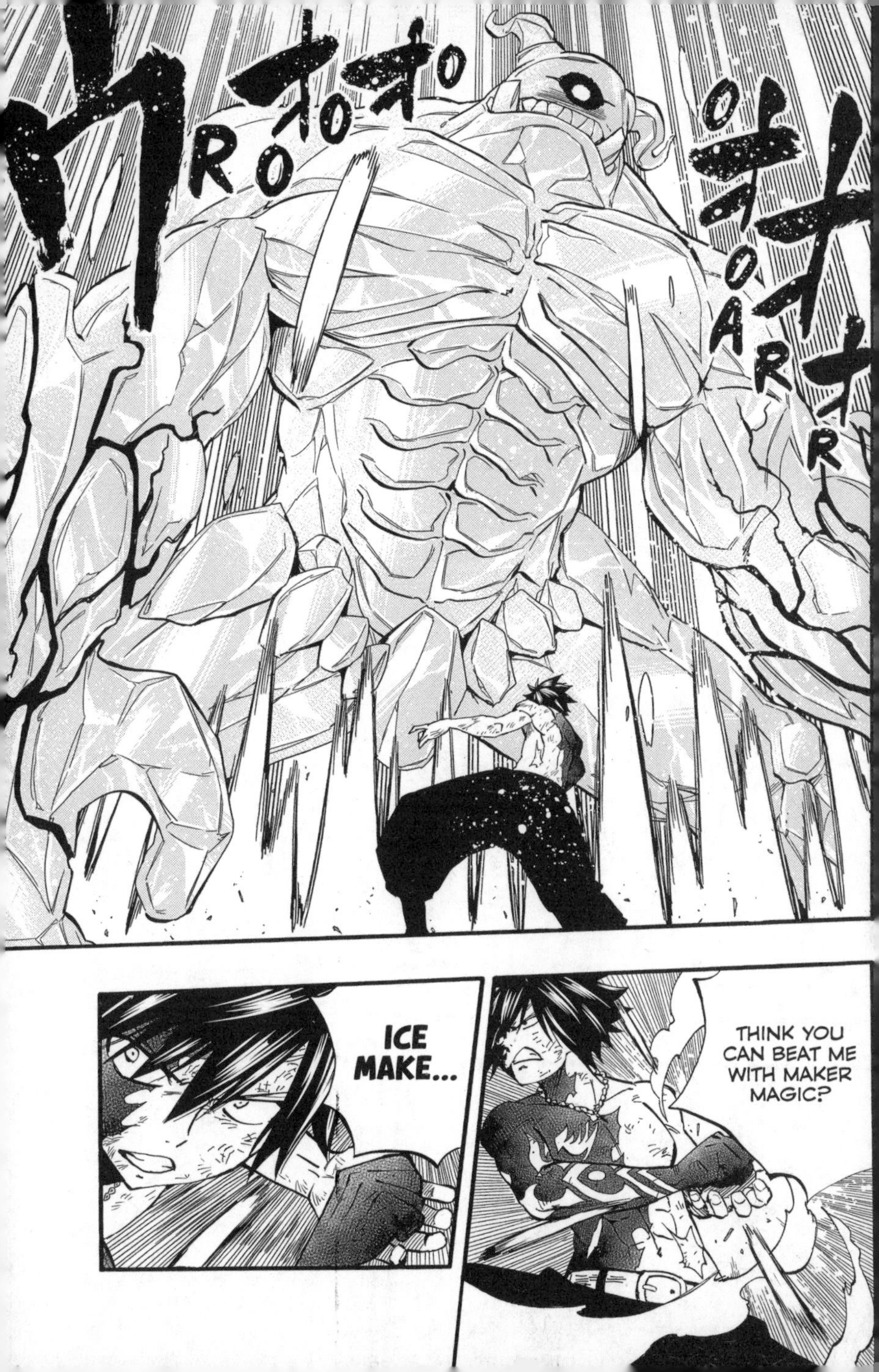
ROOOOOOOARR
THINK YOU CAN BEAT ME WITH MAKER MAGIC?
ICE MAKE...

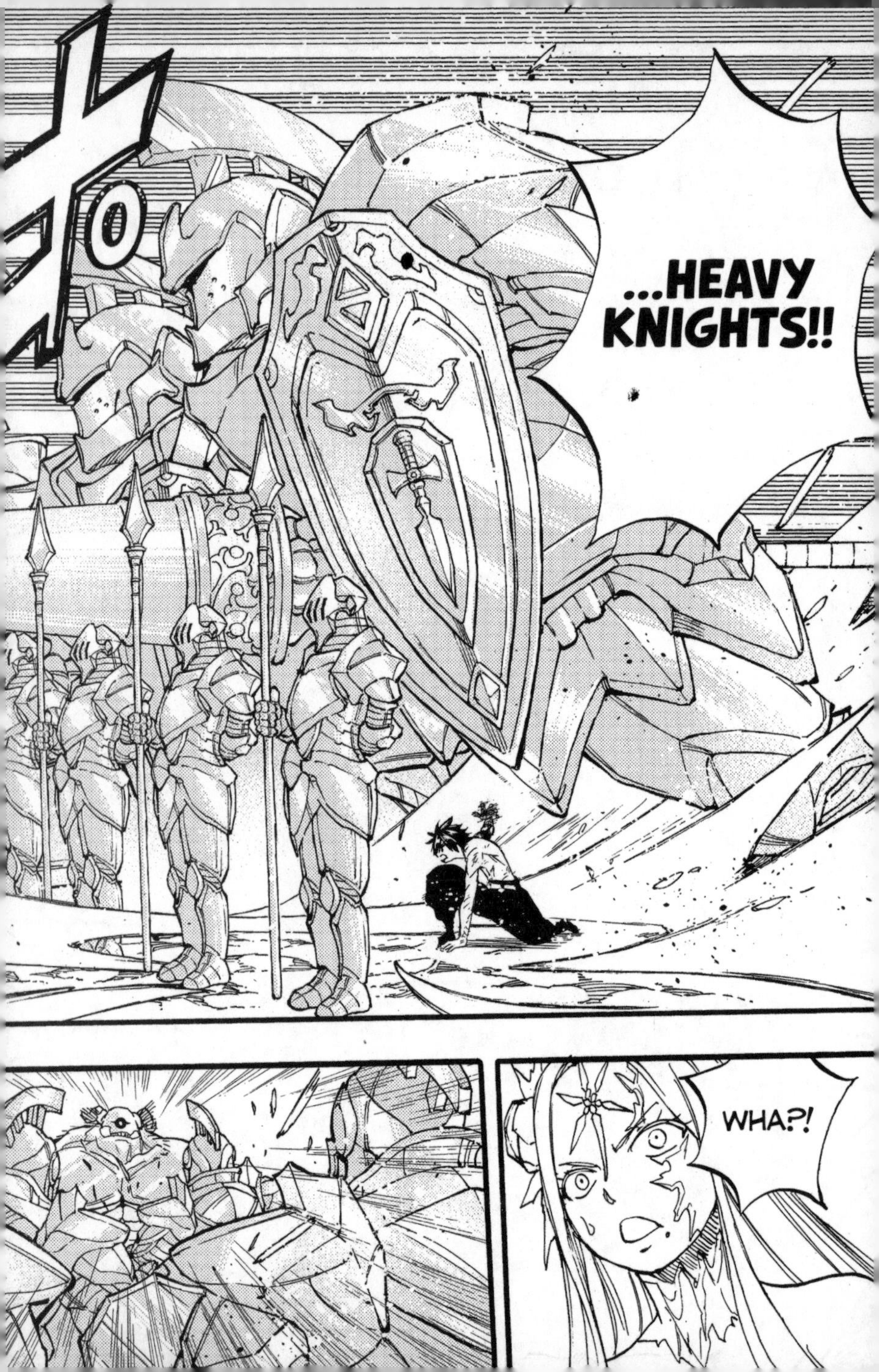
...HEAVY KNIGHTS!!
WHA?!

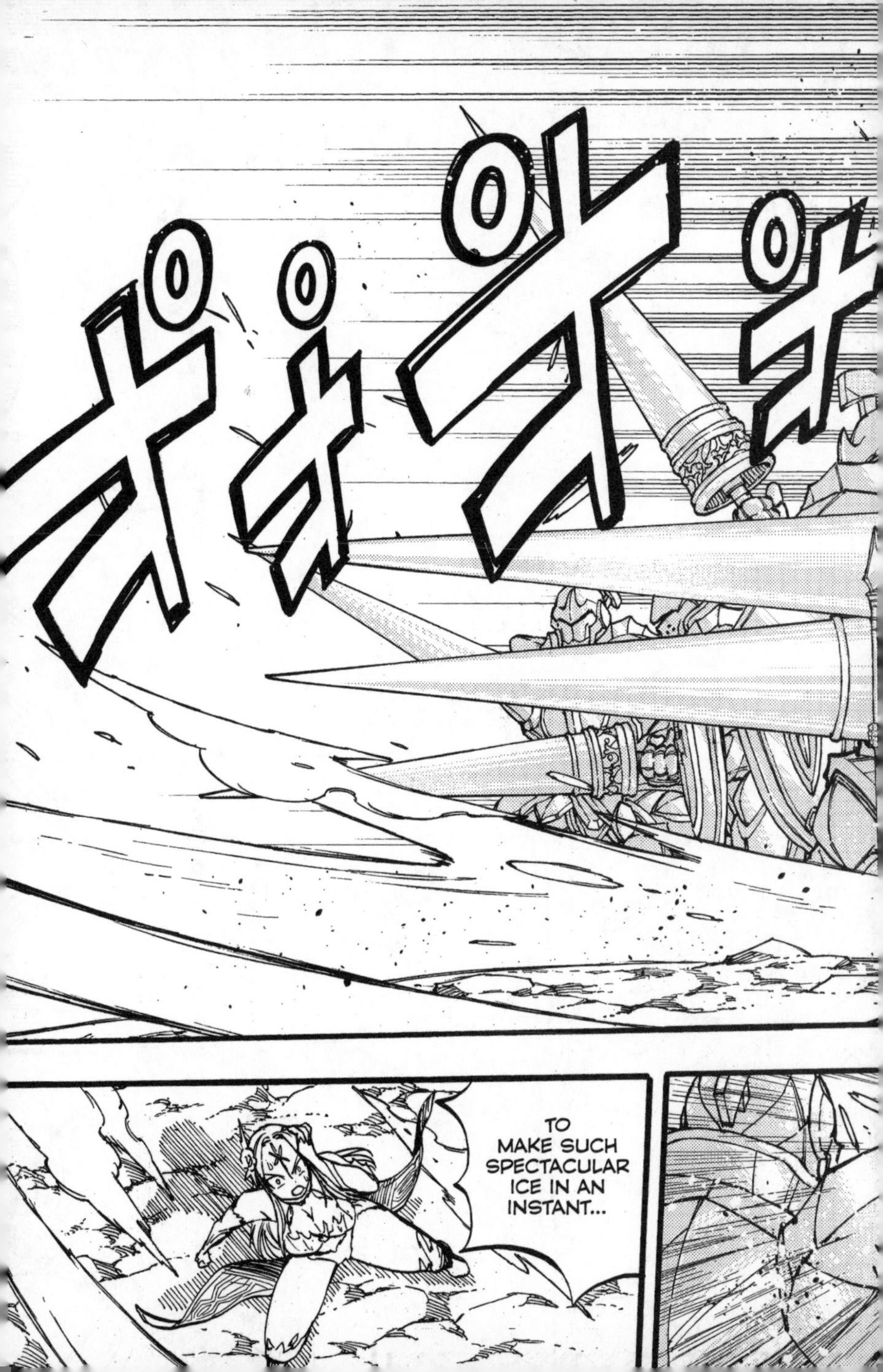
TO MAKE SUCH SPECTACULAR ICE IN AN INSTANT...

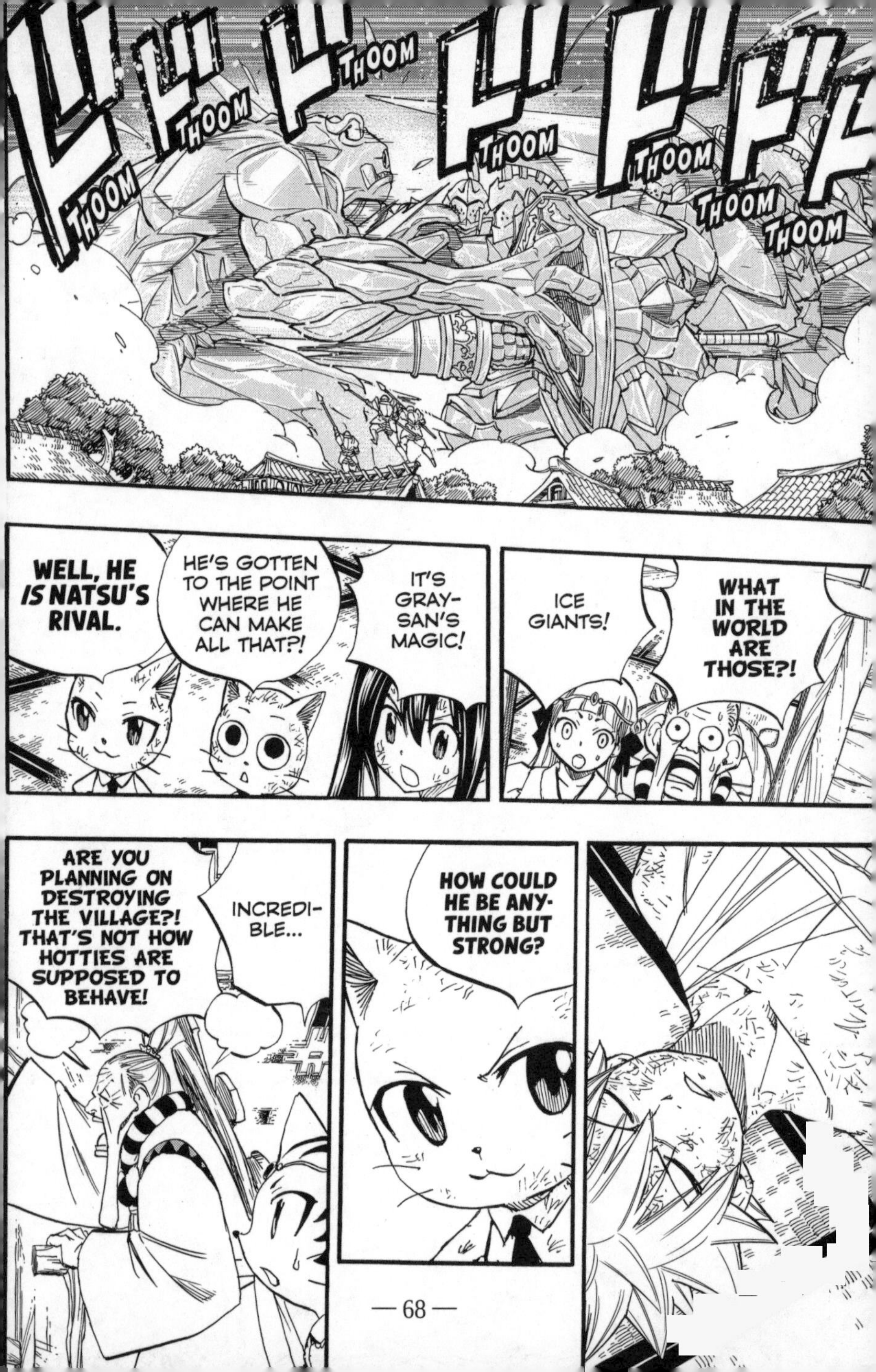
THOOM
THOOM
THOOM
THOOM
THOOM
THOOM
THOOM
WHAT IN THE WORLD ARE THOSE?!
ICE GIANTS!
IT'S GRAY-SAN'S MAGIC!
HE'S GOTTEN TO THE POINT WHERE HE CAN MAKE ALL THAT?!
WELL, HE *IS* NATSU'S RIVAL.
HOW COULD HE BE ANY-THING BUT STRONG?
INCREDI-BLE...
ARE YOU PLANNING ON DESTROYING THE VILLAGE?! THAT'S NOT HOW HOTTIES ARE SUPPOSED TO BEHAVE!

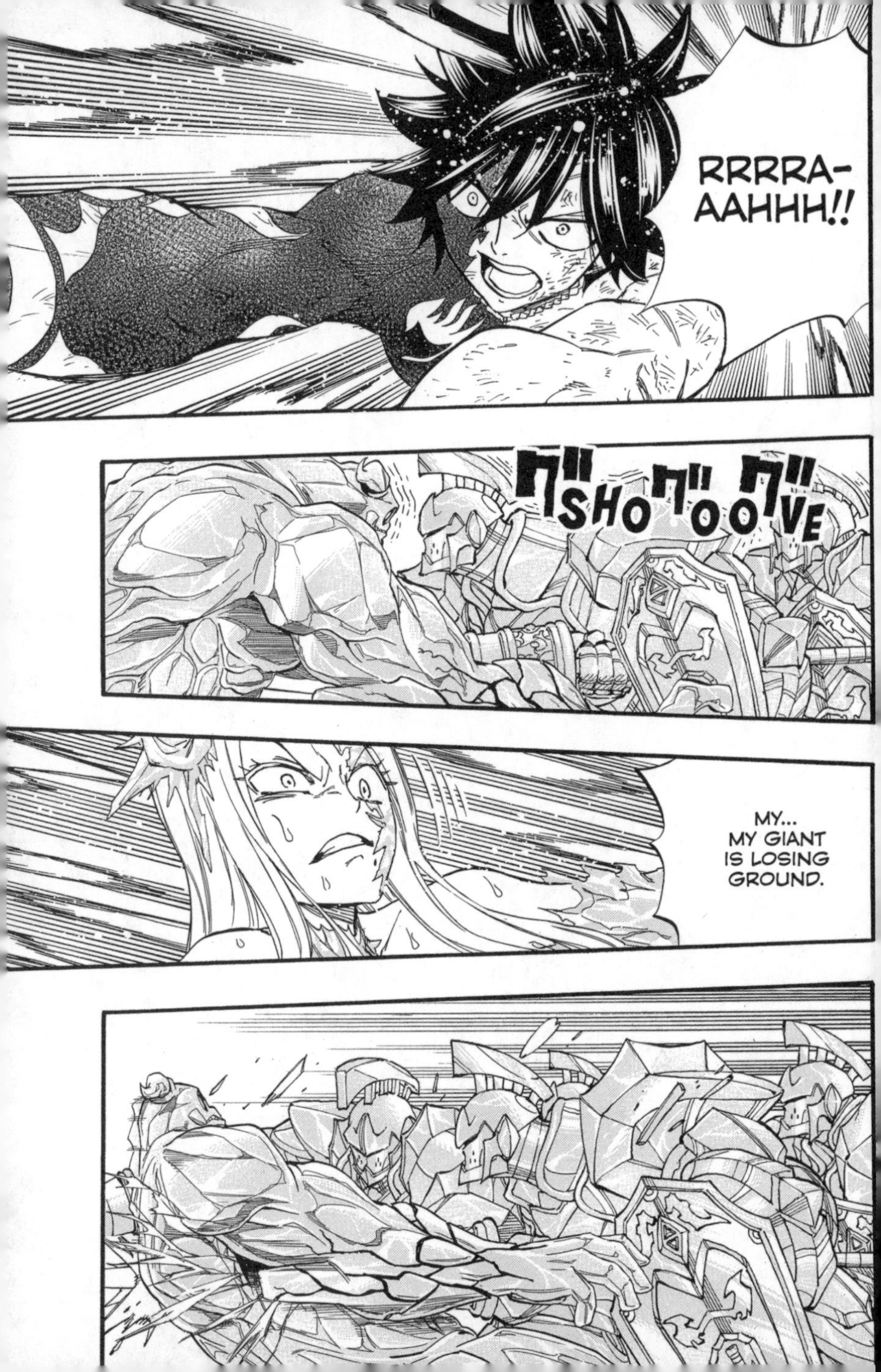
RRRRA-AAHHH!!
SHOOOVE
MY... MY GIANT IS LOSING GROUND.

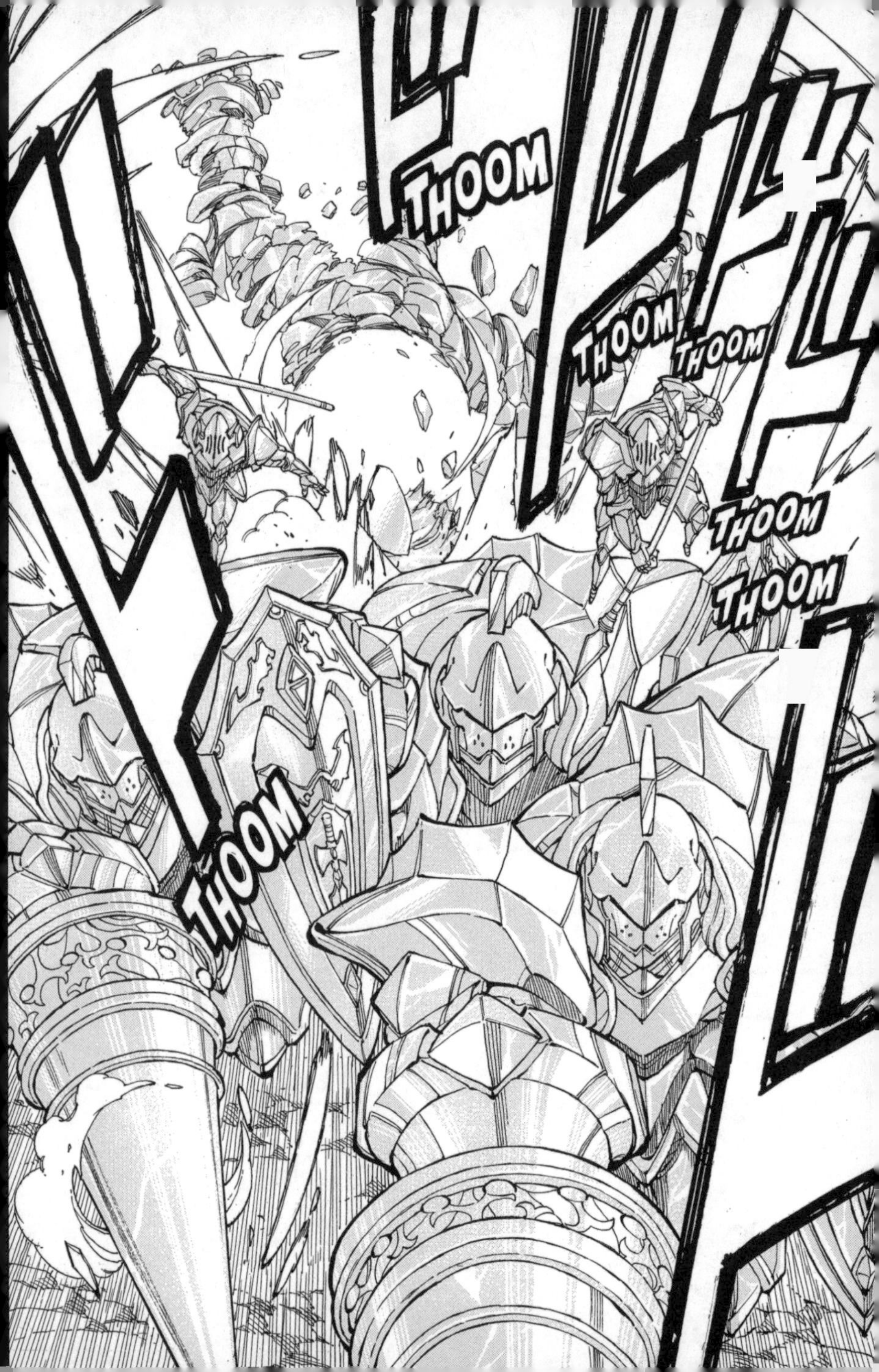
THOOM
THOOM
THOOM
THOOM
THOOM
THOOM

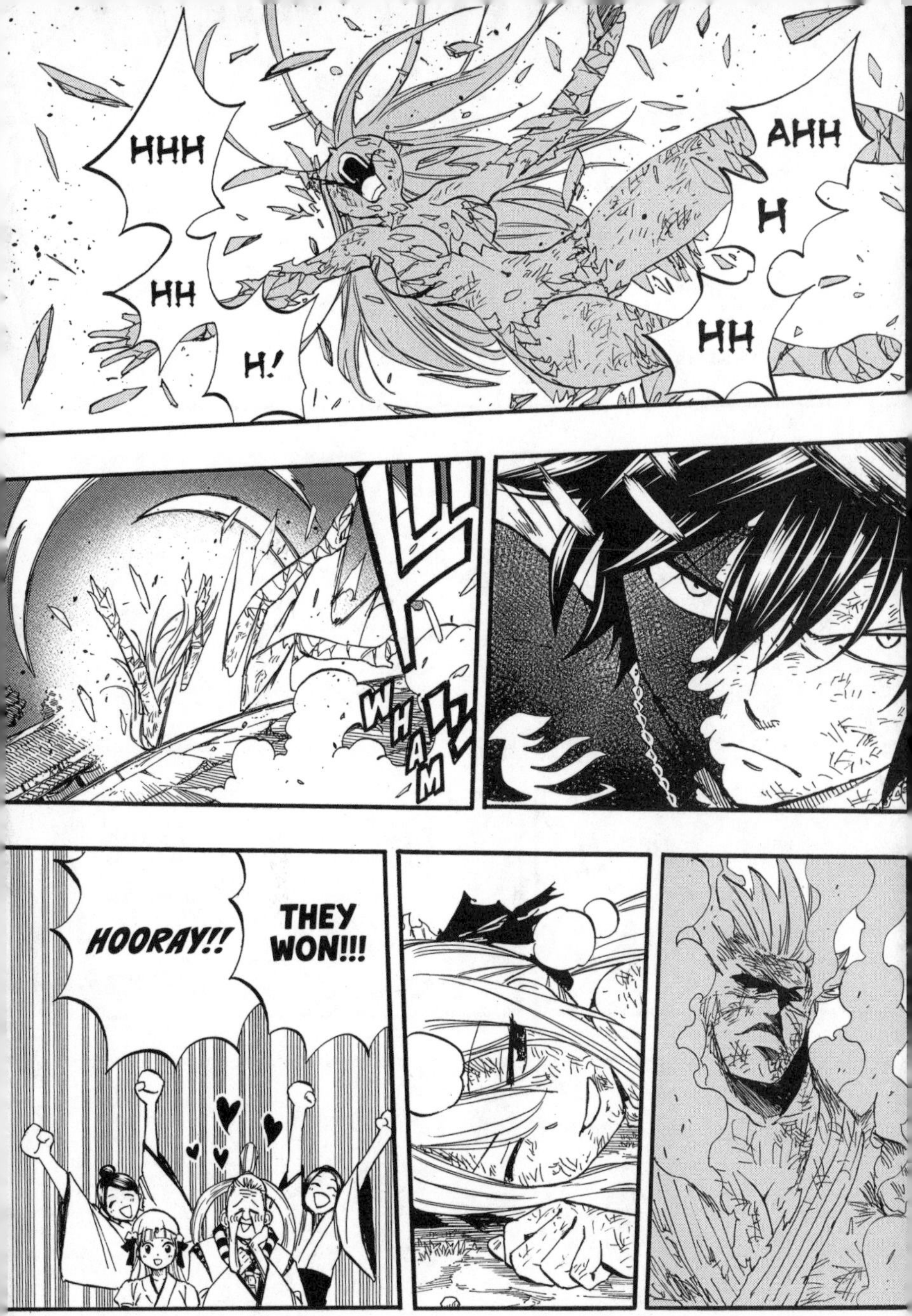
AHH
H
HH
HHH
HH
H!
WHAM
THEY WON!!!
HOORAY!!

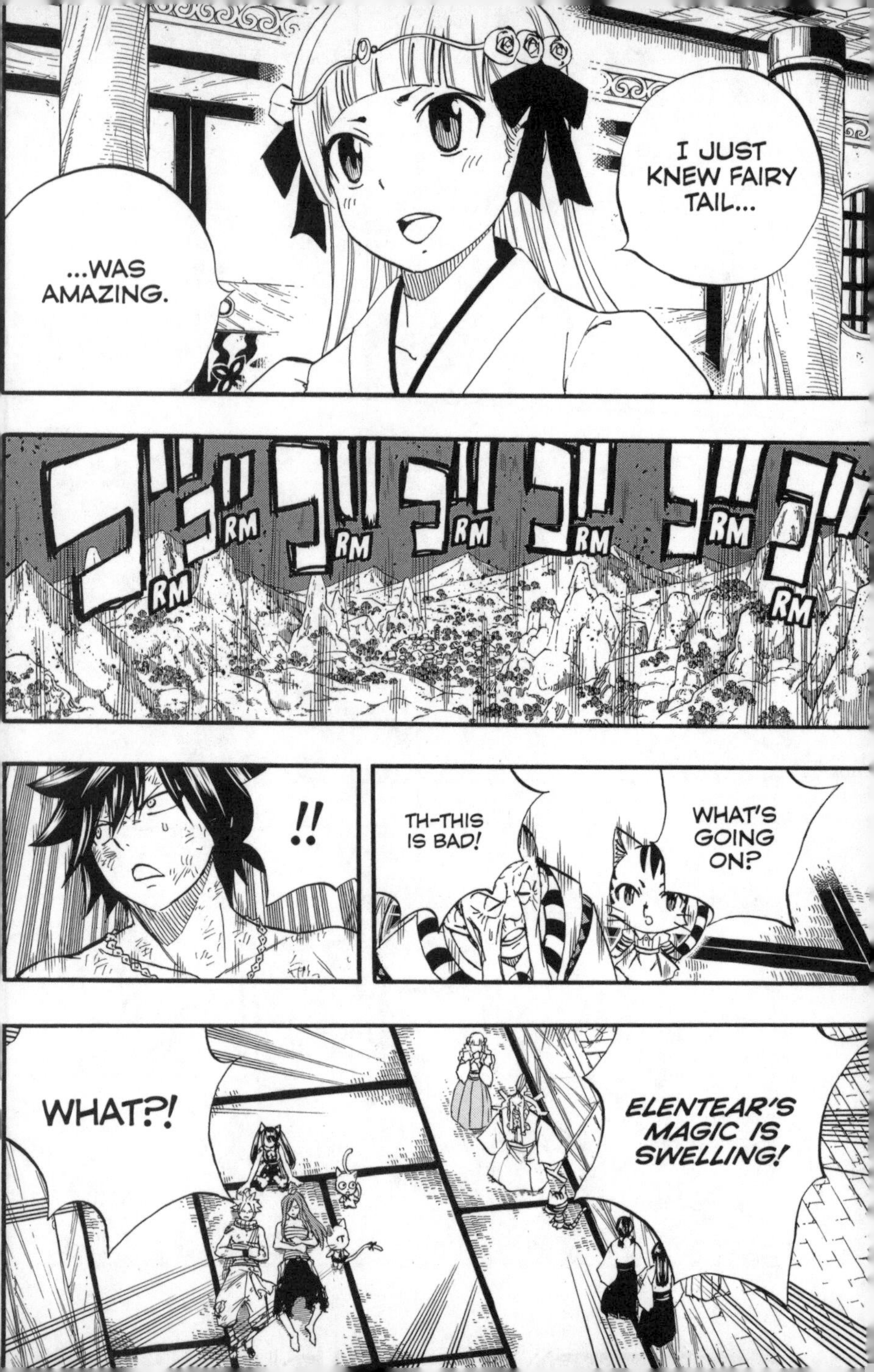
I JUST KNEW FAIRY TAIL...
...WAS AMAZING.
RM RM RM RM RM RM RM
WHAT'S GOING ON?
TH-THIS IS BAD!
!!
ELENTEAR'S MAGIC IS SWELLING!
WHAT?!

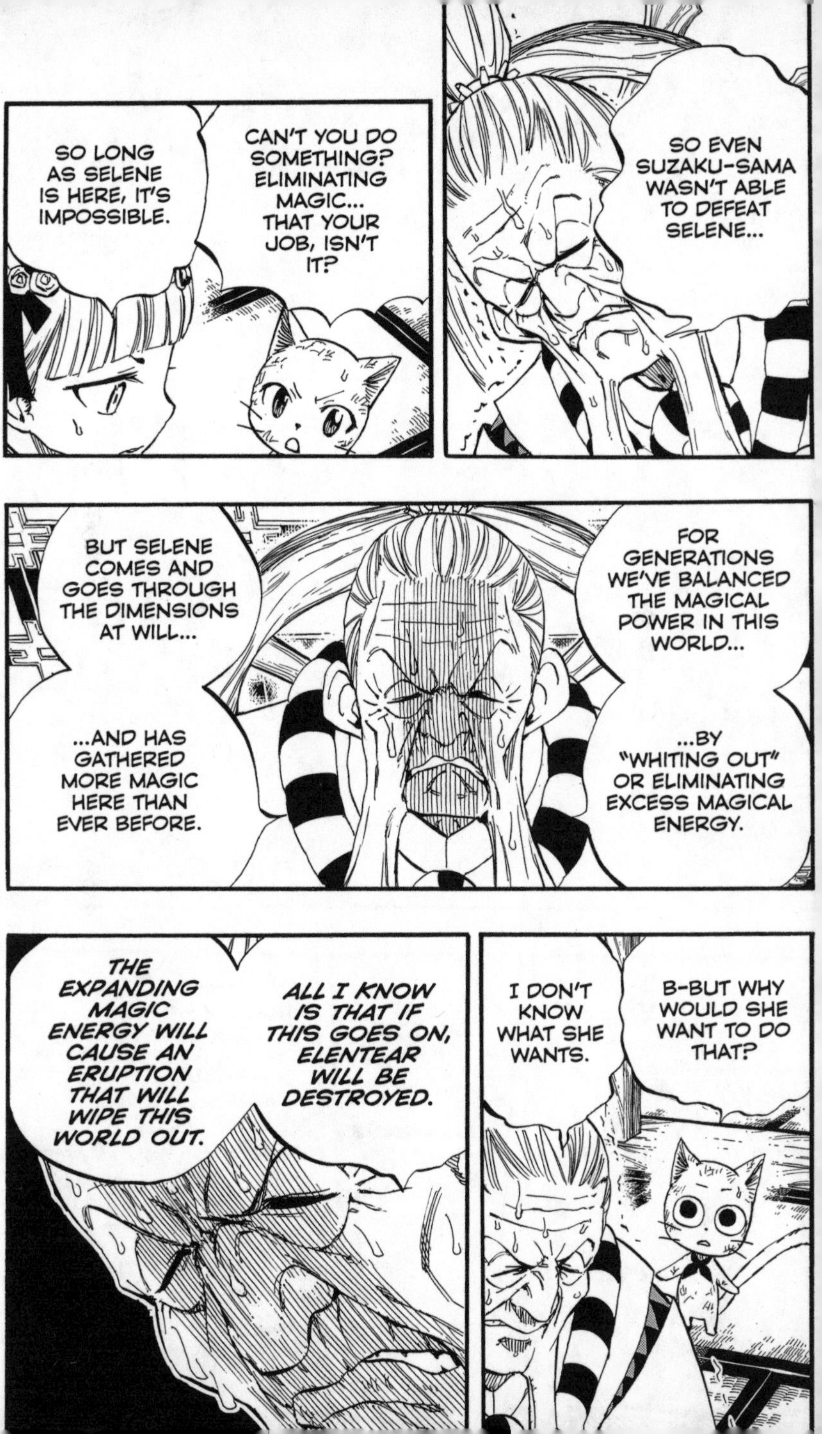
SO EVEN SUZAKU-SAMA WASN'T ABLE TO DEFEAT SELENE...
CAN'T YOU DO SOMETHING? ELIMINATING MAGIC... THAT YOUR JOB, ISN'T IT?
SO LONG AS SELENE IS HERE, IT'S IMPOSSIBLE.
FOR GENERATIONS WE'VE BALANCED THE MAGICAL POWER IN THIS WORLD...
...BY "WHITING OUT" OR ELIMINATING EXCESS MAGICAL ENERGY.
BUT SELENE COMES AND GOES THROUGH THE DIMENSIONS AT WILL...
...AND HAS GATHERED MORE MAGIC HERE THAN EVER BEFORE.
B-BUT WHY WOULD SHE WANT TO DO THAT?
I DON'T KNOW WHAT SHE WANTS.
ALL I KNOW IS THAT IF THIS GOES ON, ELENTEAR WILL BE DESTROYED.
THE EXPANDING MAGIC ENERGY WILL CAUSE AN ERUPTION THAT WILL WIPE THIS WORLD OUT.

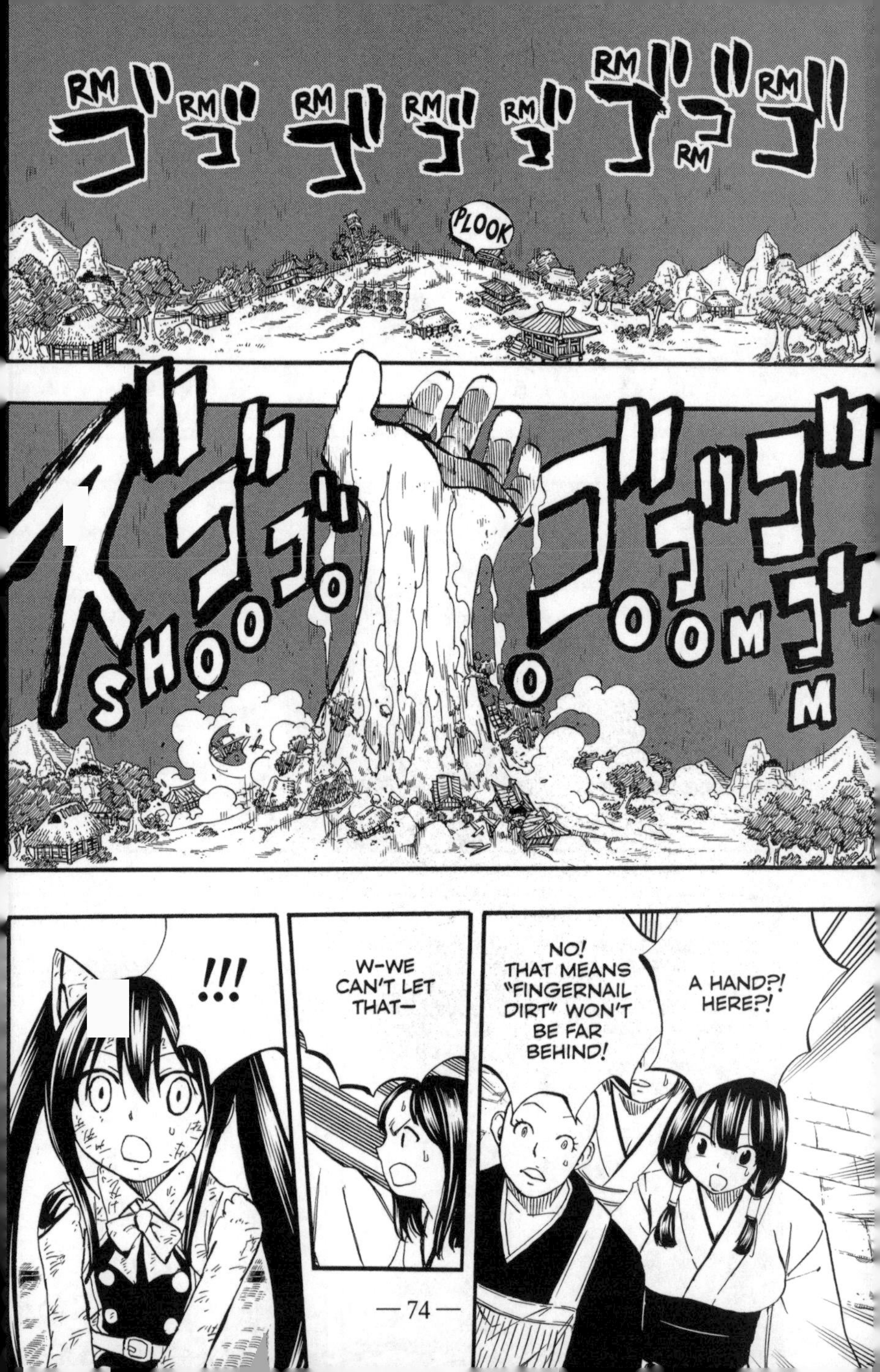
RM RM RM RM RM RM RM RM
PLOOK
SHOOOO
O
OOM
M
A HAND?! HERE?!
NO! THAT MEANS "FINGERNAIL DIRT" WON'T BE FAR BEHIND!
W-WE CAN'T LET THAT—
!!!

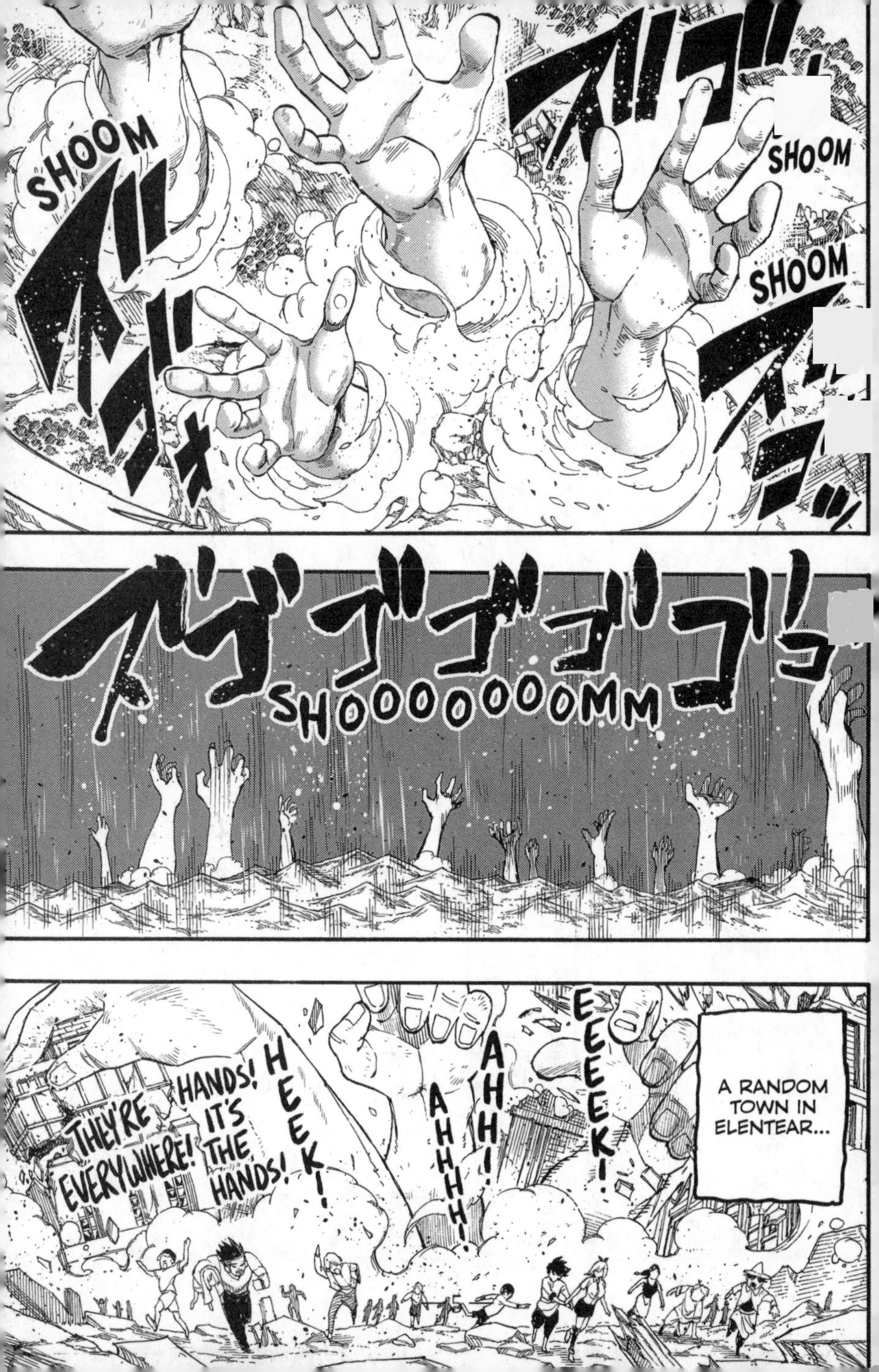
SHOOM
SHOOM
SHOOM
SHOOOOOOOOMM
A RANDOM TOWN IN ELENTEAR...
EEEEEK!
AHHH!
AHHHHH!
HEEEK!
HANDS! IT'S THE HANDS!
THEY'RE EVERYWHERE!

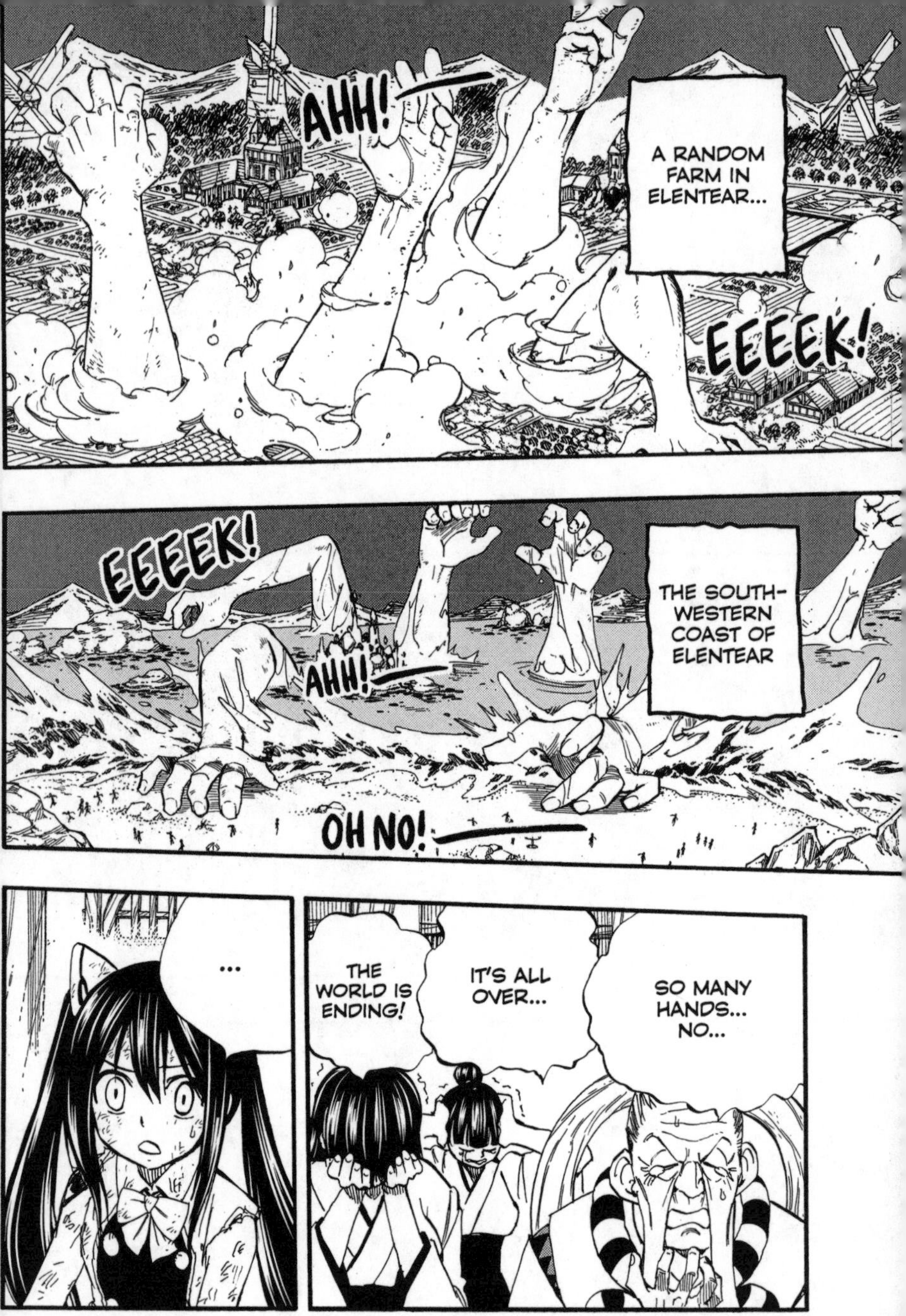
A RANDOM FARM IN ELENTEAR...
AHH!
EEEEK!
THE SOUTH-WESTERN COAST OF ELENTEAR
EEEEK!
AHH!
OH NO!
SO MANY HANDS... NO...
IT'S ALL OVER...
THE WORLD IS ENDING!
...

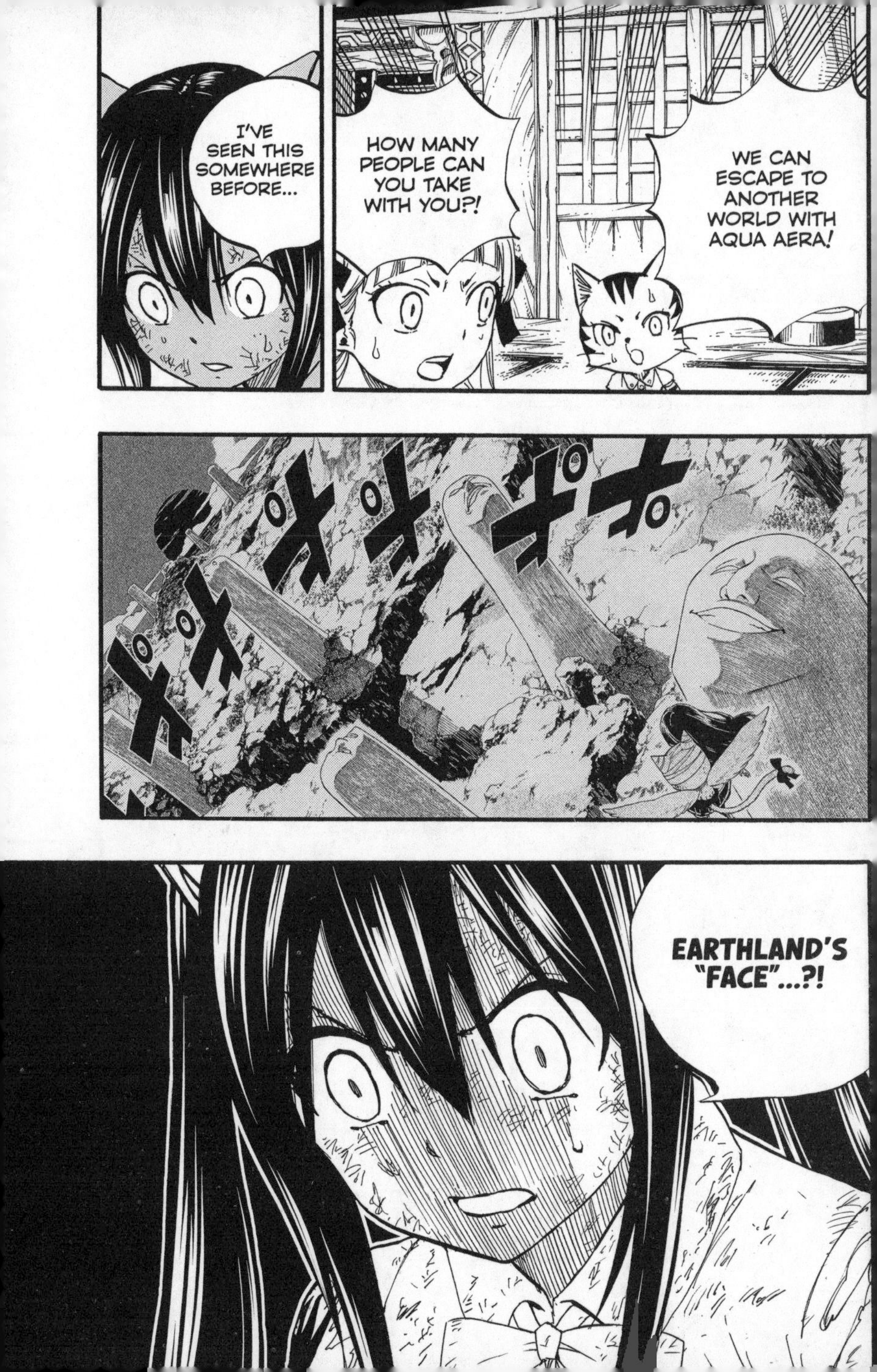
WE CAN ESCAPE TO ANOTHER WORLD WITH AQUA AERA!
HOW MANY PEOPLE CAN YOU TAKE WITH YOU?!
I'VE SEEN THIS SOMEWHERE BEFORE...
EARTHLAND'S "FACE"...?!

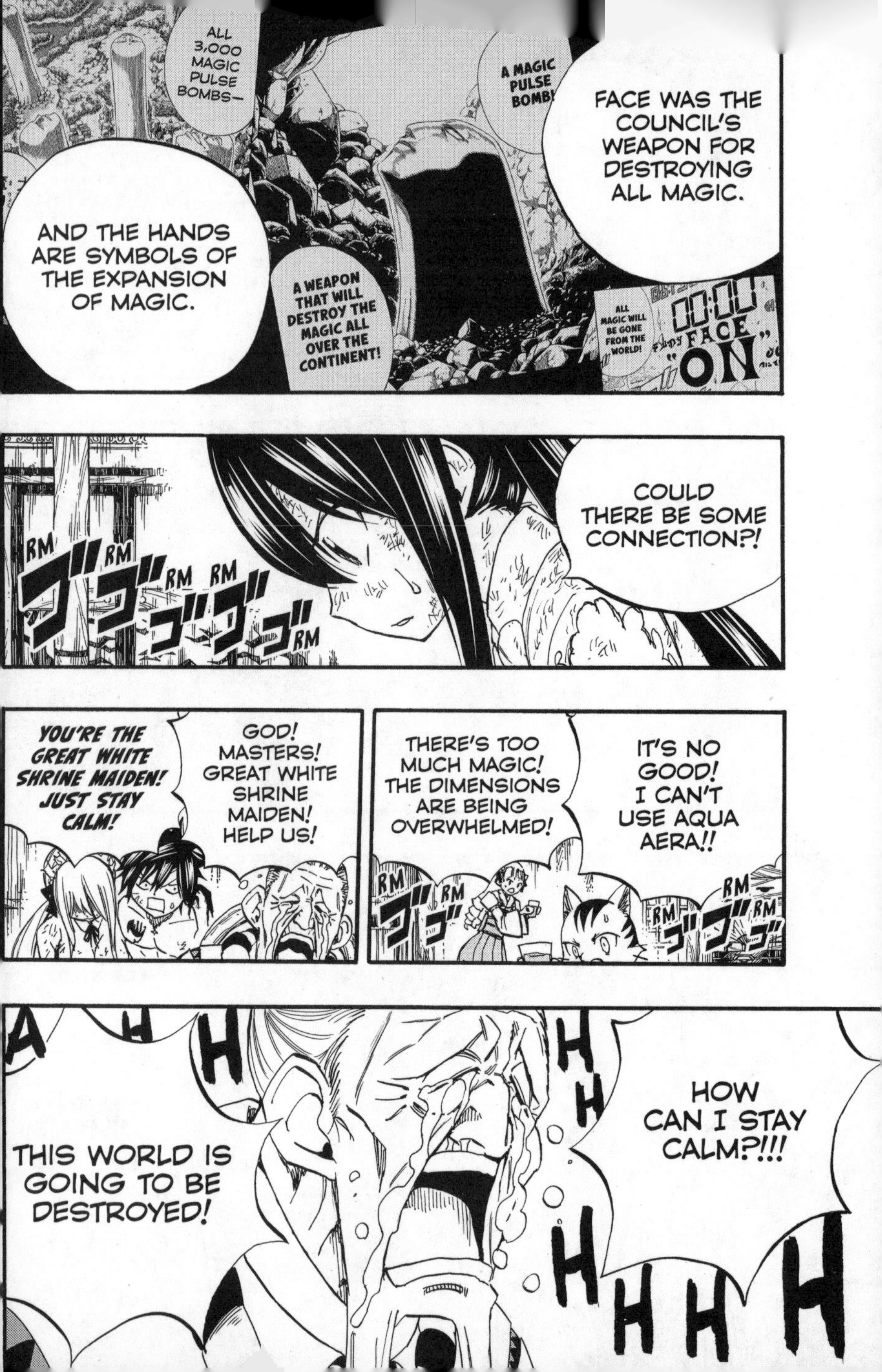
FACE WAS THE COUNCIL'S WEAPON FOR DESTROYING ALL MAGIC.
A MAGIC PULSE BOMB!
ALL 3,000 MAGIC PULSE BOMBS—
ALL MAGIC WILL BE GONE FROM THE WORLD!
FACE "ON"
A WEAPON THAT WILL DESTROY THE MAGIC ALL OVER THE CONTINENT!
AND THE HANDS ARE SYMBOLS OF THE EXPANSION OF MAGIC.
COULD THERE BE SOME CONNECTION?!
RM RM RM RM RM
IT'S NO GOOD! I CAN'T USE AQUA AERA!!
THERE'S TOO MUCH MAGIC! THE DIMENSIONS ARE BEING OVERWHELMED!
RM RM RM RM RM
GOD! MASTERS! GREAT WHITE SHRINE MAIDEN! HELP US!
YOU'RE THE GREAT WHITE SHRINE MAIDEN! JUST STAY CALM!
HOW CAN I STAY CALM?!!!
THIS WORLD IS GOING TO BE DESTROYED!

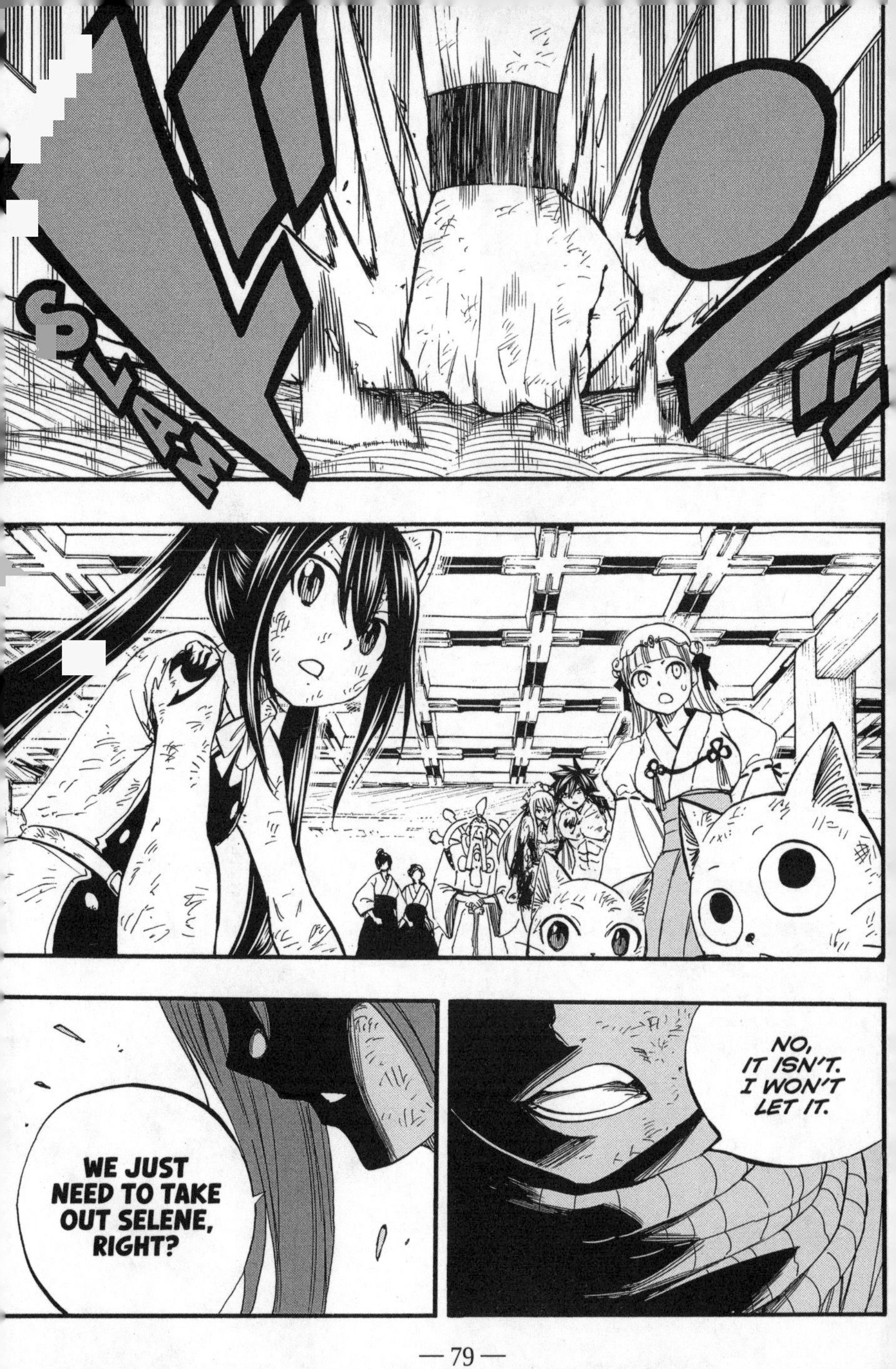
SLAM
NO, IT ISN'T. I WON'T LET IT.
WE JUST NEED TO TAKE OUT SELENE, RIGHT?

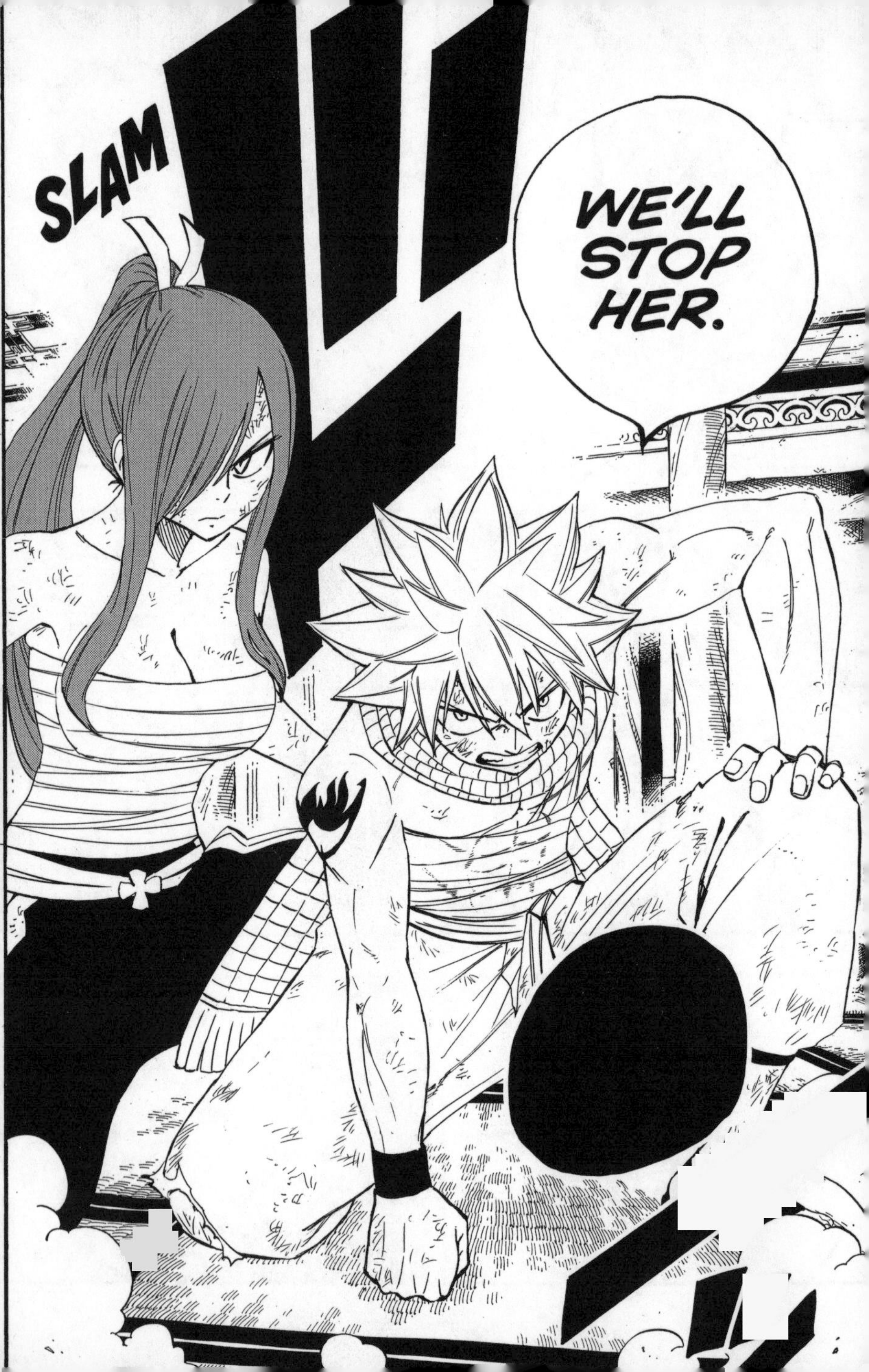
WE'LL STOP HER.
SLAM

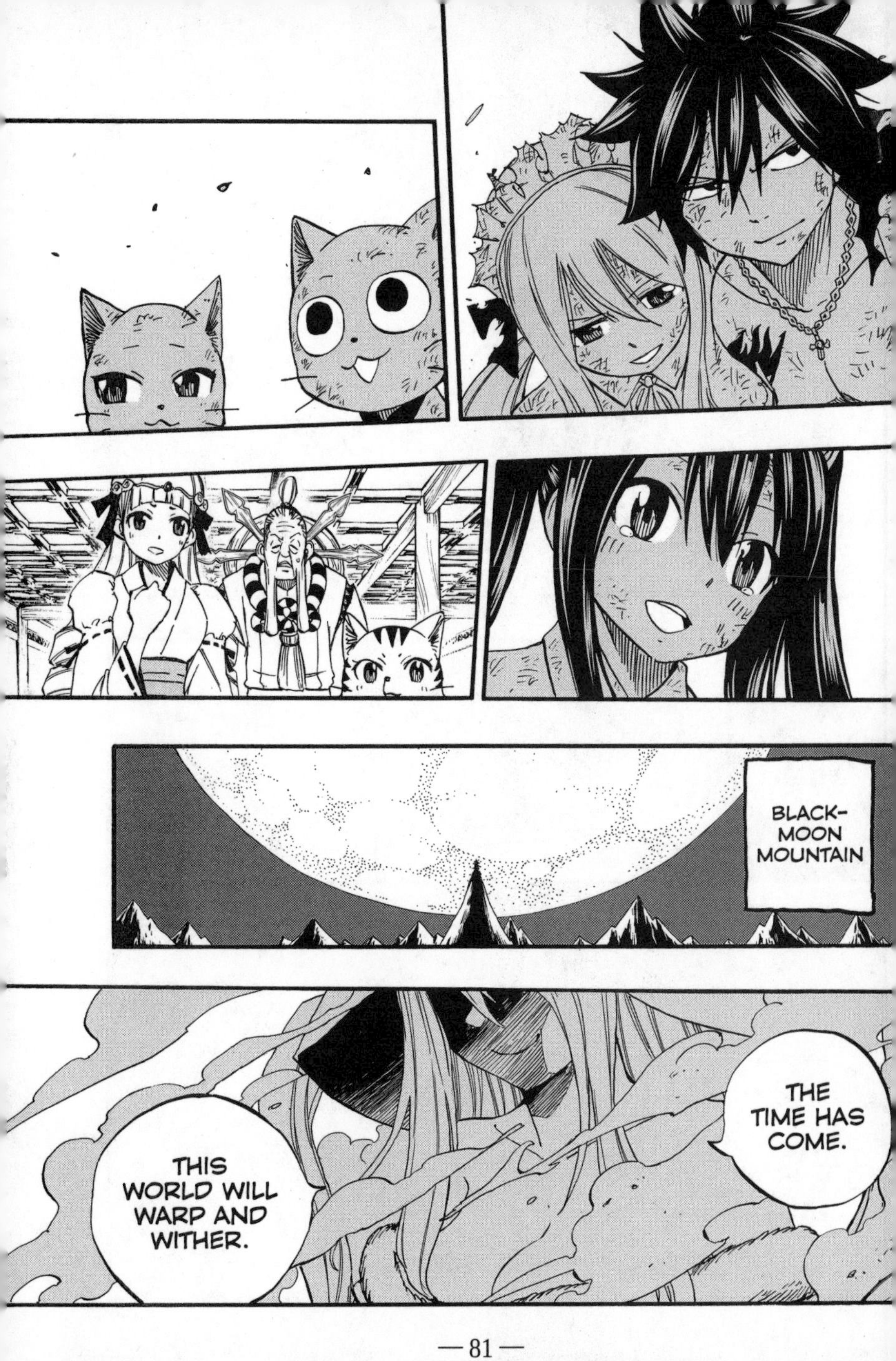
BLACK-MOON MOUNTAIN
THE TIME HAS COME.
THIS WORLD WILL WARP AND WITHER.

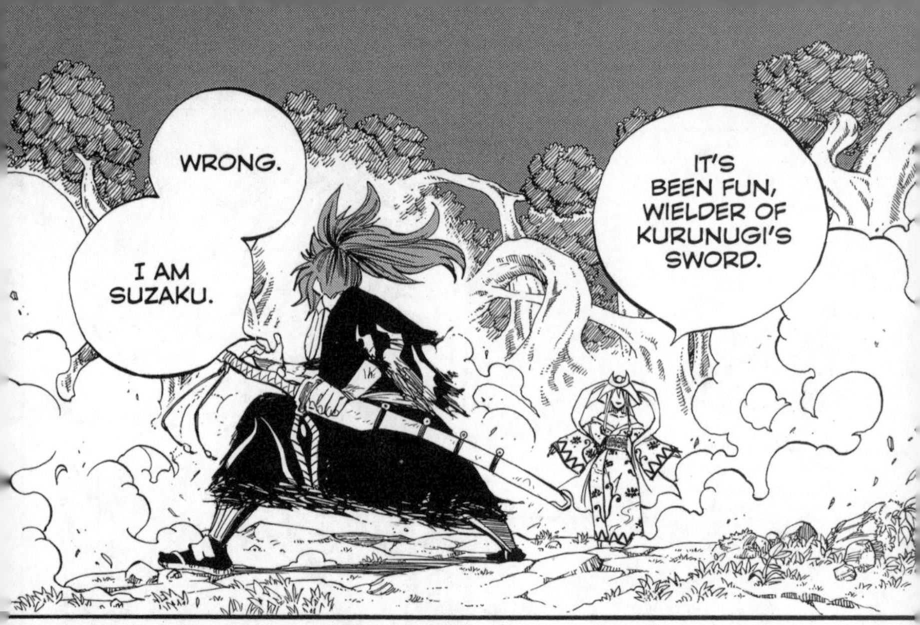
IT'S BEEN FUN, WIELDER OF KURUNUGI'S SWORD.
WRONG.
I AM SUZAKU.
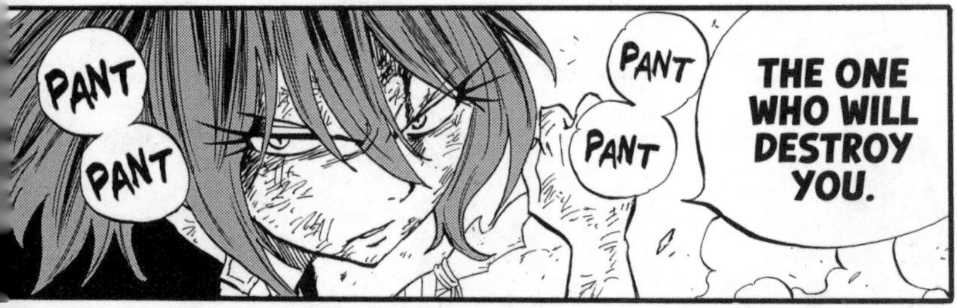
THE ONE WHO WILL DESTROY YOU.
PANT
PANT
PANT
PANT
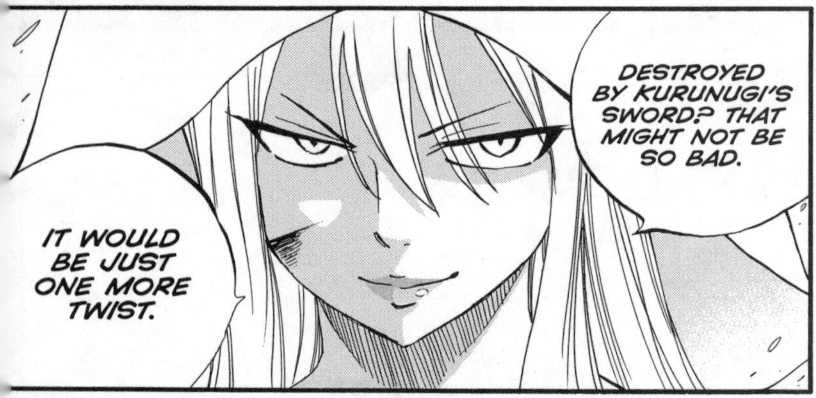
DESTROYED BY KURUNUGI'S SWORD? THAT MIGHT NOT BE SO BAD.
IT WOULD BE JUST ONE MORE TWIST.

FAIRY TAIL 100 YEARS QUEST

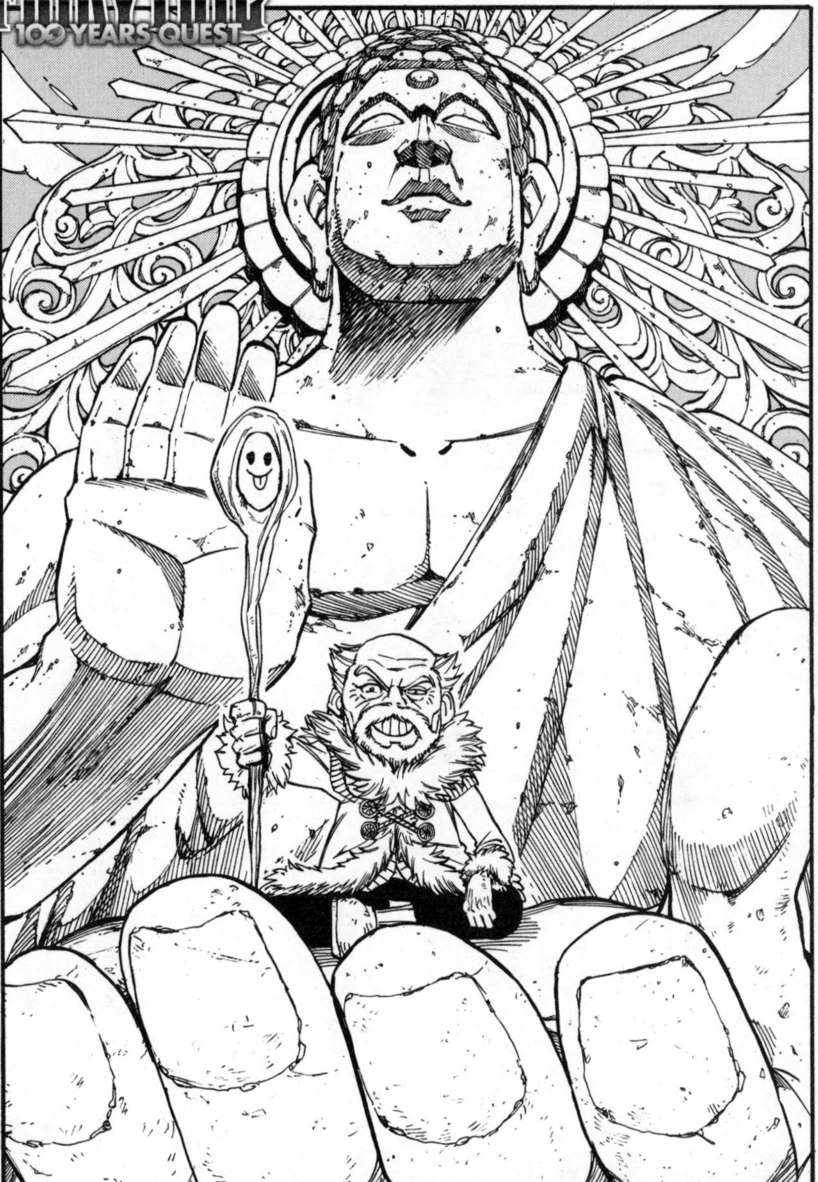

CHAPTER 86: ABYSS

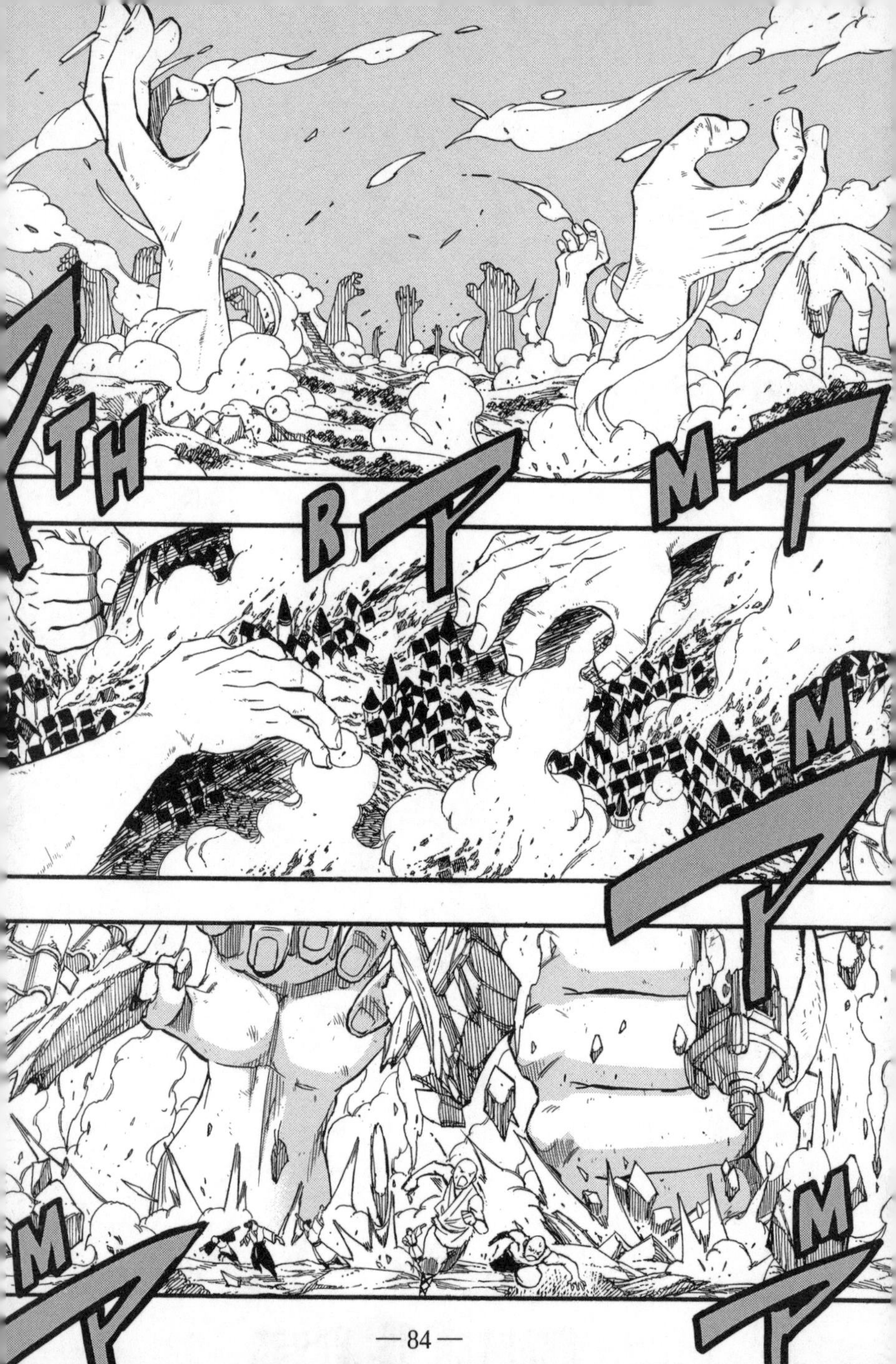
TH
R
M
M
M
M

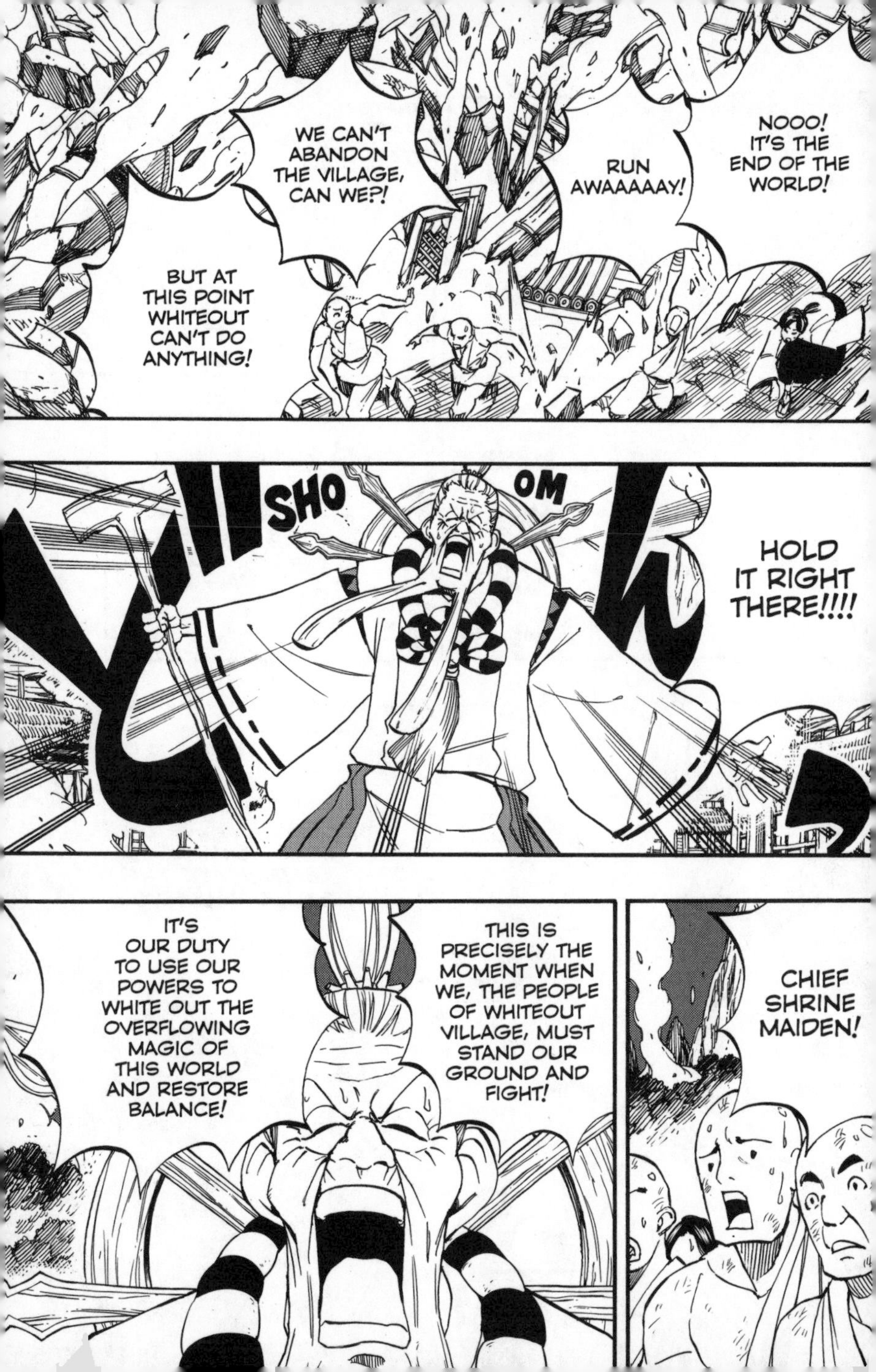
NOOO! IT'S THE END OF THE WORLD!
RUN AWAAAAAY!
WE CAN'T ABANDON THE VILLAGE, CAN WE?!
BUT AT THIS POINT WHITEOUT CAN'T DO ANYTHING!
HOLD IT RIGHT THERE!!!!
SHOOM
CHIEF SHRINE MAIDEN!
THIS IS PRECISELY THE MOMENT WHEN WE, THE PEOPLE OF WHITEOUT VILLAGE, MUST STAND OUR GROUND AND FIGHT!
IT'S OUR DUTY TO USE OUR POWERS TO WHITE OUT THE OVERFLOWING MAGIC OF THIS WORLD AND RESTORE BALANCE!

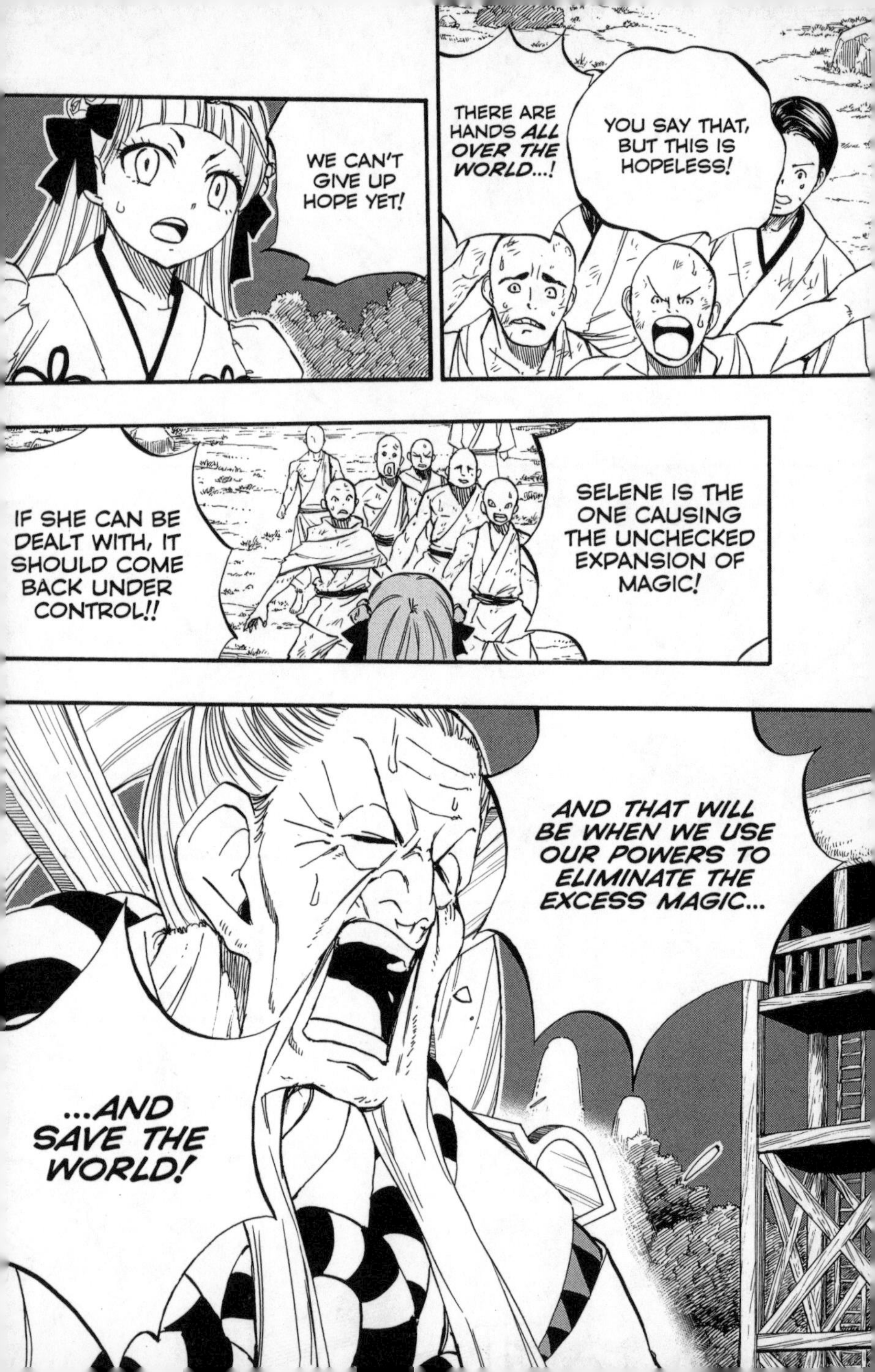
YOU SAY THAT, BUT THIS IS HOPELESS!
THERE ARE HANDS ALL OVER THE WORLD...!
WE CAN'T GIVE UP HOPE YET!
SELENE IS THE ONE CAUSING THE UNCHECKED EXPANSION OF MAGIC!
IF SHE CAN BE DEALT WITH, IT SHOULD COME BACK UNDER CONTROL!!
AND THAT WILL BE WHEN WE USE OUR POWERS TO ELIMINATE THE EXCESS MAGIC...
...AND SAVE THE WORLD!

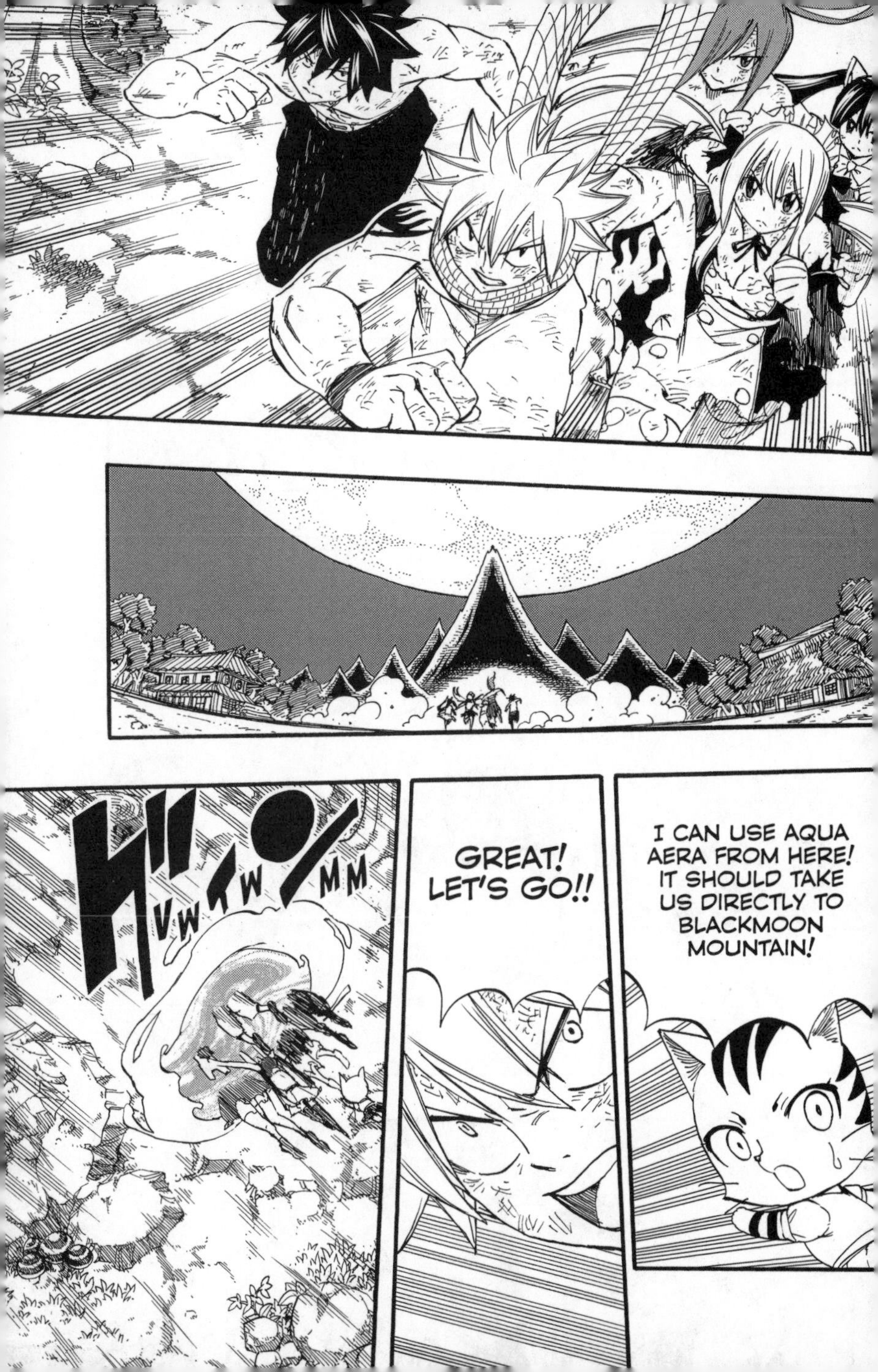
I CAN USE AQUA AERA FROM HERE! IT SHOULD TAKE US DIRECTLY TO BLACKMOON MOUNTAIN!
GREAT! LET'S GO!!

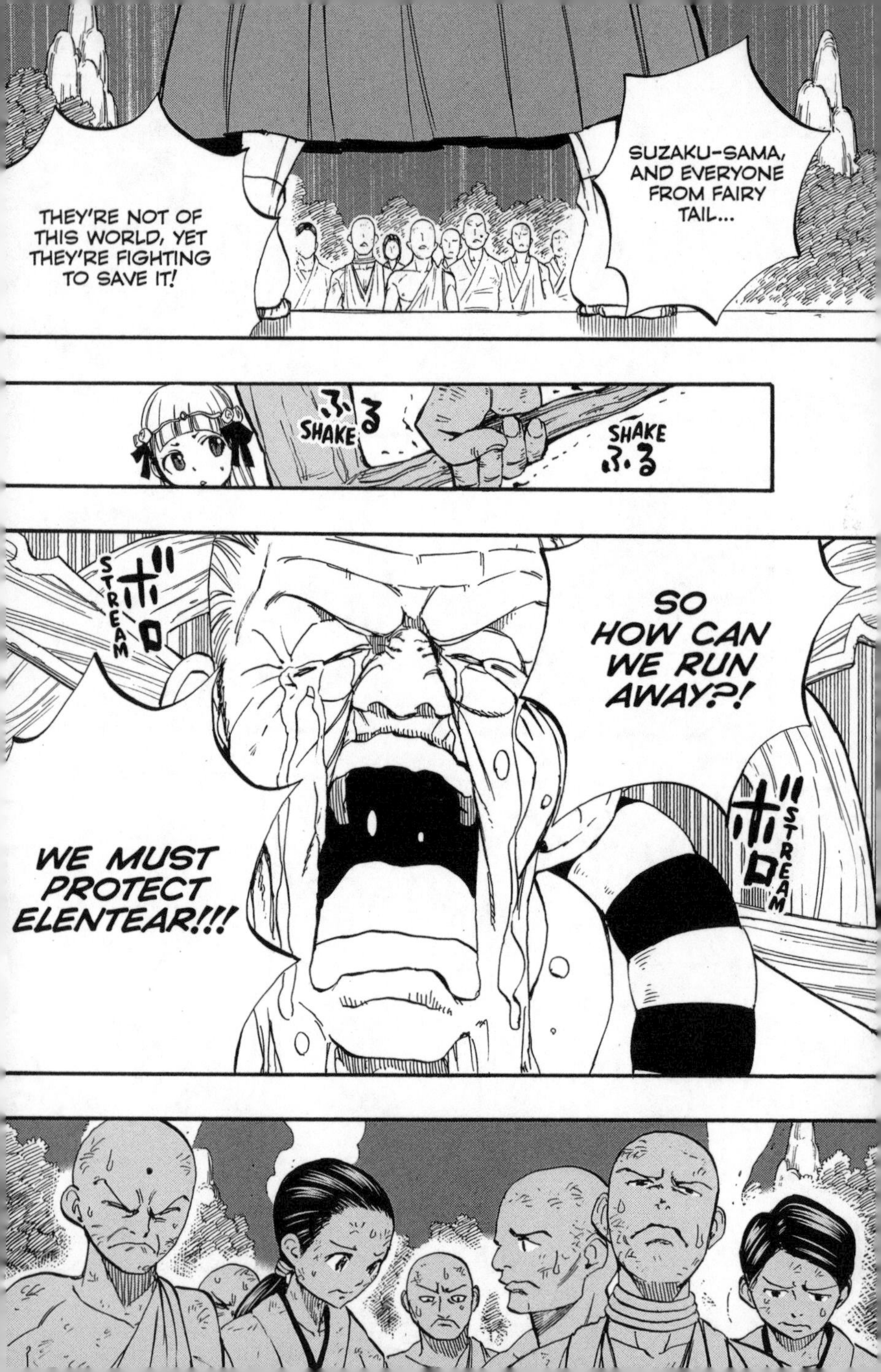
SUZAKU-SAMA, AND EVERYONE FROM FAIRY TAIL...
THEY'RE NOT OF THIS WORLD, YET THEY'RE FIGHTING TO SAVE IT!
SHAKE ふる
SHAKE ふる
SO HOW CAN WE RUN AWAY?!
STREAM ボロ
STREAM ボロ
WE MUST PROTECT ELENTEAR!!!

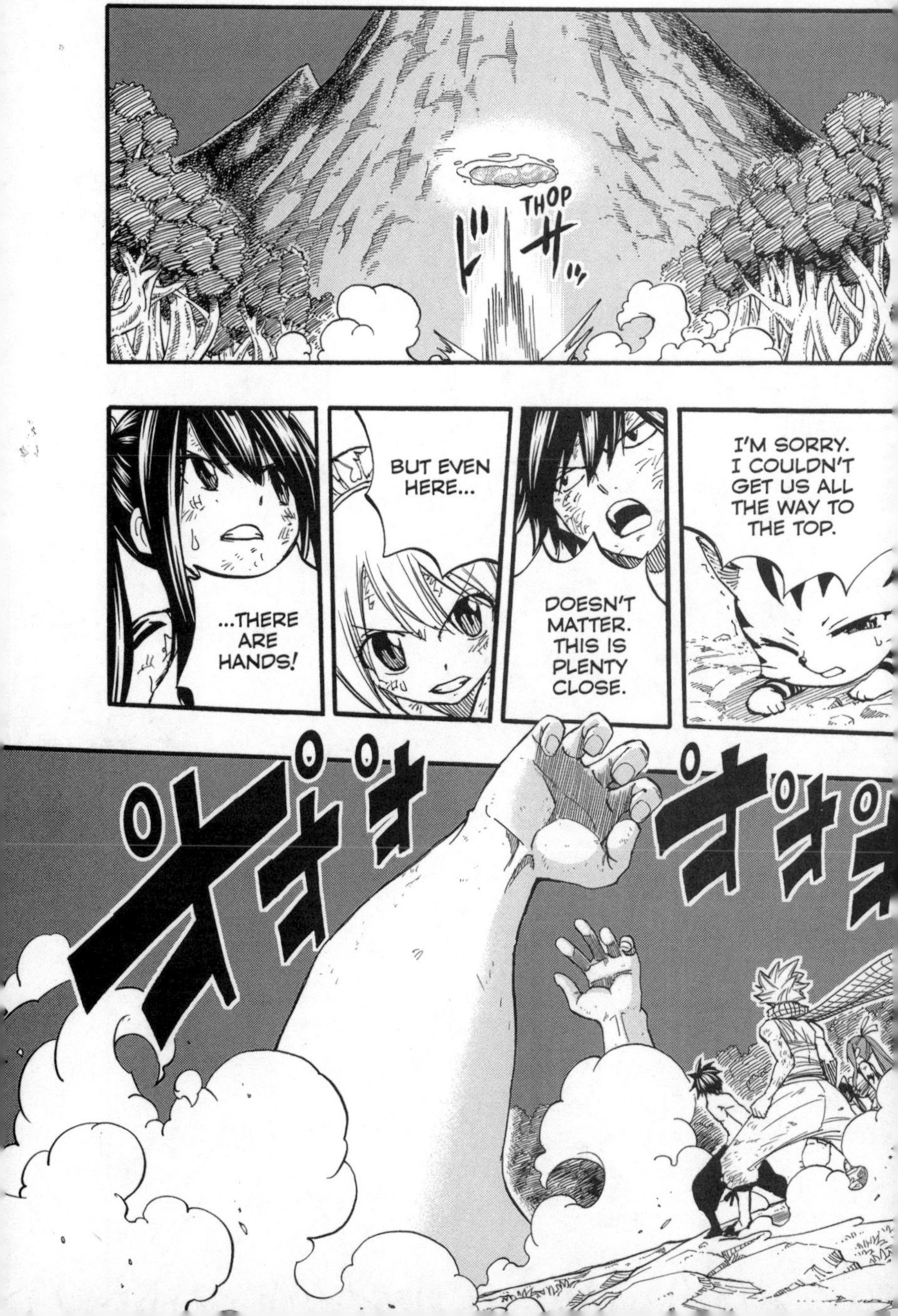
THOP
I'M SORRY. I COULDN'T GET US ALL THE WAY TO THE TOP.
DOESN'T MATTER. THIS IS PLENTY CLOSE.
BUT EVEN HERE...
...THERE ARE HANDS!

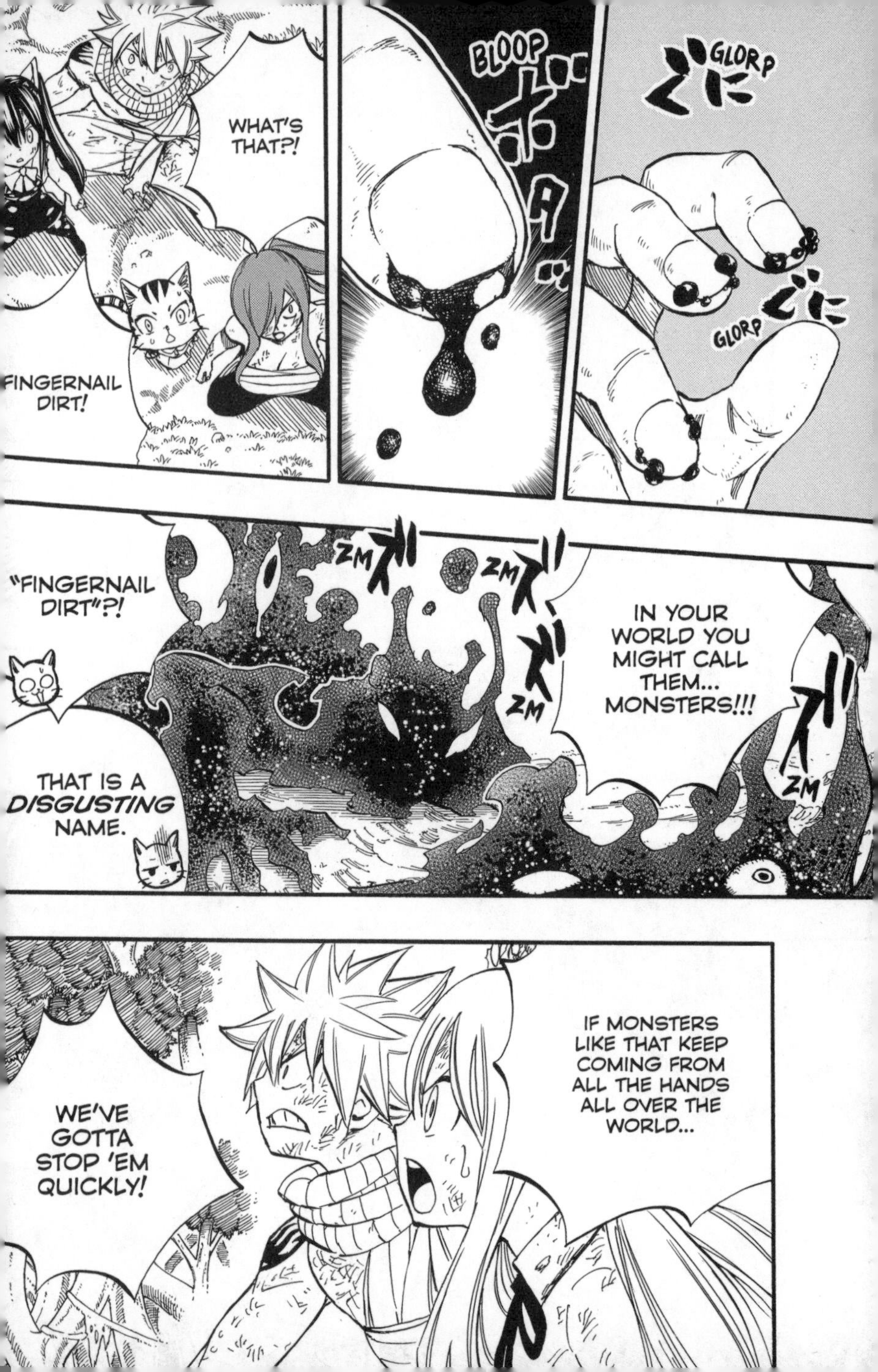
GLORP
GLORP
BLOOP
WHAT'S THAT?!
FINGERNAIL DIRT!
ZM
ZM
ZM
ZM
IN YOUR WORLD YOU MIGHT CALL THEM... MONSTERS!!!
"FINGERNAIL DIRT"?!
THAT IS A *DISGUSTING* NAME.
IF MONSTERS LIKE THAT KEEP COMING FROM ALL THE HANDS ALL OVER THE WORLD...
WE'VE GOTTA STOP 'EM QUICKLY!

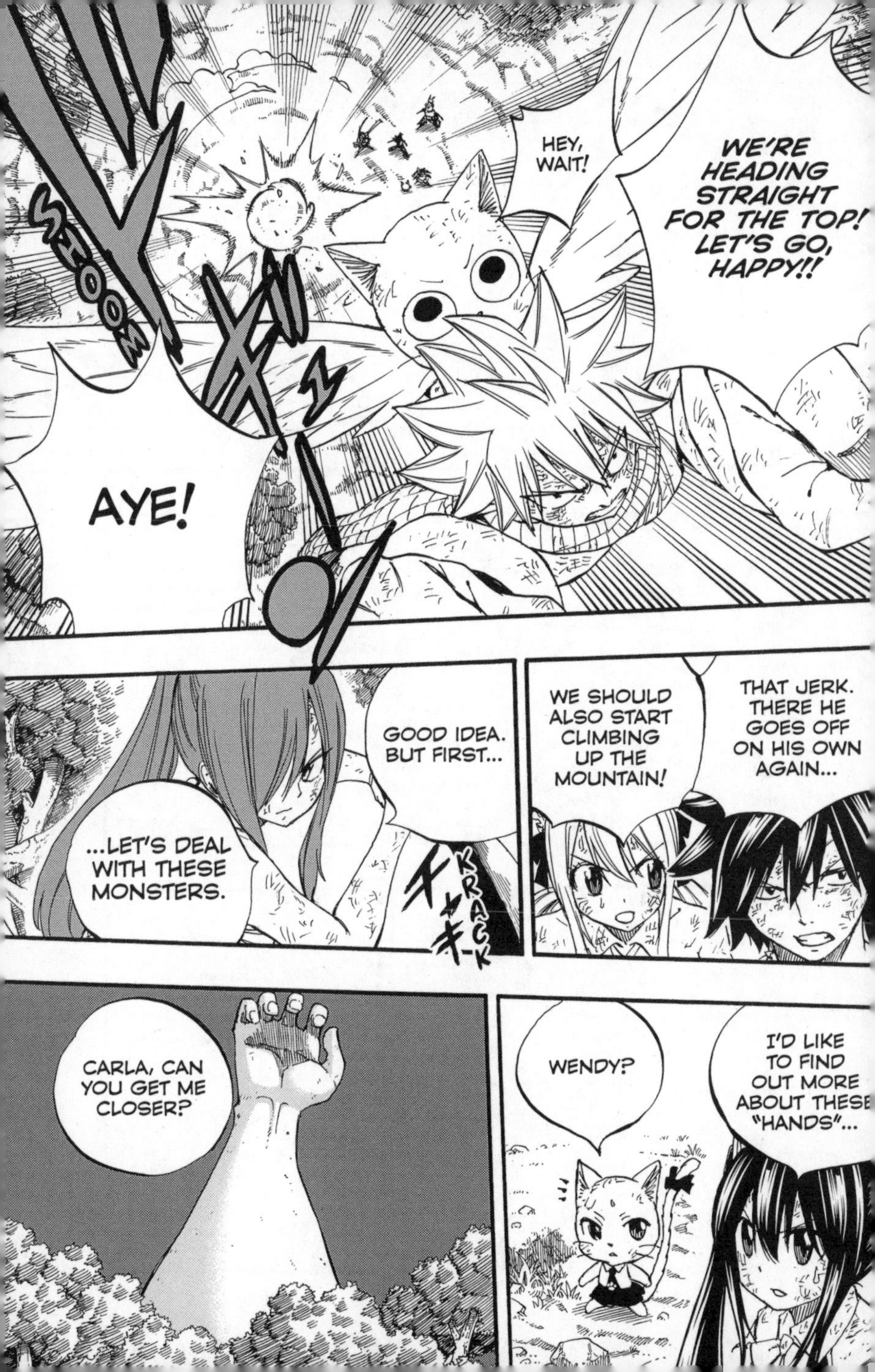
WE'RE HEADING STRAIGHT FOR THE TOP! LET'S GO, HAPPY!!
HEY, WAIT!
AYE!
THAT JERK. THERE HE GOES OFF ON HIS OWN AGAIN...
WE SHOULD ALSO START CLIMBING UP THE MOUNTAIN!
GOOD IDEA. BUT FIRST...
KRACK
...LET'S DEAL WITH THESE MONSTERS.
I'D LIKE TO FIND OUT MORE ABOUT THESE "HANDS"...
WENDY?
CARLA, CAN YOU GET ME CLOSER?

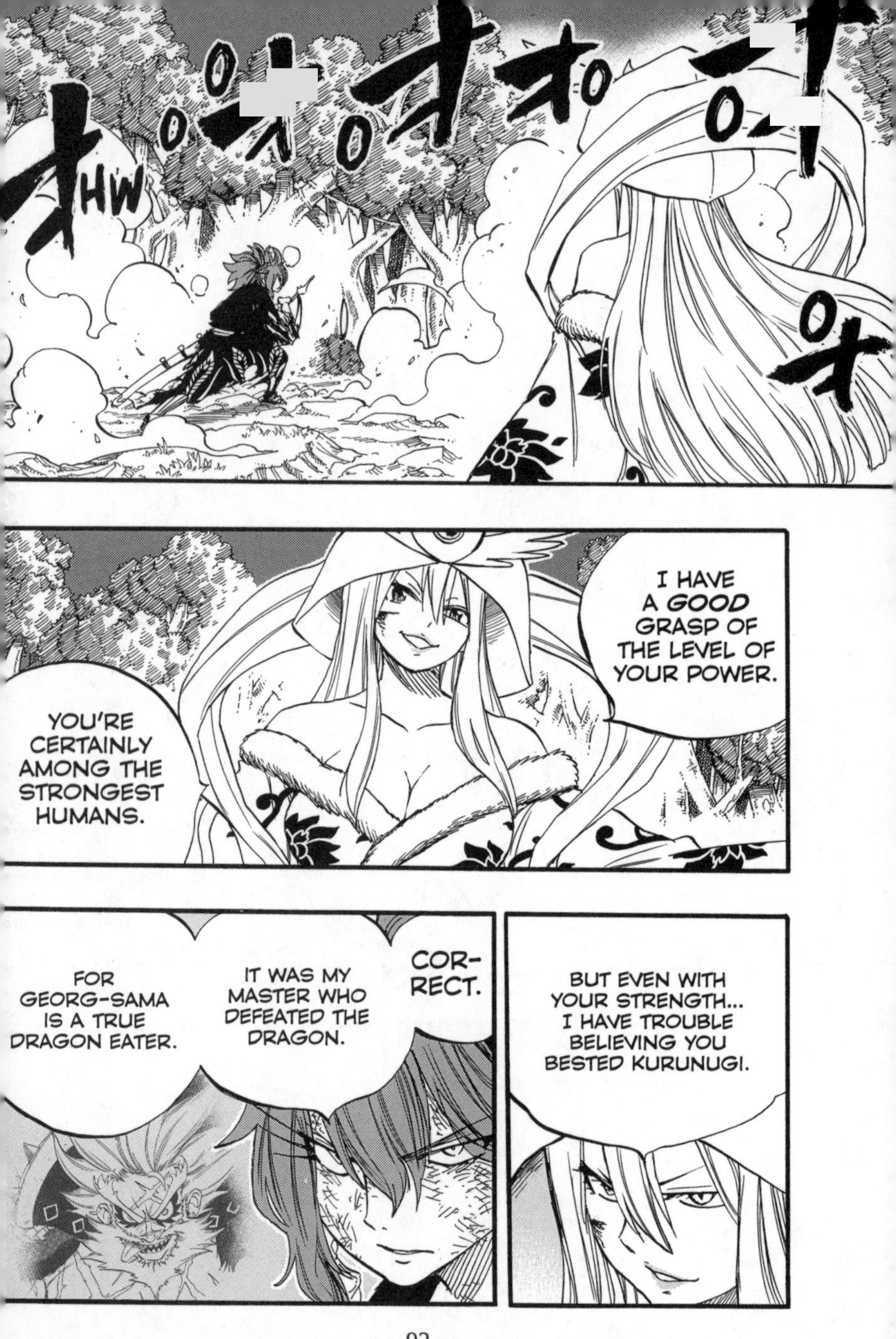
I HAVE A *GOOD* GRASP OF THE LEVEL OF YOUR POWER.
YOU'RE CERTAINLY AMONG THE STRONGEST HUMANS.
BUT EVEN WITH YOUR STRENGTH... I HAVE TROUBLE BELIEVING YOU BESTED KURUNUGI.
COR-RECT.
IT WAS MY MASTER WHO DEFEATED THE DRAGON.
FOR GEORG-SAMA IS A TRUE DRAGON EATER.

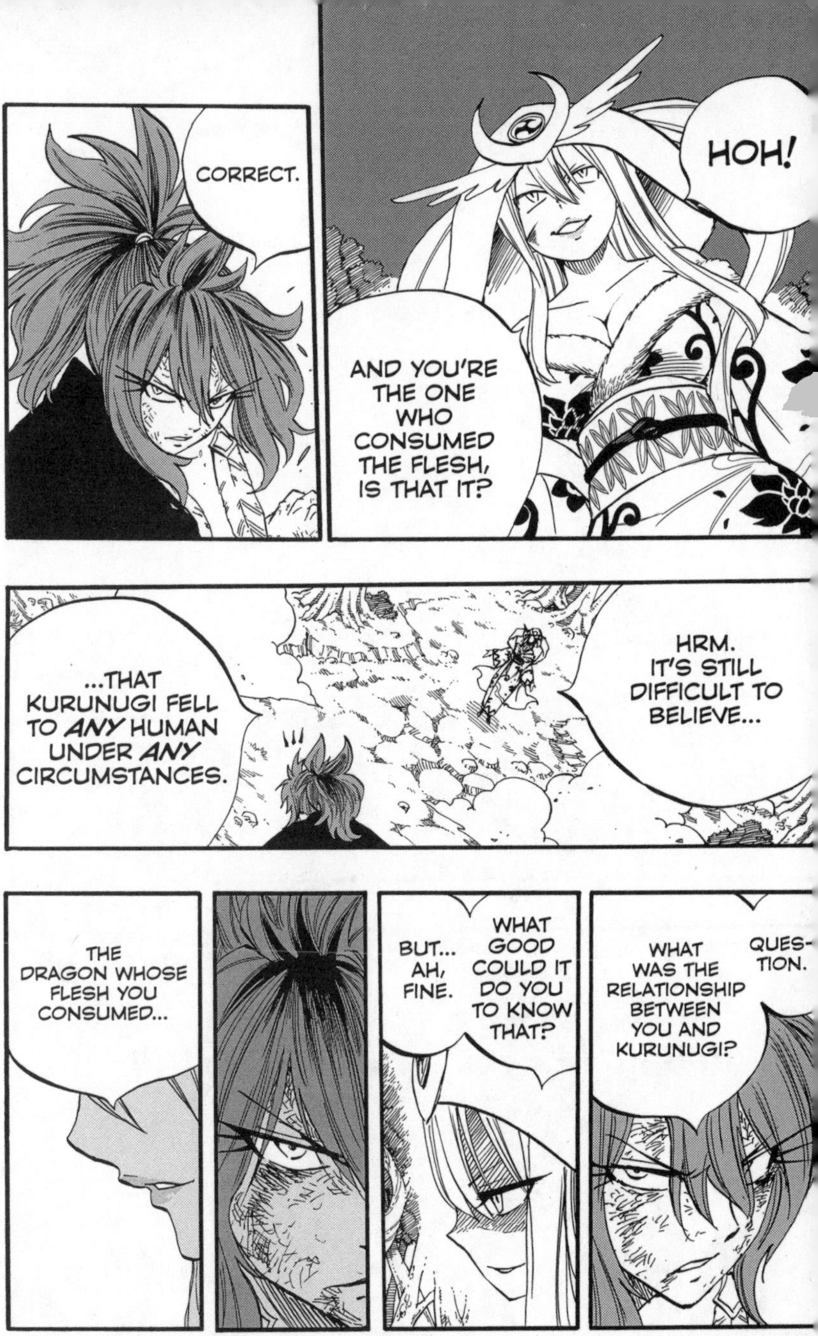
HOH!
AND YOU'RE THE ONE WHO CONSUMED THE FLESH, IS THAT IT?
CORRECT.
HRM. IT'S STILL DIFFICULT TO BELIEVE...
...THAT KURUNUGI FELL TO *ANY* HUMAN UNDER *ANY* CIRCUMSTANCES.
QUES-TION.
WHAT WAS THE RELATIONSHIP BETWEEN YOU AND KURUNUGI?
WHAT GOOD COULD IT DO YOU TO KNOW THAT?
BUT... AH, FINE.
THE DRAGON WHOSE FLESH YOU CONSUMED...

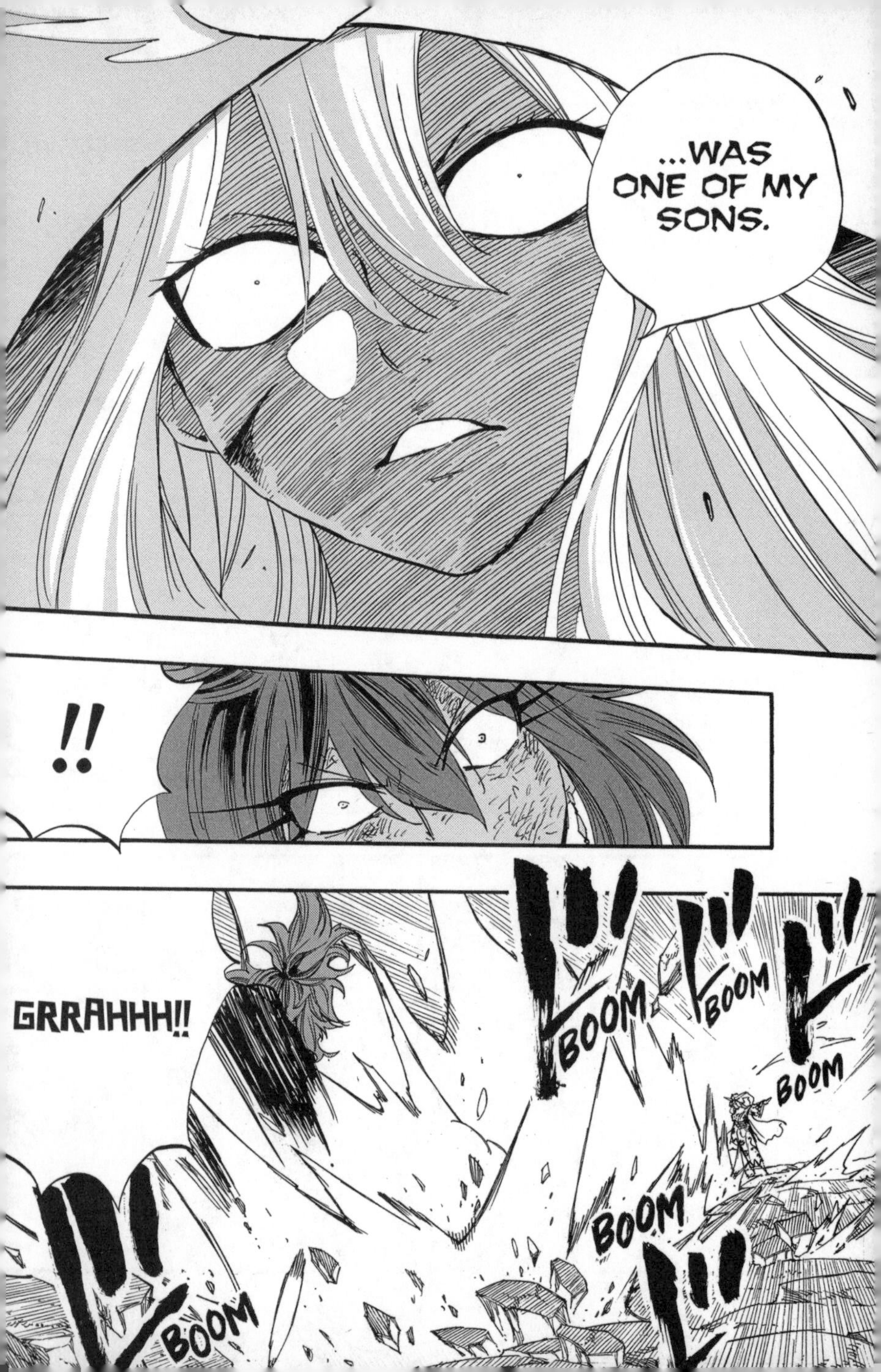
...WAS ONE OF MY SONS.
!!
BOOM
BOOM
BOOM
BOOM
GRRAHHH!!
BOOM

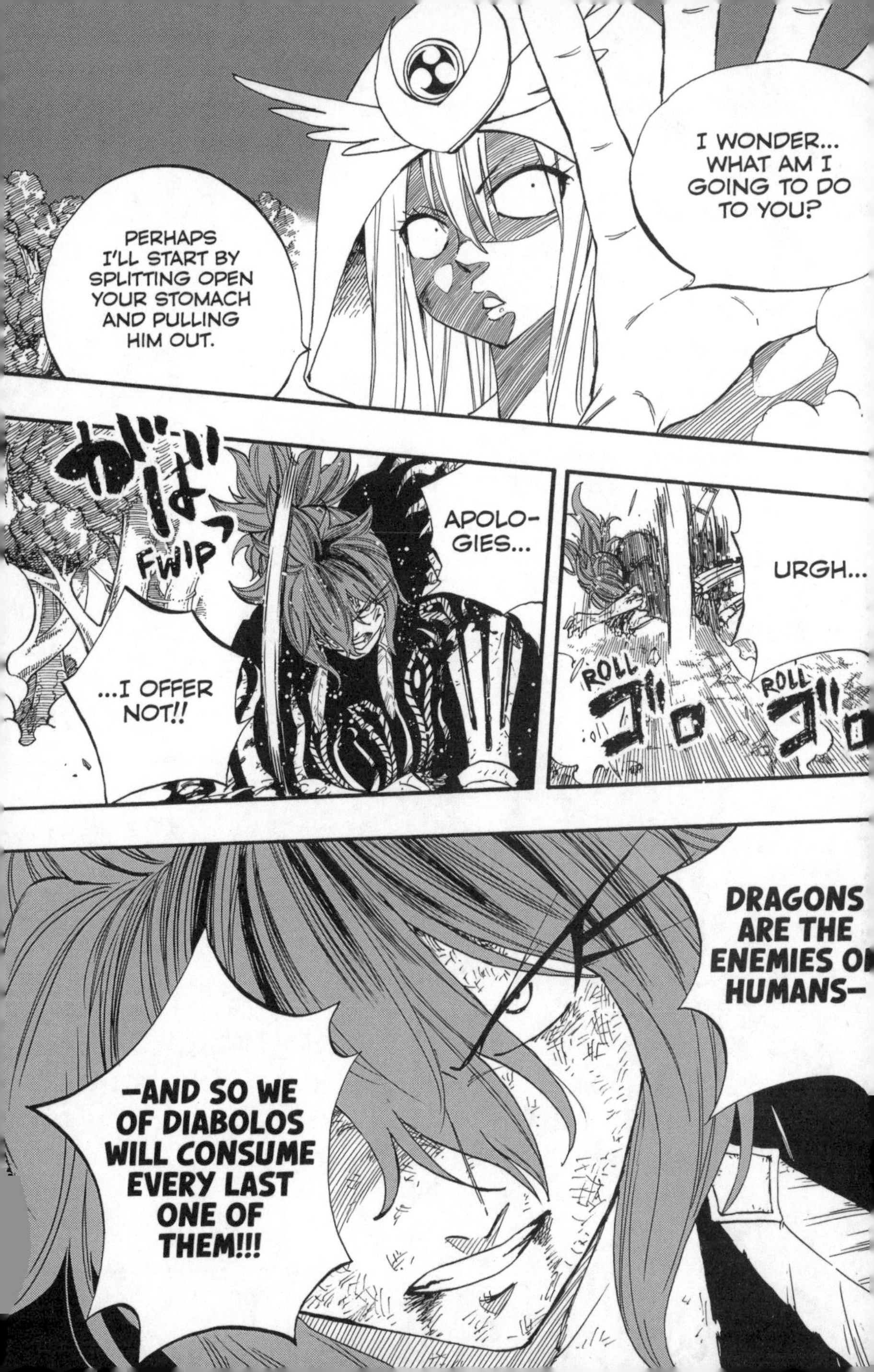
I WONDER... WHAT AM I GOING TO DO TO YOU?
PERHAPS I'LL START BY SPLITTING OPEN YOUR STOMACH AND PULLING HIM OUT.
URGH...
ROLL
ゴロ
ROLL
ゴロ
APOLO-GIES...
FWIP
...I OFFER NOT!!
DRAGONS ARE THE ENEMIES O
HUMANS—
—AND SO WE OF DIABOLOS WILL CONSUME EVERY LAST ONE OF THEM!!!

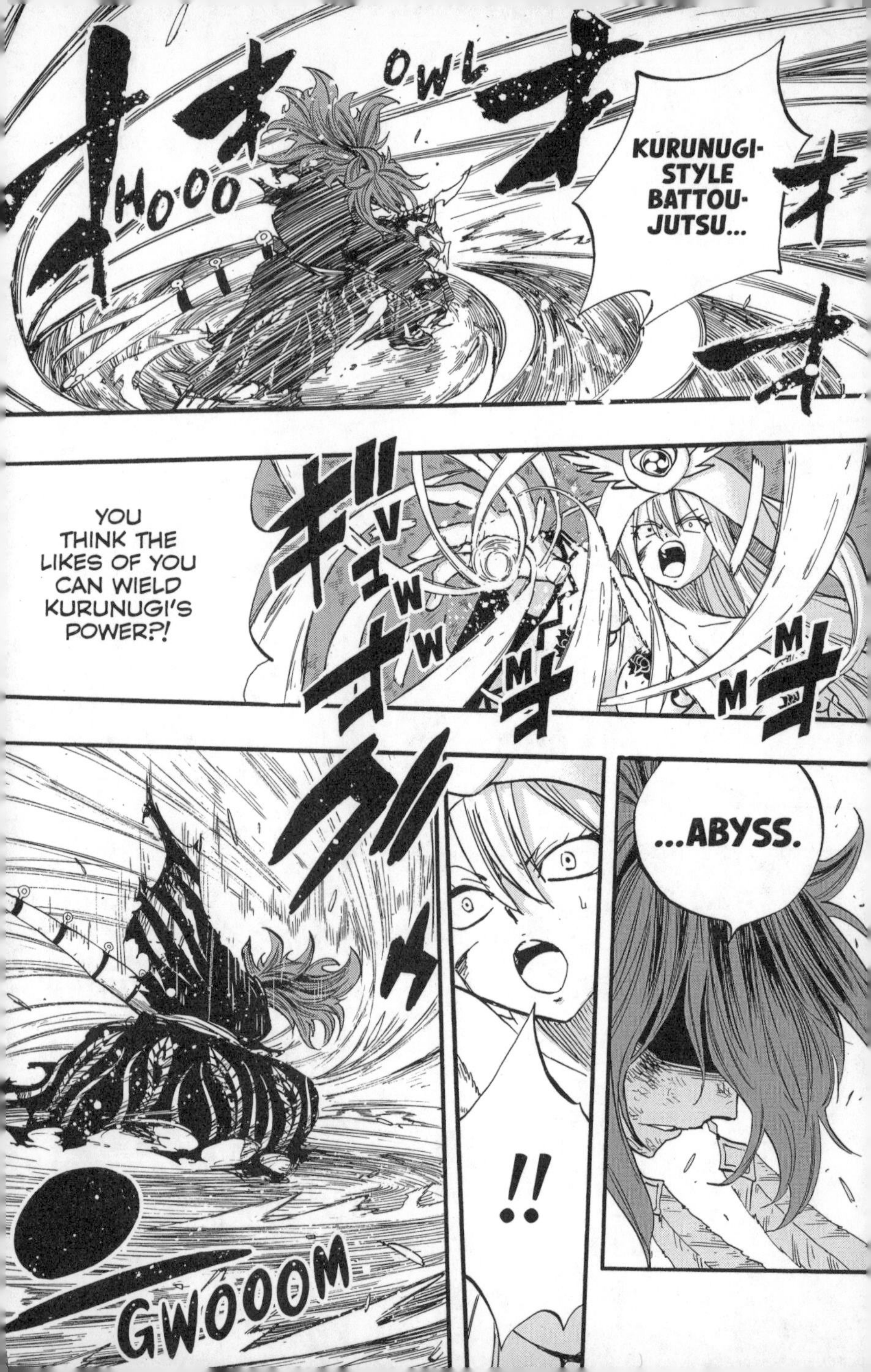
HOOOOWL
KURUNUGI-STYLE BATTOU-JUTSU...
YOU THINK THE LIKES OF YOU CAN WIELD KURUNUGI'S POWER?!
VWWMMM
...ABYSS.
!!
GWOOOM

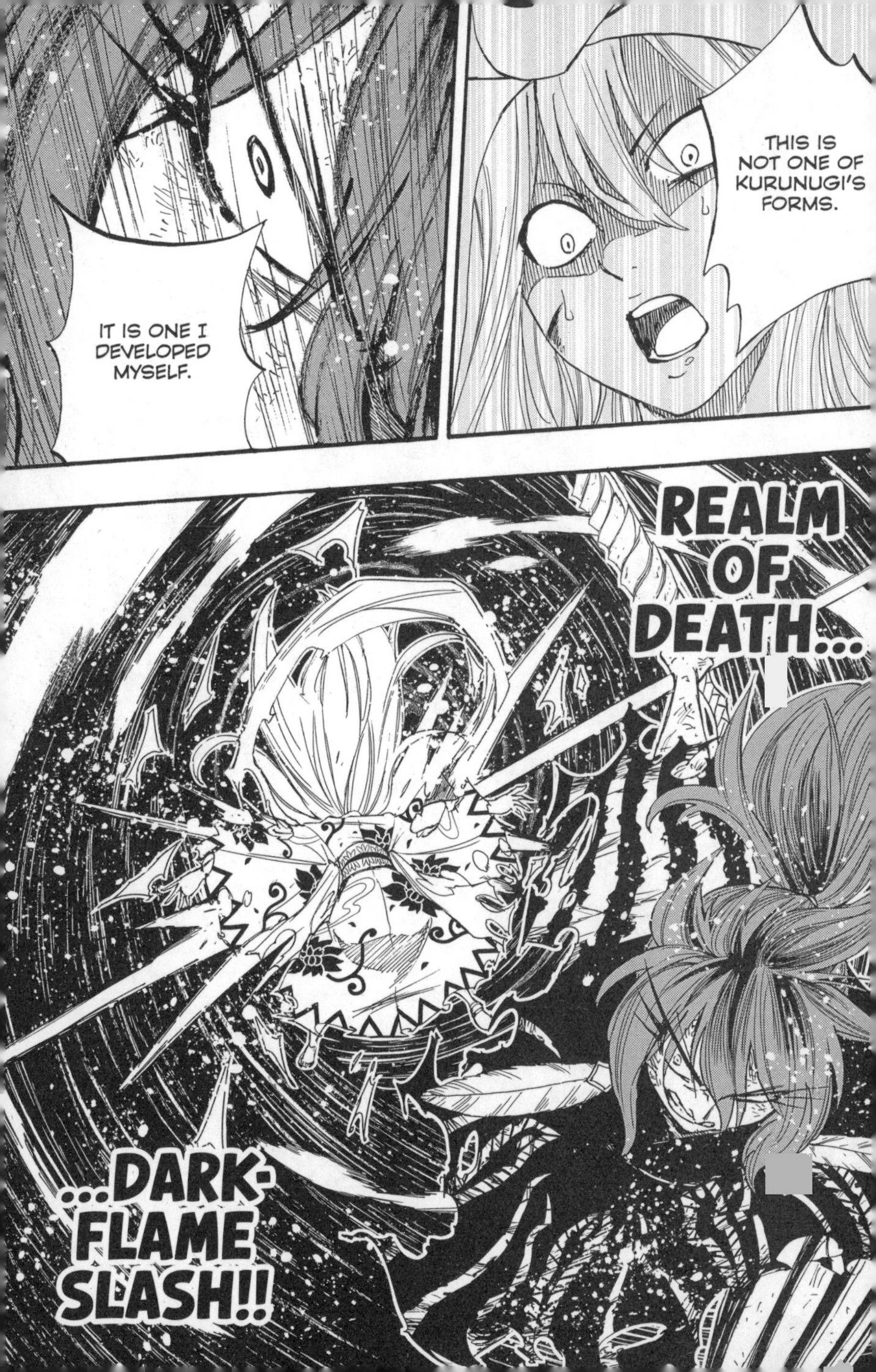
THIS IS NOT ONE OF KURUNUGI'S FORMS.
IT IS ONE I DEVELOPED MYSELF.
REALM OF DEATH...
...DARK-FLAME SLASH!!

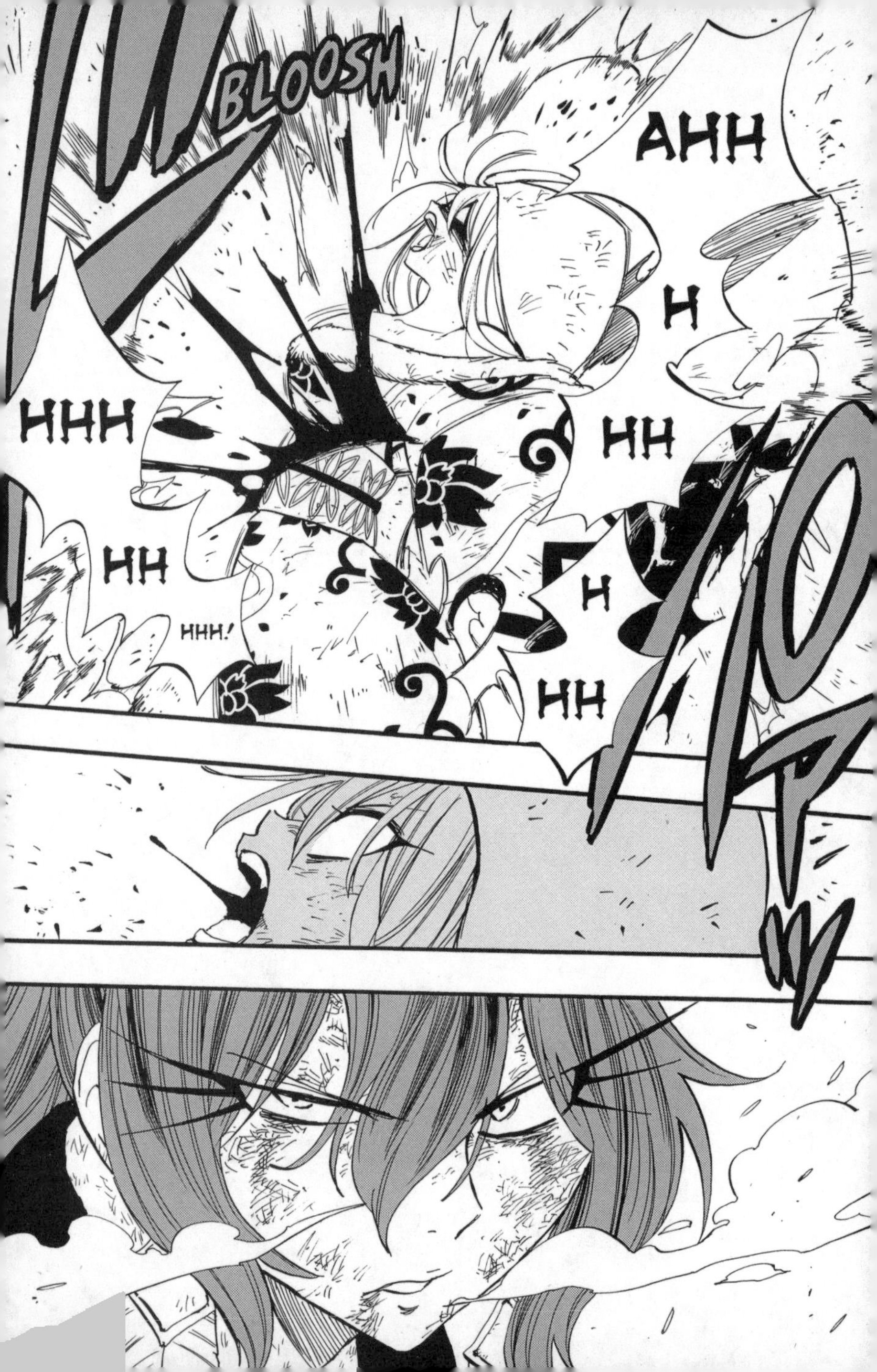
BLOOSH
AHH
H
HH
H
HH
HHH
HH
HHH!

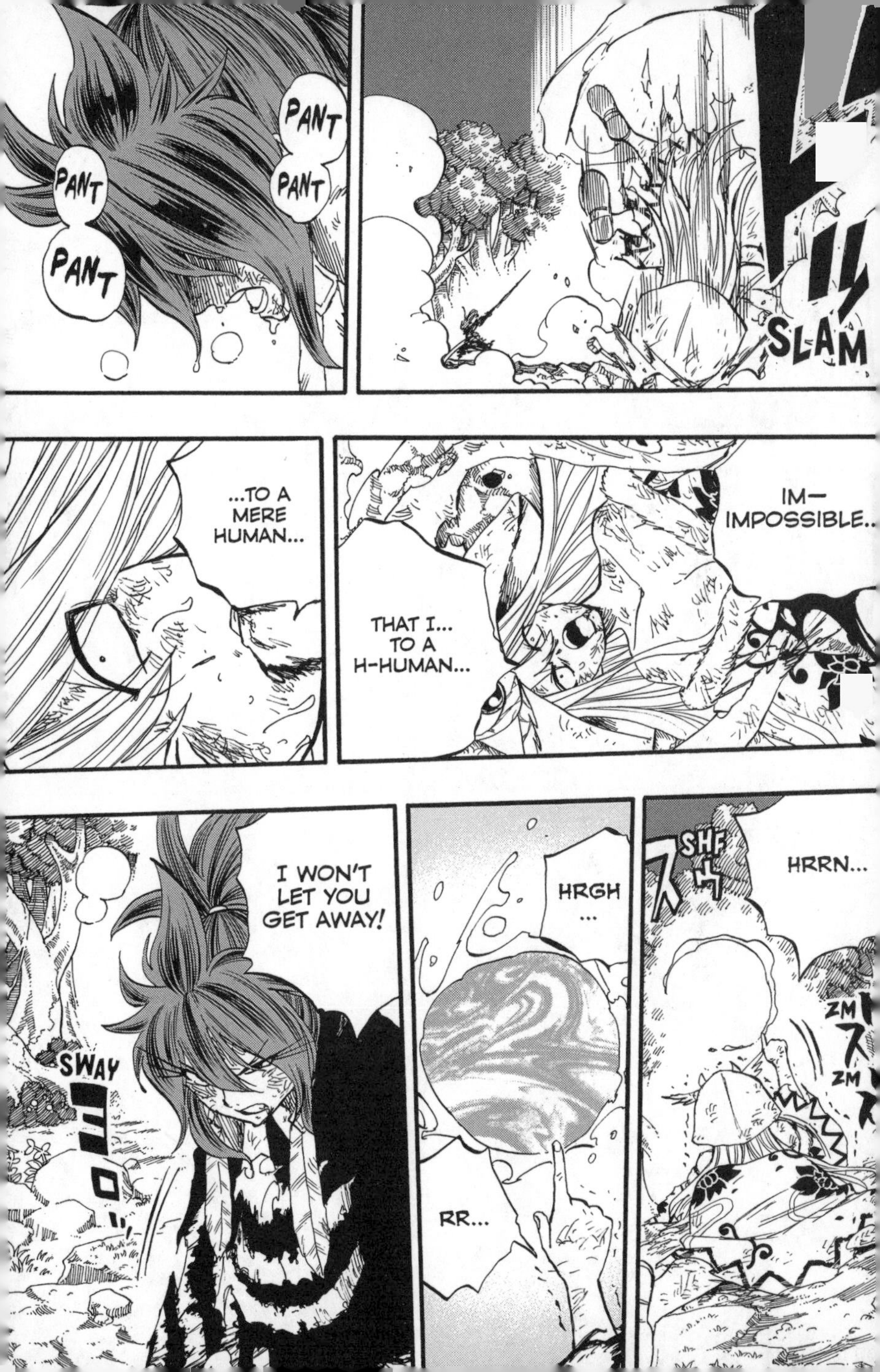
SLAM
PANT
PANT
PANT
PANT
IM— IMPOSSIBLE..
THAT I... TO A H-HUMAN...
...TO A MERE HUMAN...
SHF
HRRN...
ZM
ZM
HRGH ...
RR...
I WON'T LET YOU GET AWAY!
SWAY

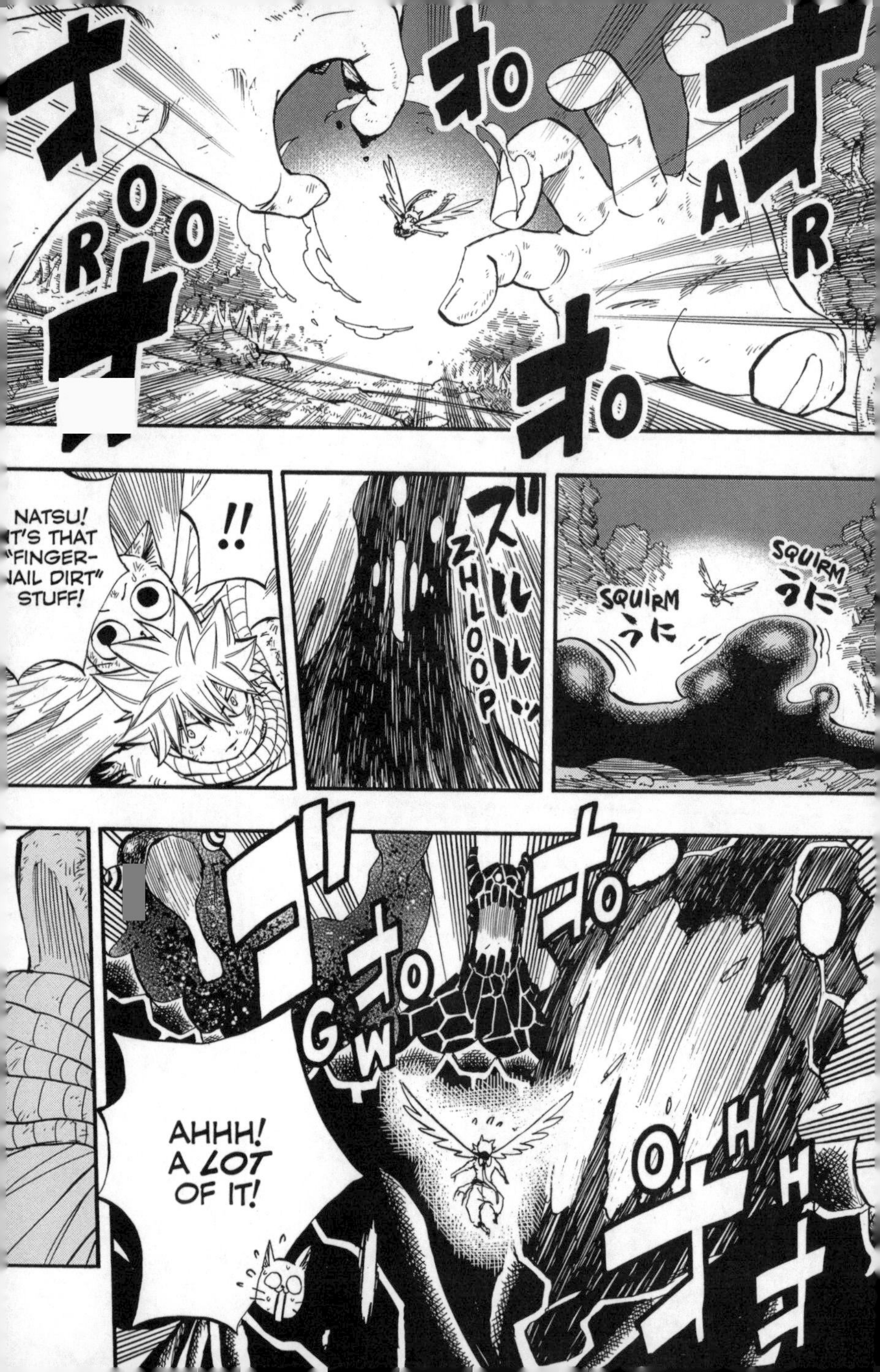

AR
ROO
SQUIRM
SQUIRM
ZHLLOOP
!!
NATSU! IT'S THAT "FINGER-NAIL DIRT" STUFF!
GWOOHH
AHHH! A LOT OF IT!

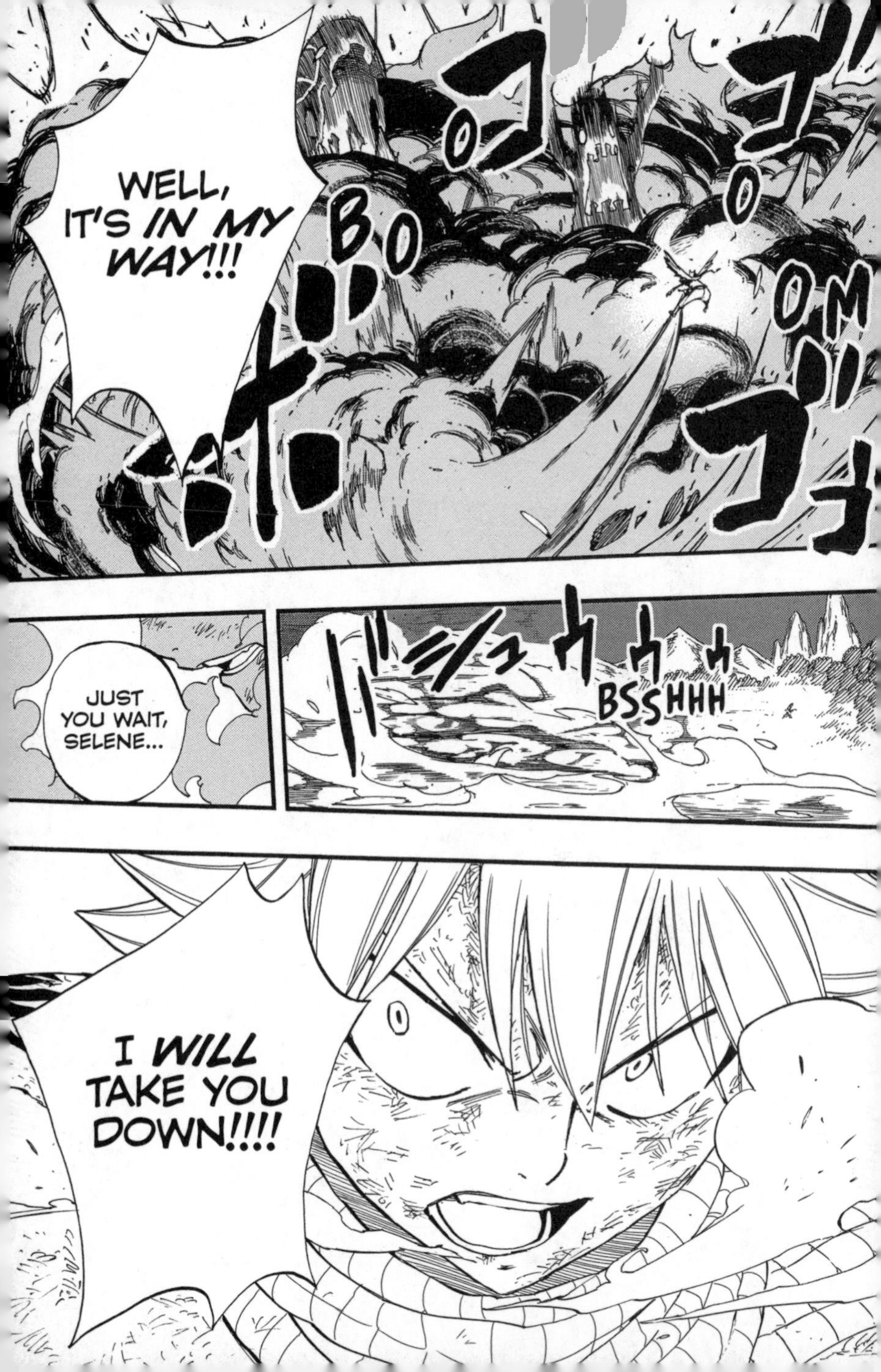
WELL, IT'S *IN MY WAY!!!*
BOOM
BSSHHH
JUST YOU WAIT, SELENE...
I *WILL* TAKE YOU DOWN!!!!

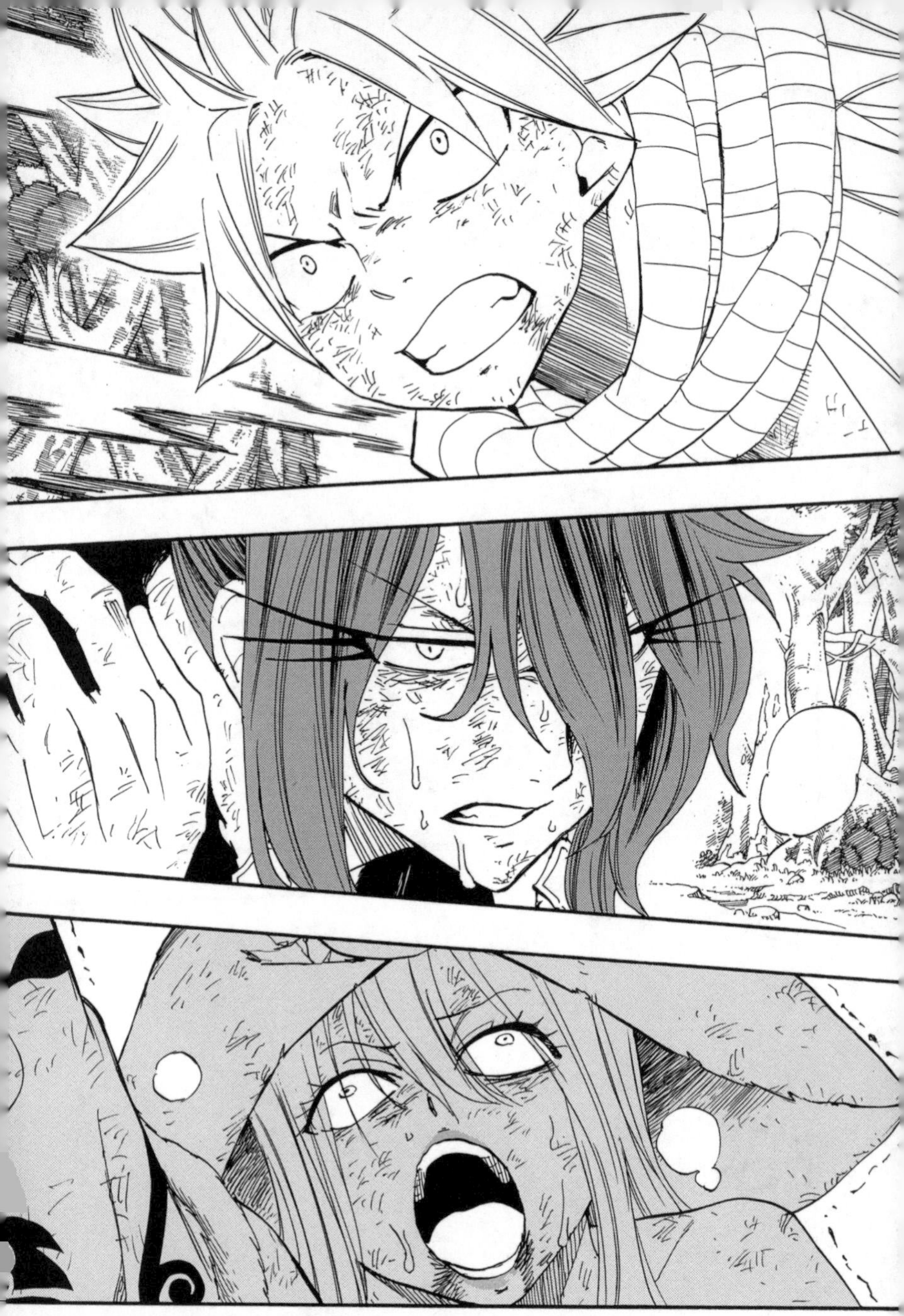

FAIRY TAIL
100 YEARS QUEST

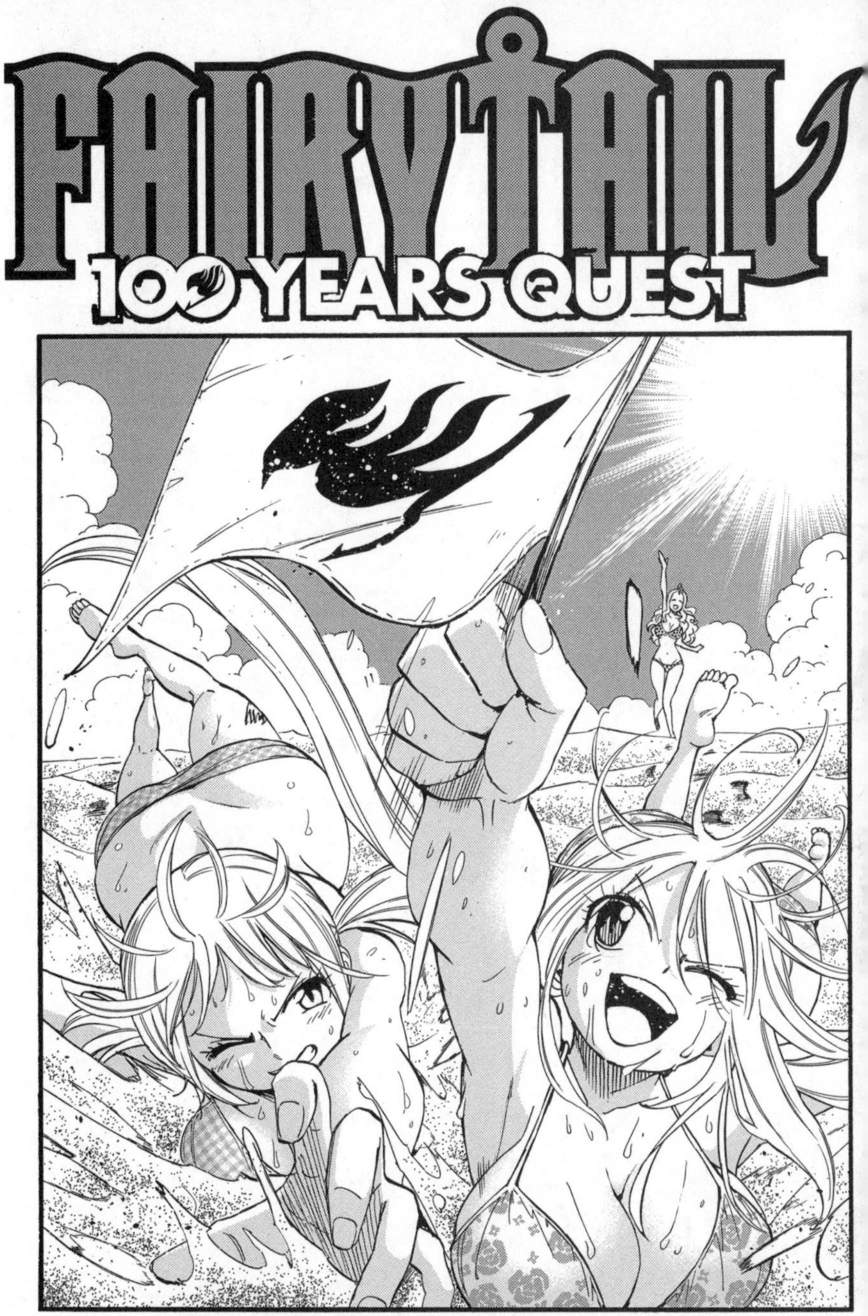

CHAPTER 87: THIS HIDEOUS WORLD

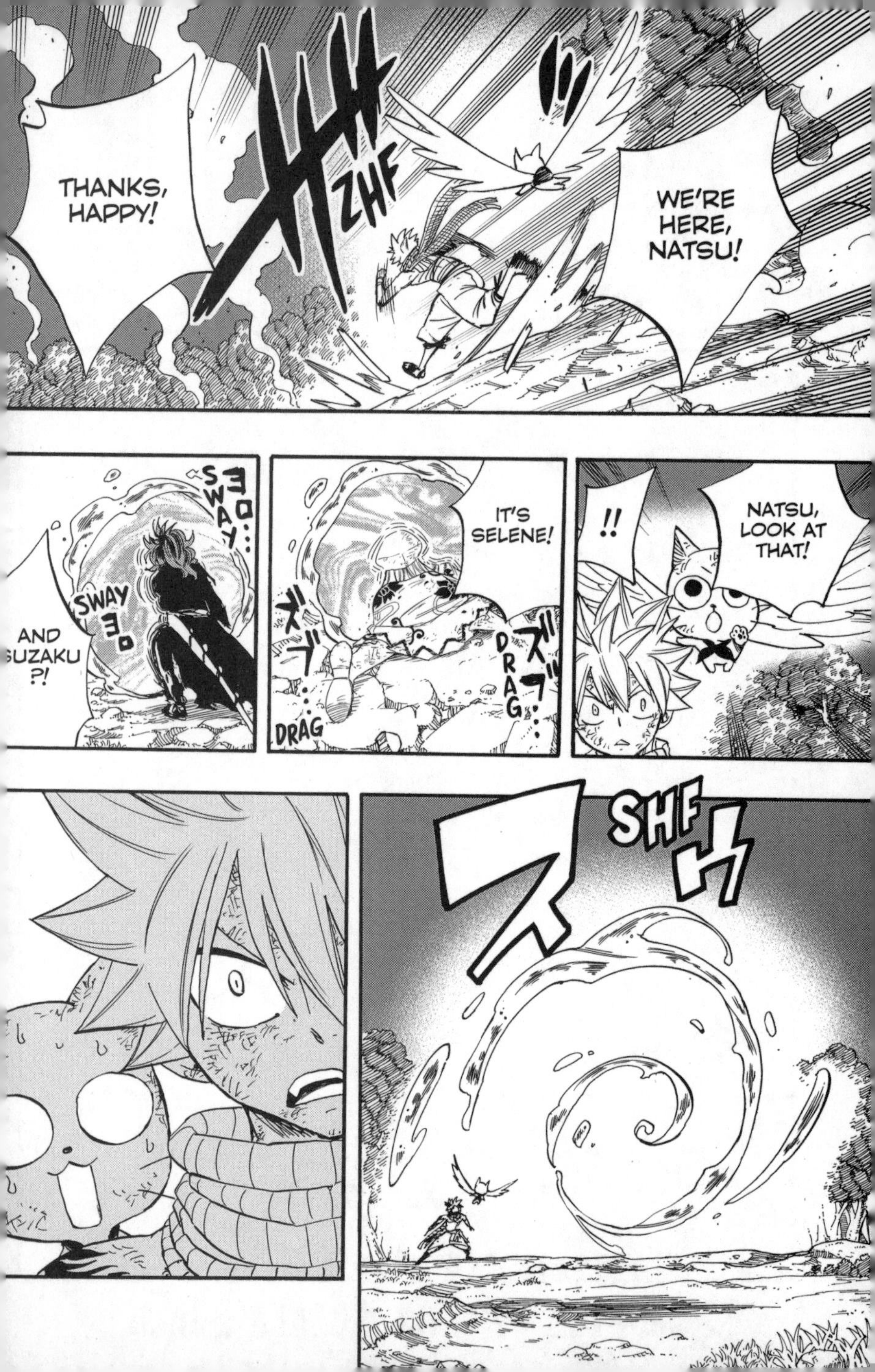
WE'RE HERE, NATSU!
ZHF
THANKS, HAPPY!
NATSU, LOOK AT THAT!
!!
IT'S SELENE!
DRAG
DRAG
SWAY...
SWAY
AND SUZAKU ?!
SHF

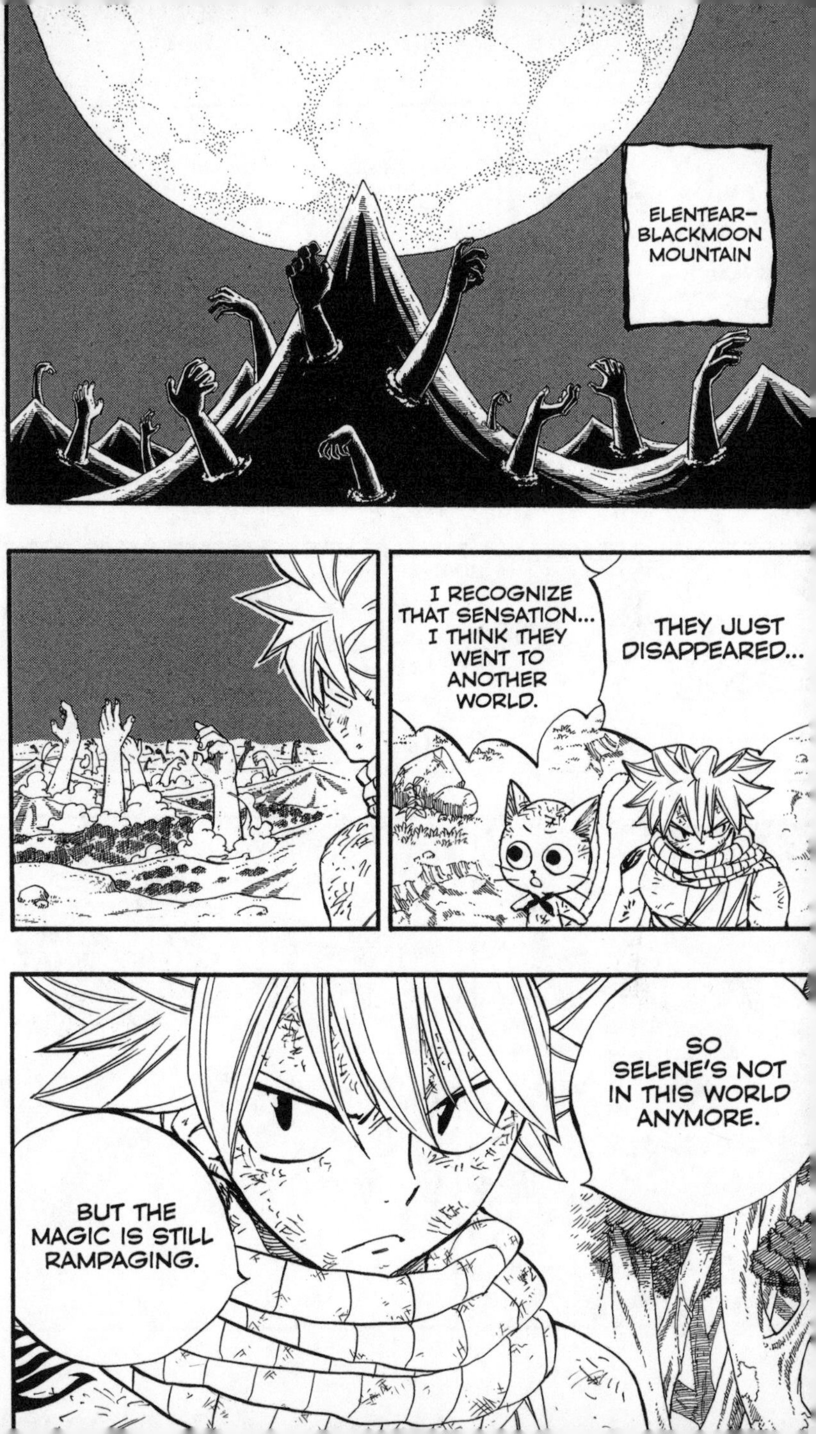
ELENTEAR—BLACKMOON MOUNTAIN
THEY JUST DISAPPEARED...
I RECOGNIZE THAT SENSATION... I THINK THEY WENT TO ANOTHER WORLD.
SO SELENE'S NOT IN THIS WORLD ANYMORE.
BUT THE MAGIC IS STILL RAMPAGING.

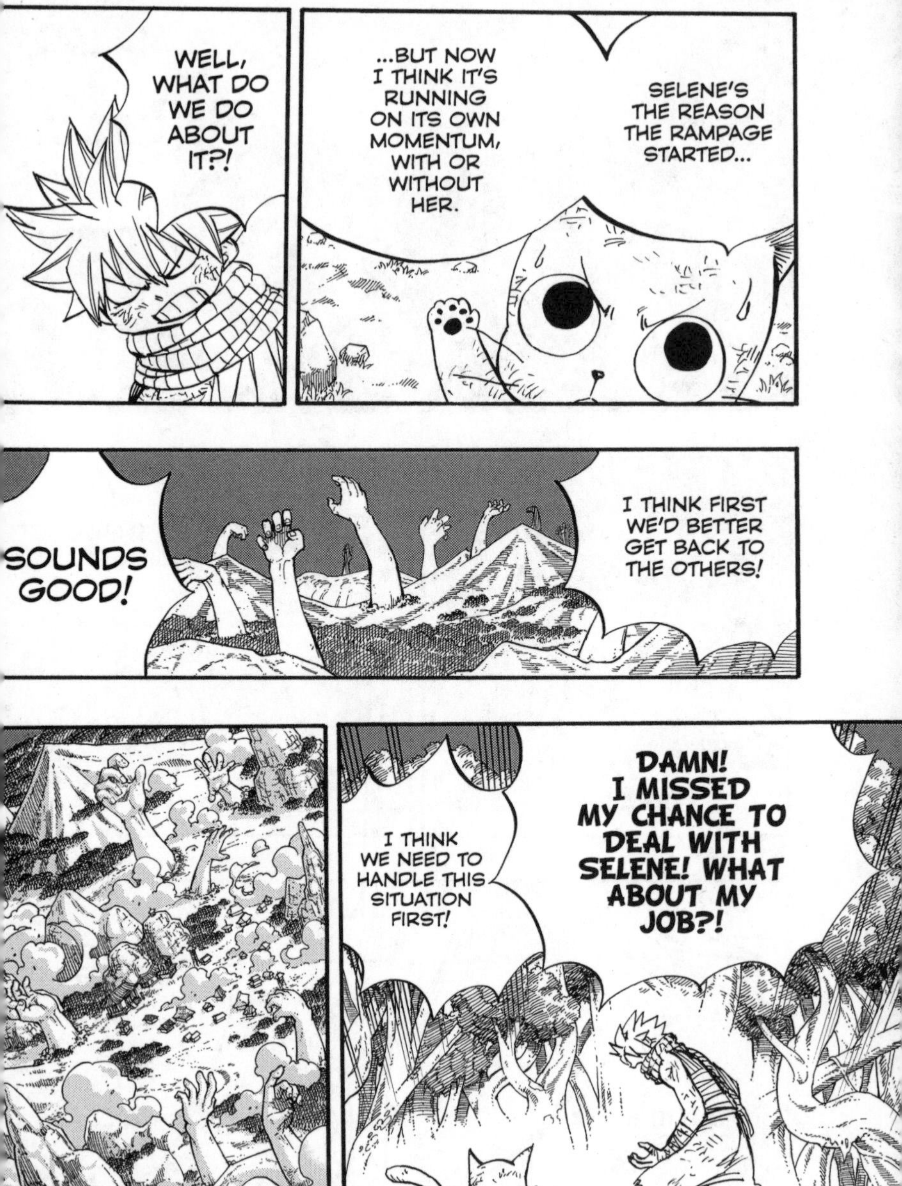
SELENE'S THE REASON THE RAMPAGE STARTED...
...BUT NOW I THINK IT'S RUNNING ON ITS OWN MOMENTUM, WITH OR WITHOUT HER.
WELL, WHAT DO WE DO ABOUT IT?!
I THINK FIRST WE'D BETTER GET BACK TO THE OTHERS!
SOUNDS GOOD!
DAMN! I MISSED MY CHANCE TO DEAL WITH SELENE! WHAT ABOUT MY JOB?!
I THINK WE NEED TO HANDLE THIS SITUATION FIRST!

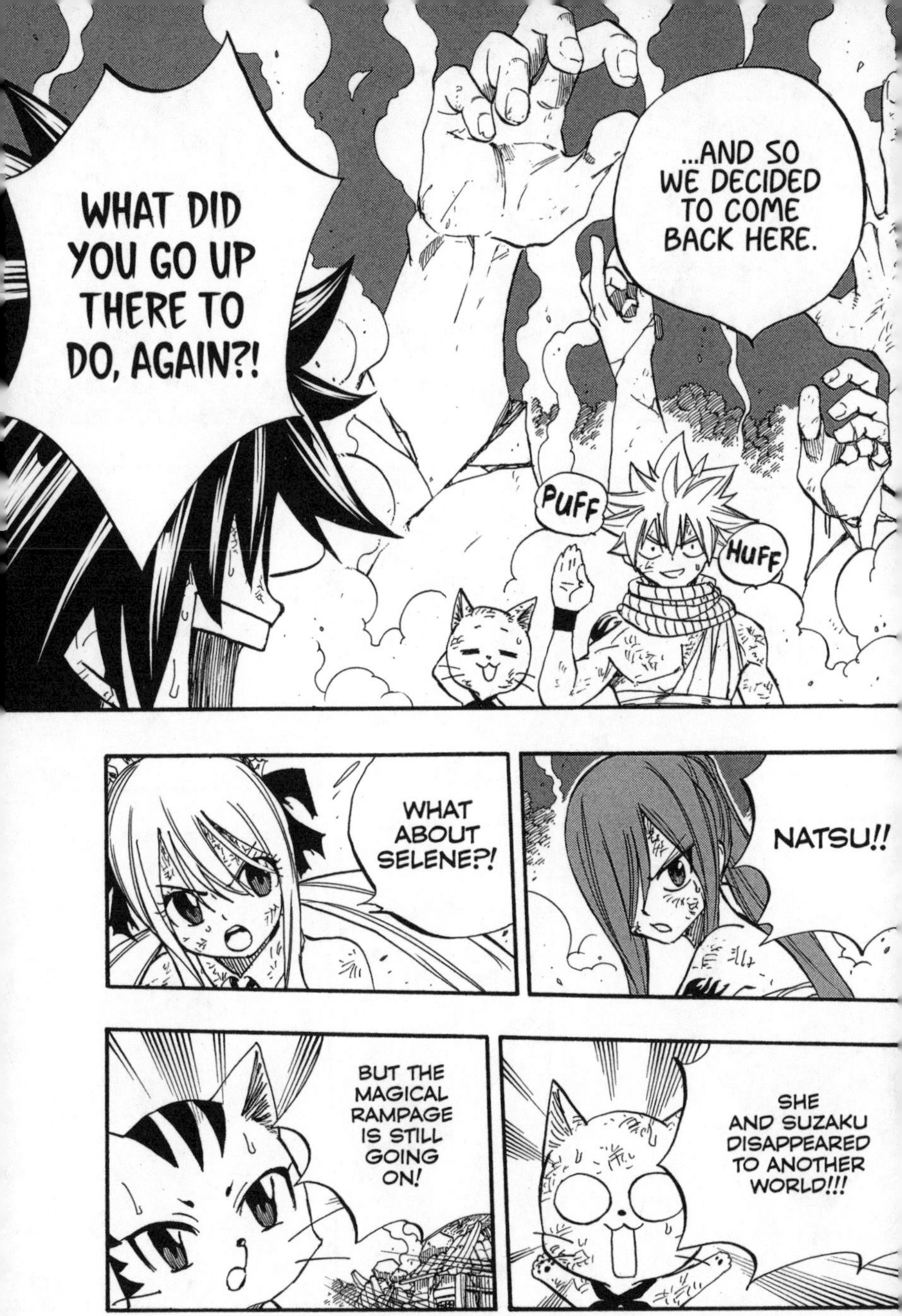
...AND SO WE DECIDED TO COME BACK HERE.
WHAT DID YOU GO UP THERE TO DO, AGAIN?!
PUFF
HUFF
NATSU!!
WHAT ABOUT SELENE?!
SHE AND SUZAKU DISAPPEARED TO ANOTHER WORLD!!!
BUT THE MAGICAL RAMPAGE IS STILL GOING ON!

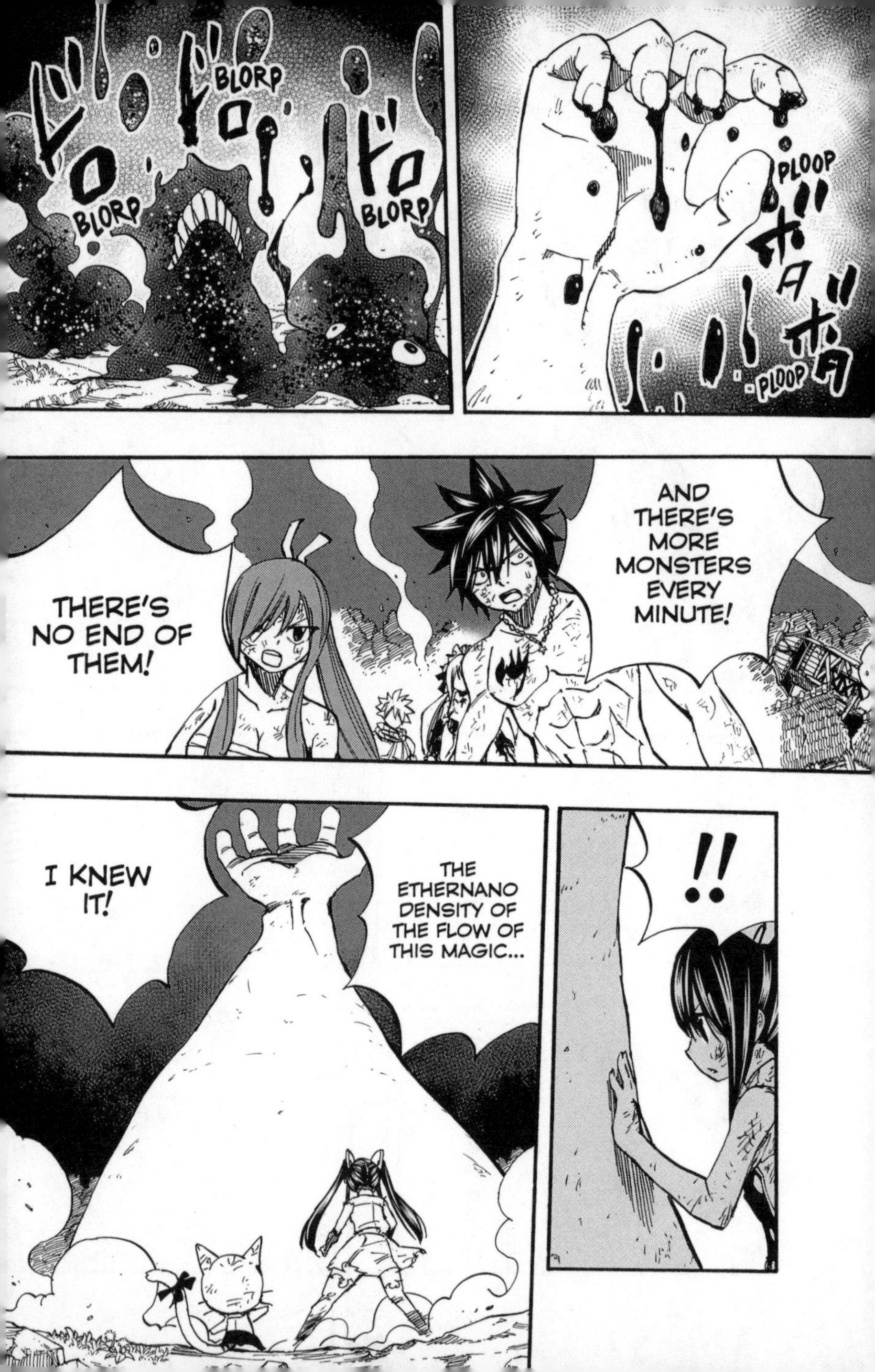
PLOOP
ボタ
ボタ
PLOOP
BLORP
BLORP
BLORP
ドロ
ドロ
ドロ
AND THERE'S MORE MONSTERS EVERY MINUTE!
THERE'S NO END OF THEM!
!!
THE ETHERNANO DENSITY OF THE FLOW OF THIS MAGIC...
I KNEW IT!

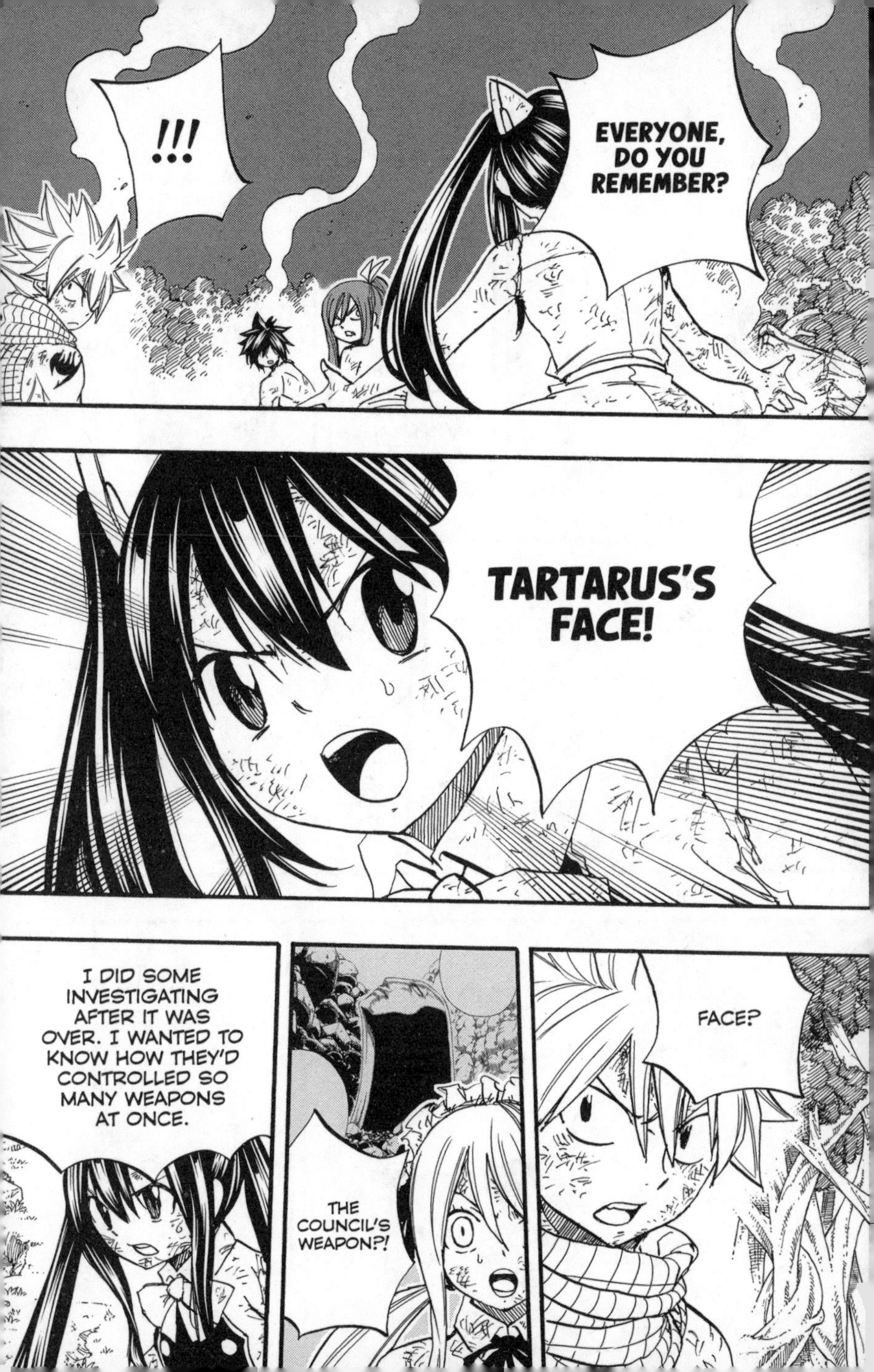
EVERYONE, DO YOU REMEMBER?
!!!
TARTARUS'S FACE!
FACE?
THE COUNCIL'S WEAPON?!
I DID SOME INVESTIGATING AFTER IT WAS OVER. I WANTED TO KNOW HOW THEY'D CONTROLLED SO MANY WEAPONS AT ONCE.

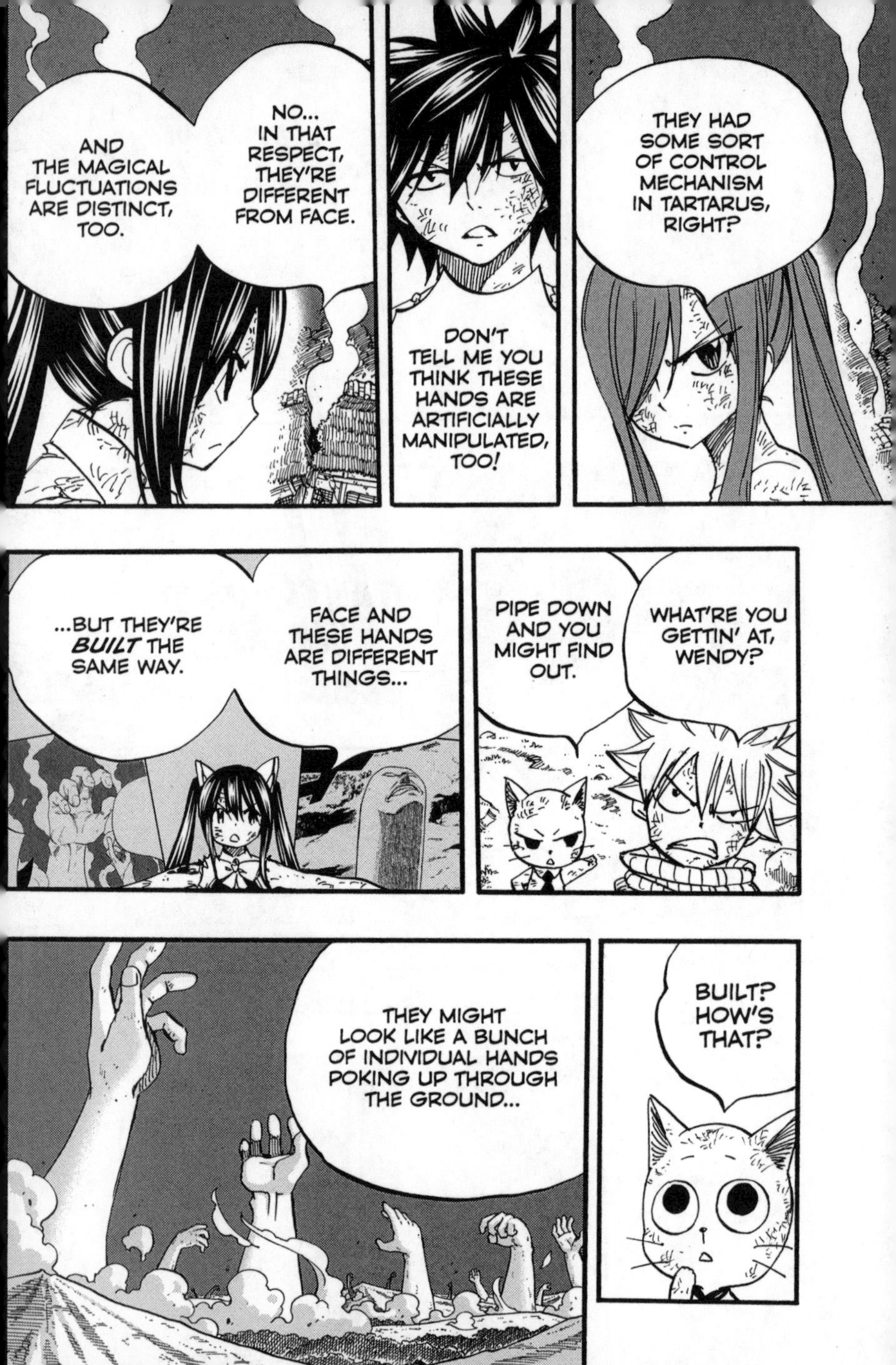

THEY HAD SOME SORT OF CONTROL MECHANISM IN TARTARUS, RIGHT?
DON'T TELL ME YOU THINK THESE HANDS ARE ARTIFICIALLY MANIPULATED, TOO!
NO... IN THAT RESPECT, THEY'RE DIFFERENT FROM FACE.
AND THE MAGICAL FLUCTUATIONS ARE DISTINCT, TOO.
WHAT'RE YOU GETTIN' AT, WENDY?
PIPE DOWN AND YOU MIGHT FIND OUT.
FACE AND THESE HANDS ARE DIFFERENT THINGS...
...BUT THEY'RE *BUILT* THE SAME WAY.
BUILT? HOW'S THAT?
THEY MIGHT LOOK LIKE A BUNCH OF INDIVIDUAL HANDS POKING UP THROUGH THE GROUND...

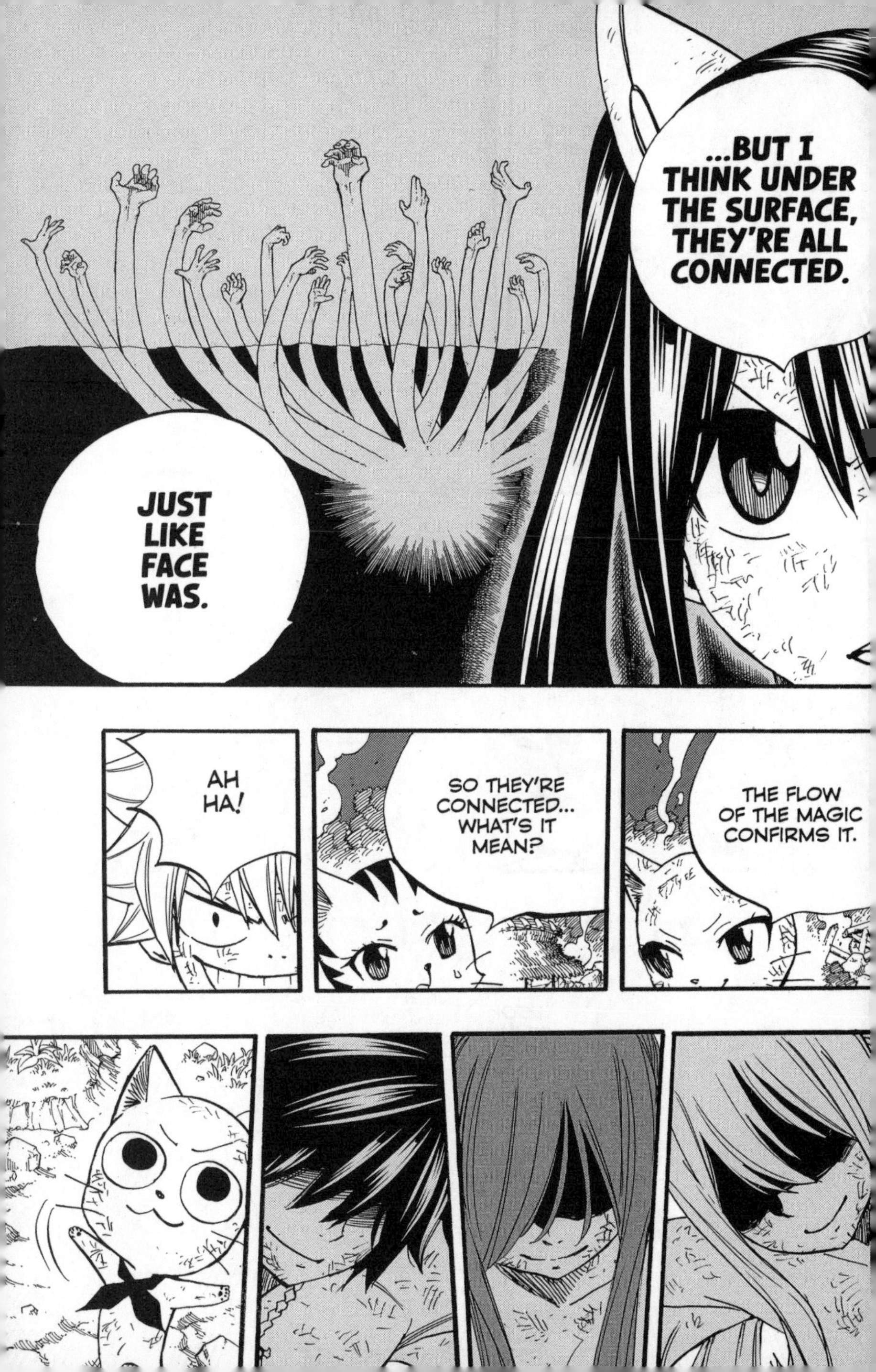
...BUT I THINK UNDER THE SURFACE, THEY'RE ALL CONNECTED.
JUST LIKE FACE WAS.
THE FLOW OF THE MAGIC CONFIRMS IT.
SO THEY'RE CONNECTED... WHAT'S IT MEAN?
AH HA!

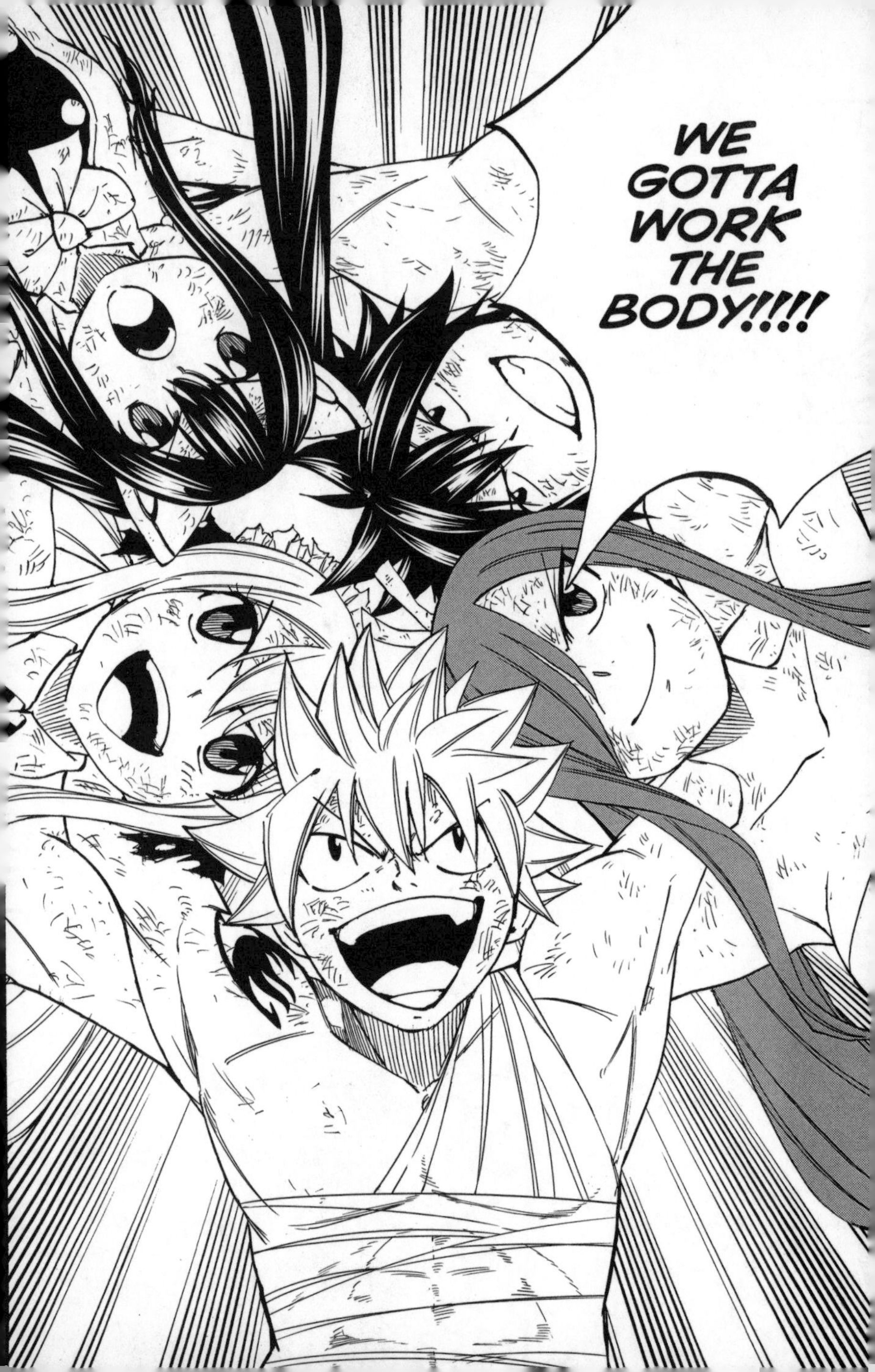
WE GOTTA WORK THE BODY!!!!

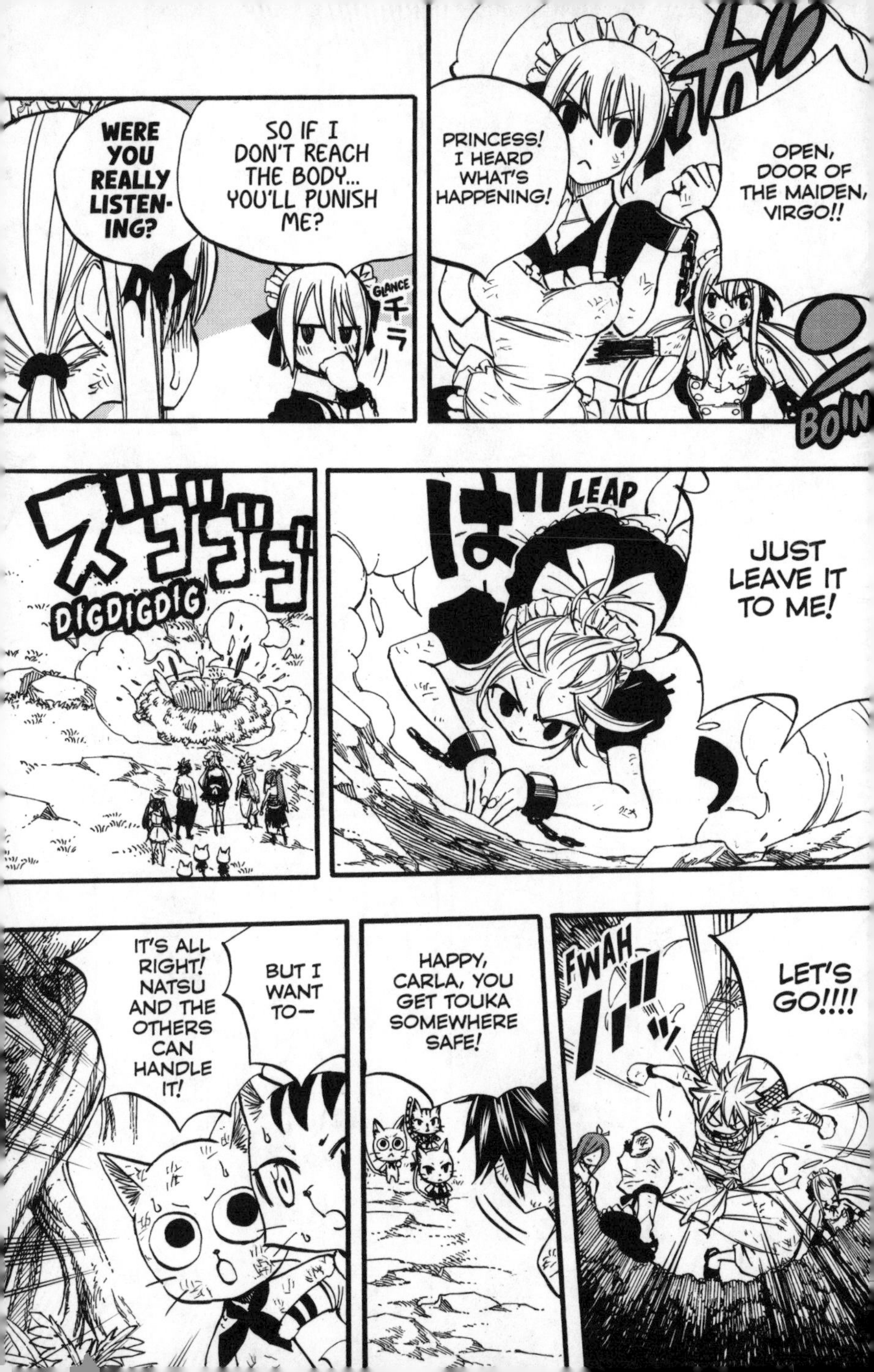
OPEN, DOOR OF THE MAIDEN, VIRGO!!
PRINCESS! I HEARD WHAT'S HAPPENING!
BOIN
SO IF I DON'T REACH THE BODY... YOU'LL PUNISH ME?
GLANCE
チラ
WERE YOU REALLY LISTEN-ING?
LEAP
JUST LEAVE IT TO ME!
DIGDIGDIG
FWAH
LET'S GO!!!!
HAPPY, CARLA, YOU GET TOUKA SOMEWHERE SAFE!
BUT I WANT TO—
IT'S ALL RIGHT! NATSU AND THE OTHERS CAN HANDLE IT!

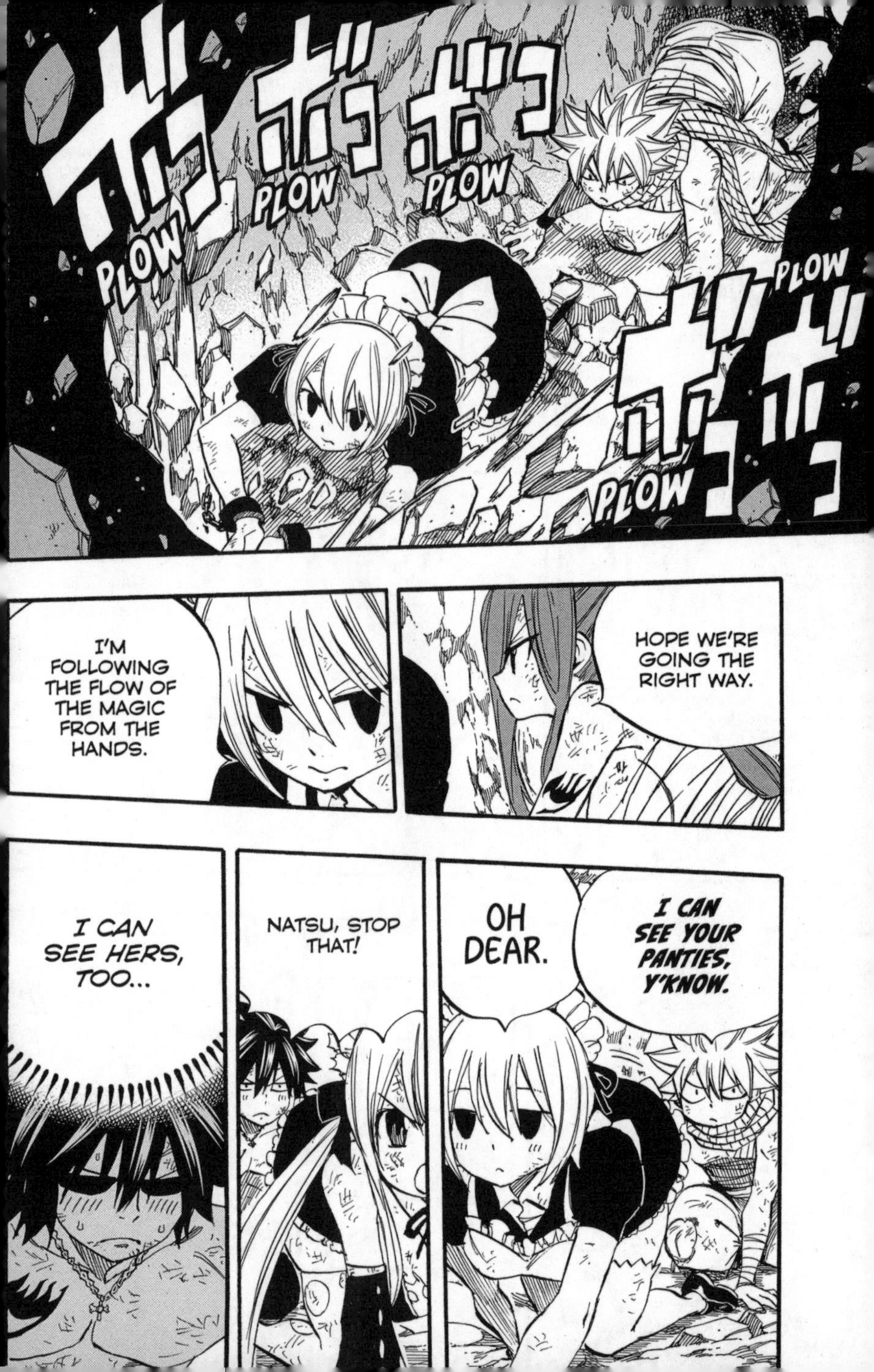
PLOW
PLOW
PLOW
PLOW
PLOW
PLOW
HOPE WE'RE GOING THE RIGHT WAY.
I'M FOLLOWING THE FLOW OF THE MAGIC FROM THE HANDS.
I CAN SEE YOUR PANTIES, Y'KNOW.
OH DEAR.
NATSU, STOP THAT!
I CAN SEE HERS, TOO...

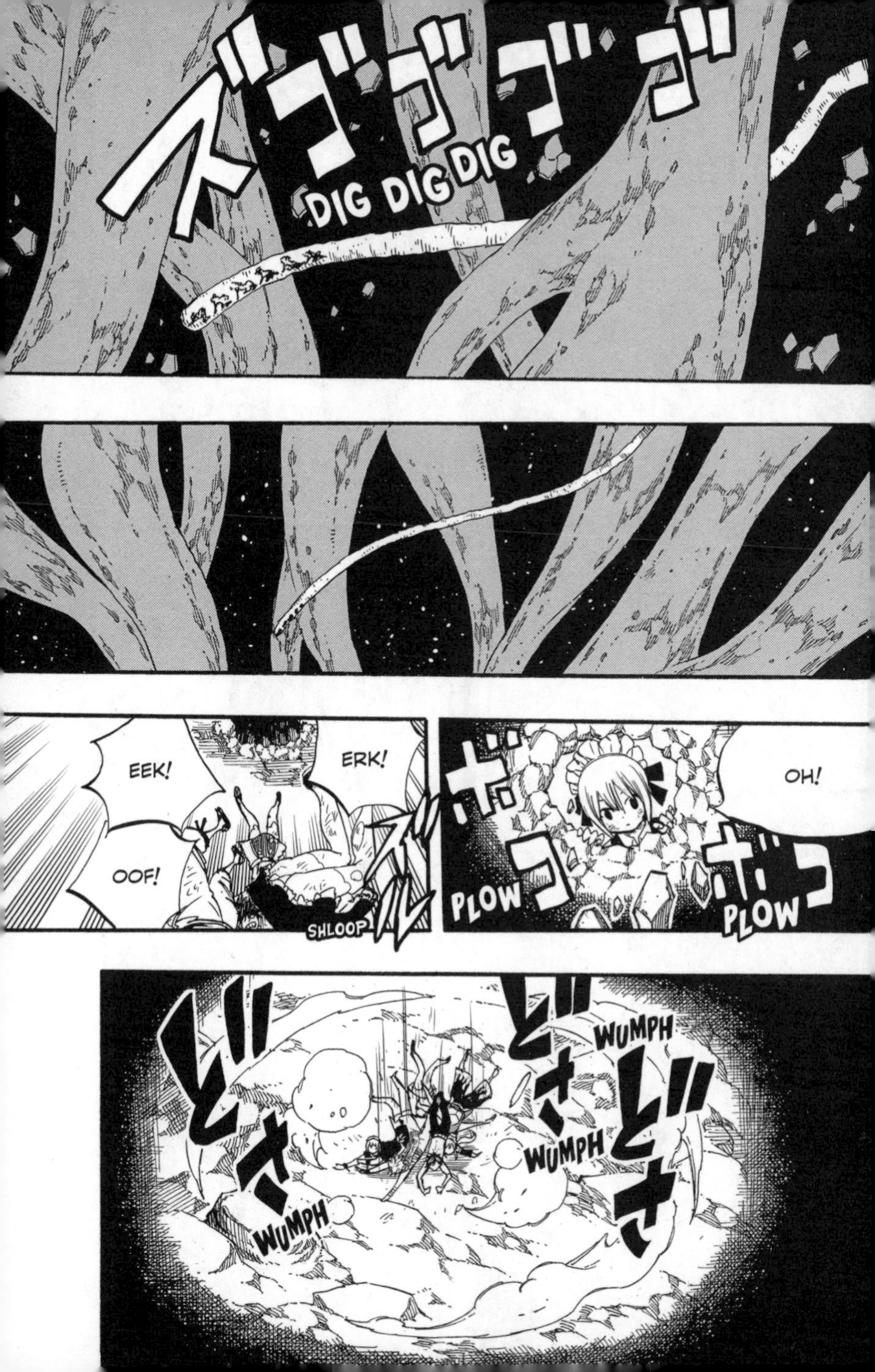
ズゴゴゴ
DIG DIG DIG
OH!
ボコッ
PLOW
ボコッ
PLOW
ERK!
EEK!
OOF!
SHLOOP
どさ
WUMPH
どさ
WUMPH
どさ
WUMPH

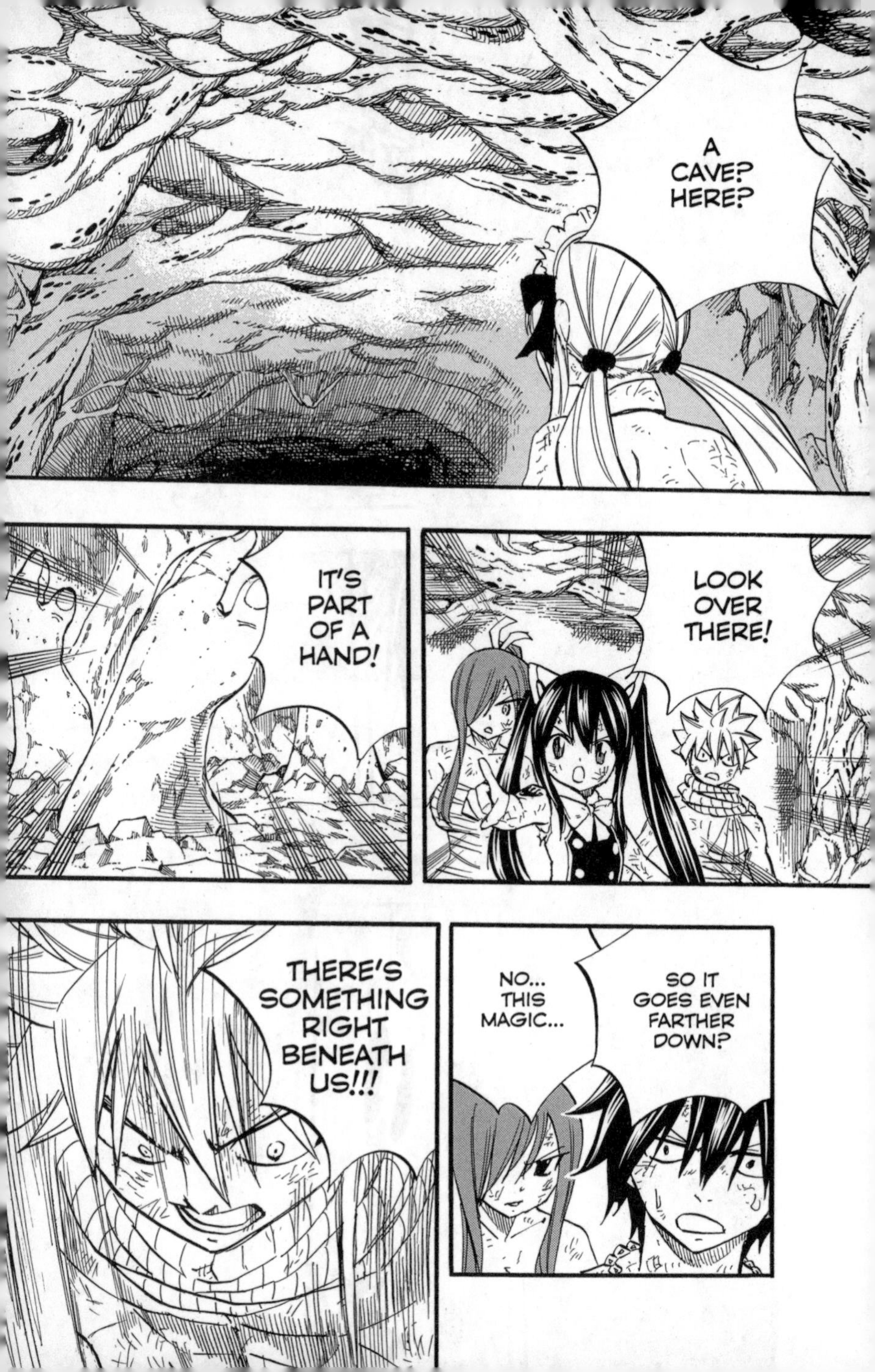
A CAVE? HERE?
LOOK OVER THERE!
IT'S PART OF A HAND!
SO IT GOES EVEN FARTHER DOWN?
NO... THIS MAGIC...
THERE'S SOMETHING RIGHT BENEATH US!!!

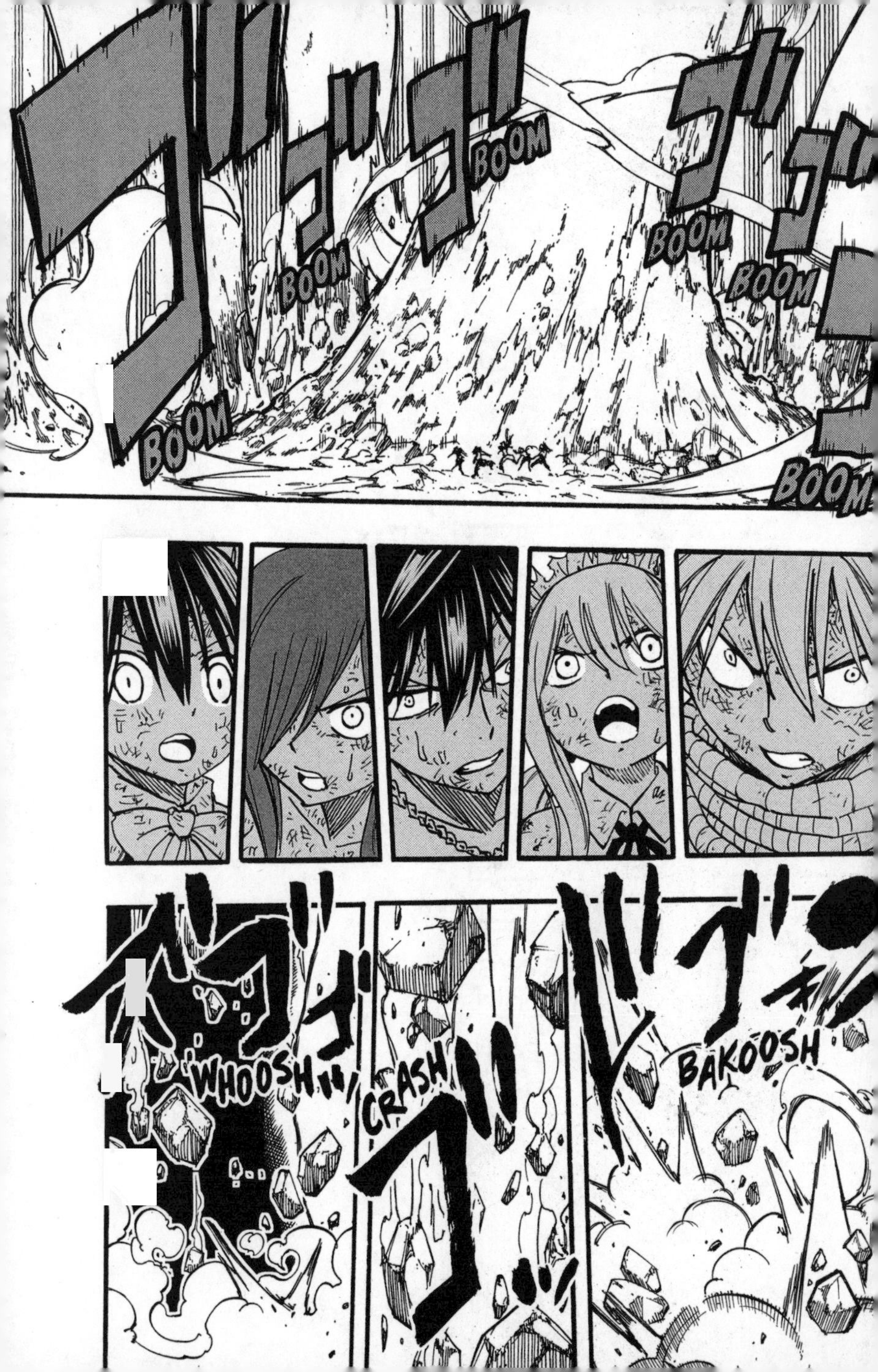
BOOM
BOOM
BOOM
BOOM
BOOM
BOOM
BAKOOSH
CRASH
WHOOSH

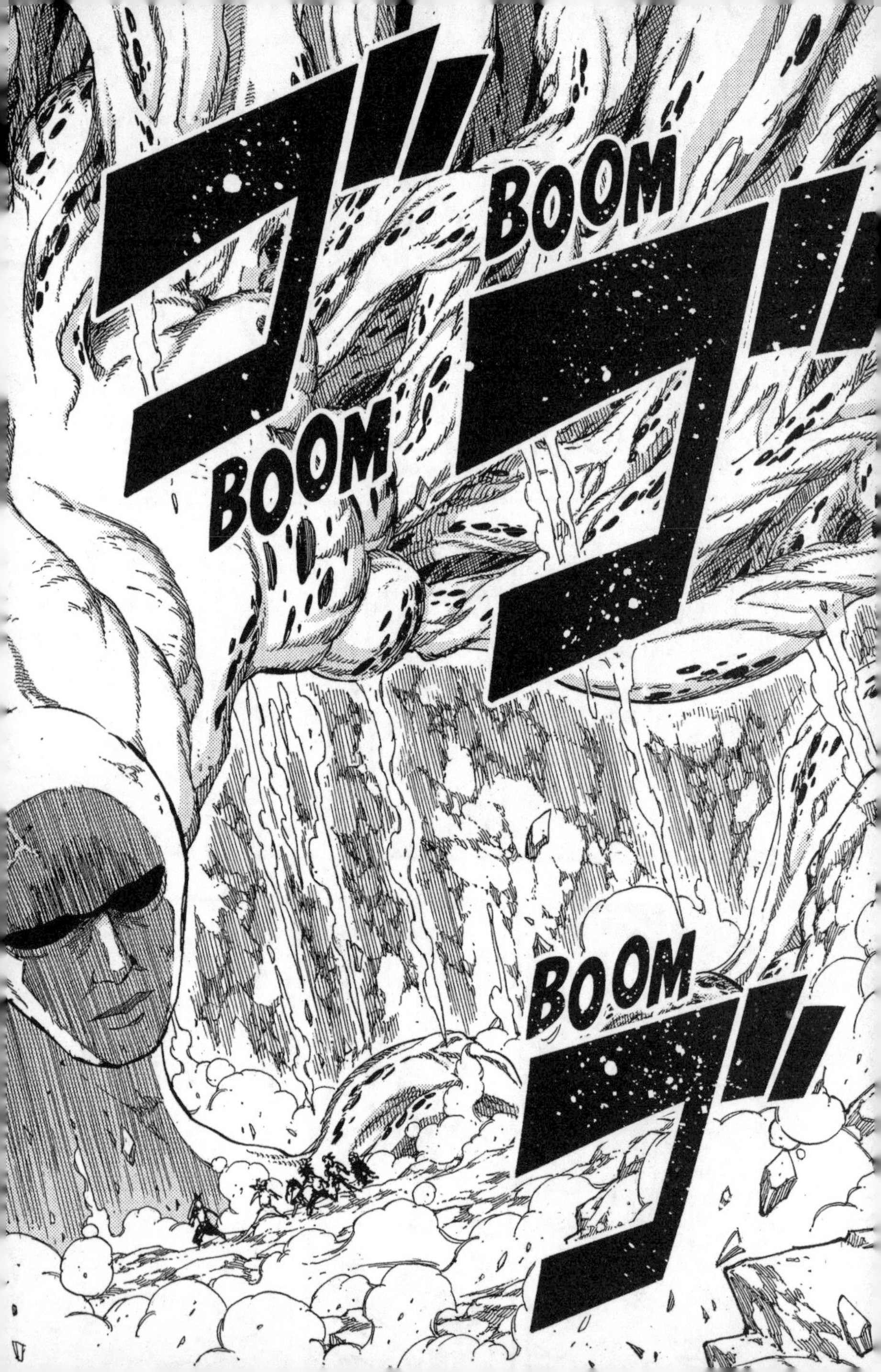
BOOM
ゴ
BOOM
ゴ
BOOM
ゴ

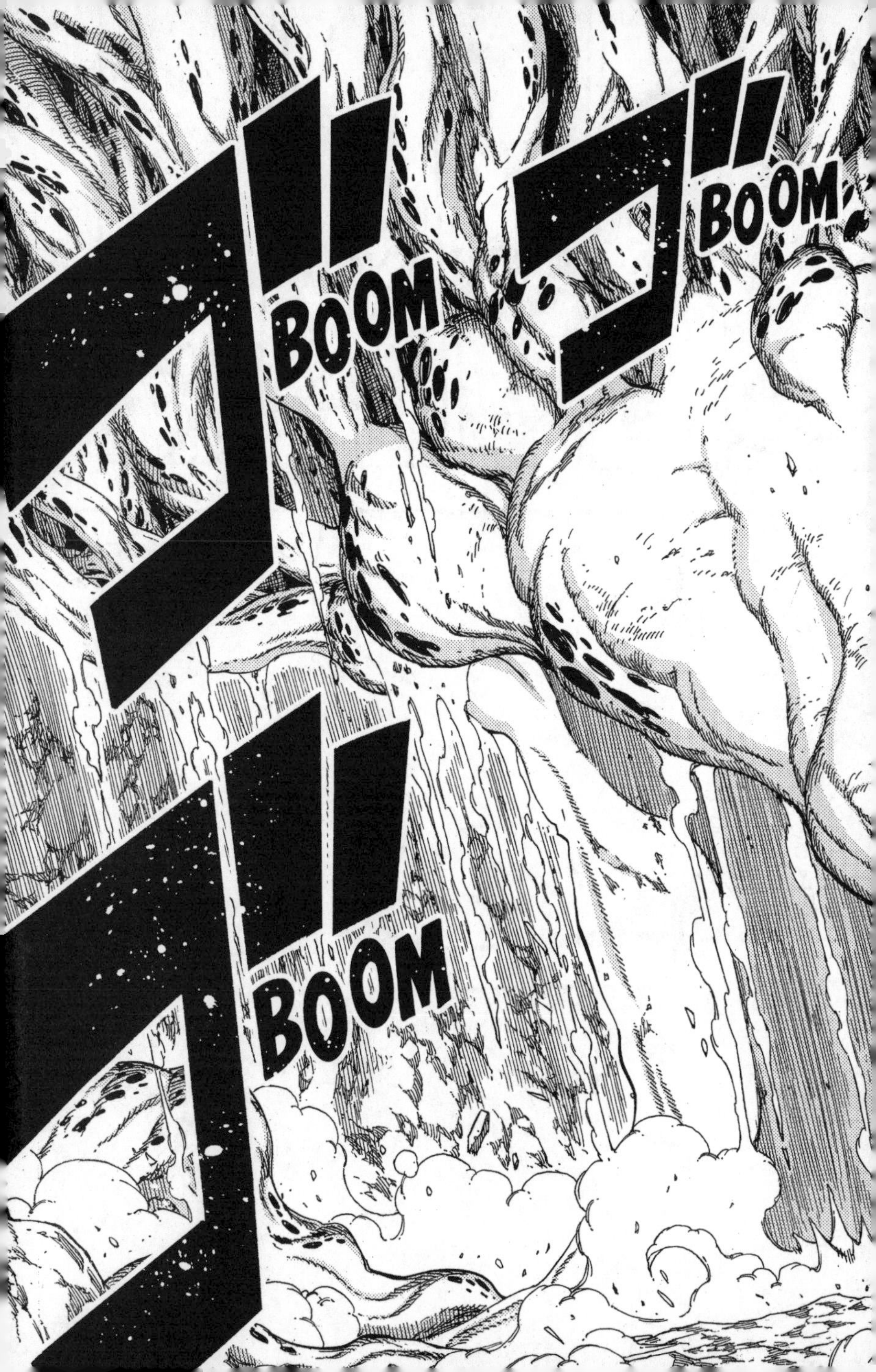
BOOM
BOOM
BOOM

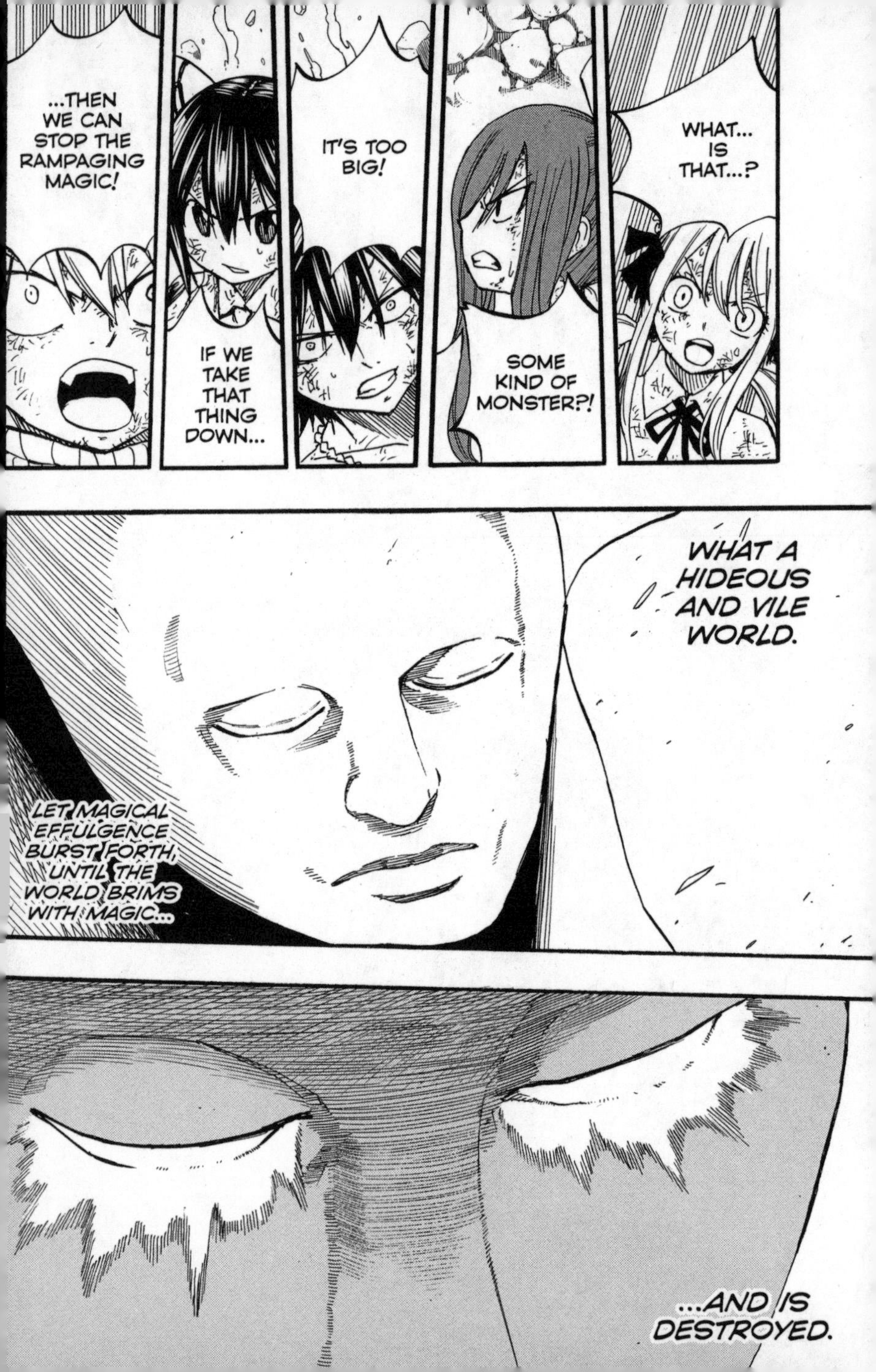
WHAT... IS THAT...?
SOME KIND OF MONSTER?!
IT'S TOO BIG!
IF WE TAKE THAT THING DOWN...
...THEN WE CAN STOP THE RAMPAGING MAGIC!
WHAT A HIDEOUS AND VILE WORLD.
LET MAGICAL EFFULGENCE BURST FORTH, UNTIL THE WORLD BRIMS WITH MAGIC...
...AND IS DESTROYED.

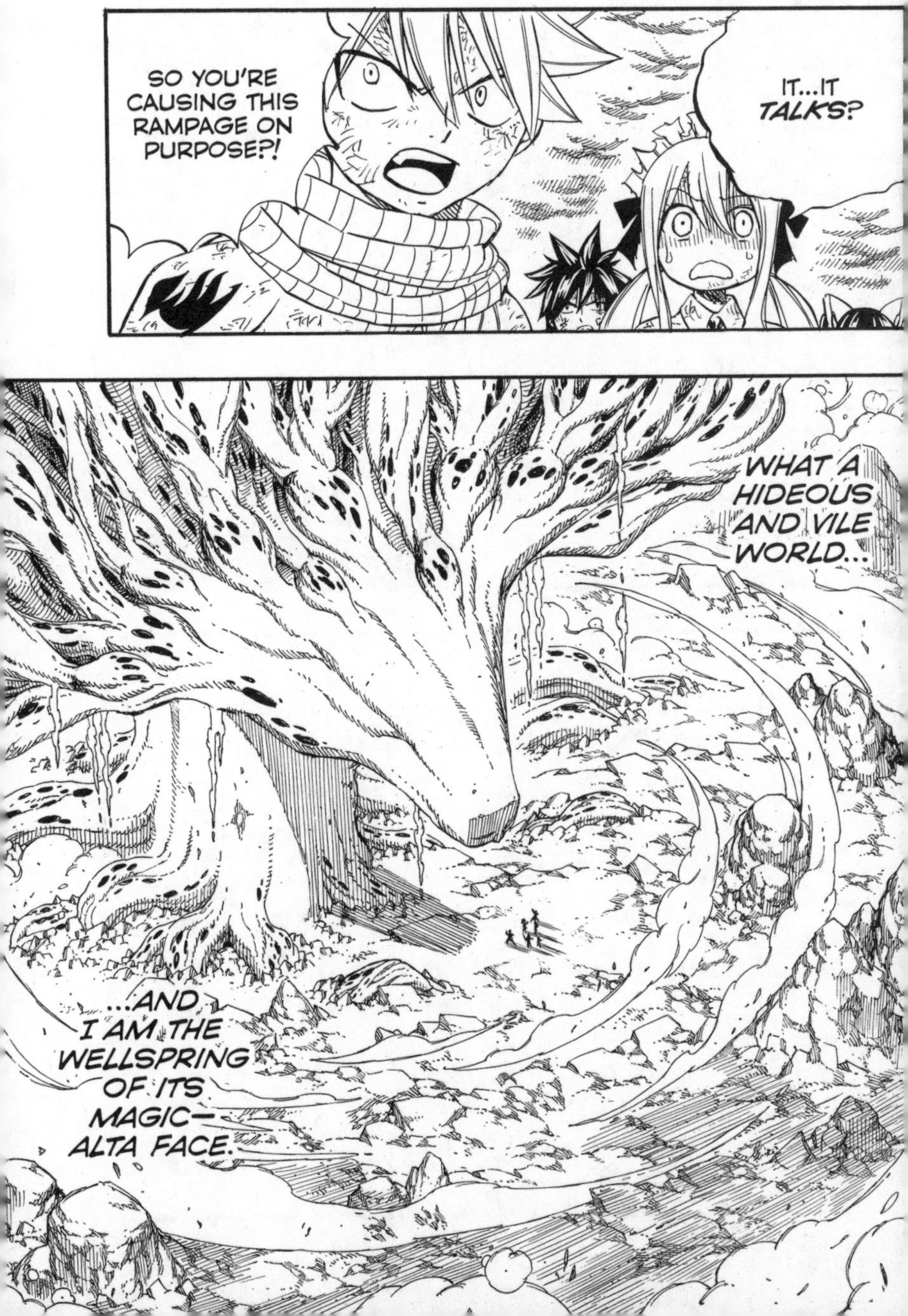
IT...IT *TALKS*?
SO YOU'RE CAUSING THIS RAMPAGE ON PURPOSE?!
WHAT A HIDEOUS AND VILE WORLD...
...AND I AM THE WELLSPRING OF ITS MAGIC—ALTA FACE.

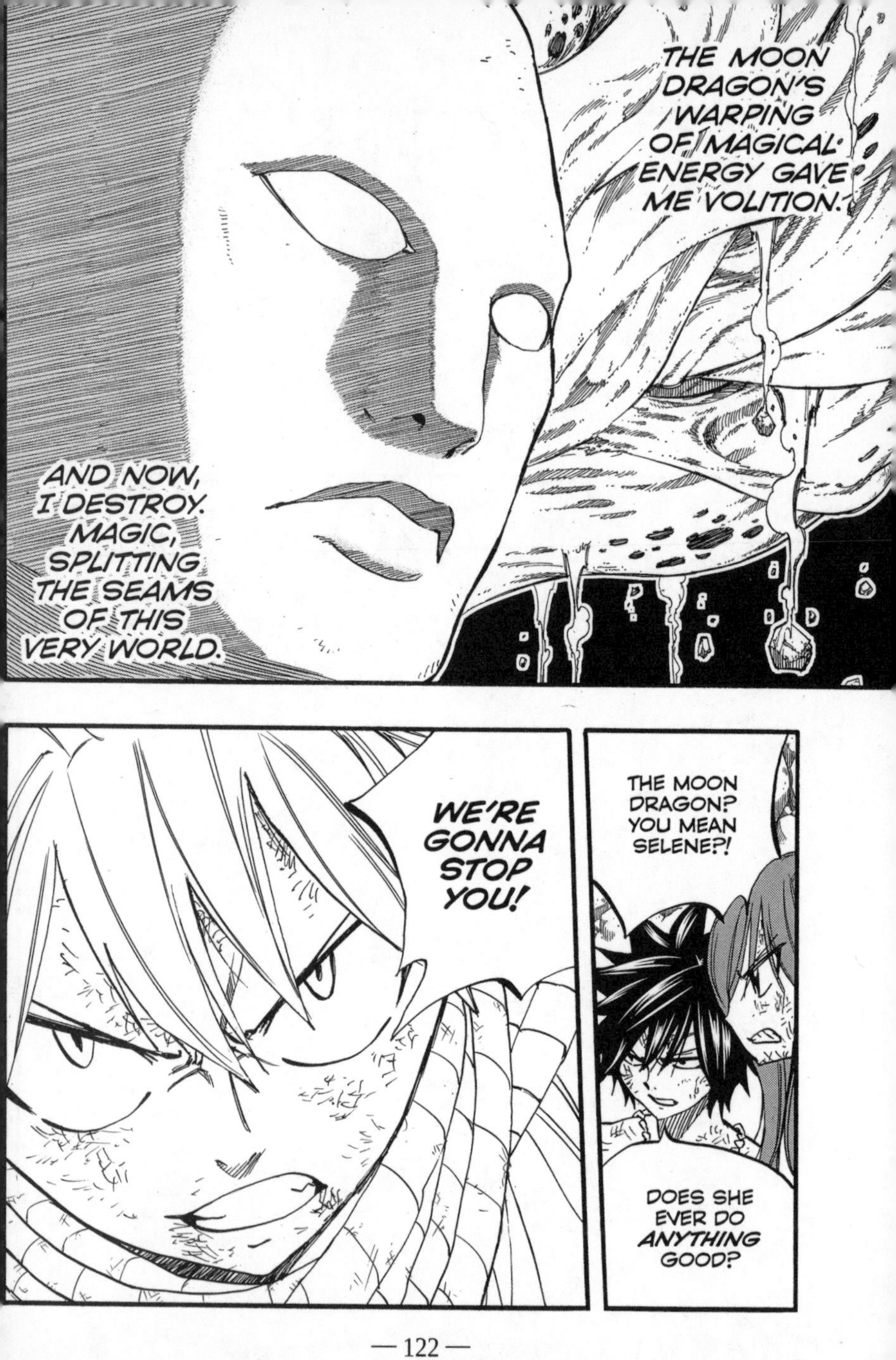
THE MOON DRAGON'S WARPING OF MAGICAL ENERGY GAVE ME VOLITION.
AND NOW, I DESTROY. MAGIC, SPLITTING THE SEAMS OF THIS VERY WORLD.
THE MOON DRAGON? YOU MEAN SELENE?!
DOES SHE EVER DO *ANYTHING* GOOD?
WE'RE GONNA STOP YOU!

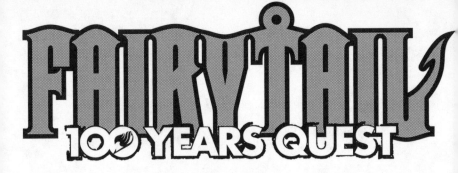

FAIRY TAIL 100 YEARS QUEST

Chapter 88: Alta Face

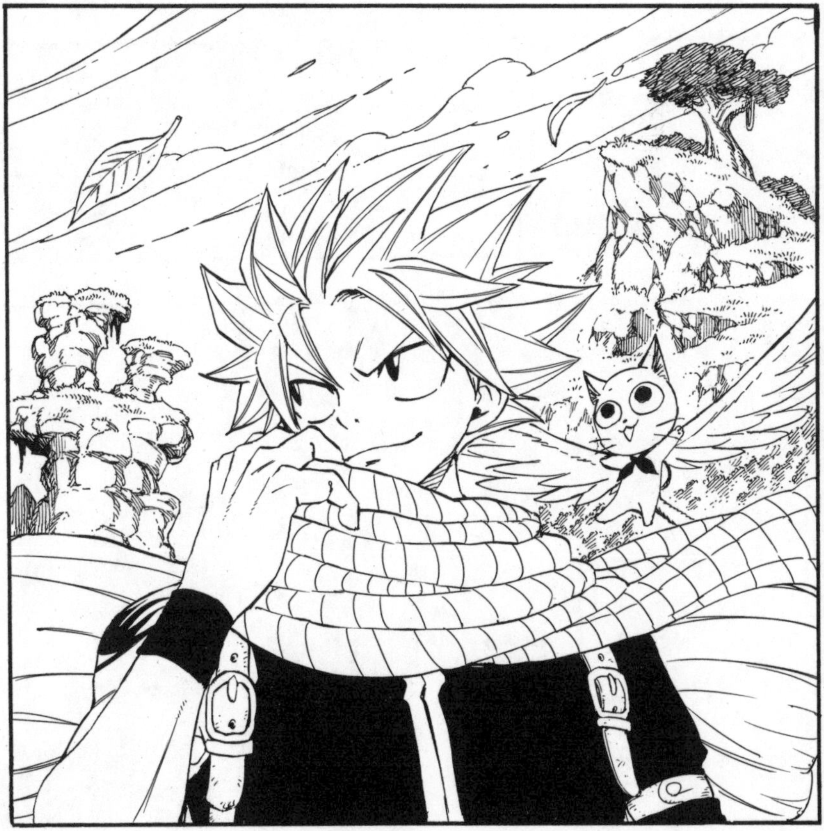

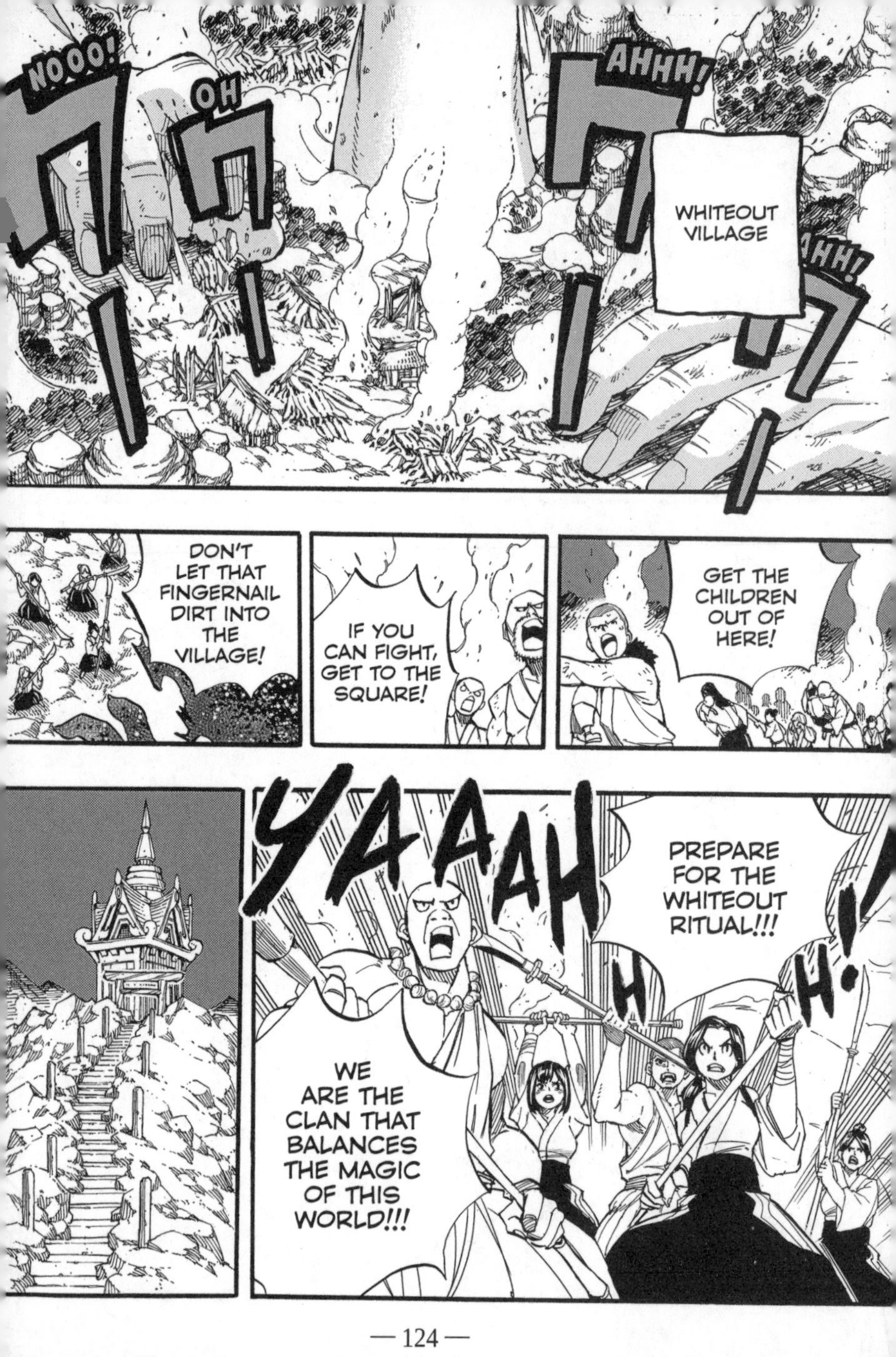
AHHH!
WHITEOUT VILLAGE
OH
NOOO!
GET THE CHILDREN OUT OF HERE!
IF YOU CAN FIGHT, GET TO THE SQUARE!
DON'T LET THAT FINGERNAIL DIRT INTO THE VILLAGE!
PREPARE FOR THE WHITEOUT RITUAL!!!
YAAAHHH!!
WE ARE THE CLAN THAT BALANCES THE MAGIC OF THIS WORLD!!!

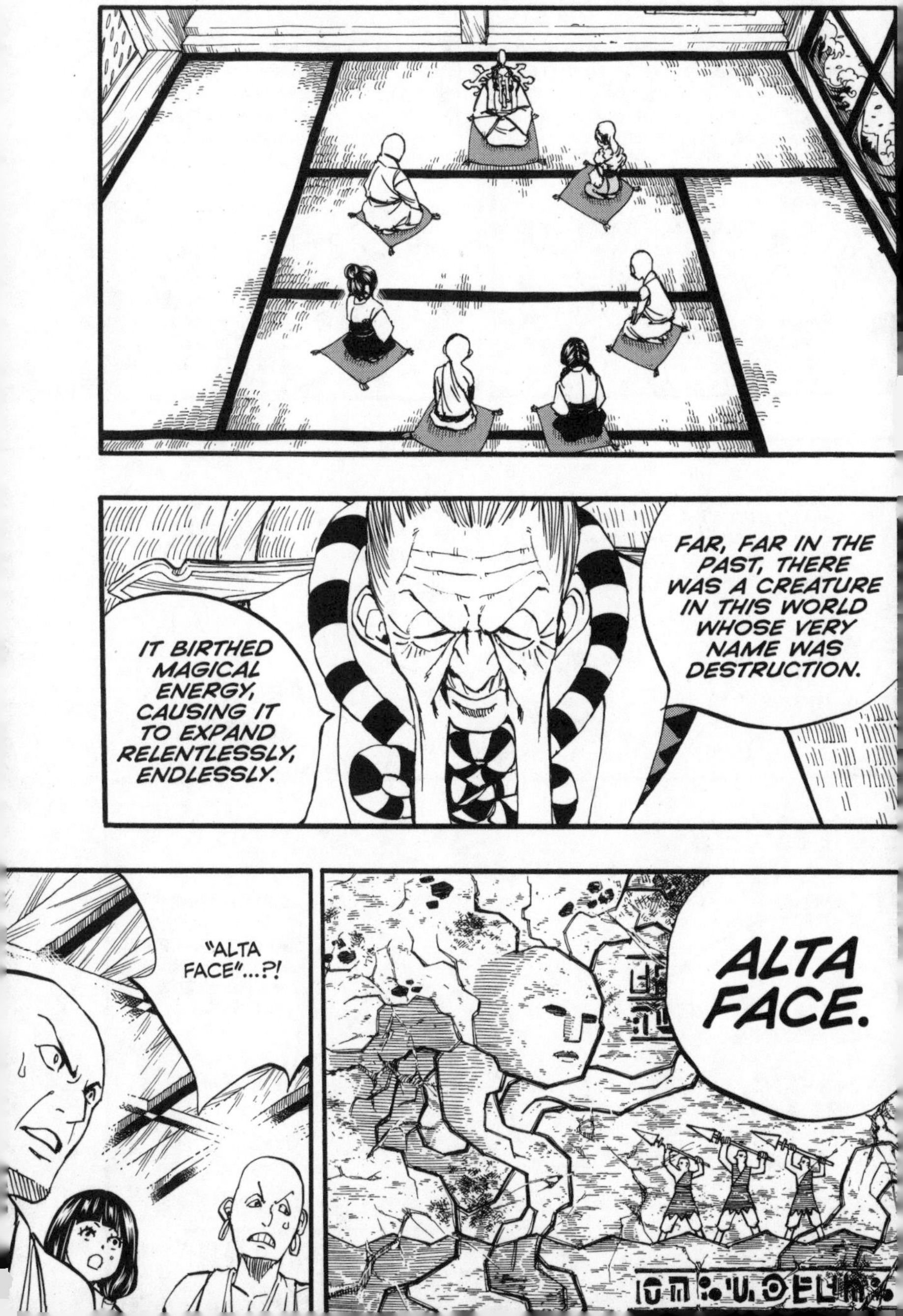
FAR, FAR IN THE PAST, THERE WAS A CREATURE IN THIS WORLD WHOSE VERY NAME WAS DESTRUCTION.
IT BIRTHED MAGICAL ENERGY, CAUSING IT TO EXPAND RELENTLESSLY, ENDLESSLY.
ALTA FACE.
"ALTA FACE"...?!

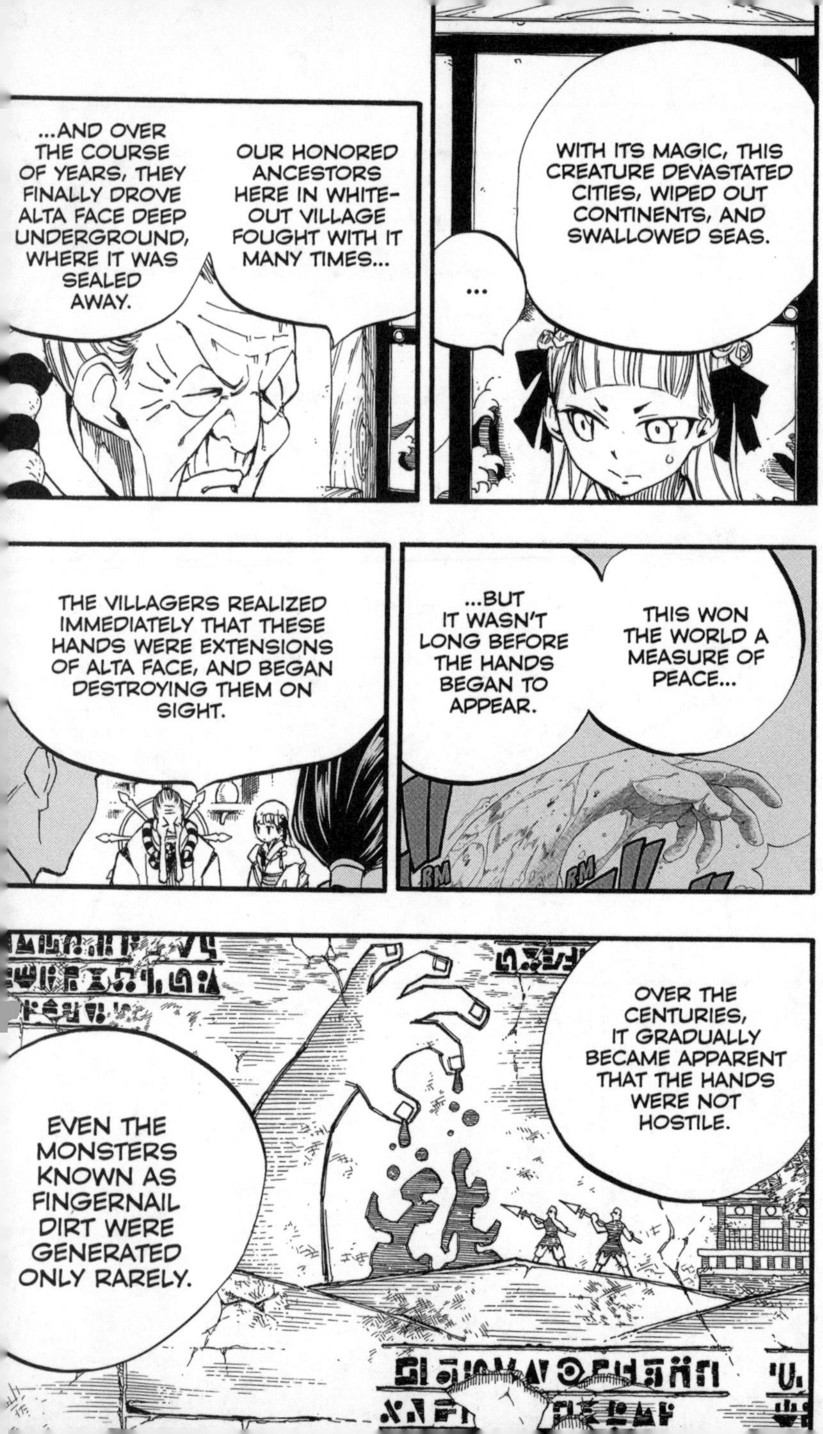
WITH ITS MAGIC, THIS CREATURE DEVASTATED CITIES, WIPED OUT CONTINENTS, AND SWALLOWED SEAS.
...
OUR HONORED ANCESTORS HERE IN WHITE-OUT VILLAGE FOUGHT WITH IT MANY TIMES...
...AND OVER THE COURSE OF YEARS, THEY FINALLY DROVE ALTA FACE DEEP UNDERGROUND, WHERE IT WAS SEALED AWAY.
THIS WON THE WORLD A MEASURE OF PEACE...
...BUT IT WASN'T LONG BEFORE THE HANDS BEGAN TO APPEAR.
RM
RM
THE VILLAGERS REALIZED IMMEDIATELY THAT THESE HANDS WERE EXTENSIONS OF ALTA FACE, AND BEGAN DESTROYING THEM ON SIGHT.
OVER THE CENTURIES, IT GRADUALLY BECAME APPARENT THAT THE HANDS WERE NOT HOSTILE.
EVEN THE MONSTERS KNOWN AS FINGERNAIL DIRT WERE GENERATED ONLY RARELY.

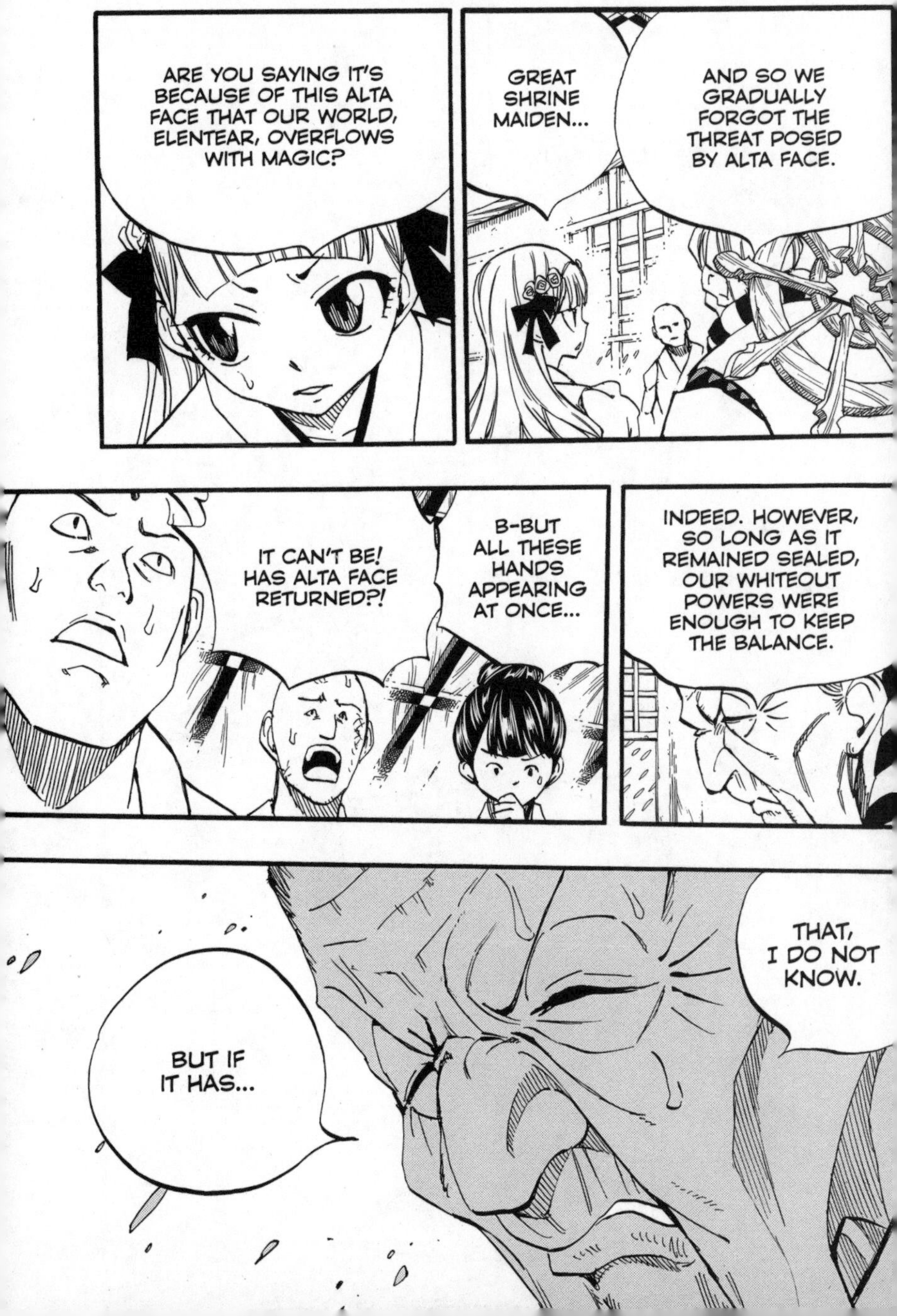
AND SO WE GRADUALLY FORGOT THE THREAT POSED BY ALTA FACE.
GREAT SHRINE MAIDEN...
ARE YOU SAYING IT'S BECAUSE OF THIS ALTA FACE THAT OUR WORLD, ELENTEAR, OVERFLOWS WITH MAGIC?
INDEED. HOWEVER, SO LONG AS IT REMAINED SEALED, OUR WHITEOUT POWERS WERE ENOUGH TO KEEP THE BALANCE.
B-BUT ALL THESE HANDS APPEARING AT ONCE...
IT CAN'T BE! HAS ALTA FACE RETURNED?!
THAT, I DO NOT KNOW.
BUT IF IT HAS...

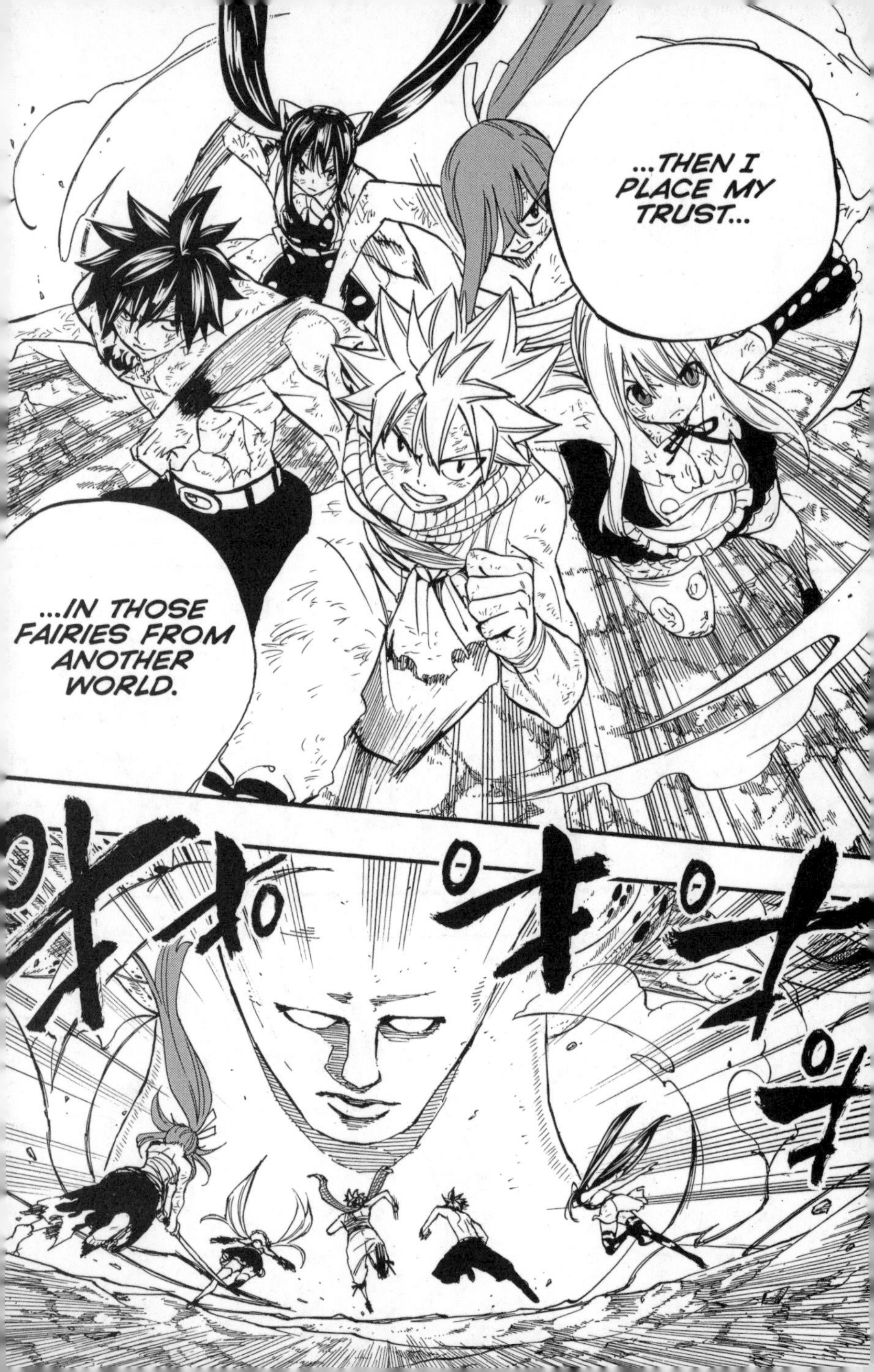
...THEN I PLACE MY TRUST...
...IN THOSE FAIRIES FROM ANOTHER WORLD.

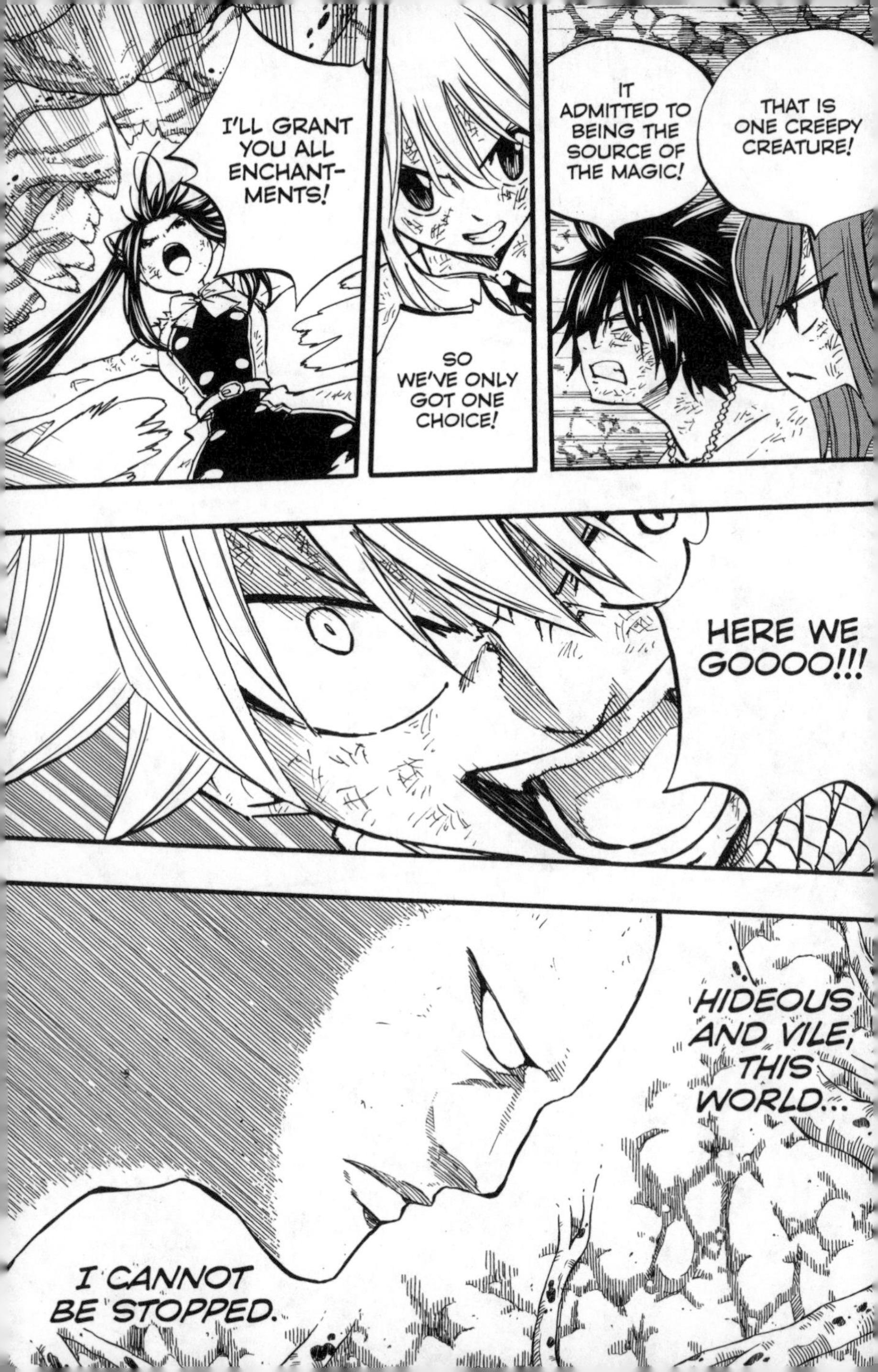
THAT IS ONE CREEPY CREATURE!
IT ADMITTED TO BEING THE SOURCE OF THE MAGIC!
SO WE'VE ONLY GOT ONE CHOICE!
I'LL GRANT YOU ALL ENCHANT-MENTS!
HERE WE GOOOO!!!
HIDEOUS AND VILE, THIS WORLD...
I CANNOT BE STOPPED.

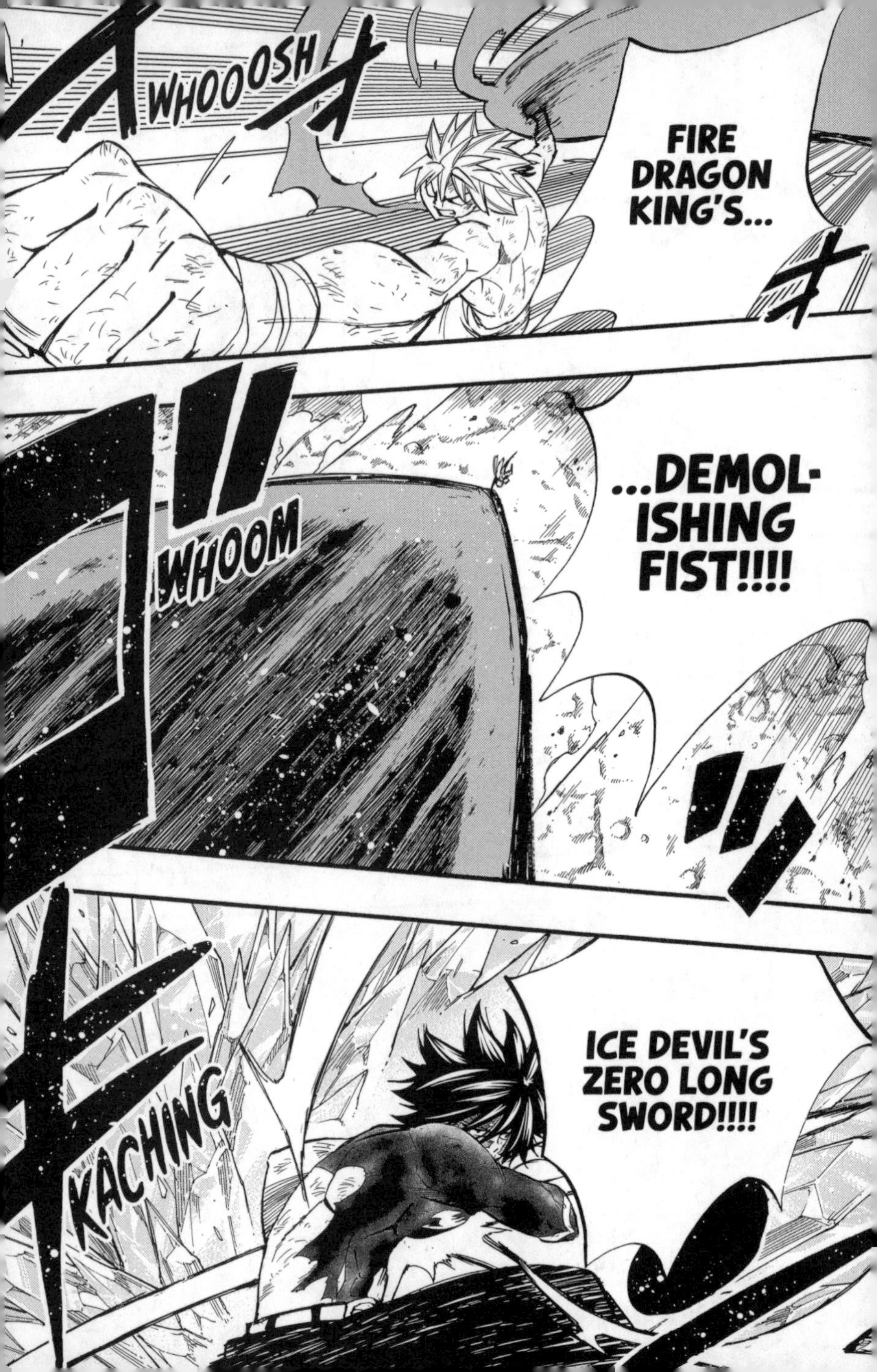
FIRE DRAGON KING'S...
WHOOOSH
...DEMOL-ISHING FIST!!!!
WHOOM
ICE DEVIL'S ZERO LONG SWORD!!!!
KACHING

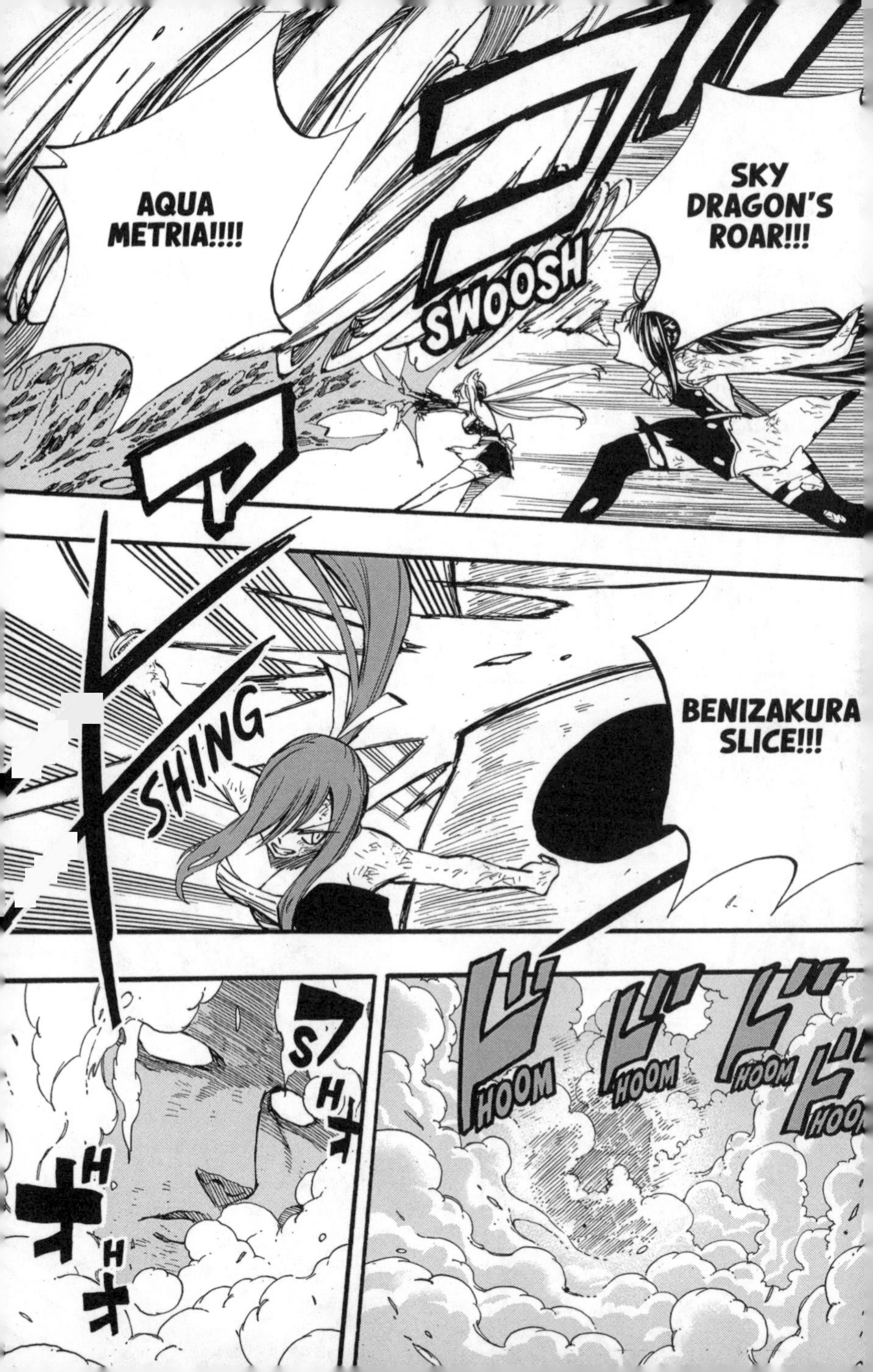
SKY DRAGON'S ROAR!!!
SWOOSH
AQUA METRIA!!!!
BENIZAKURA SLICE!!!
SHING
HOOM
HOOM
HOOM
SH
H
H

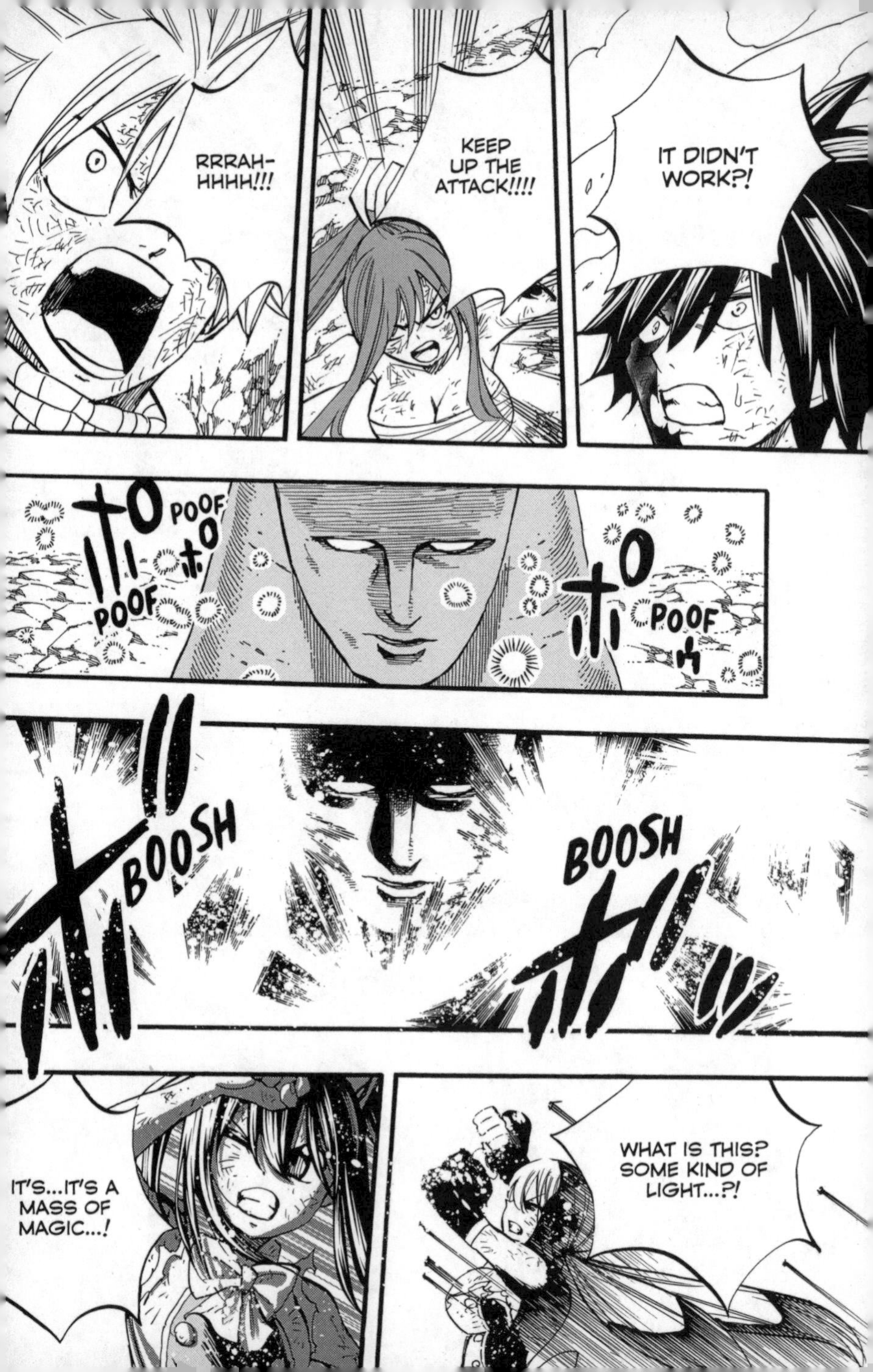
IT DIDN'T WORK?!
KEEP UP THE ATTACK!!!!
RRRAH-HHHH!!!
POOF
POOF
POOF
BOOSH
BOOSH
WHAT IS THIS? SOME KIND OF LIGHT...?!
IT'S...IT'S A MASS OF MAGIC...!

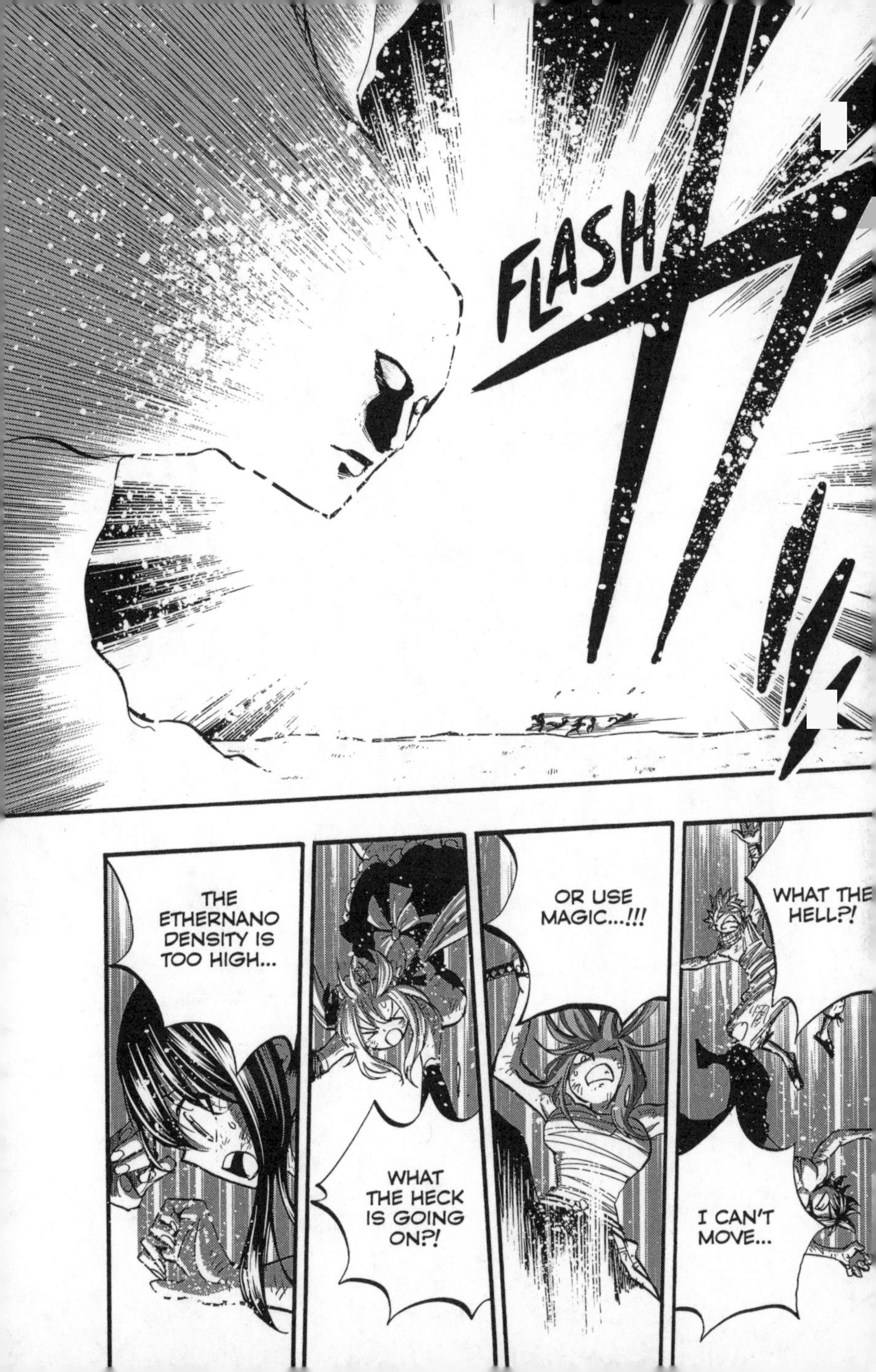
FLASH
WHAT THE HELL?!
I CAN'T MOVE...
OR USE MAGIC...!!!
WHAT THE HECK IS GOING ON?!
THE ETHERNANO DENSITY IS TOO HIGH...

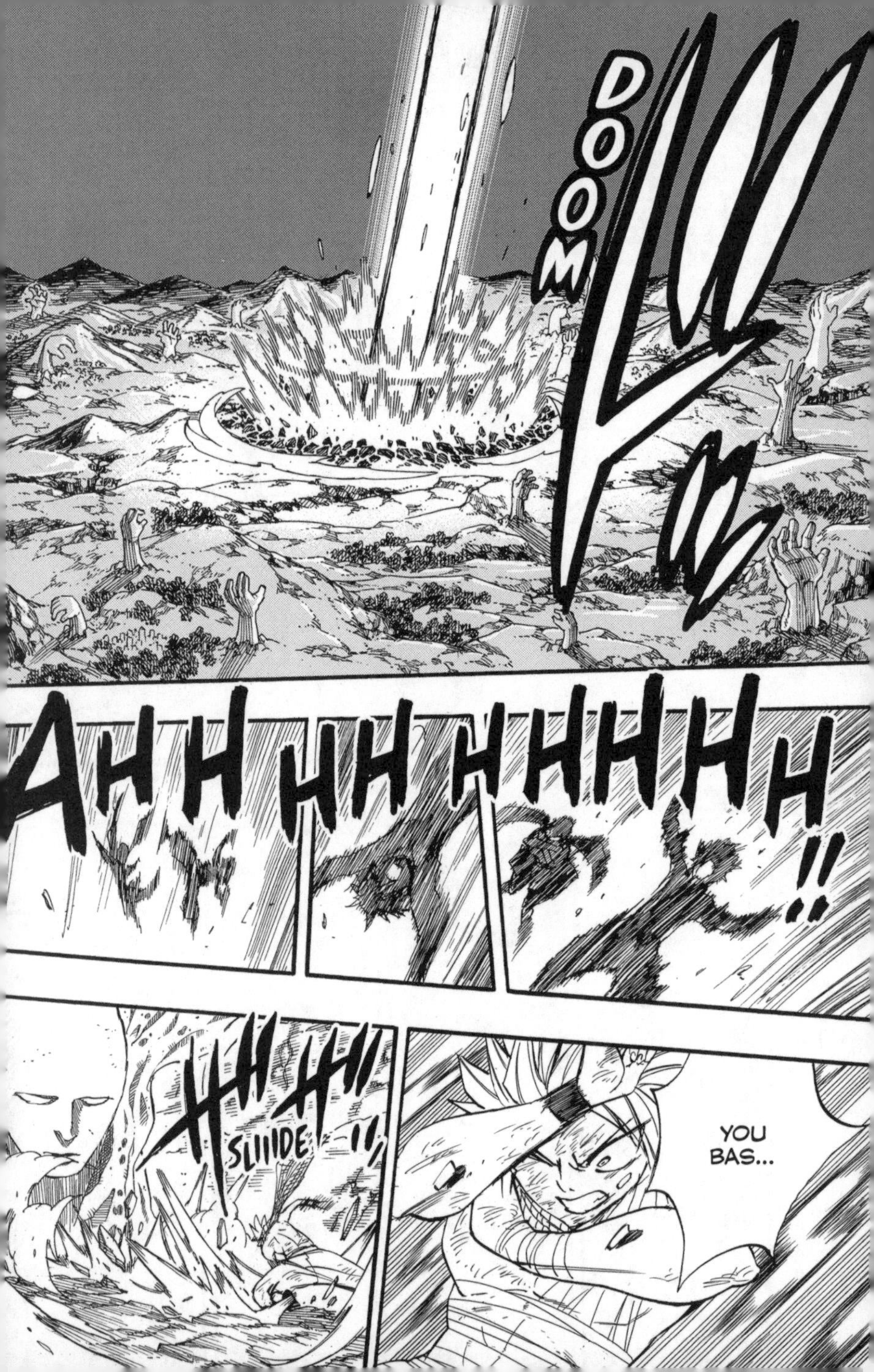
DOOM
AHHHHHHHHH!!
YOU BAS...
SLIIIDE

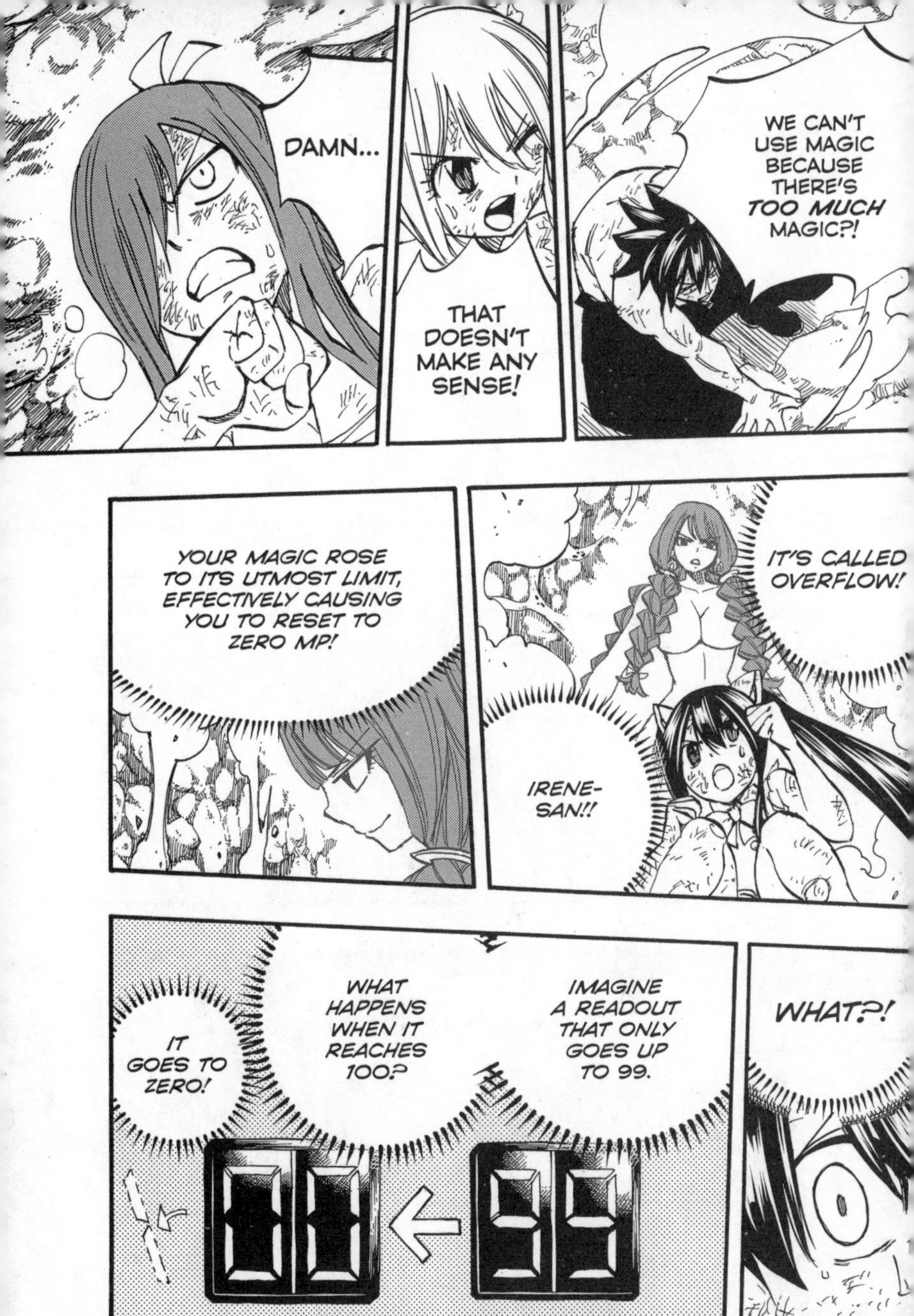
WE CAN'T USE MAGIC BECAUSE THERE'S *TOO MUCH* MAGIC?!
THAT DOESN'T MAKE ANY SENSE!
DAMN...
IT'S CALLED OVERFLOW!
IRENE-SAN!!
YOUR MAGIC ROSE TO ITS UTMOST LIMIT, EFFECTIVELY CAUSING YOU TO RESET TO ZERO MP!
WHAT?!
IMAGINE A READOUT THAT ONLY GOES UP TO 99.
WHAT HAPPENS WHEN IT REACHES 100?
IT GOES TO ZERO!

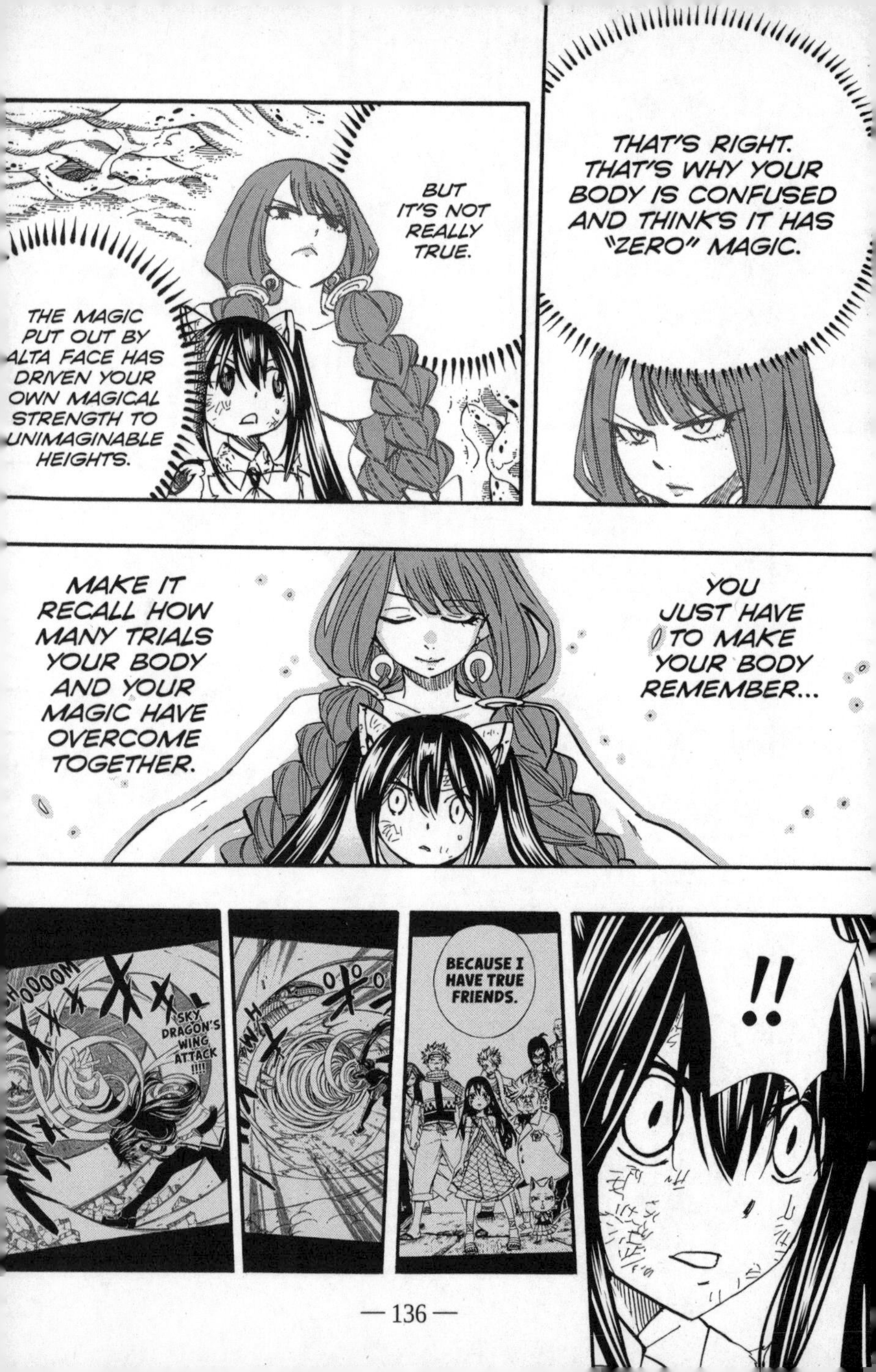
THAT'S RIGHT. THAT'S WHY YOUR BODY IS CONFUSED AND THINKS IT HAS "ZERO" MAGIC.
BUT IT'S NOT REALLY TRUE.
THE MAGIC PUT OUT BY ALTA FACE HAS DRIVEN YOUR OWN MAGICAL STRENGTH TO UNIMAGINABLE HEIGHTS.
YOU JUST HAVE TO MAKE YOUR BODY REMEMBER...
MAKE IT RECALL HOW MANY TRIALS YOUR BODY AND YOUR MAGIC HAVE OVERCOME TOGETHER.
!!
BECAUSE I HAVE TRUE FRIENDS.
SKY DRAGON'S WING ATTACK !!!!

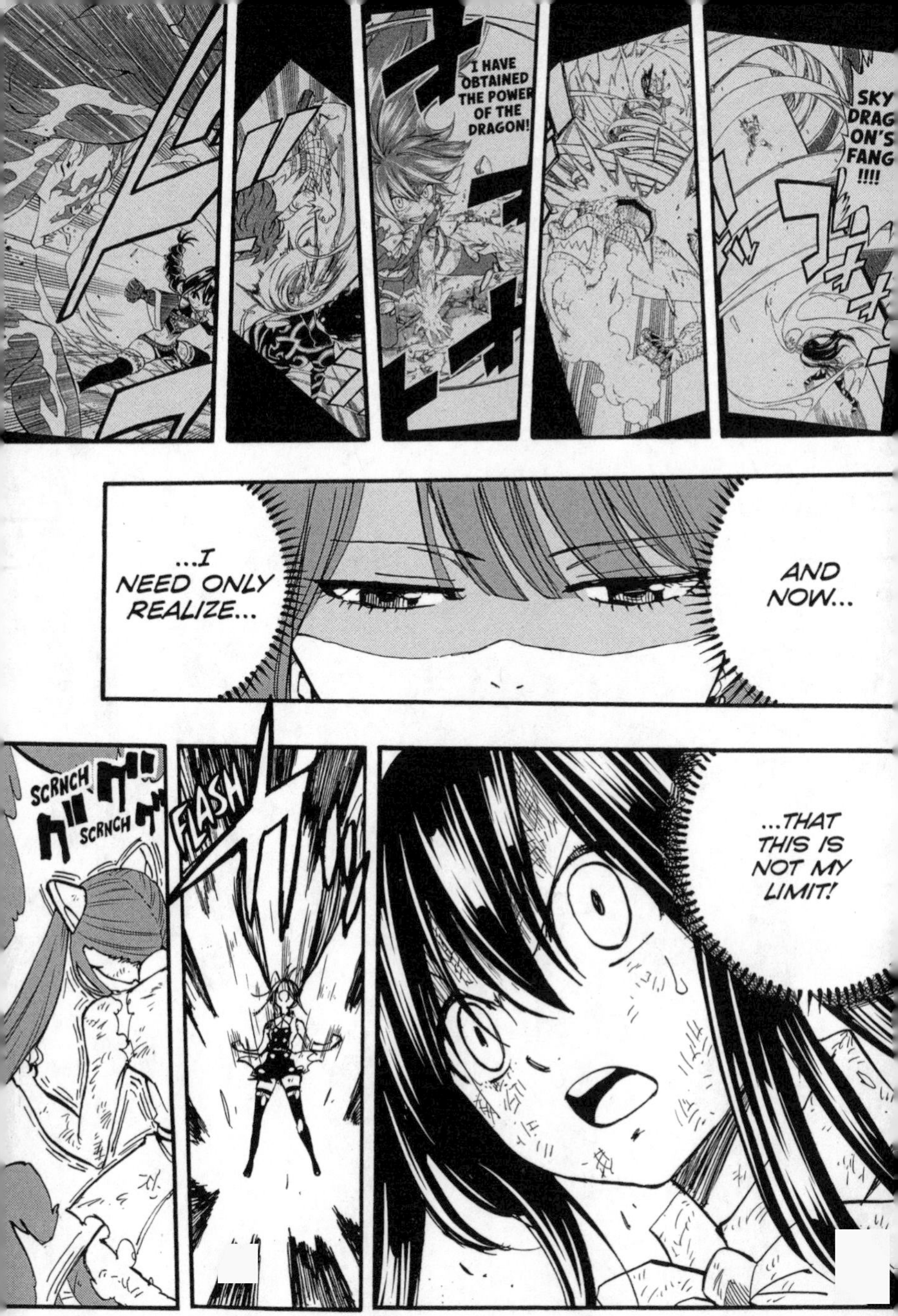
SKY DRAGON'S FANG!!!!
I HAVE OBTAINED THE POWER OF THE DRAGON!
AND NOW...
...I NEED ONLY REALIZE...
...THAT THIS IS NOT MY LIMIT!
FLASH
SCRNCH
SCRNCH

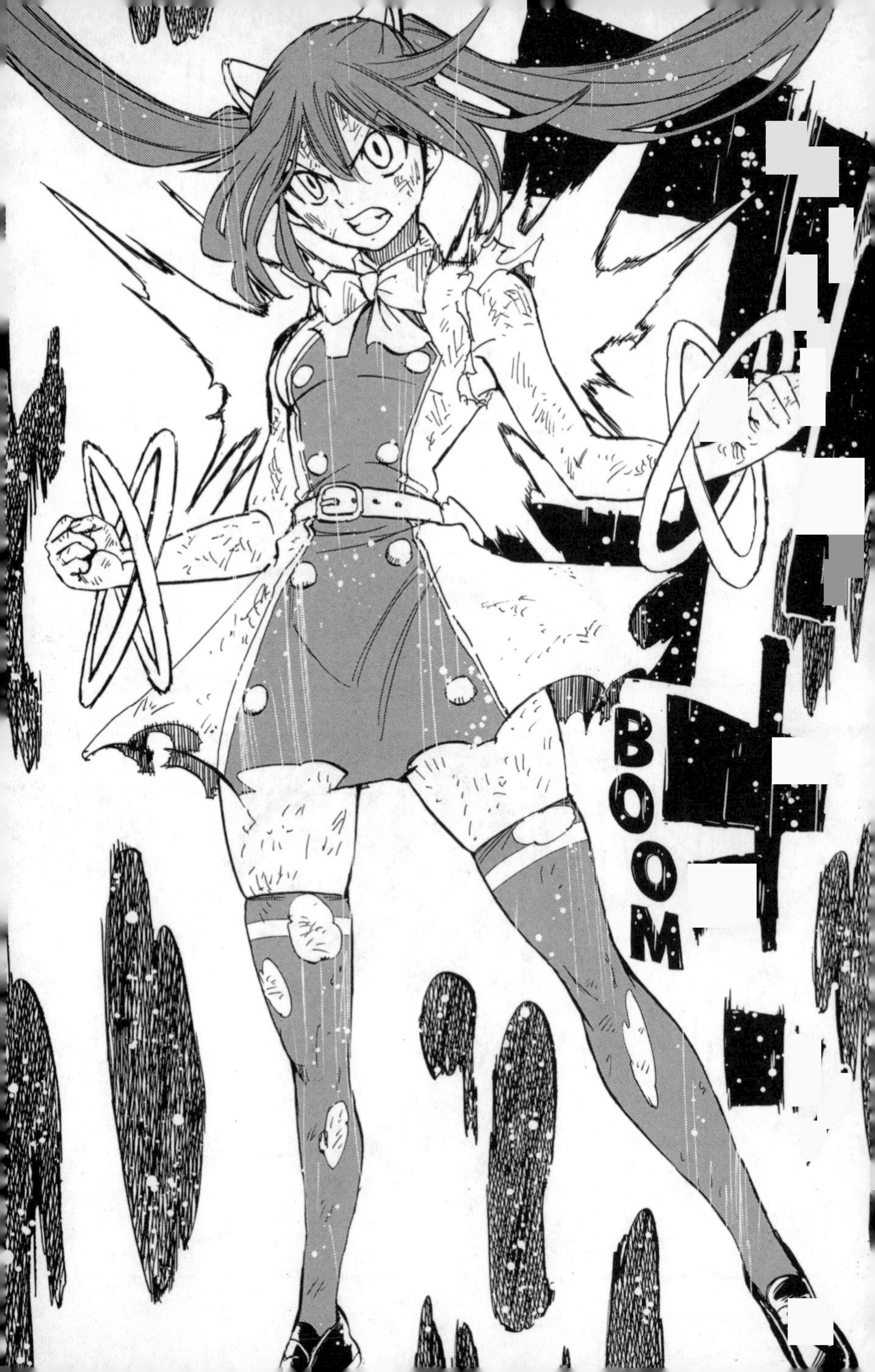
BOOM

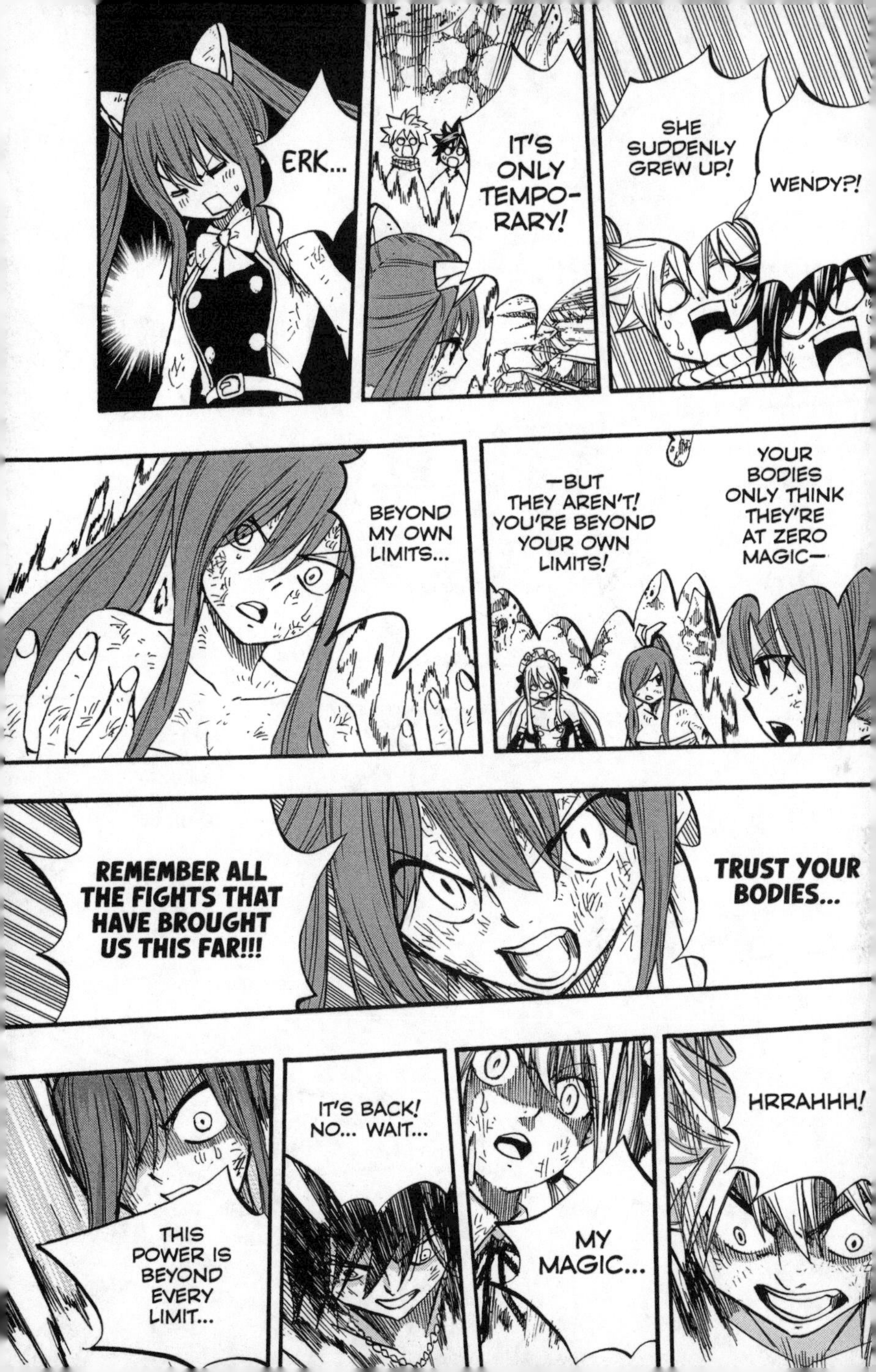
WENDY?!
SHE SUDDENLY GREW UP!
IT'S ONLY TEMPORARY!
ERK...
YOUR BODIES ONLY THINK THEY'RE AT ZERO MAGIC—
—BUT THEY AREN'T! YOU'RE BEYOND YOUR OWN LIMITS!
BEYOND MY OWN LIMITS...
TRUST YOUR BODIES...
REMEMBER ALL THE FIGHTS THAT HAVE BROUGHT US THIS FAR!!!
HRRAHHH!
MY MAGIC...
IT'S BACK! NO... WAIT...
THIS POWER IS BEYOND EVERY LIMIT...

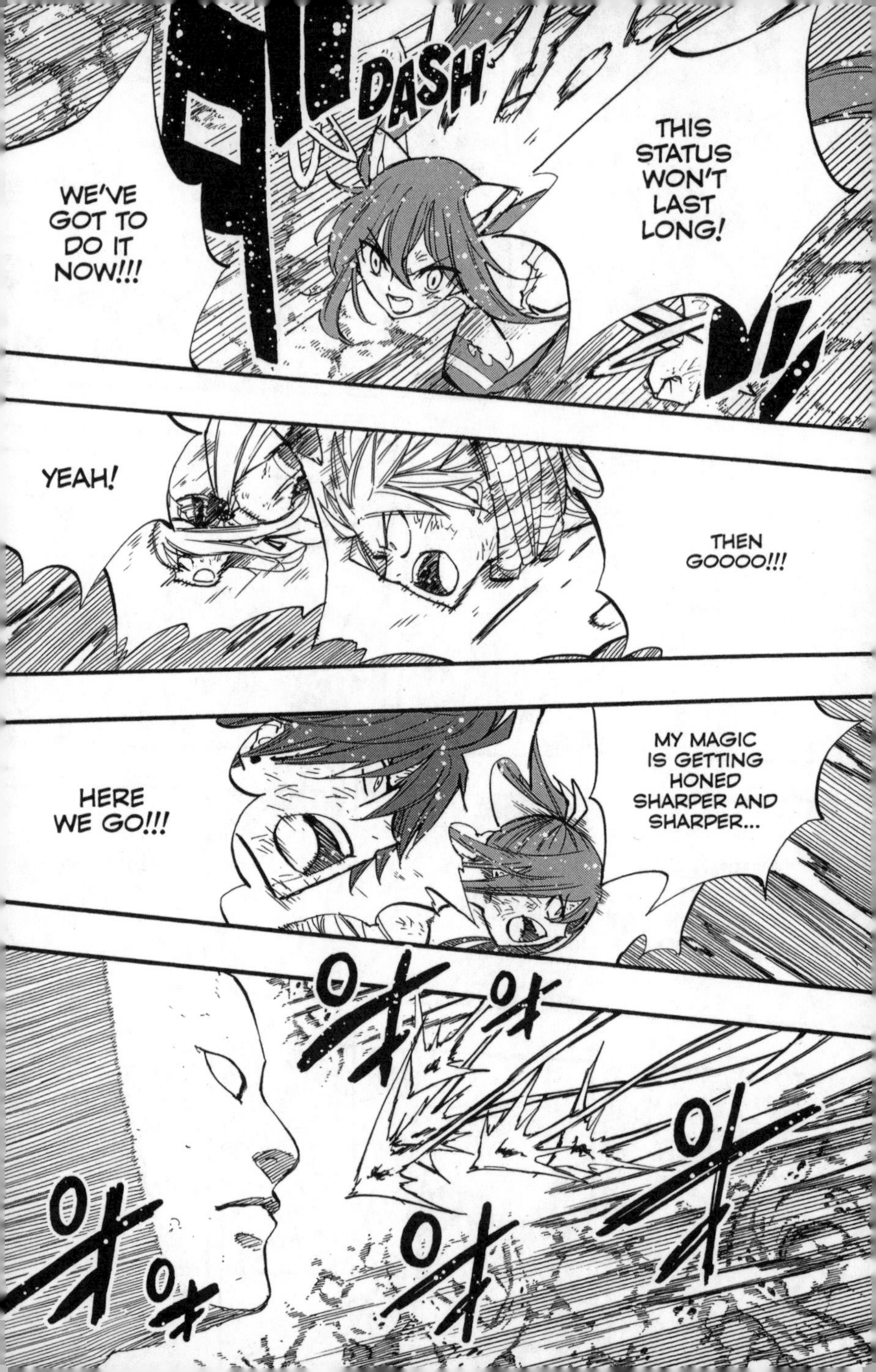
THIS STATUS WON'T LAST LONG!
DASH
WE'VE GOT TO DO IT NOW!!!
THEN GOOOO!!!
YEAH!
MY MAGIC IS GETTING HONED SHARPER AND SHARPER...
HERE WE GO!!!

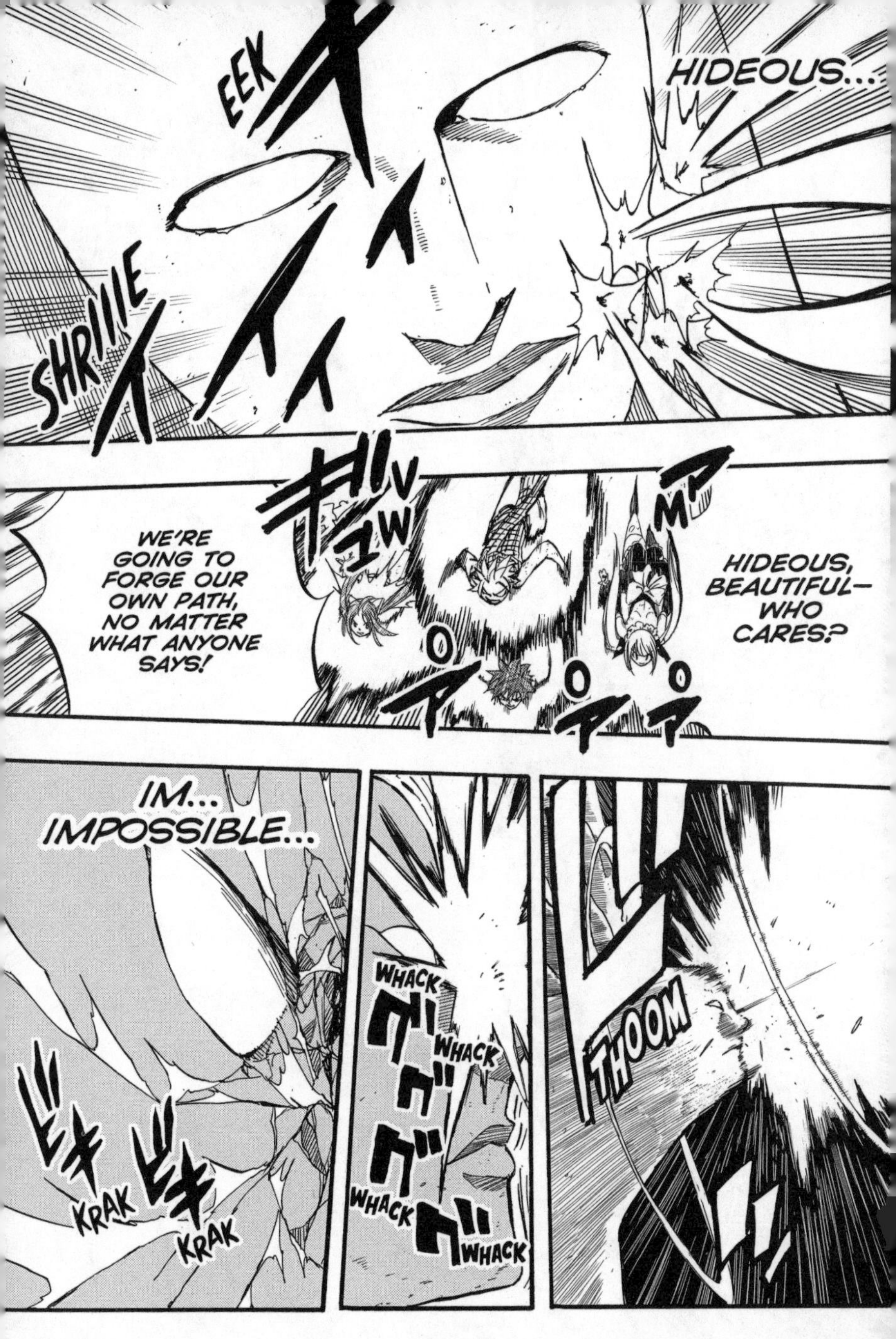
HIDEOUS...
EEK
SHRIIIE
HIDEOUS, BEAUTIFUL— WHO CARES?
VWMP
WE'RE GOING TO FORGE OUR OWN PATH, NO MATTER WHAT ANYONE SAYS!
THOOM
WHACK
WHACK
WHACK
WHACK
IM... IMPOSSIBLE...
KRAK
KRAK

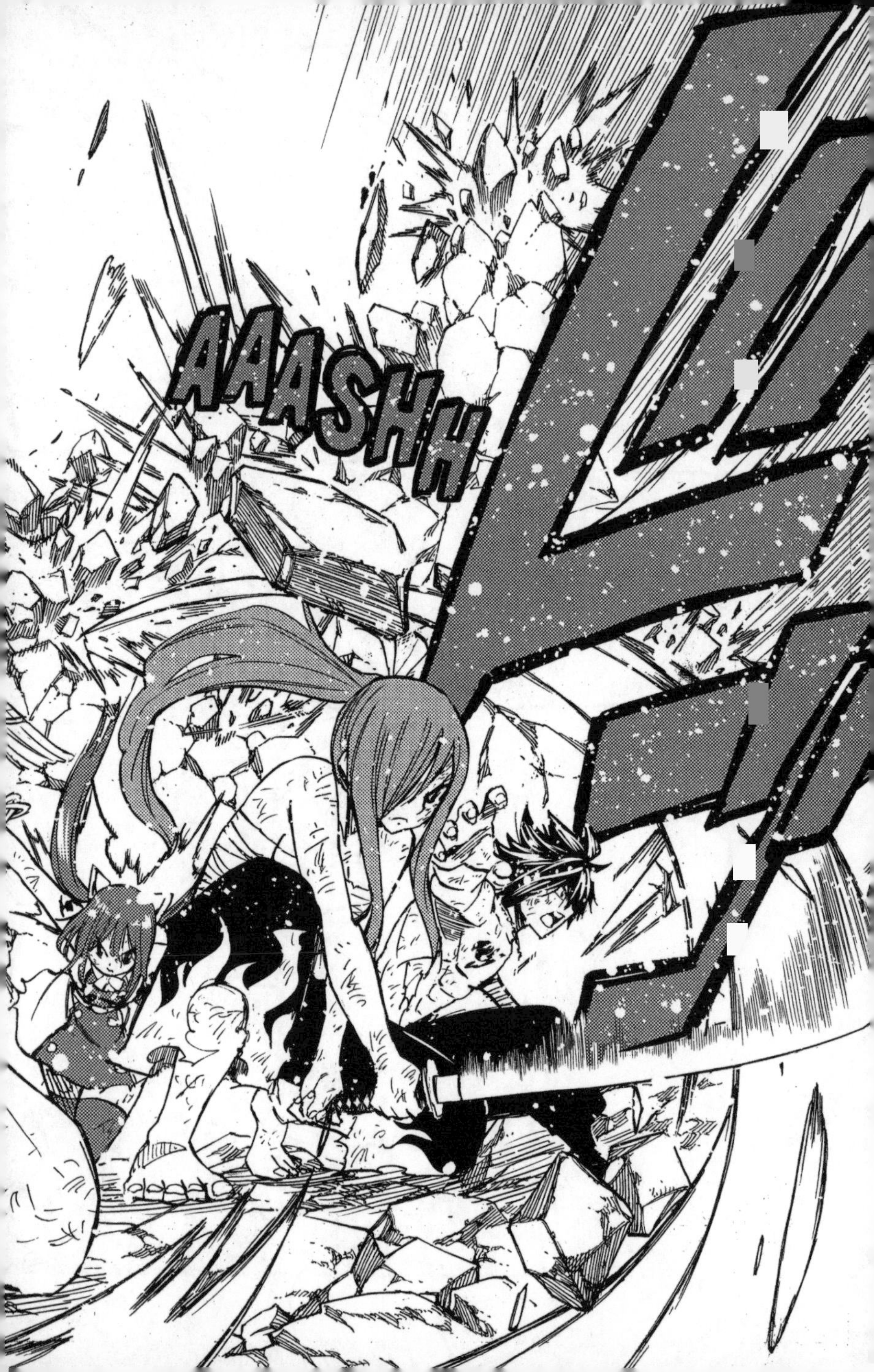
AAASHH

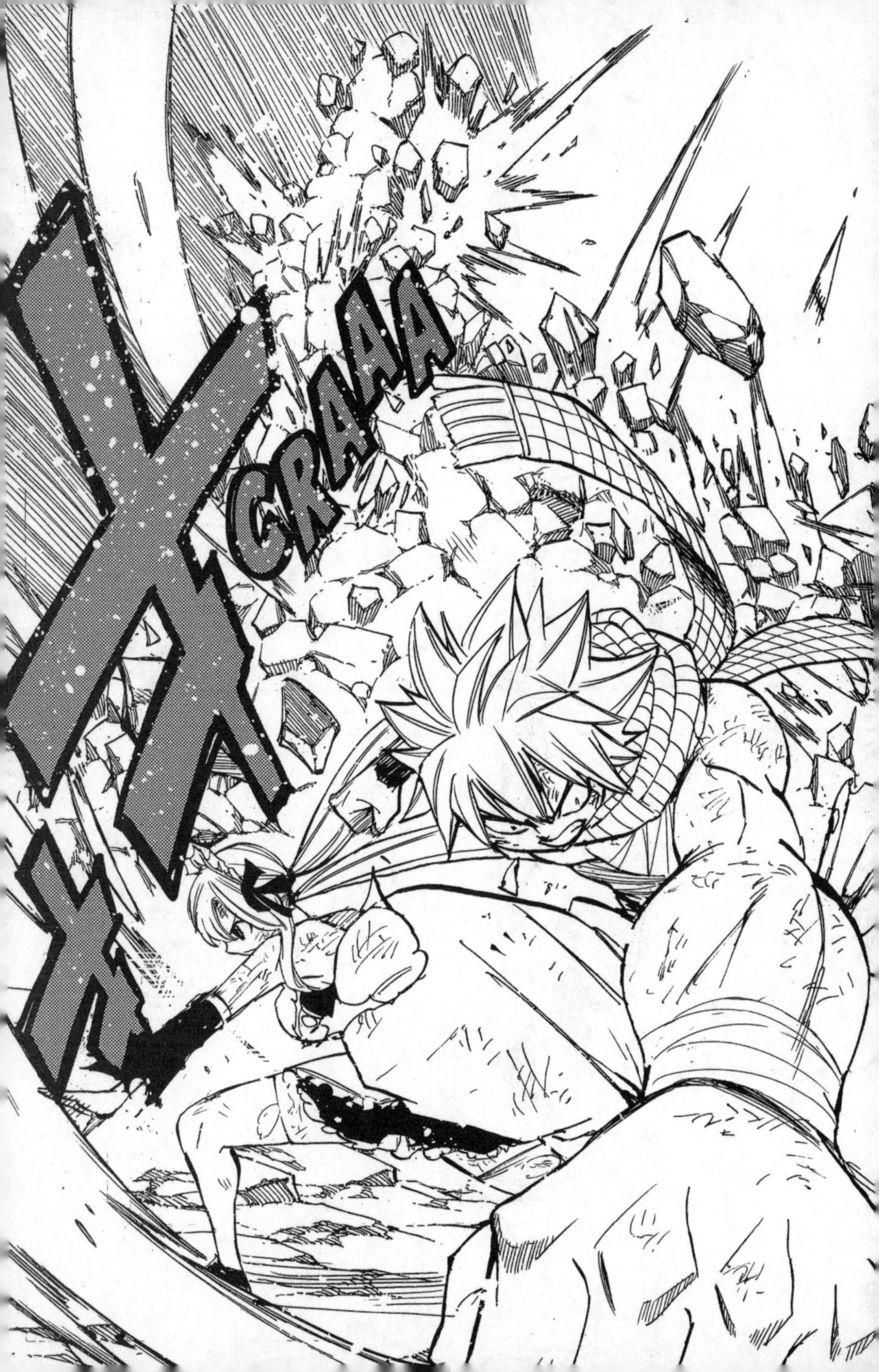
CRAAA
K

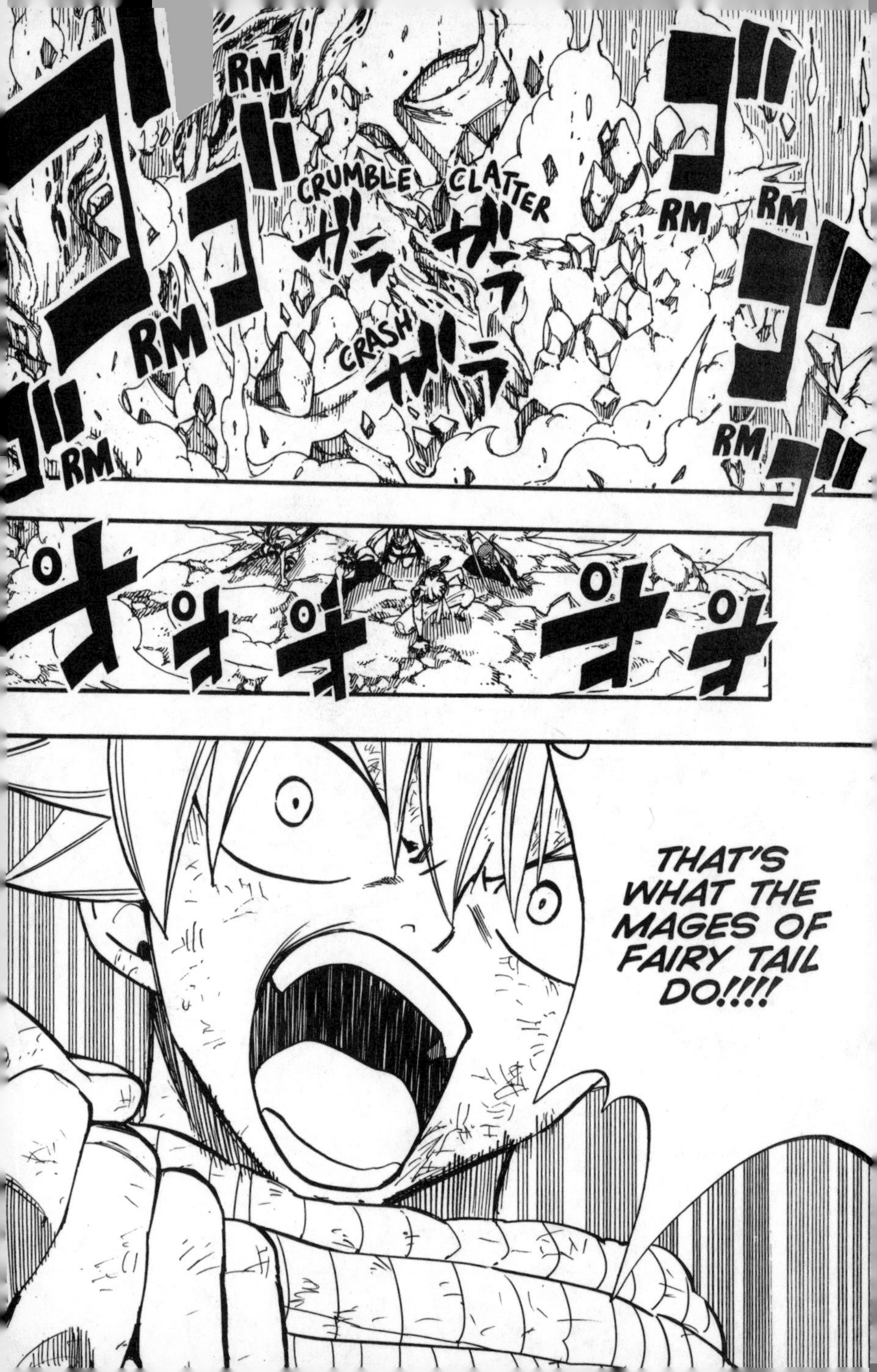
RM
RM
CLATTER
RM
CRUMBLE
CRASH
RM
RM
RM
THAT'S WHAT THE MAGES OF FAIRY TAIL DO!!!!

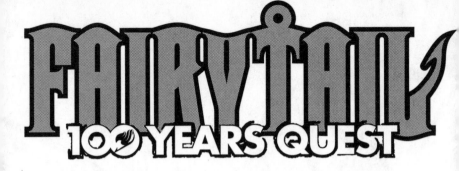

FAIRY TAIL 100 YEARS QUEST

Chapter 89: An Elentear Evening

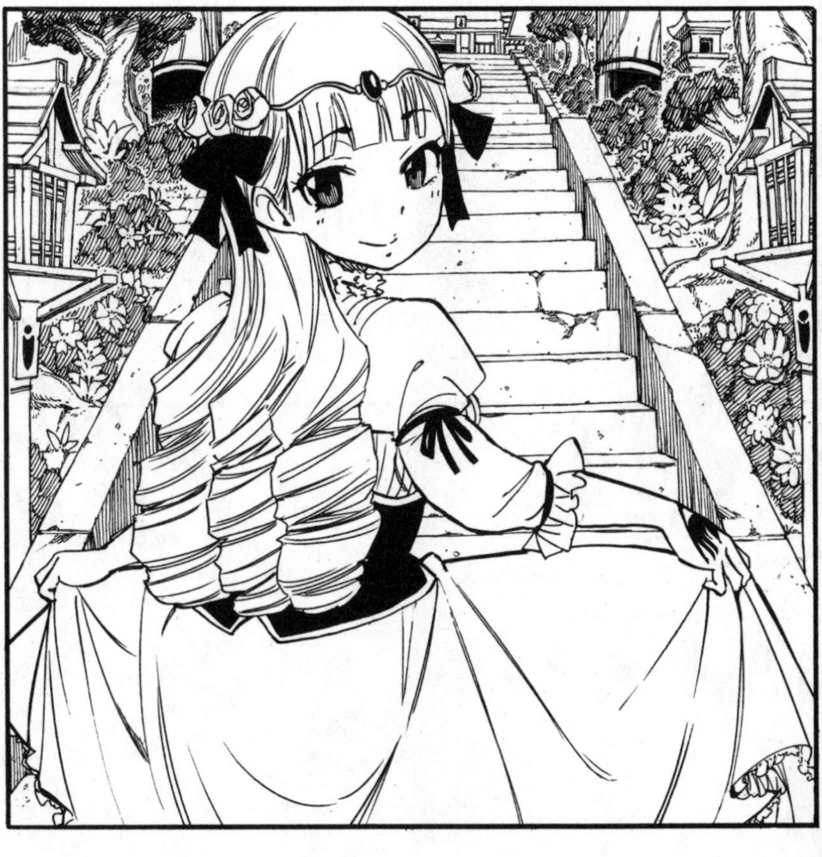

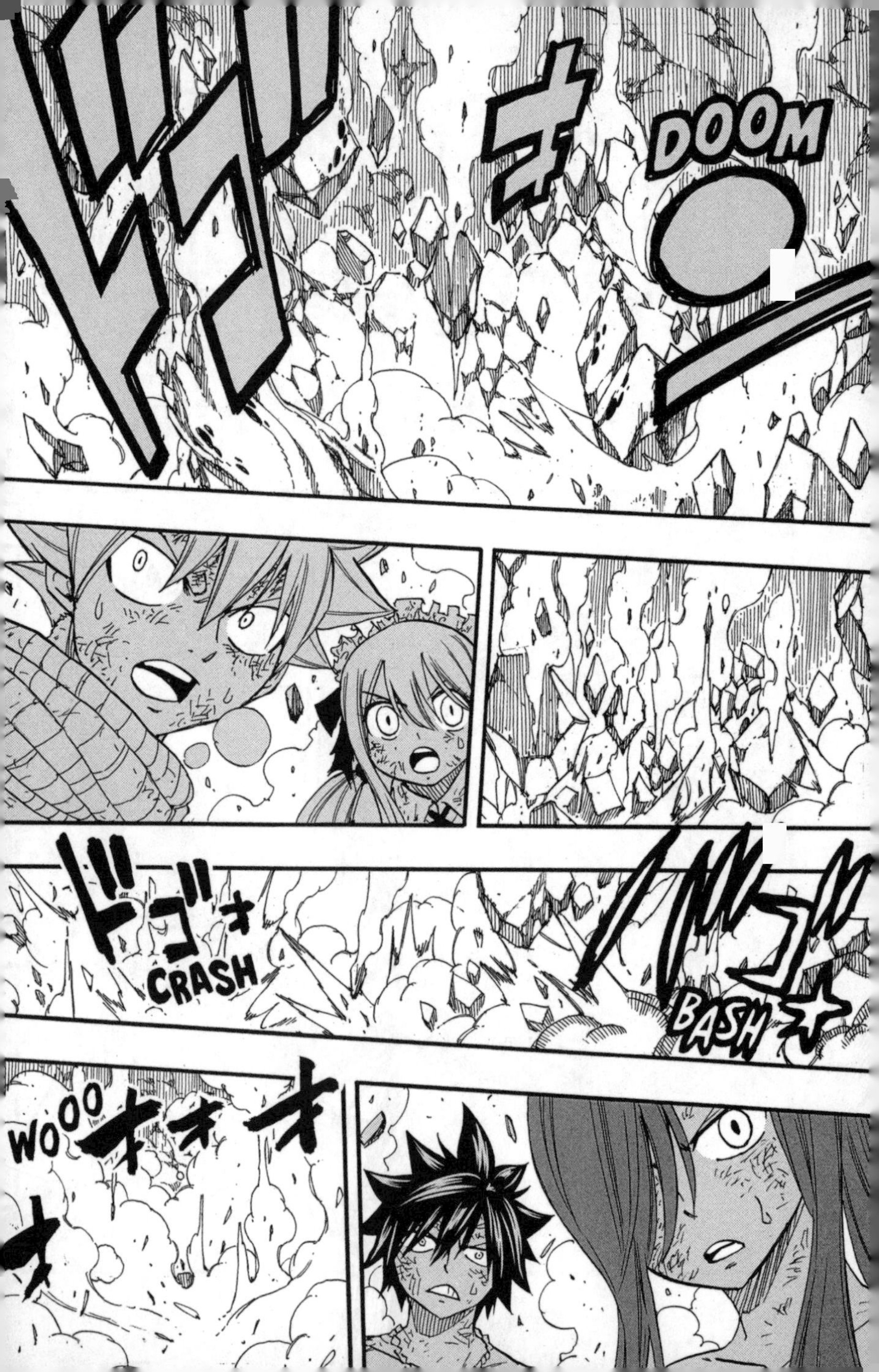
DOOM
BASH
CRASH
WOOO

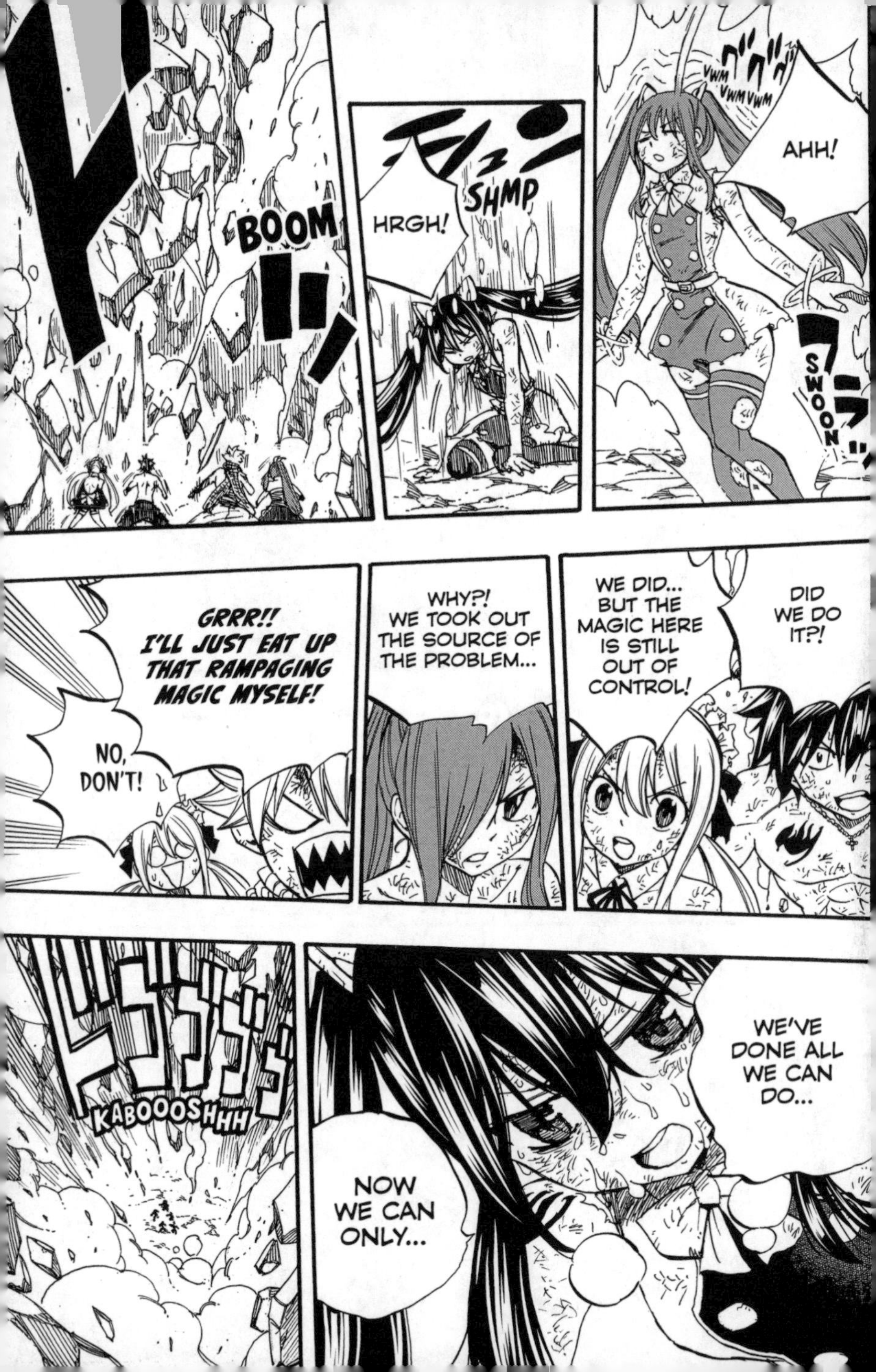
VWM VWMVWM
AHH!
SWOON
SHMP
HRGH!
BOOM
DID WE DO IT?!
WE DID... BUT THE MAGIC HERE IS STILL OUT OF CONTROL!
WHY?! WE TOOK OUT THE SOURCE OF THE PROBLEM...
GRRR!! I'LL JUST EAT UP THAT RAMPAGING MAGIC MYSELF!
NO, DON'T!
WE'VE DONE ALL WE CAN DO...
NOW WE CAN ONLY...
KABOOOSHHH

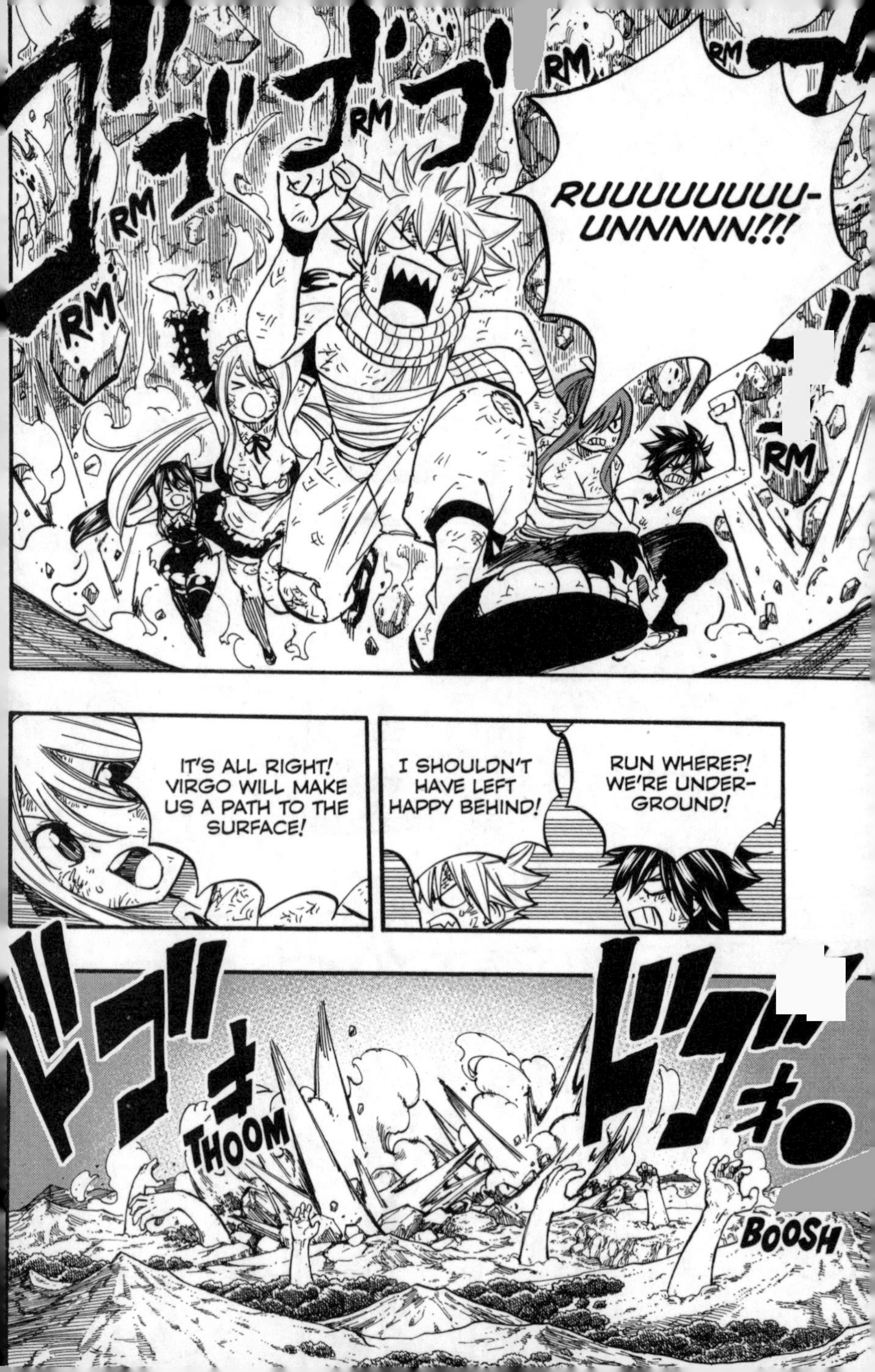
RM
RM
RUUUUUUUUU-UNNNNNN!!!
RM
RM
RM
RM
RM
RUN WHERE?! WE'RE UNDER-GROUND!
I SHOULDN'T HAVE LEFT HAPPY BEHIND!
IT'S ALL RIGHT! VIRGO WILL MAKE US A PATH TO THE SURFACE!
BOOSH
THOOM

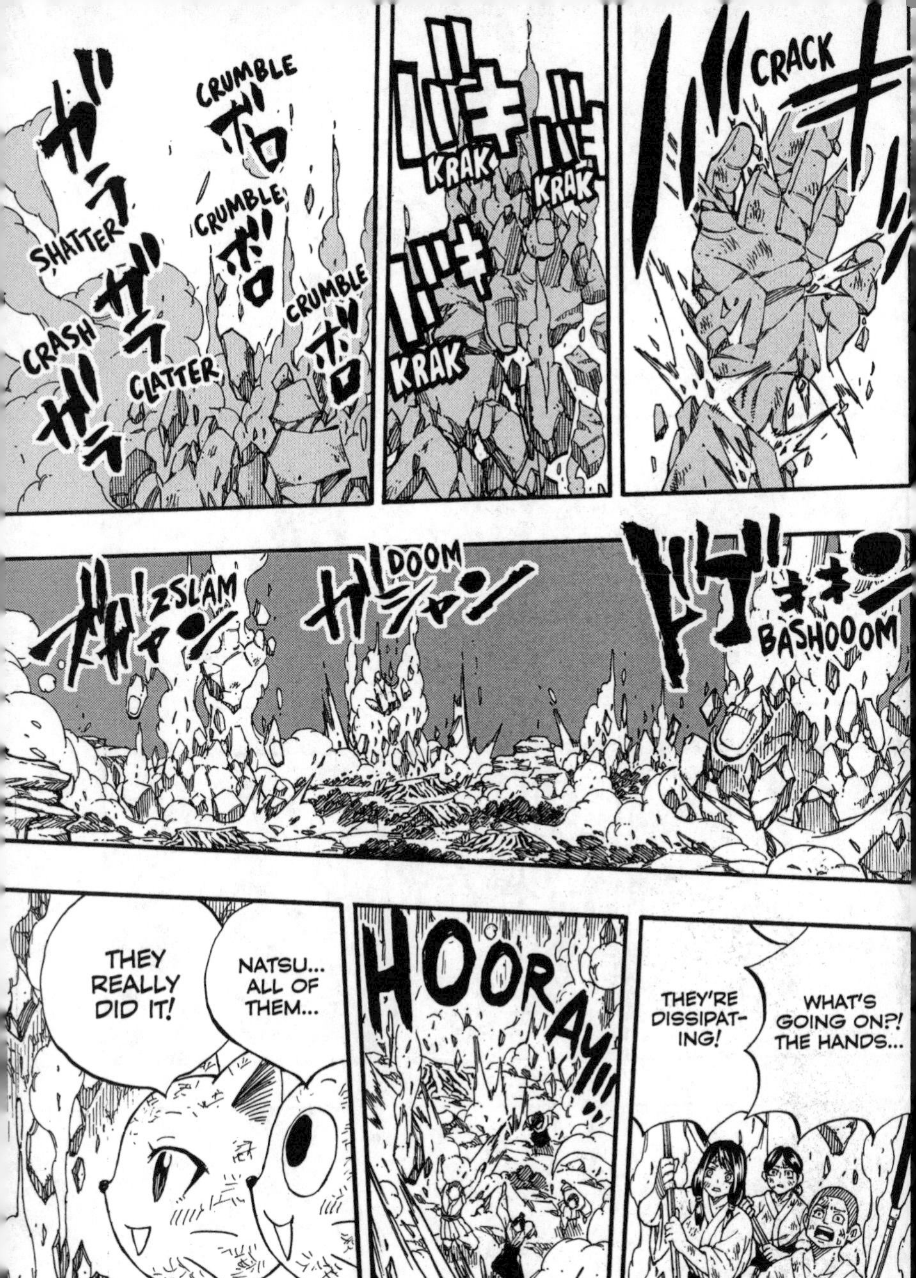
CRACK
KRAK
KRAK
KRAK
CRUMBLE
SHATTER
CRUMBLE
CRUMBLE
CRASH
CLATTER
BASHOOOM
DOOM
ZSLAM
WHAT'S GOING ON?! THE HANDS...
THEY'RE DISSIPAT-ING!
HOORAY!!!
NATSU... ALL OF THEM...
THEY REALLY DID IT!

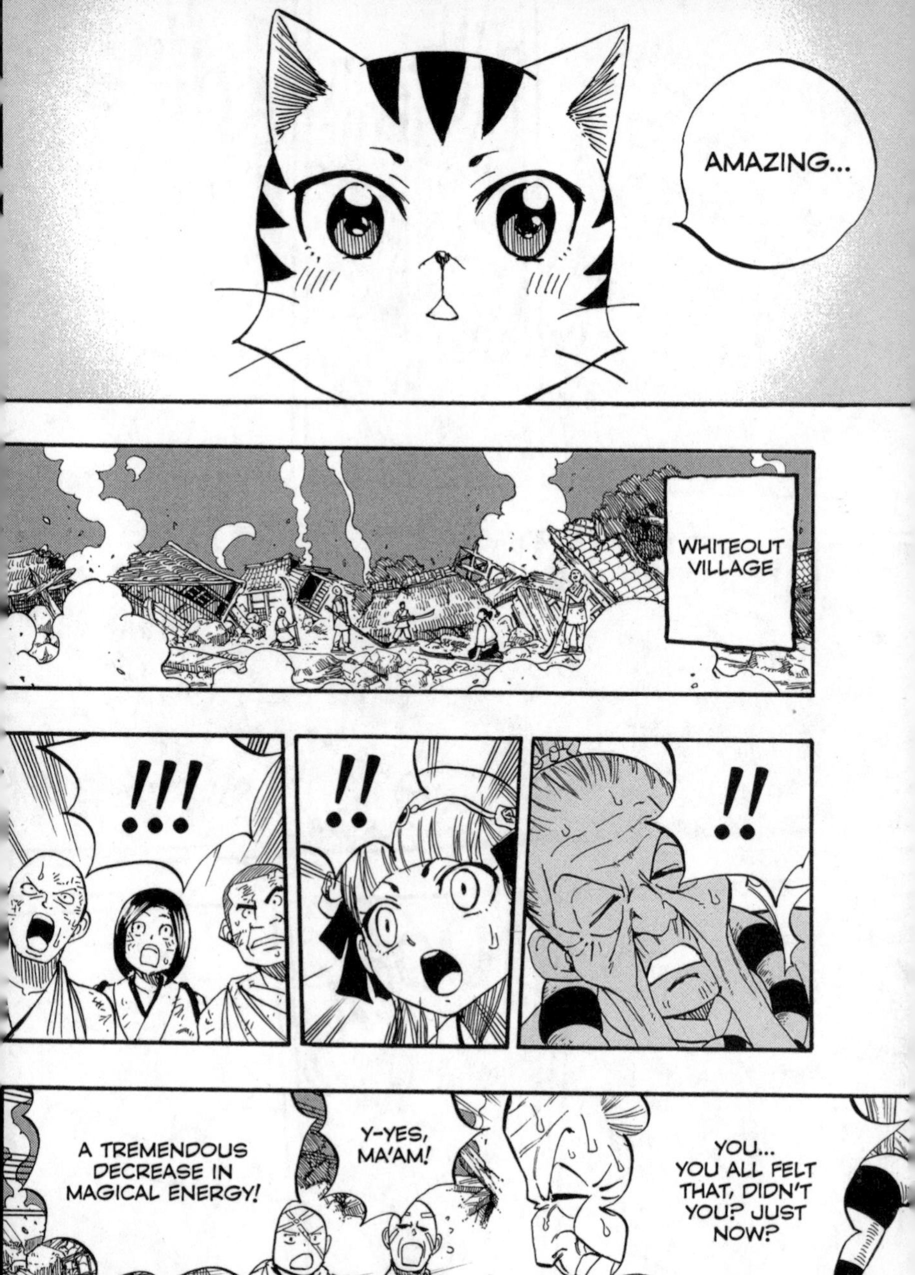
AMAZING...
WHITEOUT VILLAGE
!!
!!
!!!
YOU... YOU ALL FELT THAT, DIDN'T YOU? JUST NOW?
Y-YES, MA'AM!
A TREMENDOUS DECREASE IN MAGICAL ENERGY!

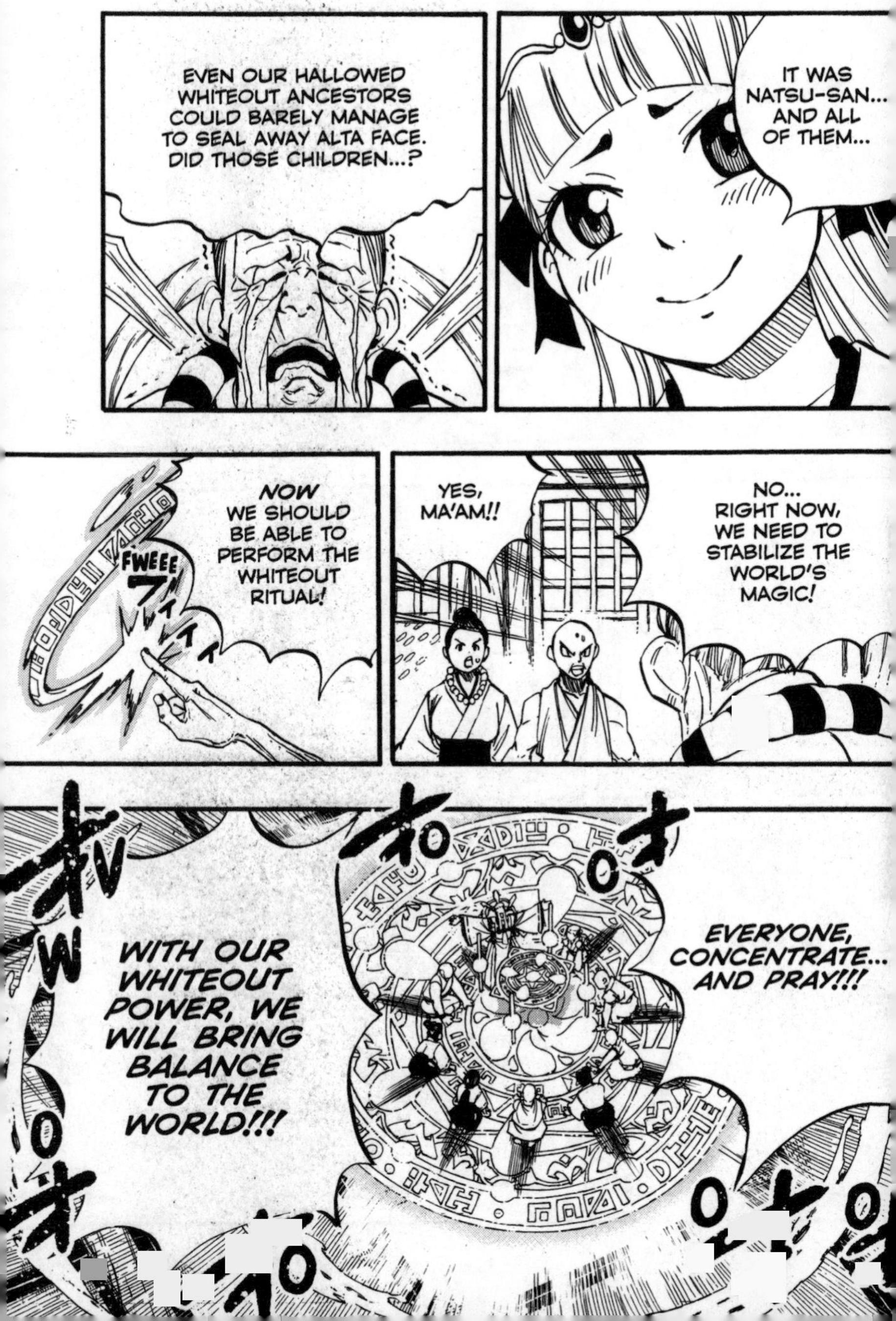
IT WAS NATSU-SAN... AND ALL OF THEM...
EVEN OUR HALLOWED WHITEOUT ANCESTORS COULD BARELY MANAGE TO SEAL AWAY ALTA FACE. DID THOSE CHILDREN...?
NO... RIGHT NOW, WE NEED TO STABILIZE THE WORLD'S MAGIC!
YES, MA'AM!!
NOW WE SHOULD BE ABLE TO PERFORM THE WHITEOUT RITUAL!
FWEEE
EVERYONE, CONCENTRATE... AND PRAY!!!
WITH OUR WHITEOUT POWER, WE WILL BRING BALANCE TO THE WORLD!!!

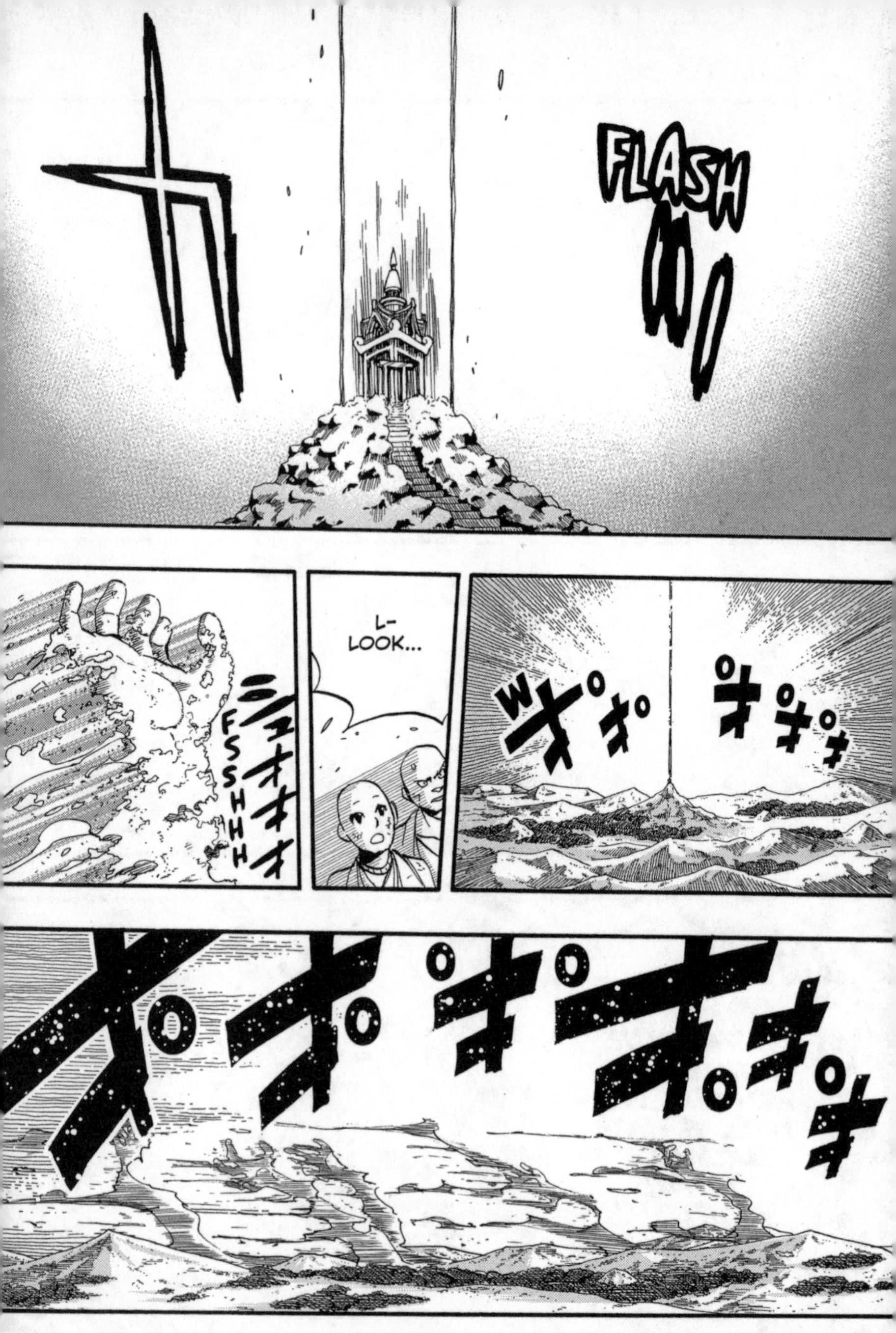
FLASH
W
L-
LOOK...
FSSHHH

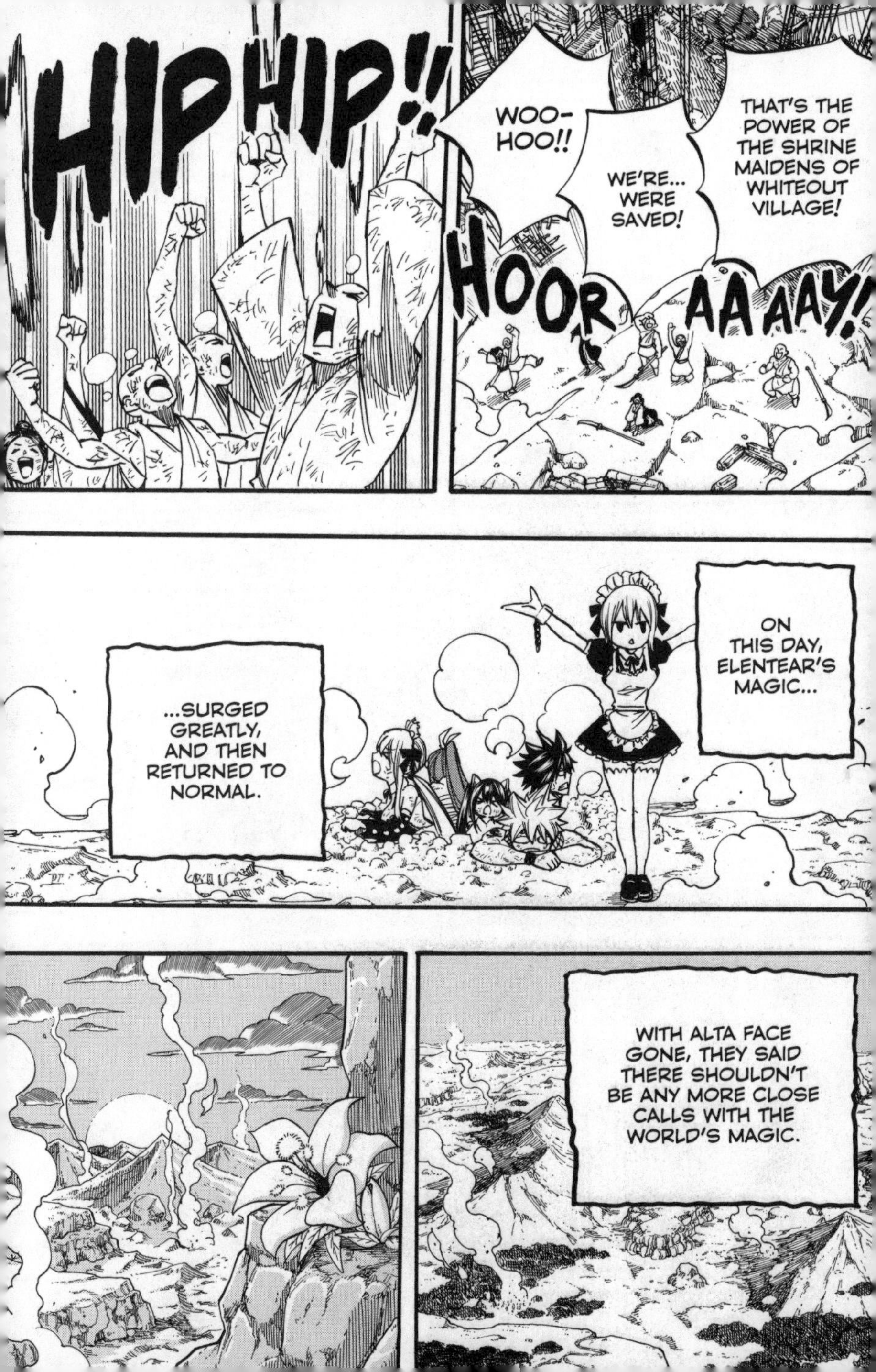
THAT'S THE POWER OF THE SHRINE MAIDENS OF WHITEOUT VILLAGE!
WE'RE... WERE SAVED!
WOO-HOO!!
HOORAAAAY!!
HIP HIP!!
ON THIS DAY, ELENTEAR'S MAGIC...
...SURGED GREATLY, AND THEN RETURNED TO NORMAL.
WITH ALTA FACE GONE, THEY SAID THERE SHOULDN'T BE ANY MORE CLOSE CALLS WITH THE WORLD'S MAGIC.

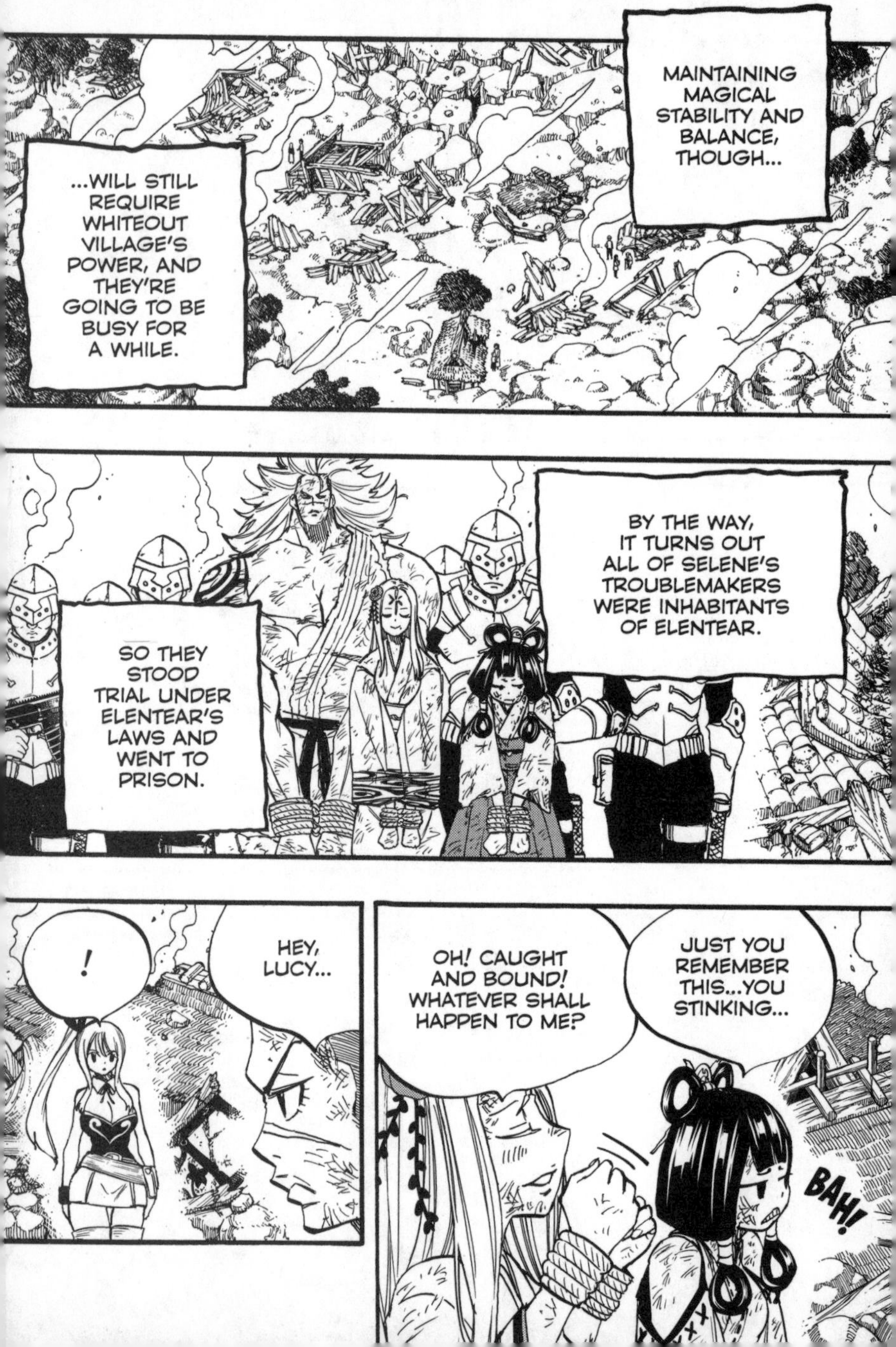
MAINTAINING MAGICAL STABILITY AND BALANCE, THOUGH...
...WILL STILL REQUIRE WHITEOUT VILLAGE'S POWER, AND THEY'RE GOING TO BE BUSY FOR A WHILE.
BY THE WAY, IT TURNS OUT ALL OF SELENE'S TROUBLEMAKERS WERE INHABITANTS OF ELENTEAR.
SO THEY STOOD TRIAL UNDER ELENTEAR'S LAWS AND WENT TO PRISON.
JUST YOU REMEMBER THIS...YOU STINKING...
OH! CAUGHT AND BOUND! WHATEVER SHALL HAPPEN TO ME?
BAH!
HEY, LUCY...
!

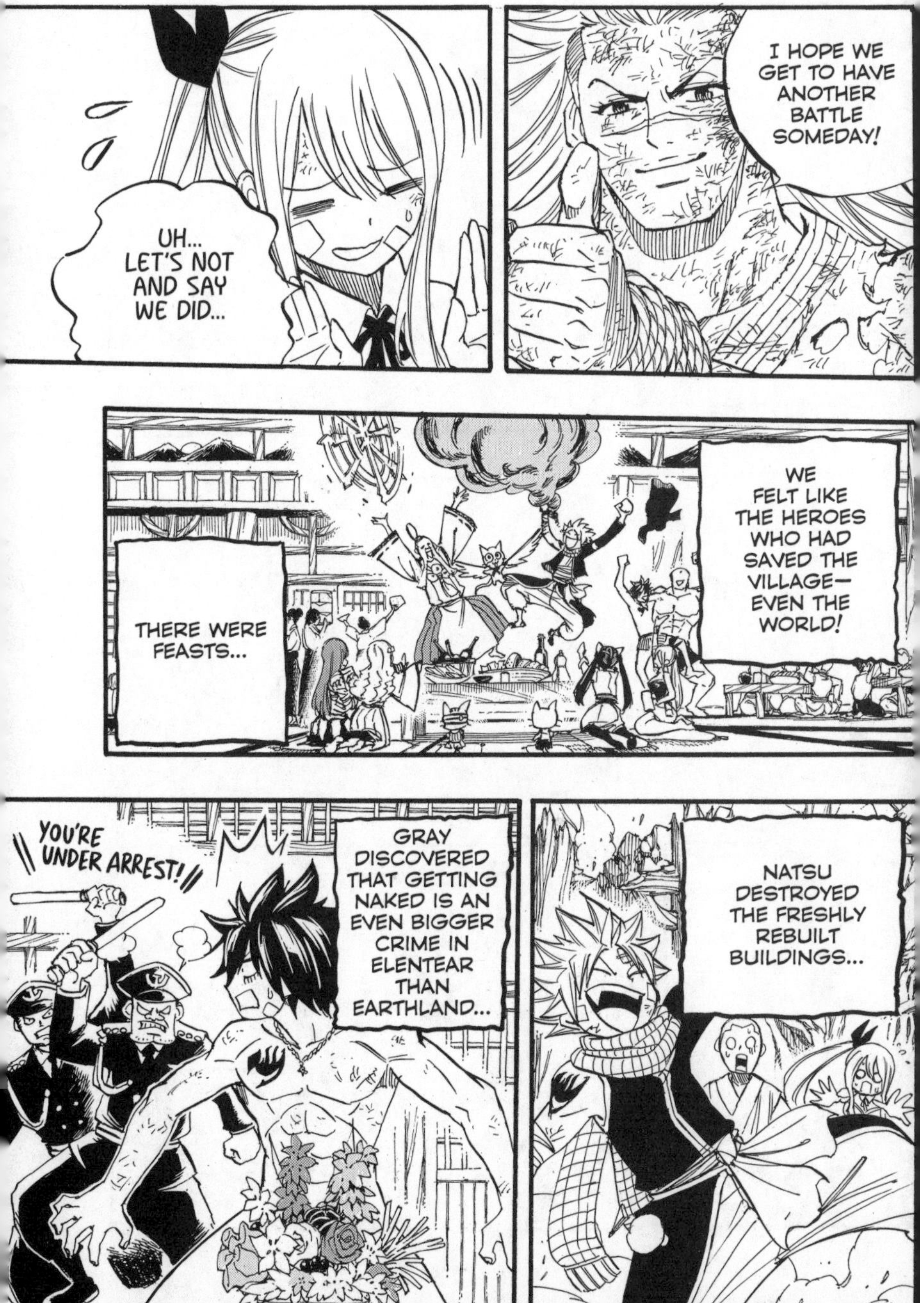

I HOPE WE GET TO HAVE ANOTHER BATTLE SOMEDAY!
UH... LET'S NOT AND SAY WE DID...
WE FELT LIKE THE HEROES WHO HAD SAVED THE VILLAGE—EVEN THE WORLD!
THERE WERE FEASTS...
NATSU DESTROYED THE FRESHLY REBUILT BUILDINGS...
GRAY DISCOVERED THAT GETTING NAKED IS AN EVEN BIGGER CRIME IN ELENTEAR THAN EARTHLAND...
YOU'RE UNDER ARREST!

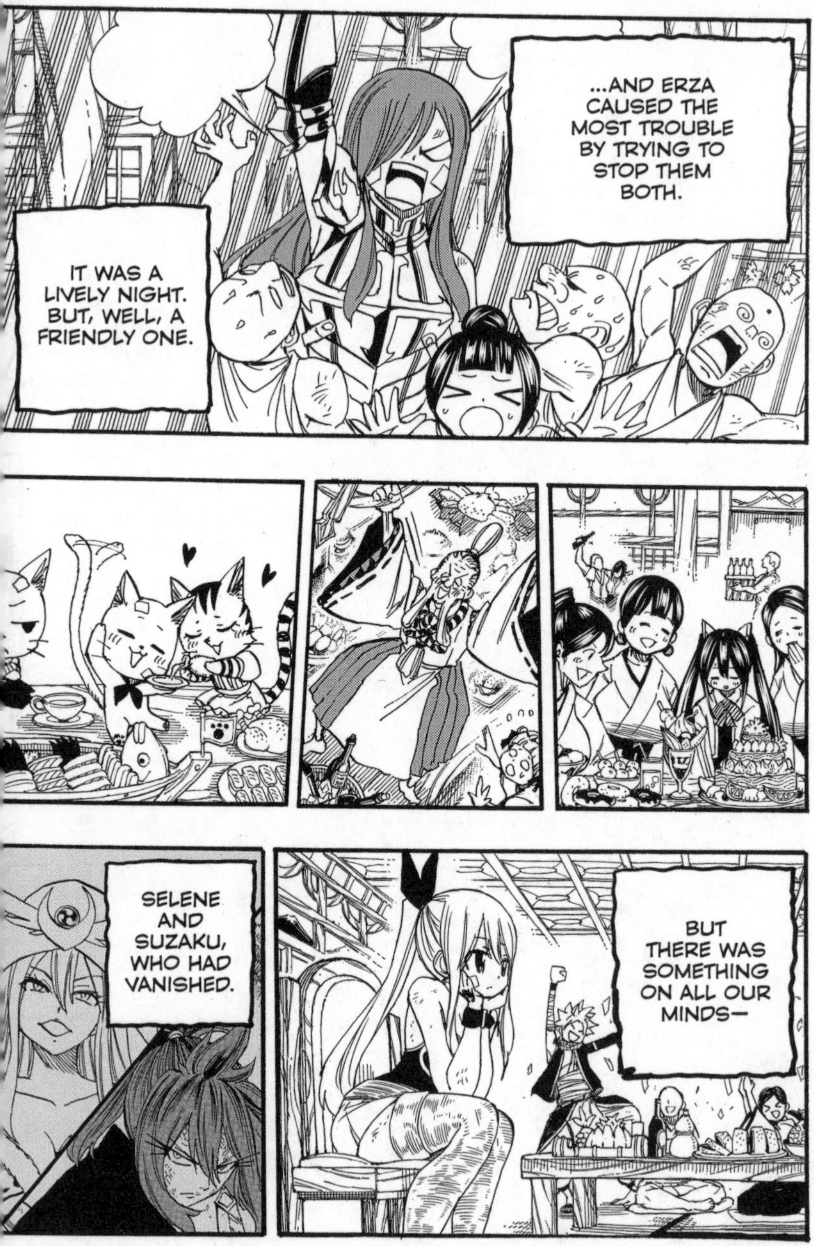
...AND ERZA CAUSED THE MOST TROUBLE BY TRYING TO STOP THEM BOTH.
IT WAS A LIVELY NIGHT. BUT, WELL, A FRIENDLY ONE.
BUT THERE WAS SOMETHING ON ALL OUR MINDS—
SELENE AND SUZAKU, WHO HAD VANISHED.

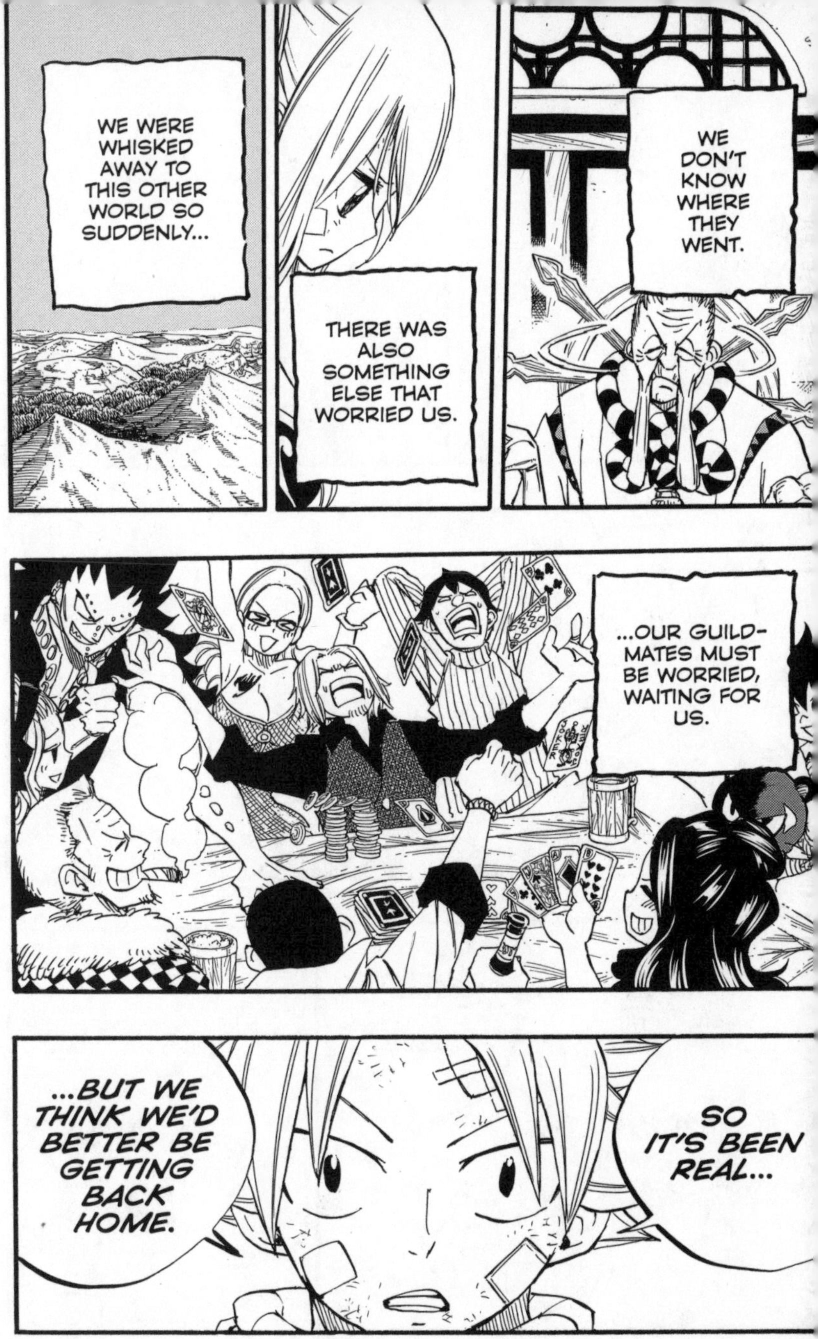
WE DON'T KNOW WHERE THEY WENT.
THERE WAS ALSO SOMETHING ELSE THAT WORRIED US.
WE WERE WHISKED AWAY TO THIS OTHER WORLD SO SUDDENLY...
...OUR GUILD-MATES MUST BE WORRIED, WAITING FOR US.
JOKER
SO IT'S BEEN REAL...
...BUT WE THINK WE'D BETTER BE GETTING BACK HOME.

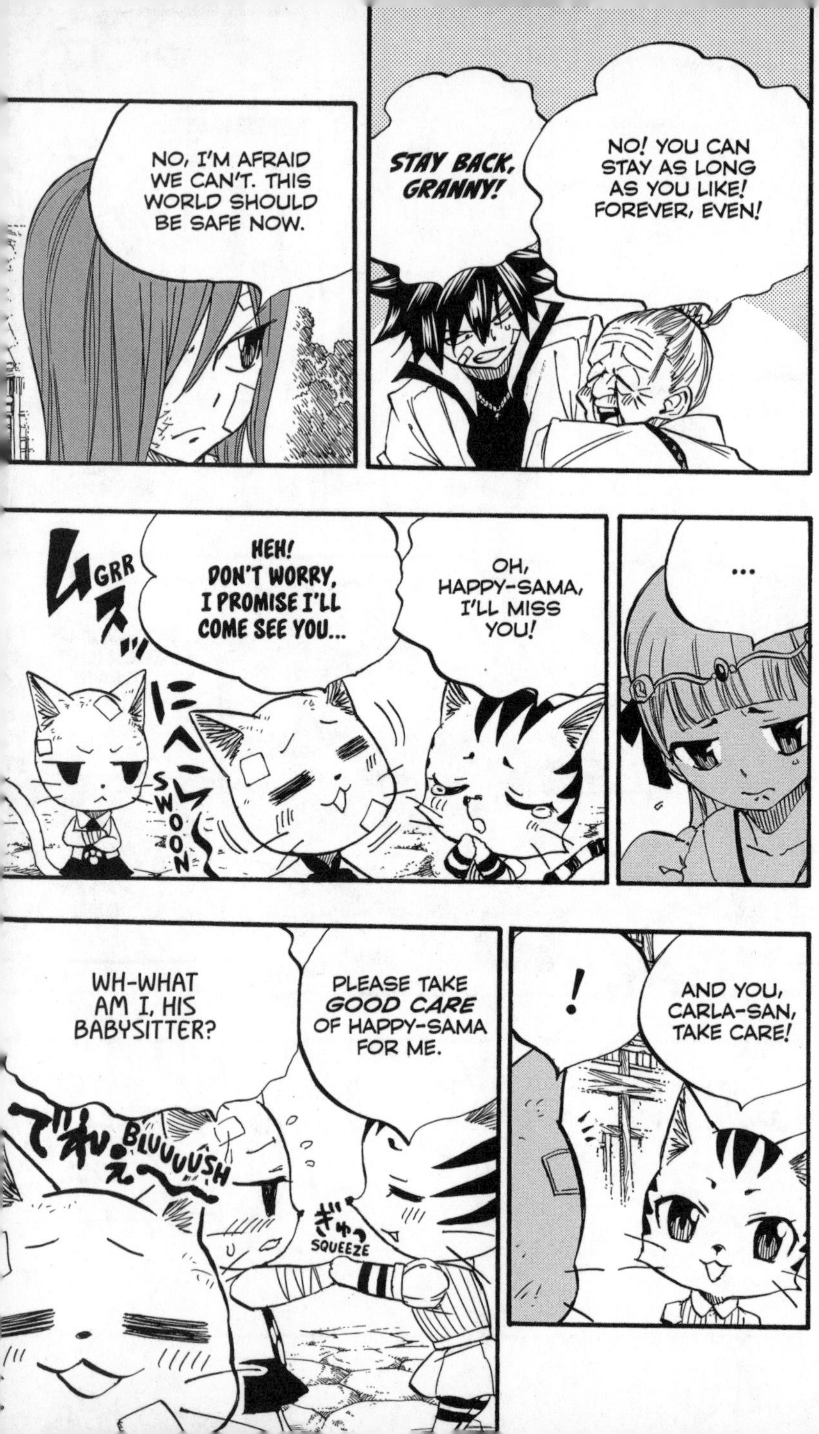
NO! YOU CAN STAY AS LONG AS YOU LIKE! FOREVER, EVEN!
STAY BACK, GRANNY!
NO, I'M AFRAID WE CAN'T. THIS WORLD SHOULD BE SAFE NOW.
...
OH, HAPPY-SAMA, I'LL MISS YOU!
HEH! DON'T WORRY, I PROMISE I'LL COME SEE YOU...
SWOON
GRR
AND YOU, CARLA-SAN, TAKE CARE!
!
PLEASE TAKE *GOOD CARE* OF HAPPY-SAMA FOR ME.
ぎゅっ
SQUEEZE
WH-WHAT AM I, HIS BABYSITTER?
BLUUUUSH

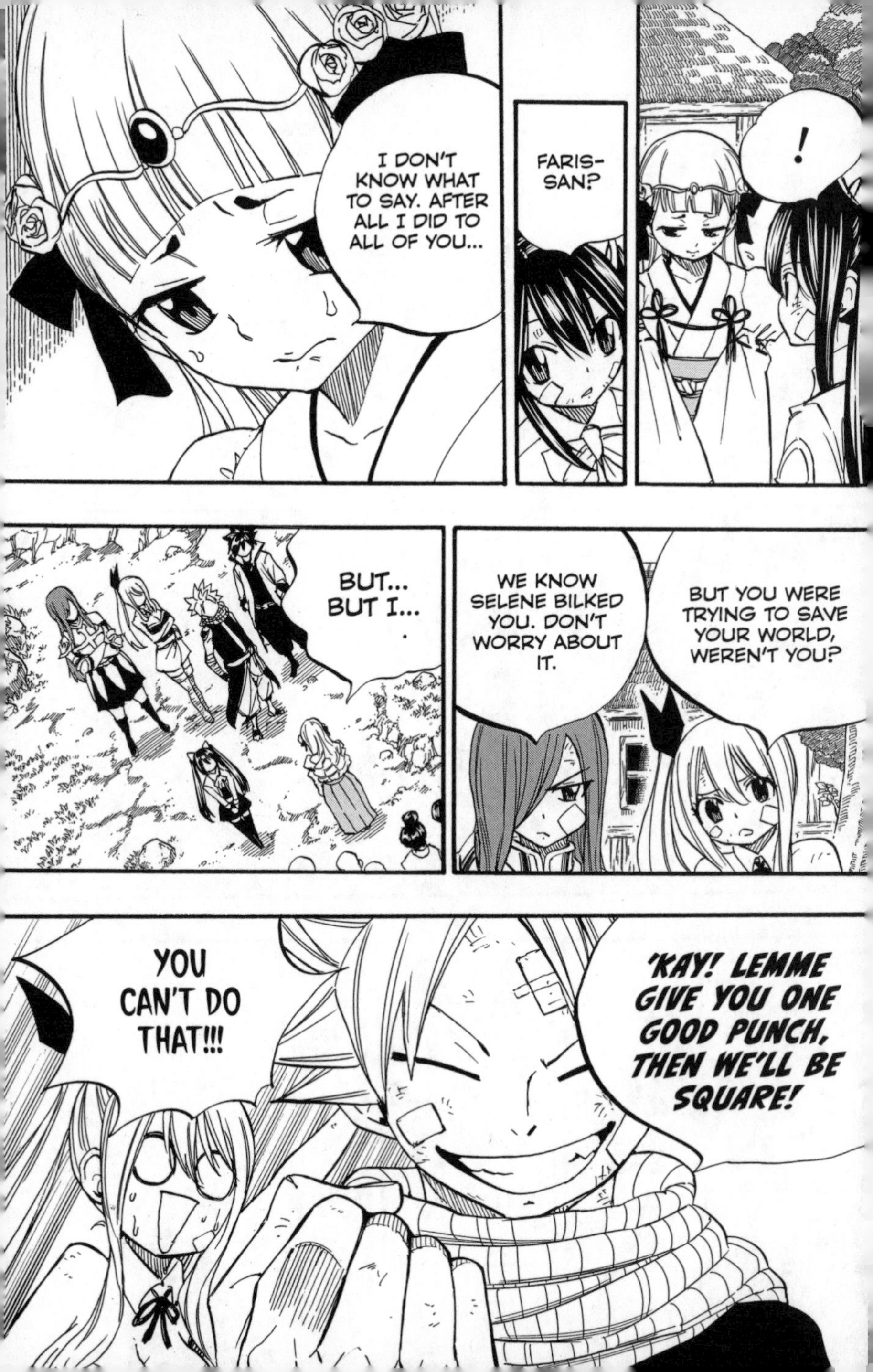
!
FARIS-SAN?
I DON'T KNOW WHAT TO SAY. AFTER ALL I DID TO ALL OF YOU...
BUT YOU WERE TRYING TO SAVE YOUR WORLD, WEREN'T YOU?
WE KNOW SELENE BILKED YOU. DON'T WORRY ABOUT IT.
BUT... BUT I...
'KAY! LEMME GIVE YOU ONE GOOD PUNCH, THEN WE'LL BE SQUARE!
YOU CAN'T DO THAT!!!

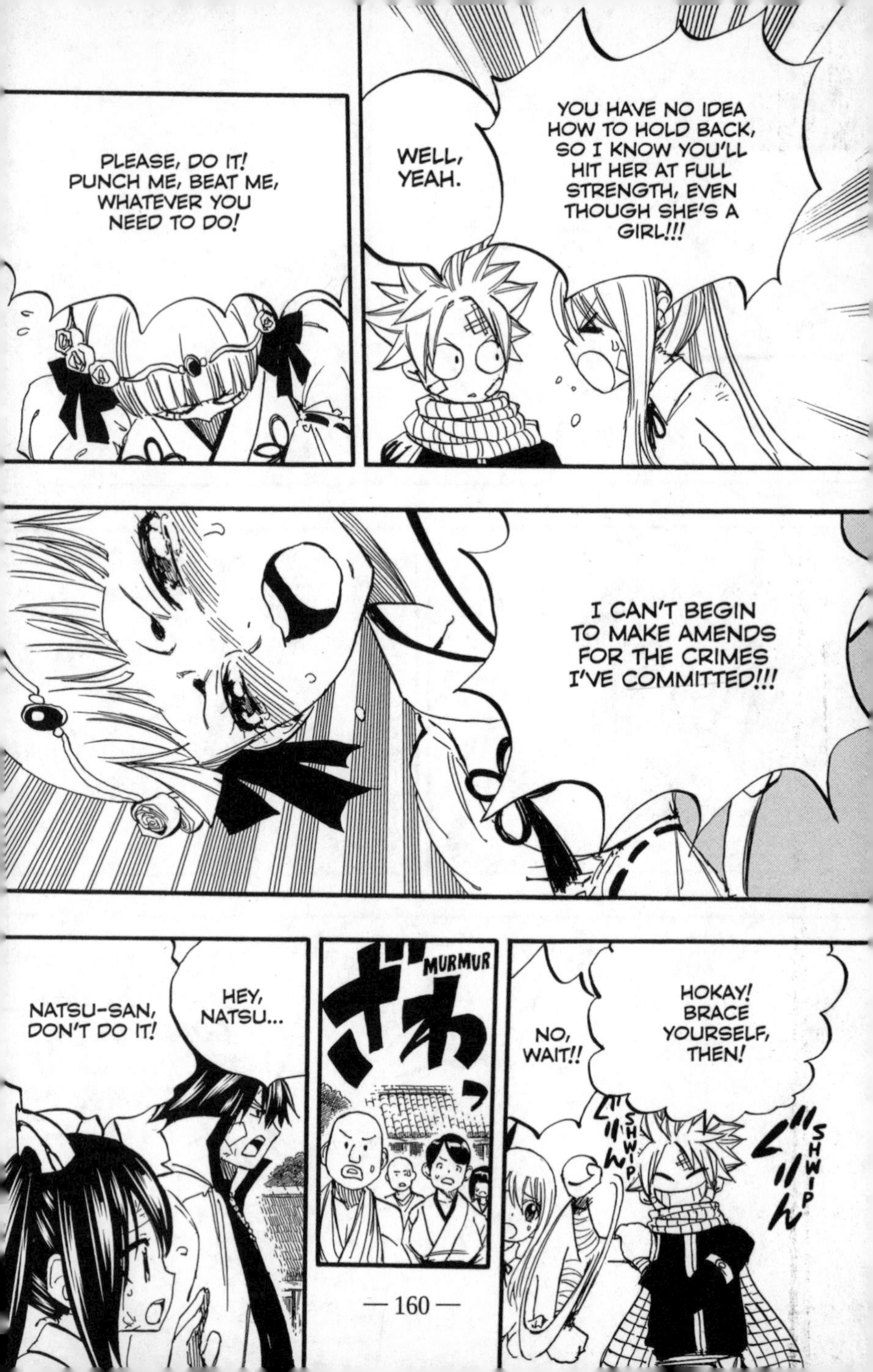
YOU HAVE NO IDEA HOW TO HOLD BACK, SO I KNOW YOU'LL HIT HER AT FULL STRENGTH, EVEN THOUGH SHE'S A GIRL!!!
WELL, YEAH.
PLEASE, DO IT! PUNCH ME, BEAT ME, WHATEVER YOU NEED TO DO!
I CAN'T BEGIN TO MAKE AMENDS FOR THE CRIMES I'VE COMMITTED!!!
HOKAY! BRACE YOURSELF, THEN!
NO, WAIT!!
SHWIP
SHWIP
ざわっ
MURMUR
HEY, NATSU...
NATSU-SAN, DON'T DO IT!

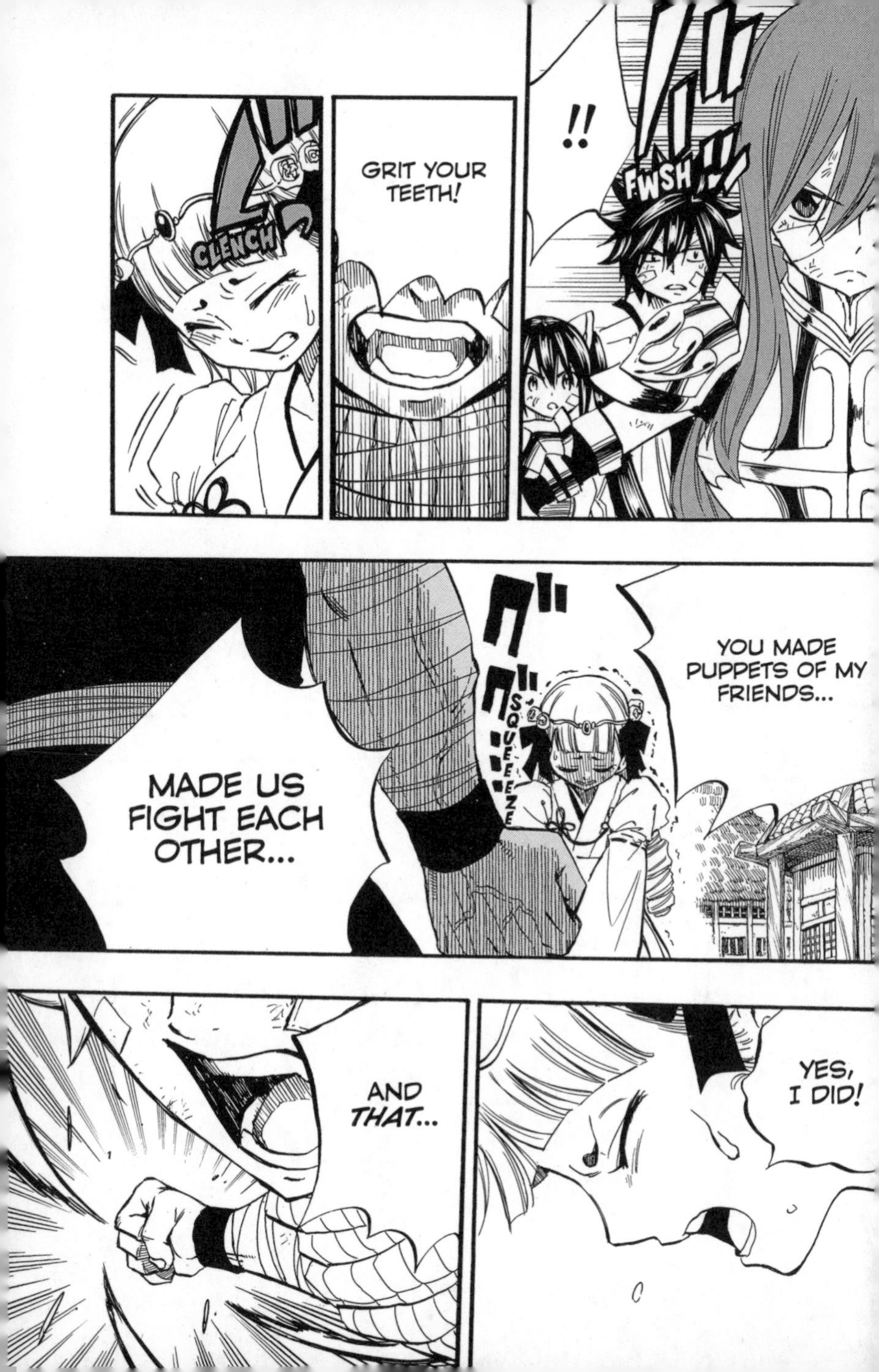
!!
FWSH
GRIT YOUR TEETH!
CLENCH
YOU MADE PUPPETS OF MY FRIENDS...
SQUEEEZE
MADE US FIGHT EACH OTHER...
YES, I DID!
AND THAT...

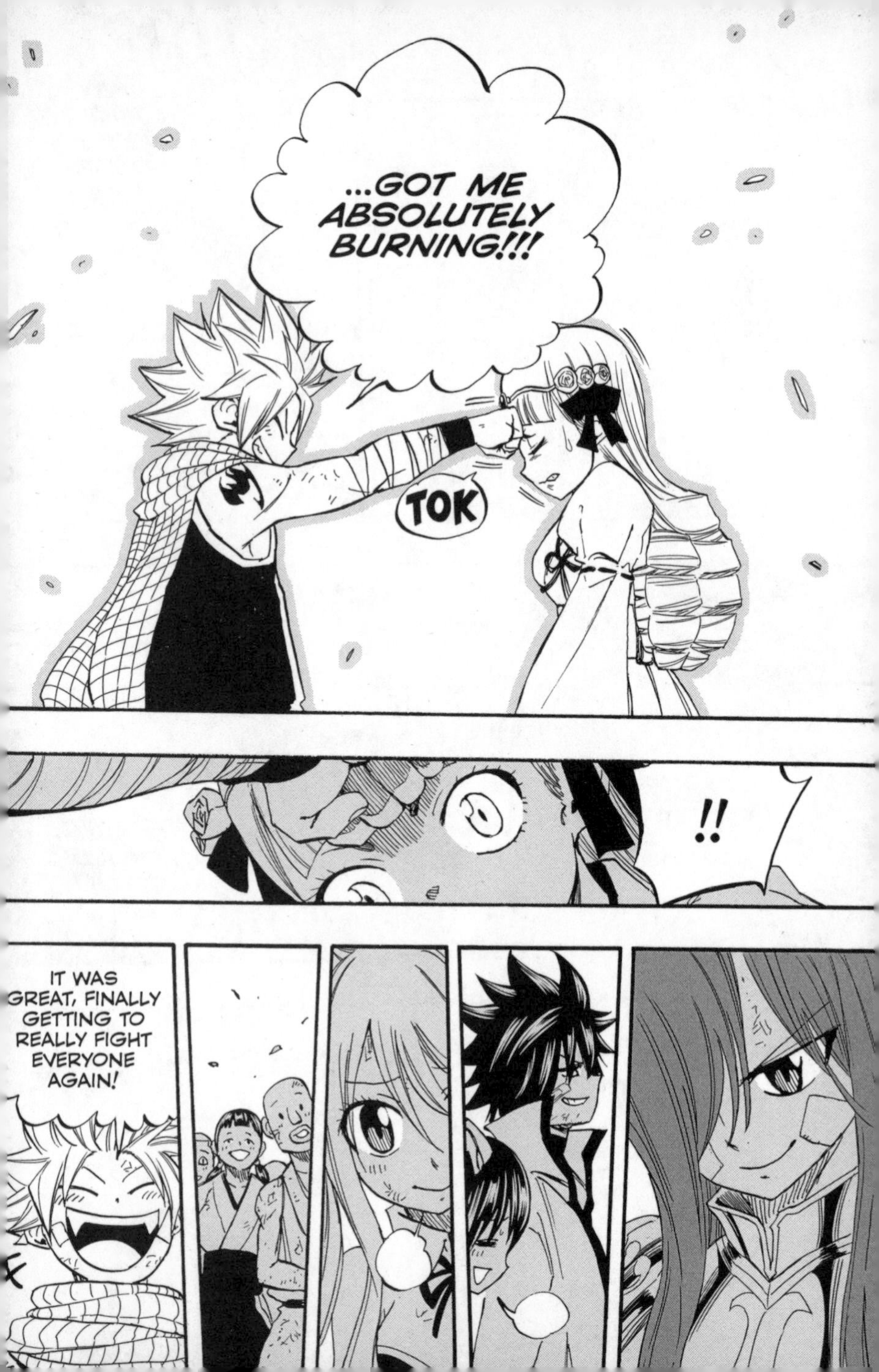
...GOT ME ABSOLUTELY BURNING!!!
TOK
!!
IT WAS GREAT, FINALLY GETTING TO REALLY FIGHT EVERYONE AGAIN!

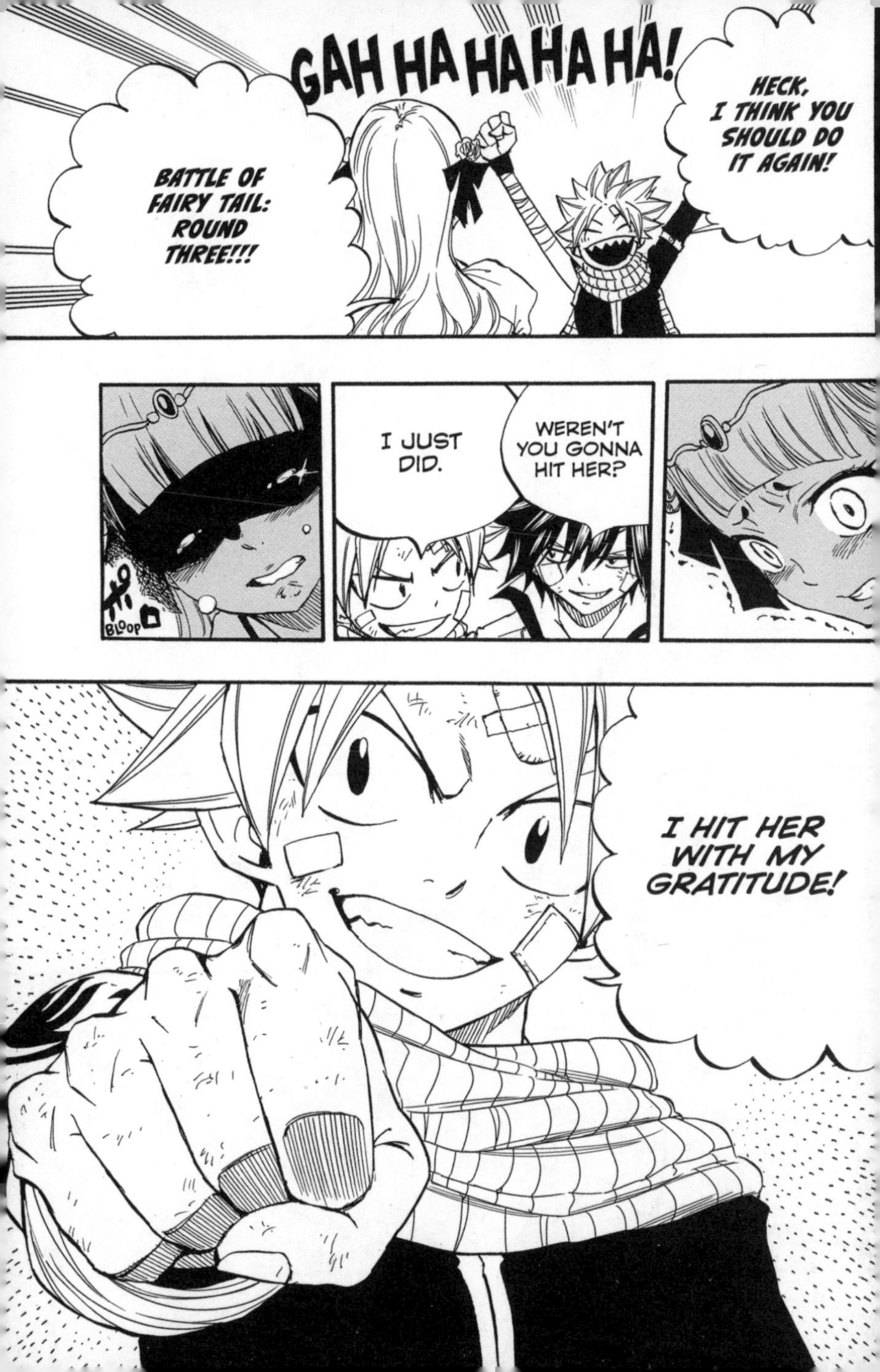
HECK, I THINK YOU SHOULD DO IT AGAIN!
GAH HA HA HA HA HA!
BATTLE OF FAIRY TAIL: ROUND THREE!!!
WEREN'T YOU GONNA HIT HER?
I JUST DID.
BLOOP
I HIT HER WITH MY GRATITUDE!

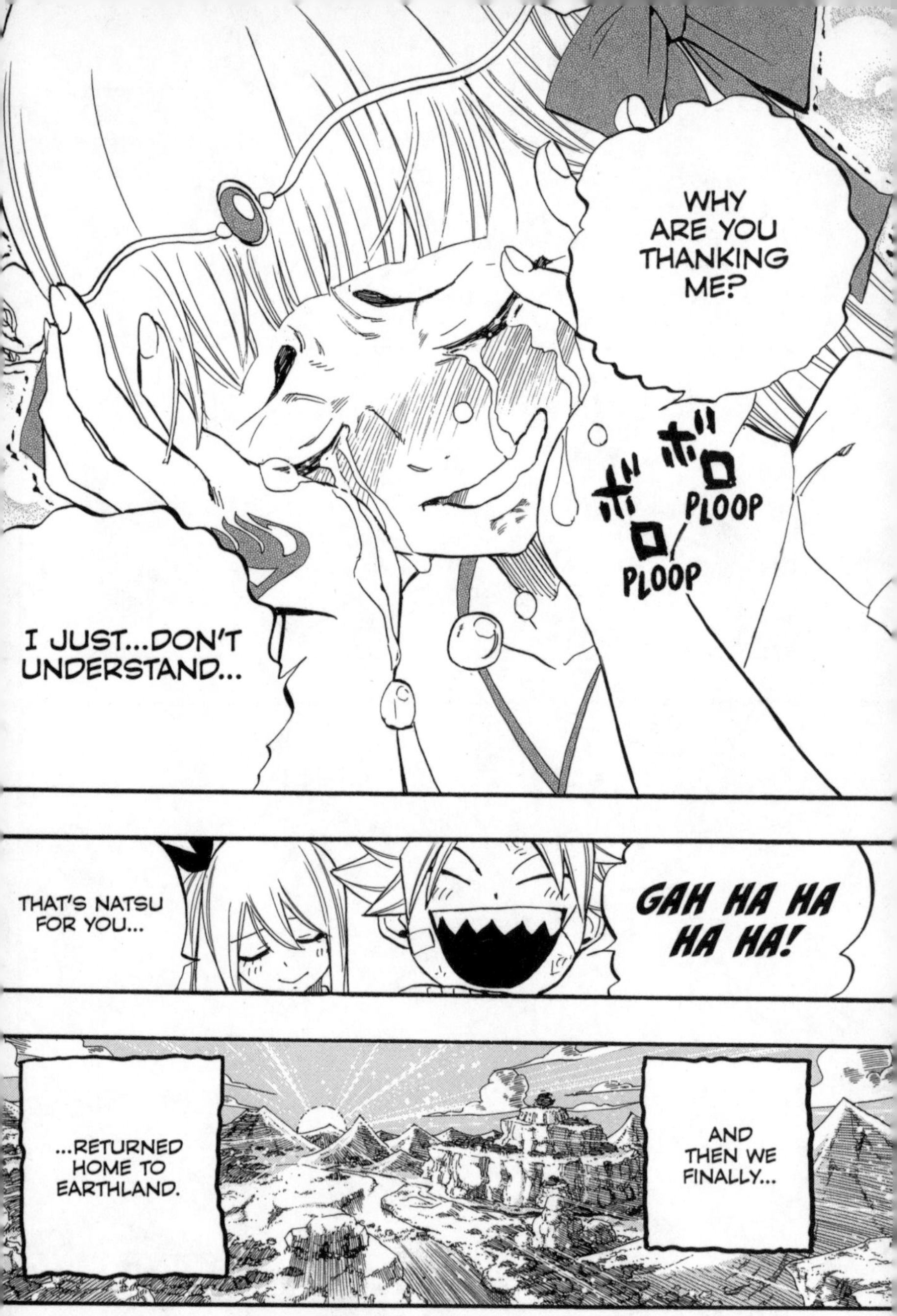
WHY ARE YOU THANKING ME?
PLOOP
PLOOP
I JUST...DON'T UNDERSTAND...
GAH HA HA HA HA!
THAT'S NATSU FOR YOU...
AND THEN WE FINALLY...
...RETURNED HOME TO EARTHLAND.

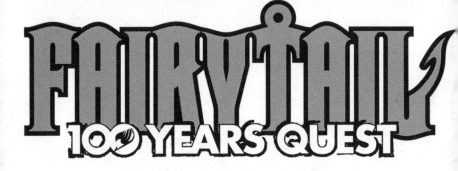

FAIRY TAIL 100 YEARS QUEST

Chapter 98: Homecoming

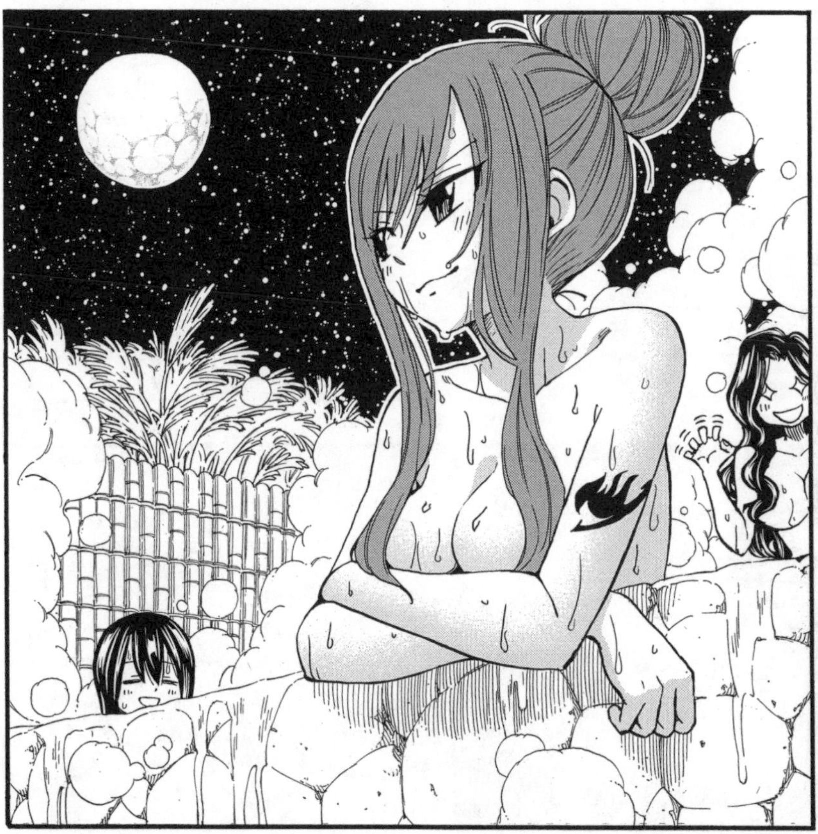

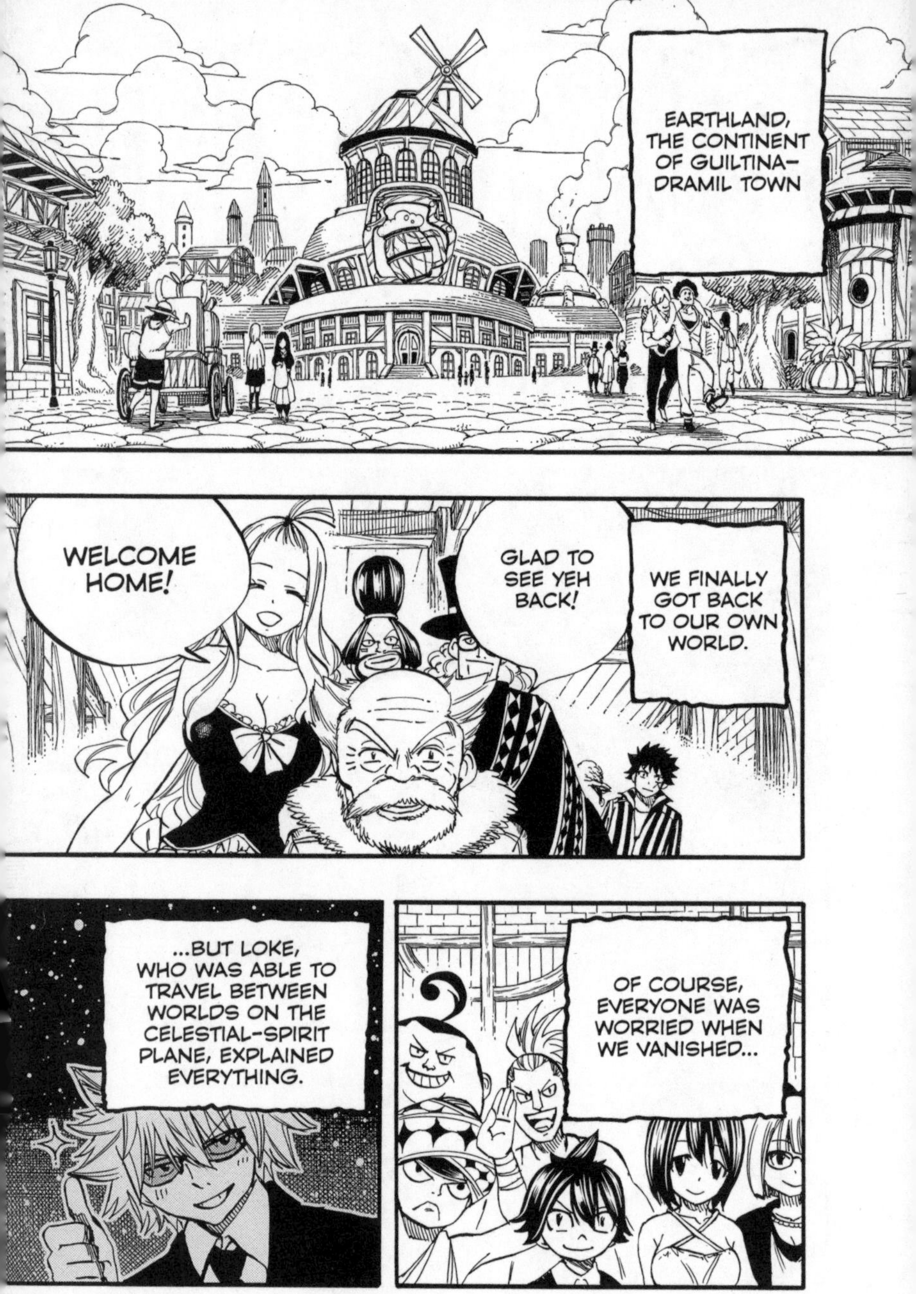
EARTHLAND, THE CONTINENT OF GUILTINA— DRAMIL TOWN
WE FINALLY GOT BACK TO OUR OWN WORLD.
GLAD TO SEE YEH BACK!
WELCOME HOME!
OF COURSE, EVERYONE WAS WORRIED WHEN WE VANISHED...
...BUT LOKE, WHO WAS ABLE TO TRAVEL BETWEEN WORLDS ON THE CELESTIAL-SPIRIT PLANE, EXPLAINED EVERYTHING.

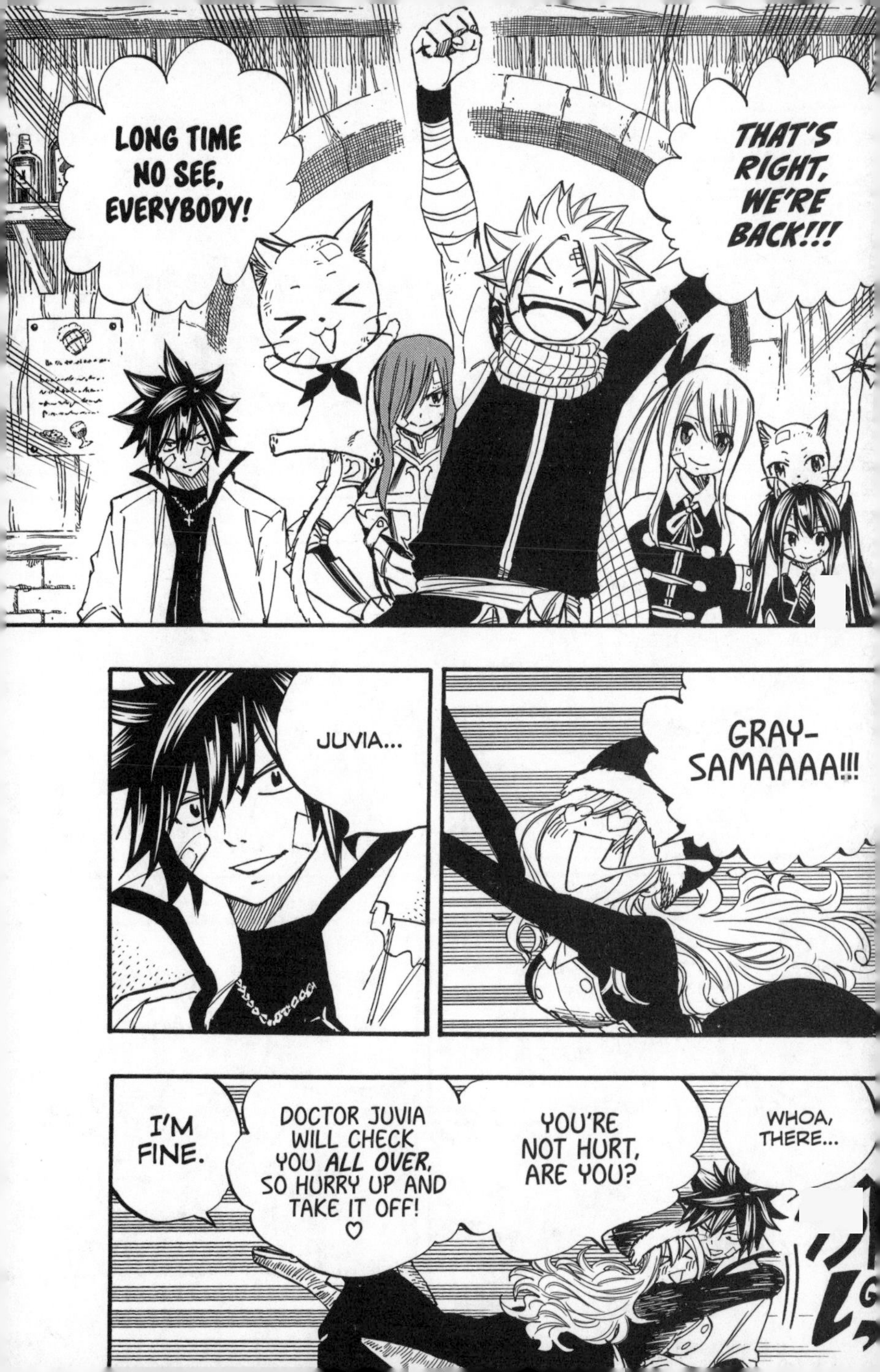
THAT'S RIGHT, WE'RE BACK!!!
LONG TIME NO SEE, EVERYBODY!
GRAY-SAMAAAA!!!
JUVIA...
WHOA, THERE...
YOU'RE NOT HURT, ARE YOU?
DOCTOR JUVIA WILL CHECK YOU ALL OVER, SO HURRY UP AND TAKE IT OFF! ♡
I'M FINE.

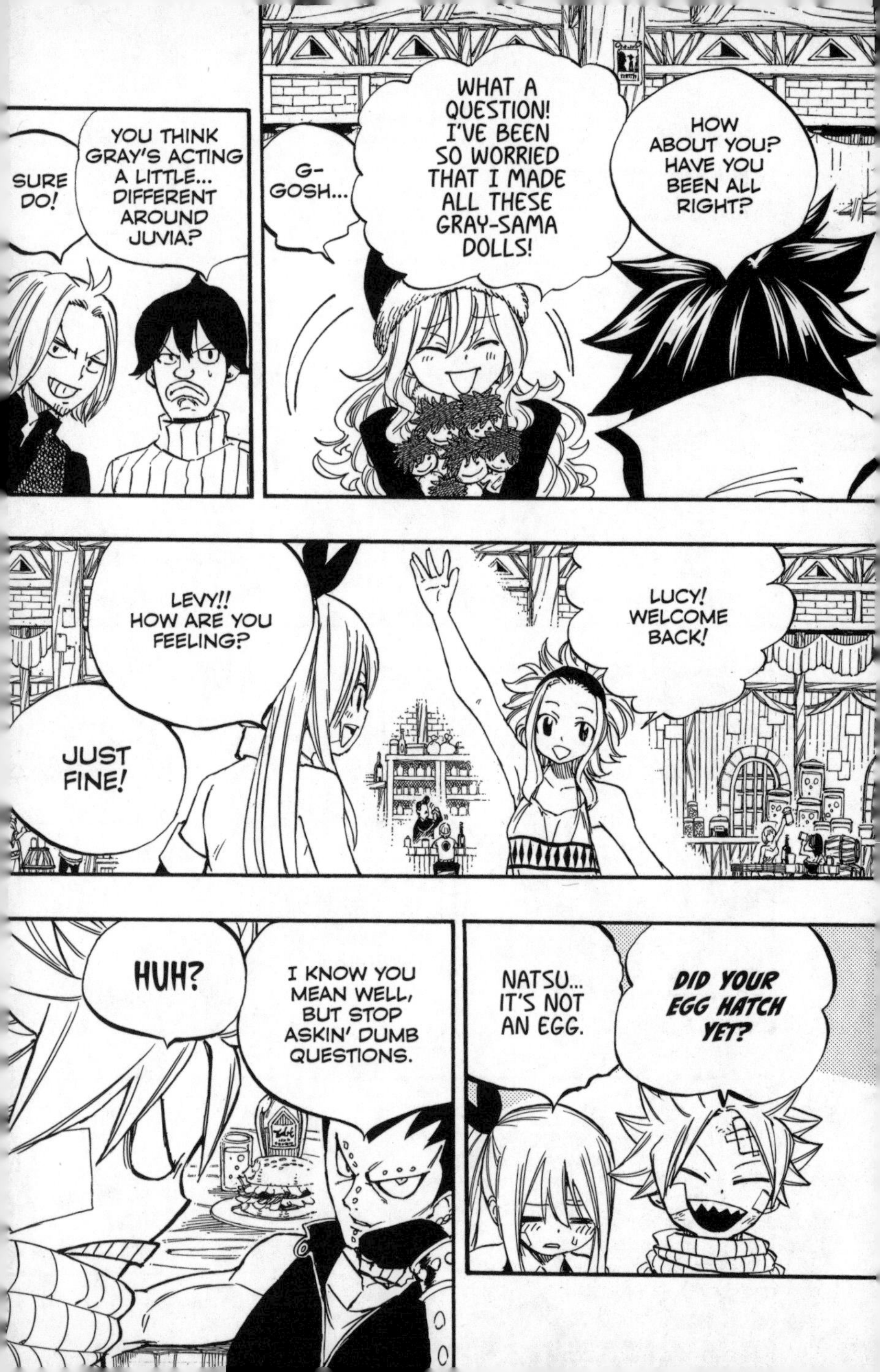
HOW ABOUT YOU? HAVE YOU BEEN ALL RIGHT?
WHAT A QUESTION! I'VE BEEN SO WORRIED THAT I MADE ALL THESE GRAY-SAMA DOLLS!
G-GOSH...
YOU THINK GRAY'S ACTING A LITTLE... DIFFERENT AROUND JUVIA?
SURE DO!
LUCY! WELCOME BACK!
LEVY!! HOW ARE YOU FEELING?
JUST FINE!
DID YOUR EGG HATCH YET?
NATSU... IT'S NOT AN EGG.
I KNOW YOU MEAN WELL, BUT STOP ASKIN' DUMB QUESTIONS.
HUH?

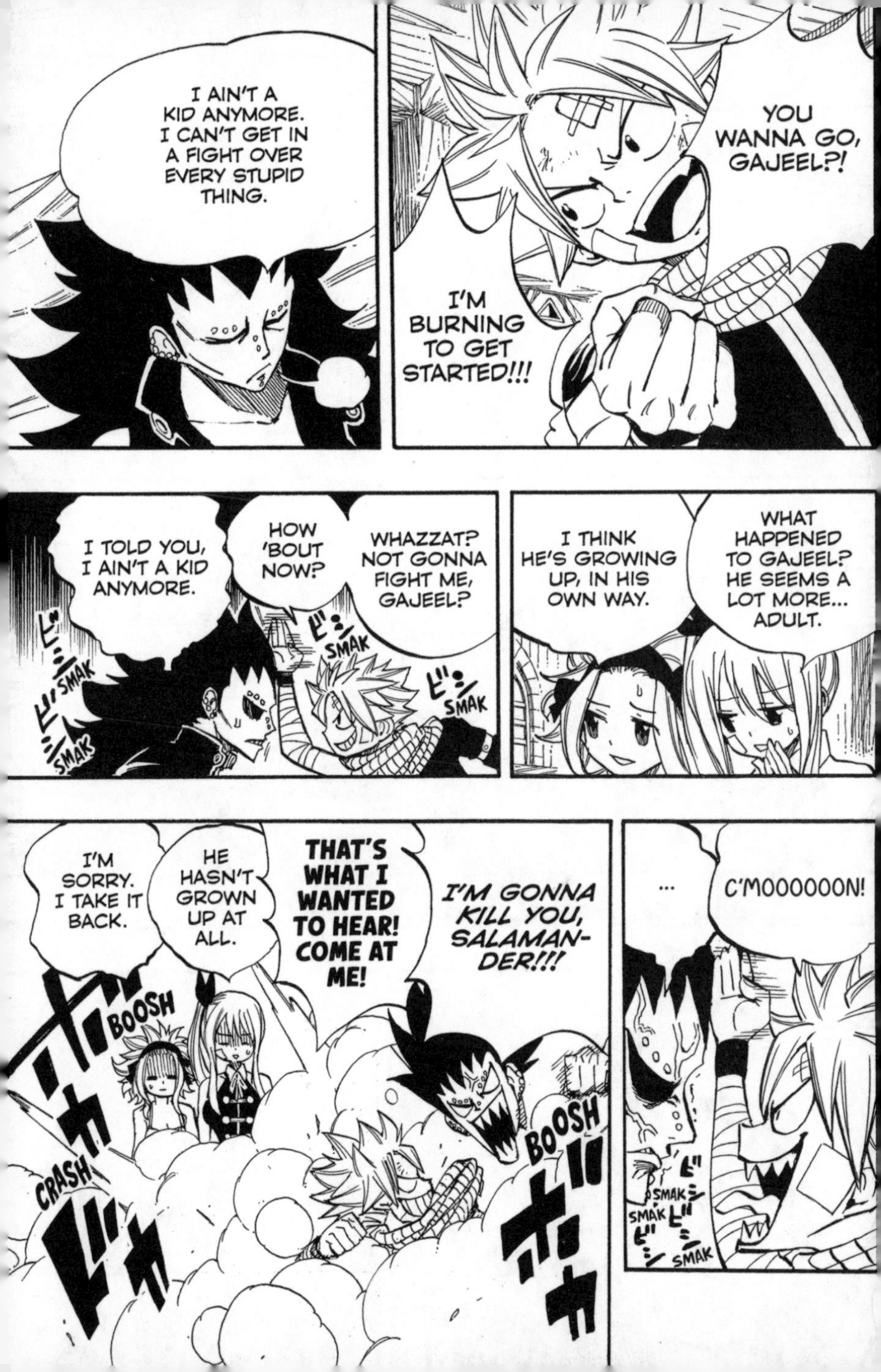
YOU WANNA GO, GAJEEL?!
I'M BURNING TO GET STARTED!!!
I AIN'T A KID ANYMORE. I CAN'T GET IN A FIGHT OVER EVERY STUPID THING.
WHAT HAPPENED TO GAJEEL? HE SEEMS A LOT MORE... ADULT.
I THINK HE'S GROWING UP, IN HIS OWN WAY.
WHAZZAT? NOT GONNA FIGHT ME, GAJEEL?
SMAK
SMAK
HOW 'BOUT NOW?
I TOLD YOU, I AIN'T A KID ANYMORE.
SMAK
SMAK
C'MOOOOOON!
...
SMAK
SMAK
SMAK
I'M GONNA KILL YOU, SALAMANDER!!!
THAT'S WHAT I WANTED TO HEAR! COME AT ME!
BOOSH
HE HASN'T GROWN UP AT ALL.
I'M SORRY. I TAKE IT BACK.
BOOSH
CRASH

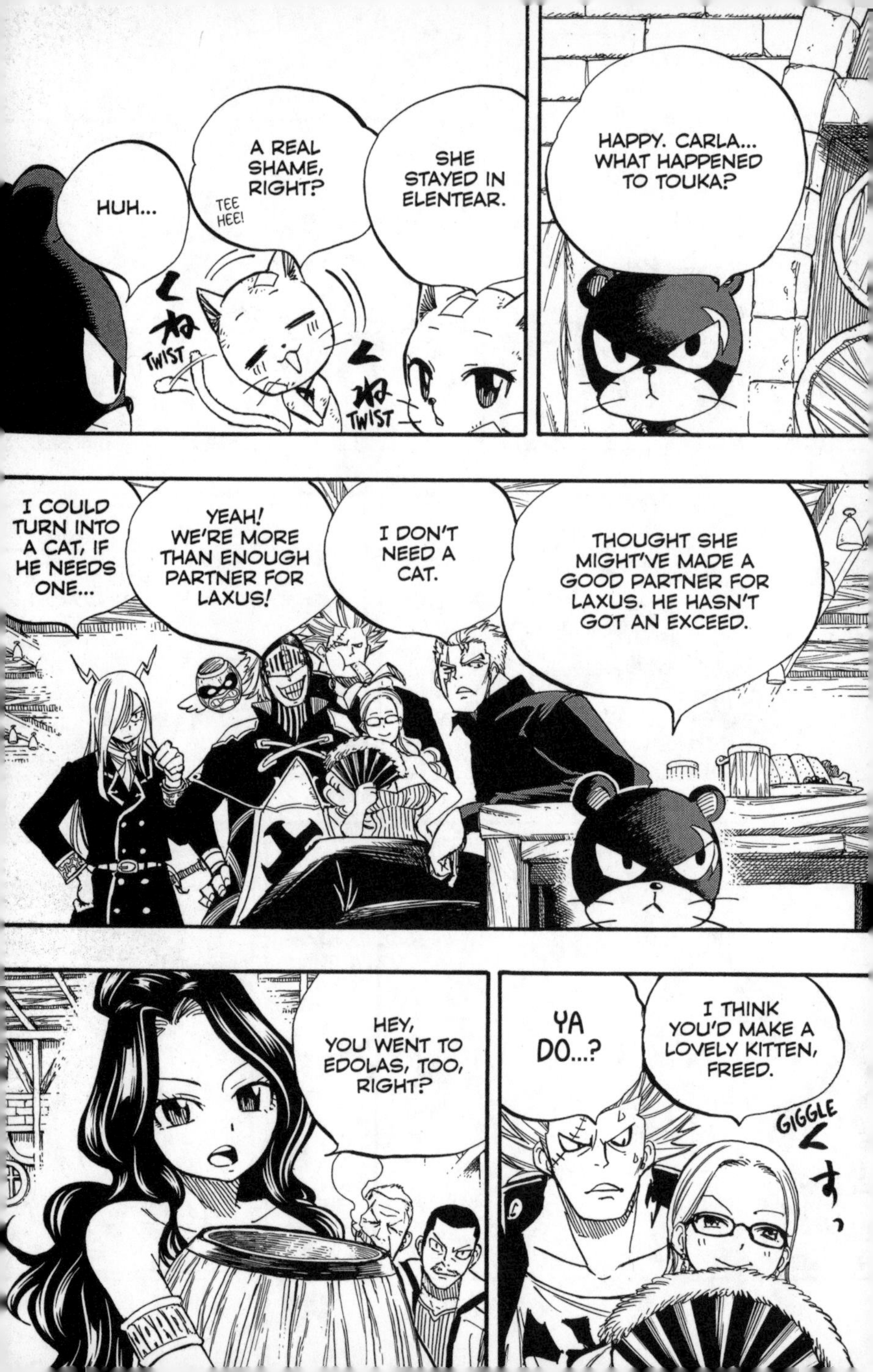
HAPPY. CARLA... WHAT HAPPENED TO TOUKA?
SHE STAYED IN ELENTEAR.
くね
TWIST
A REAL SHAME, RIGHT?
TEE HEE!
くね
TWIST
HUH...
THOUGHT SHE MIGHT'VE MADE A GOOD PARTNER FOR LAXUS. HE HASN'T GOT AN EXCEED.
I DON'T NEED A CAT.
YEAH! WE'RE MORE THAN ENOUGH PARTNER FOR LAXUS!
I COULD TURN INTO A CAT, IF HE NEEDS ONE...
I THINK YOU'D MAKE A LOVELY KITTEN, FREED.
GIGGLE
くすっ
YA DO...?
HEY, YOU WENT TO EDOLAS, TOO, RIGHT?

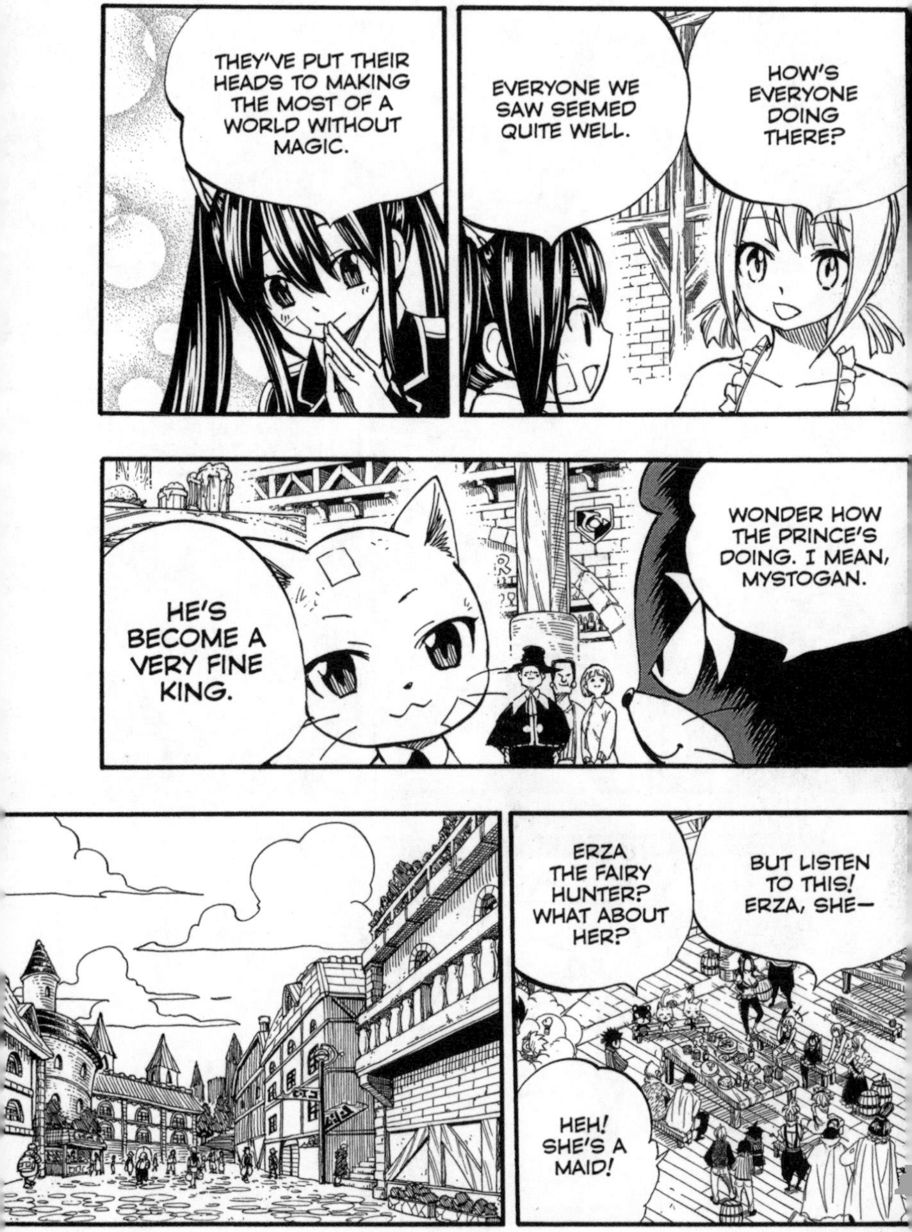
HOW'S EVERYONE DOING THERE?
EVERYONE WE SAW SEEMED QUITE WELL.
THEY'VE PUT THEIR HEADS TO MAKING THE MOST OF A WORLD WITHOUT MAGIC.
WONDER HOW THE PRINCE'S DOING. I MEAN, MYSTOGAN.
HE'S BECOME A VERY FINE KING.
BUT LISTEN TO THIS! ERZA, SHE—
ERZA THE FAIRY HUNTER? WHAT ABOUT HER?
HEH! SHE'S A MAID!

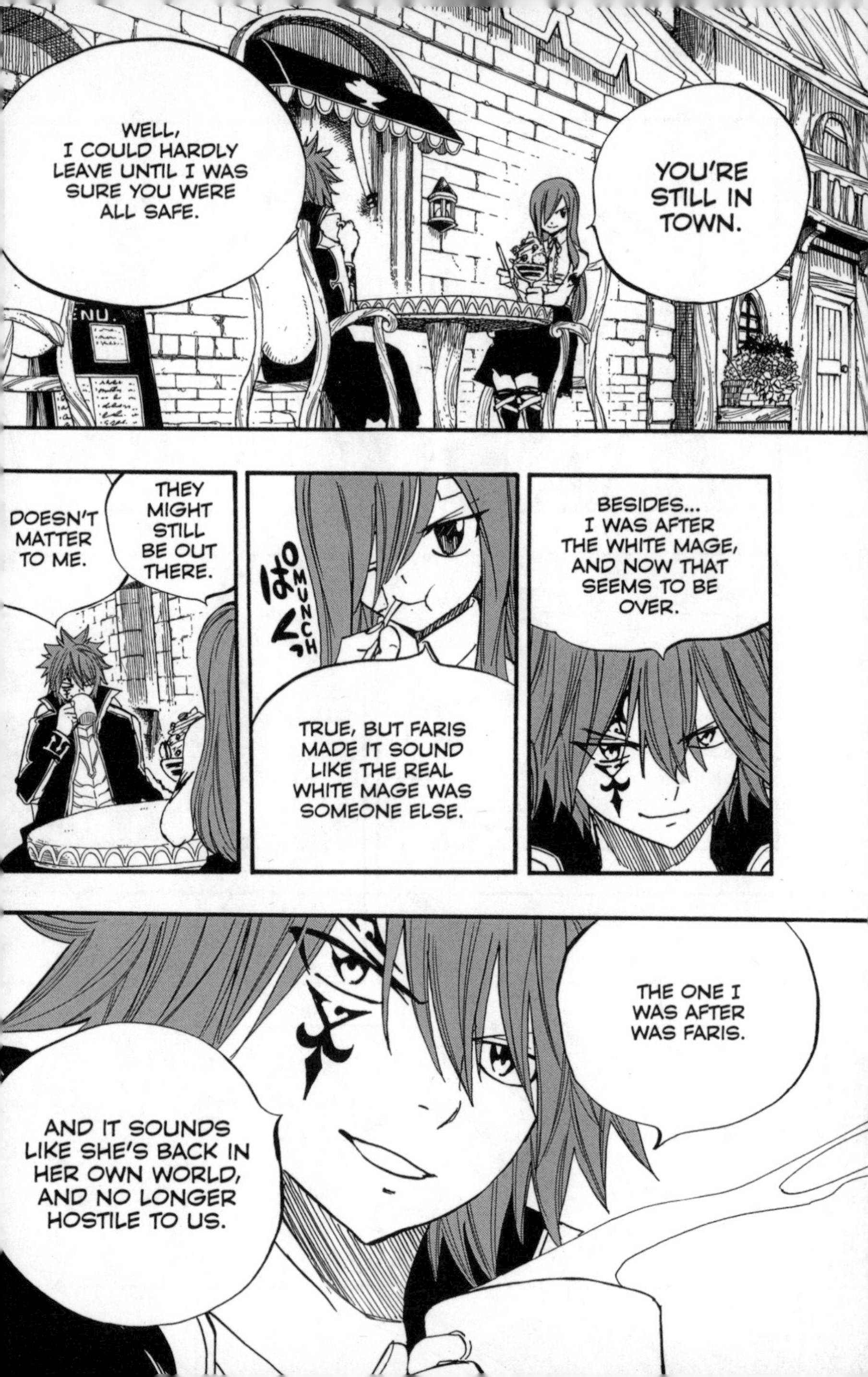
YOU'RE STILL IN TOWN.
WELL, I COULD HARDLY LEAVE UNTIL I WAS SURE YOU WERE ALL SAFE.
BESIDES... I WAS AFTER THE WHITE MAGE, AND NOW THAT SEEMS TO BE OVER.
MUNCH
TRUE, BUT FARIS MADE IT SOUND LIKE THE REAL WHITE MAGE WAS SOMEONE ELSE.
THEY MIGHT STILL BE OUT THERE.
DOESN'T MATTER TO ME.
THE ONE I WAS AFTER WAS FARIS.
AND IT SOUNDS LIKE SHE'S BACK IN HER OWN WORLD, AND NO LONGER HOSTILE TO US.

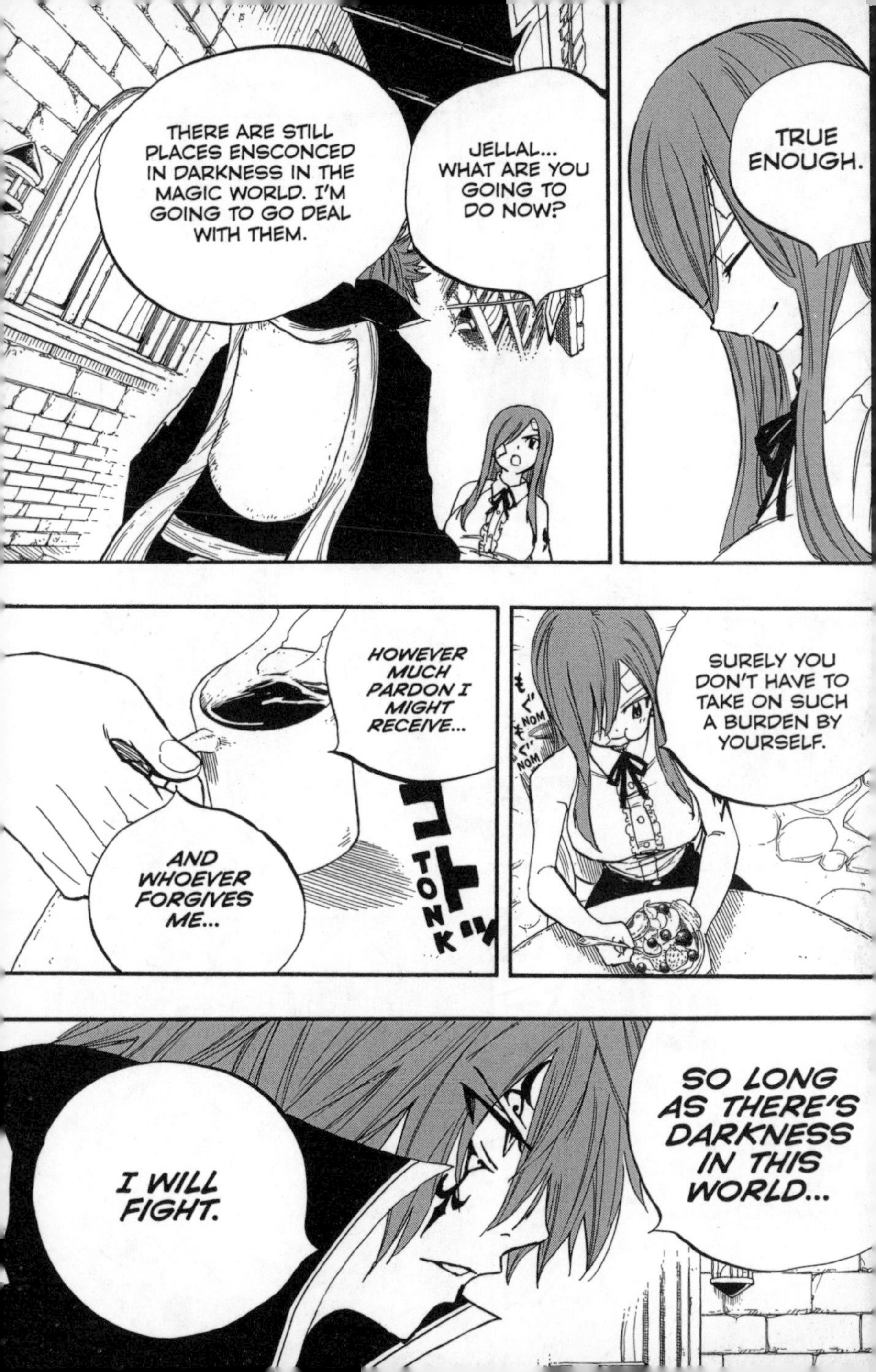
TRUE ENOUGH.
JELLAL... WHAT ARE YOU GOING TO DO NOW?
THERE ARE STILL PLACES ENSCONCED IN DARKNESS IN THE MAGIC WORLD. I'M GOING TO GO DEAL WITH THEM.
SURELY YOU DON'T HAVE TO TAKE ON SUCH A BURDEN BY YOURSELF.
NOM NOM
HOWEVER MUCH PARDON I MIGHT RECEIVE...
TONK
AND WHOEVER FORGIVES ME...
SO LONG AS THERE'S DARKNESS IN THIS WORLD...
I WILL FIGHT.

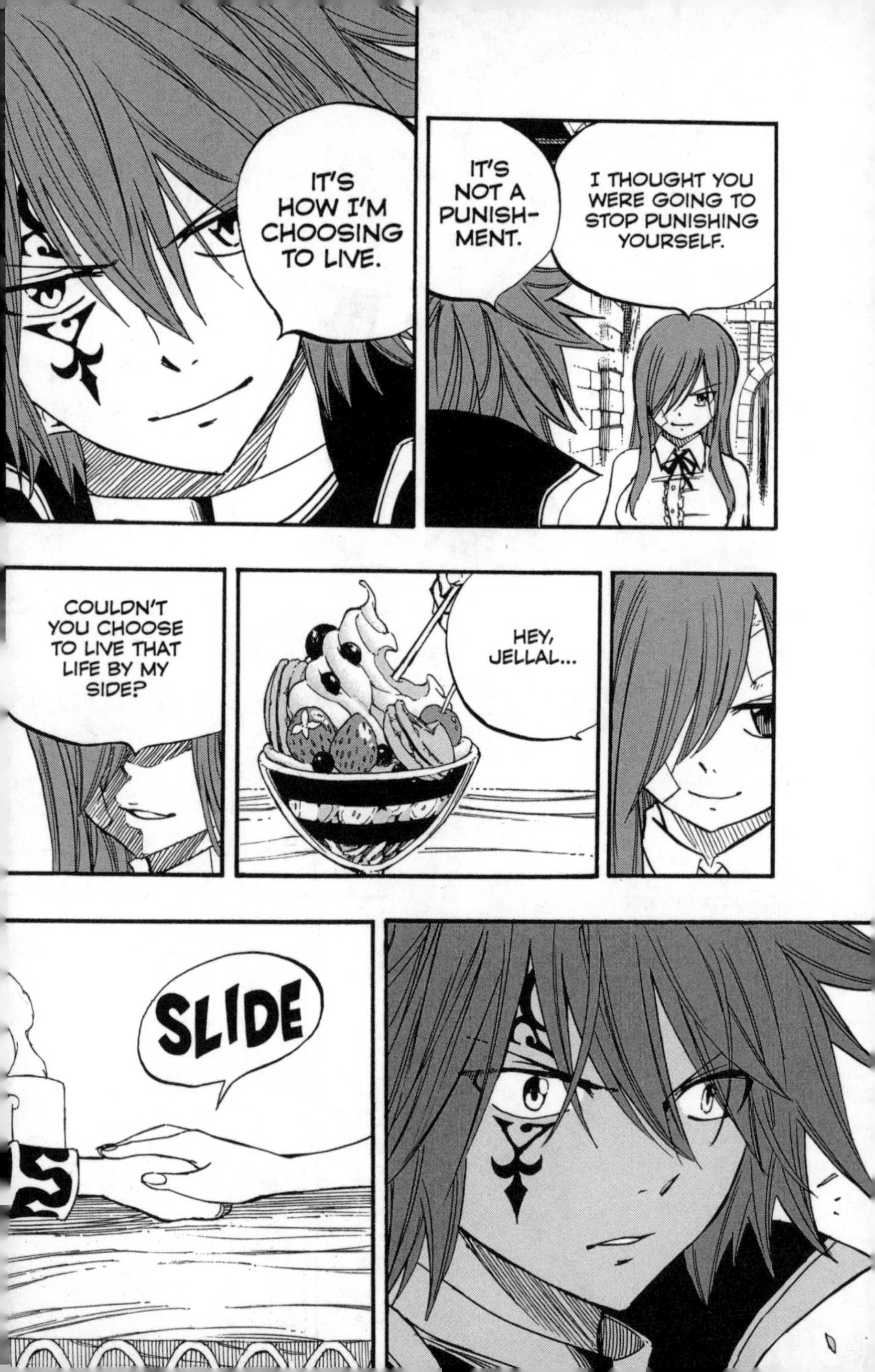
I THOUGHT YOU WERE GOING TO STOP PUNISHING YOURSELF.
IT'S NOT A PUNISH-MENT.
IT'S HOW I'M CHOOSING TO LIVE.
HEY, JELLAL...
COULDN'T YOU CHOOSE TO LIVE THAT LIFE BY MY SIDE?
SLIDE

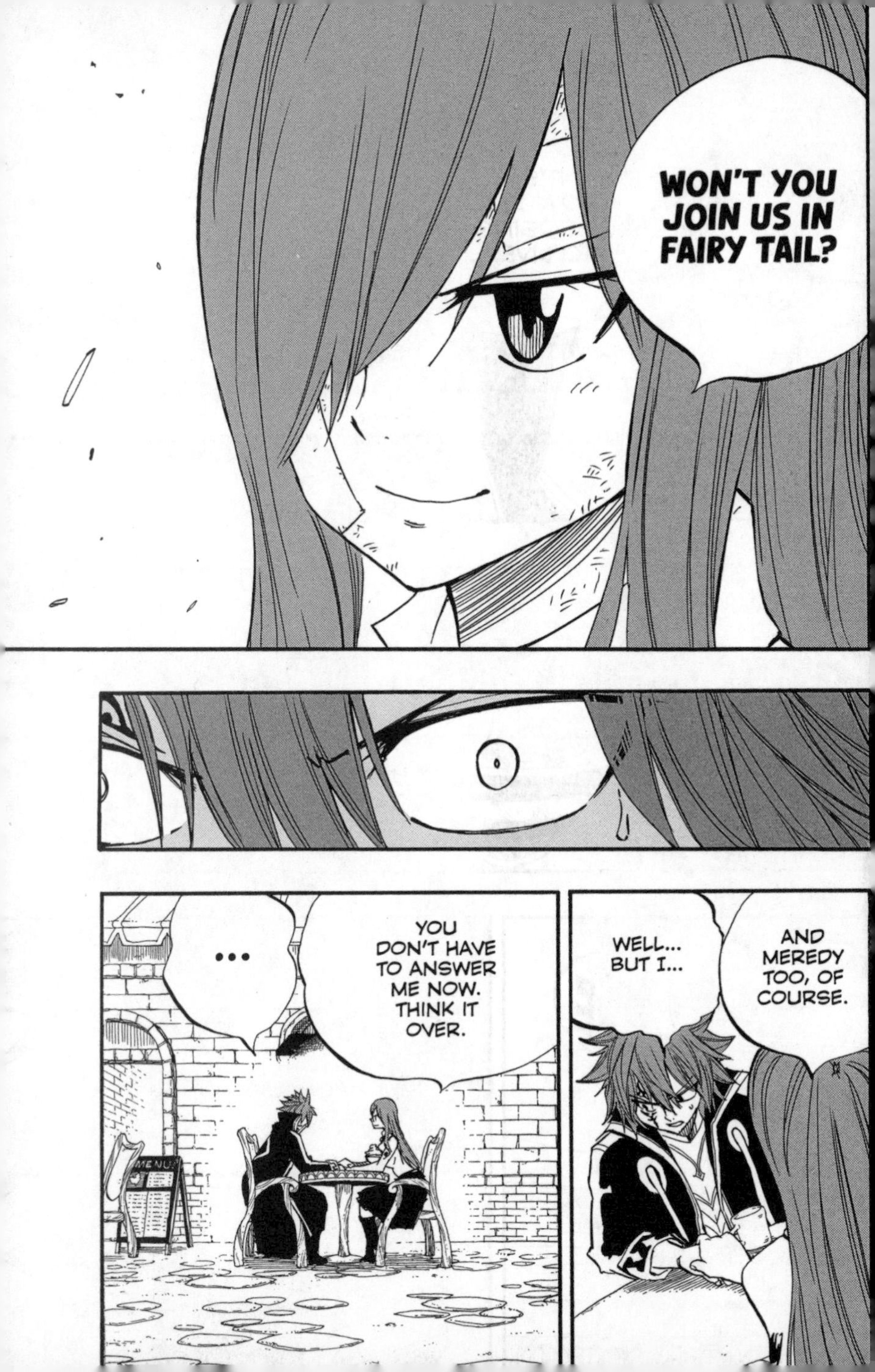
WON'T YOU JOIN US IN FAIRY TAIL?
AND MEREDY TOO, OF COURSE.
WELL... BUT I...
YOU DON'T HAVE TO ANSWER ME NOW. THINK IT OVER.
...
MENU

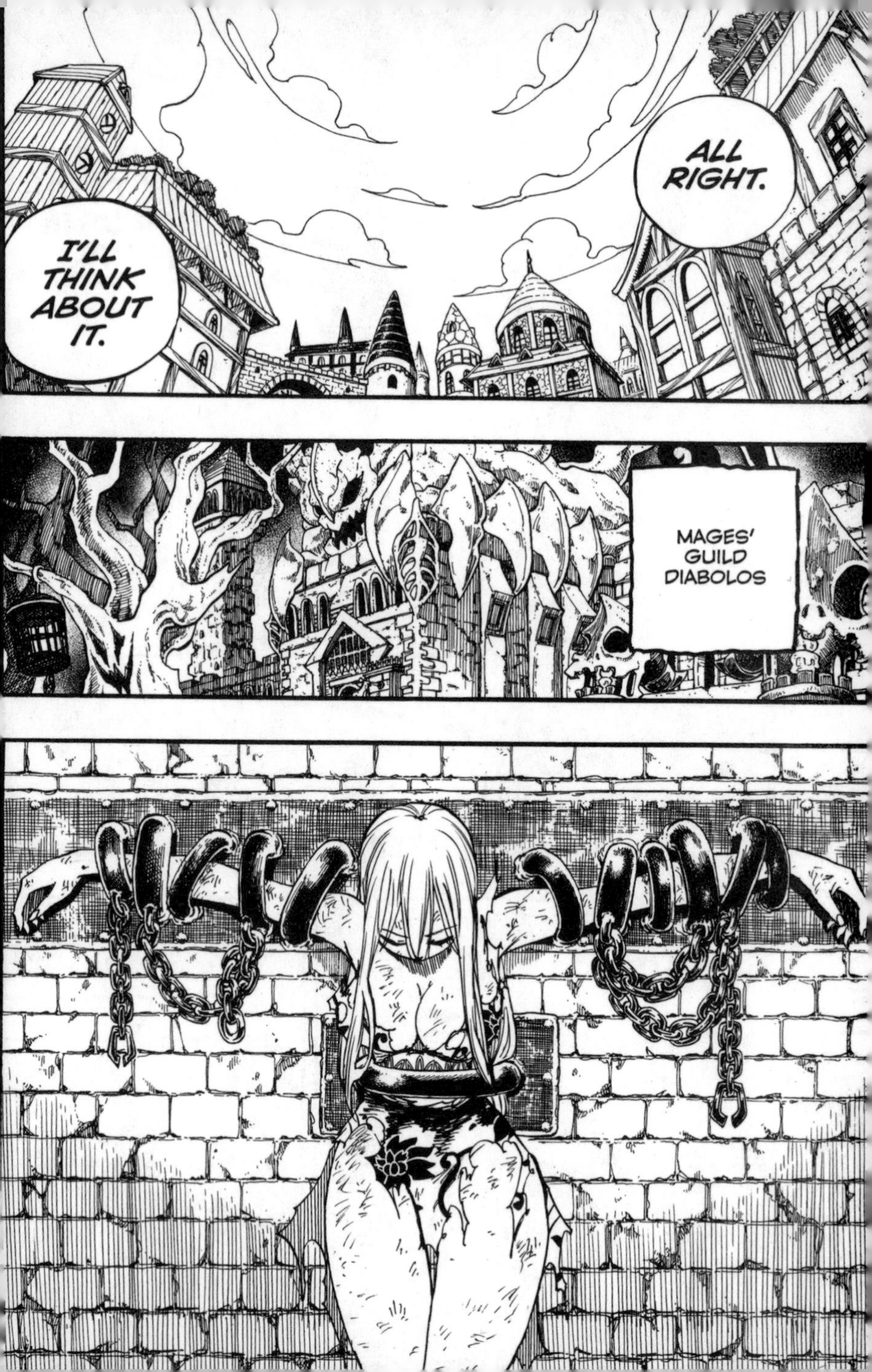
ALL RIGHT.
I'LL THINK ABOUT IT.
MAGES' GUILD DIABOLOS

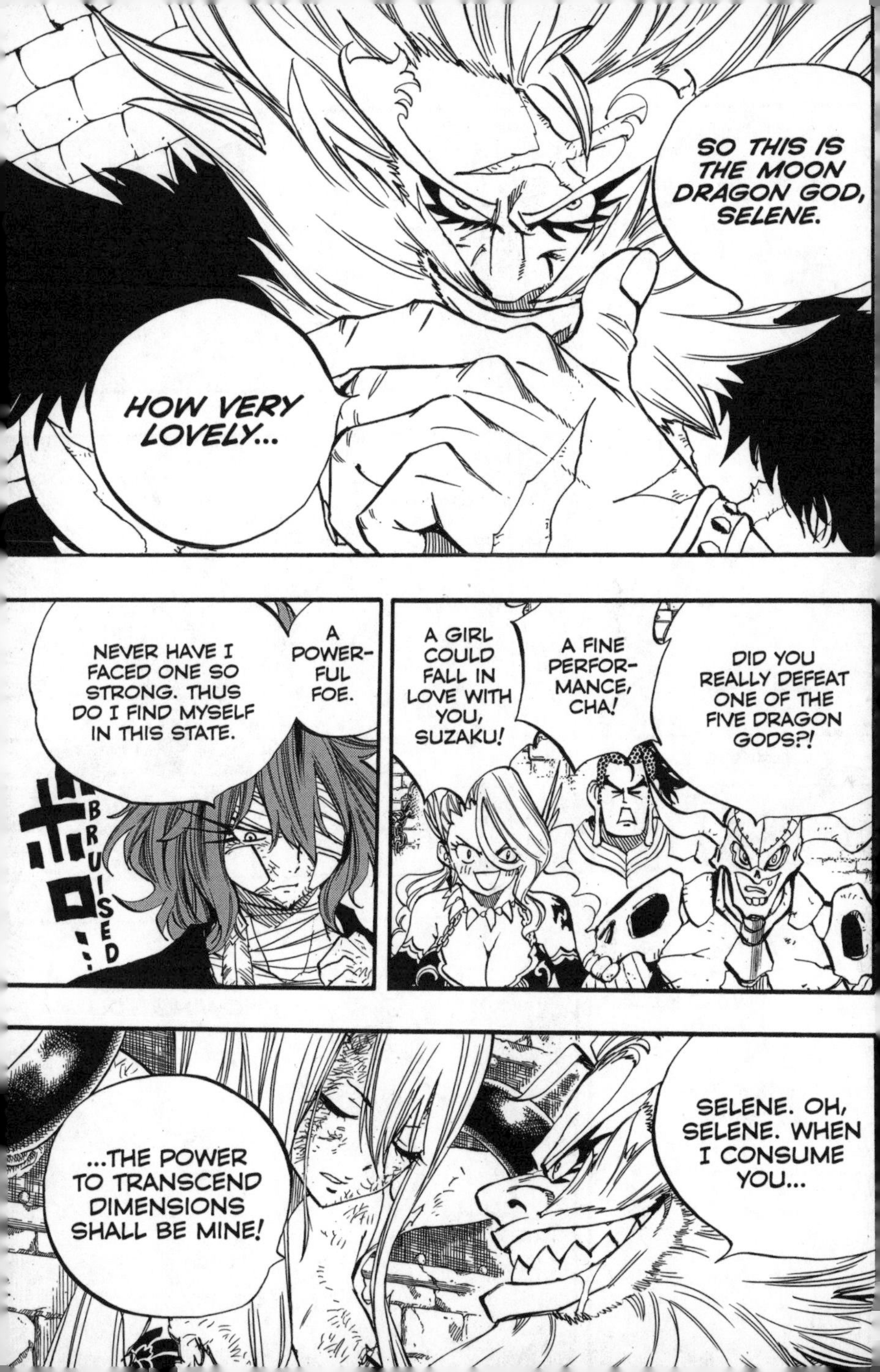
SO THIS IS THE MOON DRAGON GOD, SELENE.
HOW VERY LOVELY...
DID YOU REALLY DEFEAT ONE OF THE FIVE DRAGON GODS?!
A FINE PERFORMANCE, CHA!
A GIRL COULD FALL IN LOVE WITH YOU, SUZAKU!
A POWERFUL FOE.
NEVER HAVE I FACED ONE SO STRONG. THUS DO I FIND MYSELF IN THIS STATE.
BRUISED
SELENE. OH, SELENE. WHEN I CONSUME YOU...
...THE POWER TO TRANSCEND DIMENSIONS SHALL BE MINE!

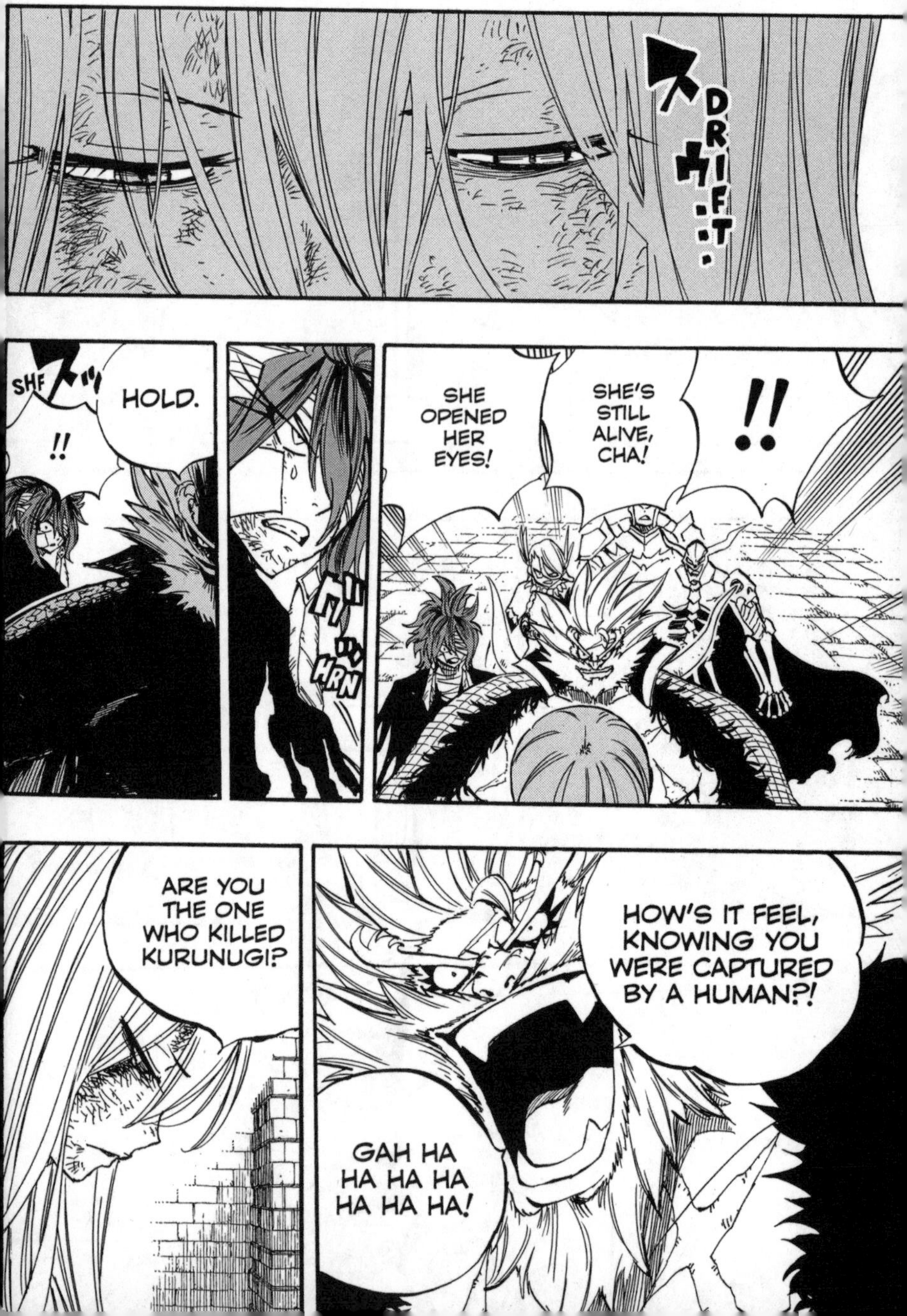
DRIFT...
!!
SHE'S STILL ALIVE, CHA!
SHE OPENED HER EYES!
HRN
HOLD.
SHF
!!
HOW'S IT FEEL, KNOWING YOU WERE CAPTURED BY A HUMAN?!
GAH HA HA HA HA HA HA HA!
ARE YOU THE ONE WHO KILLED KURUNUGI?

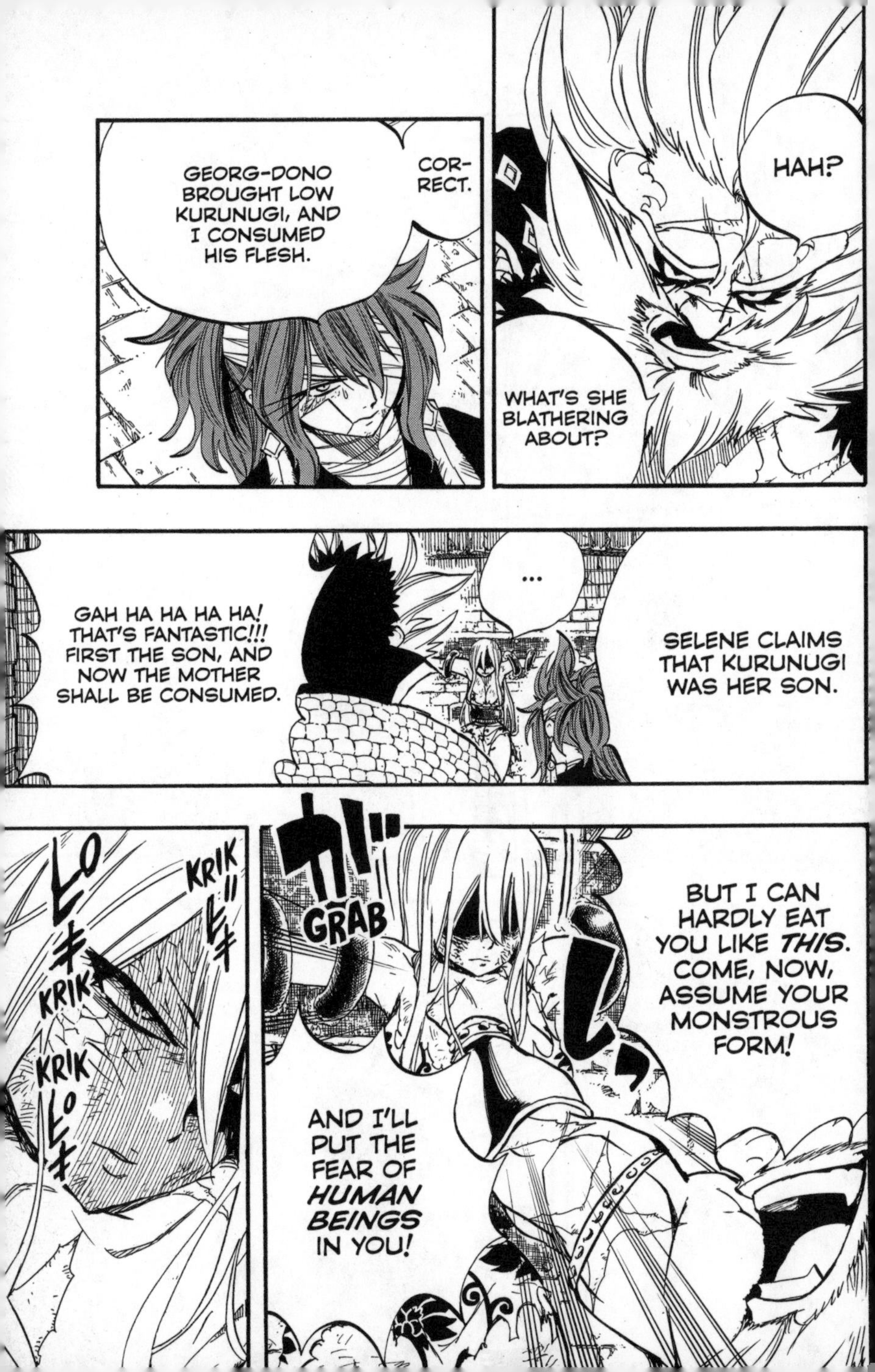
HAH?
WHAT'S SHE BLATHERING ABOUT?
COR-RECT.
GEORG-DONO BROUGHT LOW KURUNUGI, AND I CONSUMED HIS FLESH.
SELENE CLAIMS THAT KURUNUGI WAS HER SON.
...
GAH HA HA HA HA! THAT'S FANTASTIC!!! FIRST THE SON, AND NOW THE MOTHER SHALL BE CONSUMED.
BUT I CAN HARDLY EAT YOU LIKE *THIS*. COME, NOW, ASSUME YOUR MONSTROUS FORM!
GRAB
AND I'LL PUT THE FEAR OF *HUMAN BEINGS* IN YOU!
KRIK
KRIK
KRIK

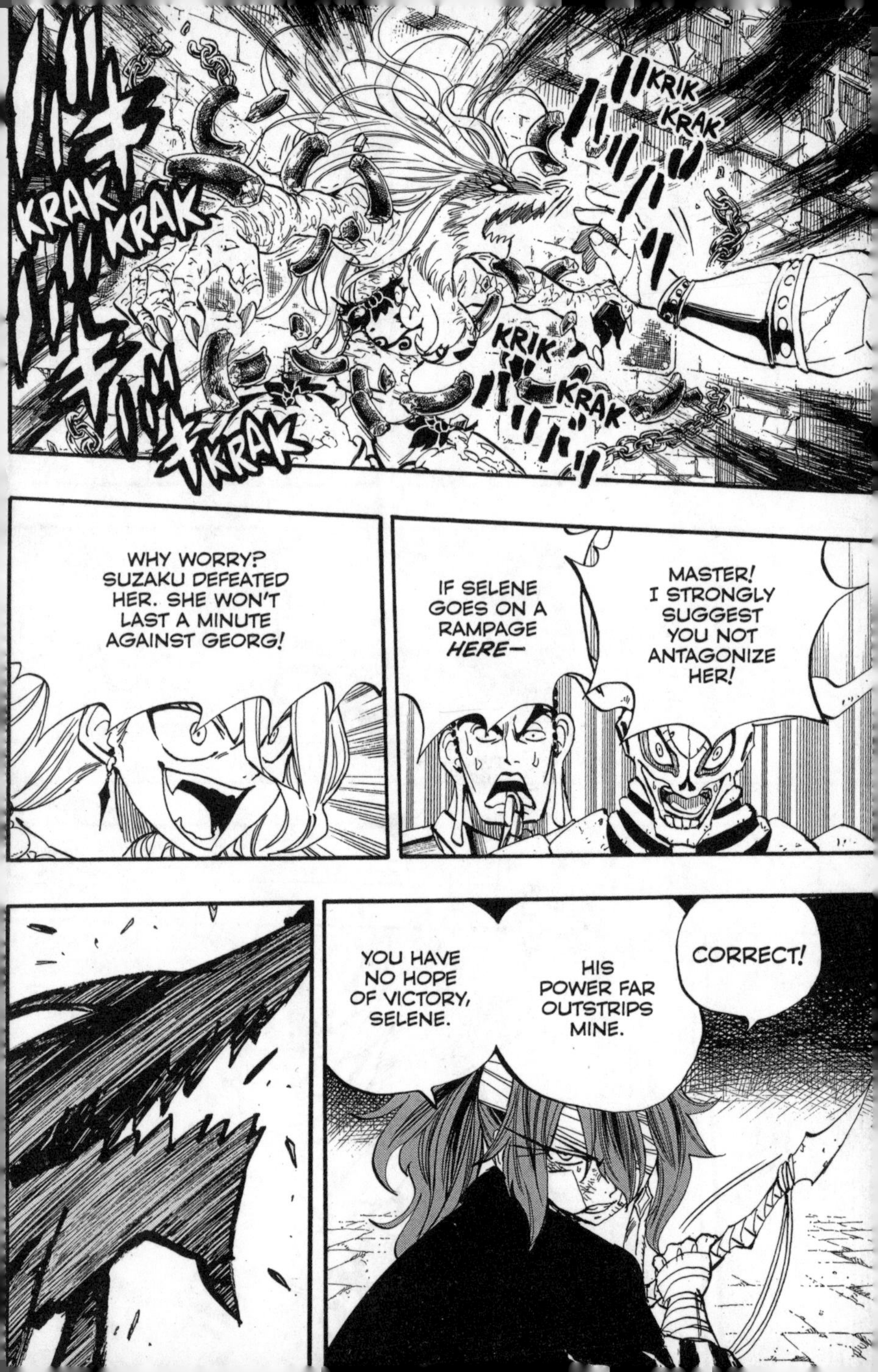
KRIK KRAK
KRIK KRAK
KRAK KRAK
KRAK
MASTER! I STRONGLY SUGGEST YOU NOT ANTAGONIZE HER!
IF SELENE GOES ON A RAMPAGE *HERE*—
WHY WORRY? SUZAKU DEFEATED HER. SHE WON'T LAST A MINUTE AGAINST GEORG!
CORRECT!
HIS POWER FAR OUTSTRIPS MINE.
YOU HAVE NO HOPE OF VICTORY, SELENE.

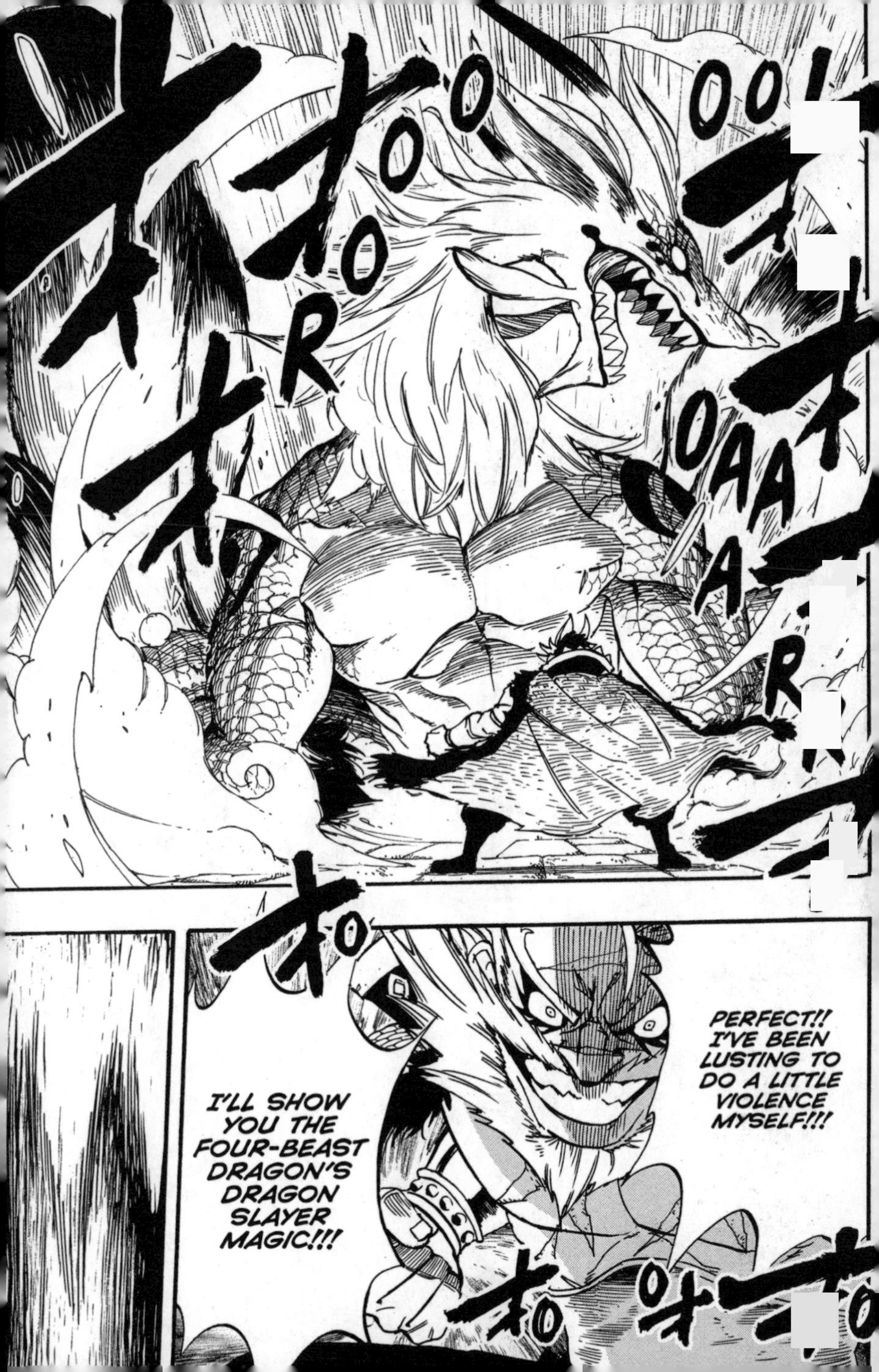
PERFECT!! I'VE BEEN LUSTING TO DO A LITTLE VIOLENCE MYSELF!!!
I'LL SHOW YOU THE FOUR-BEAST DRAGON'S DRAGON SLAYER MAGIC!!!

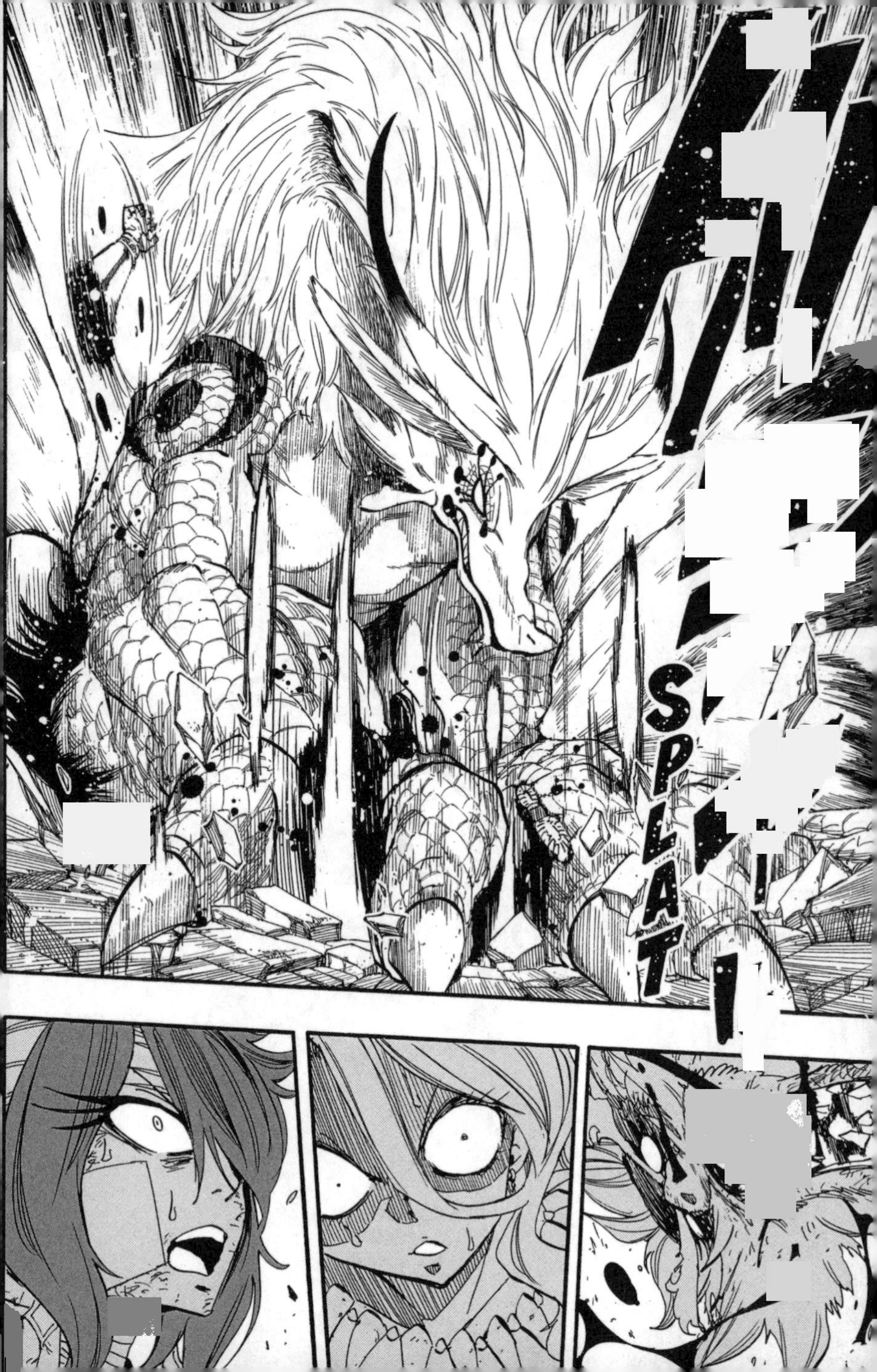
SPLAT

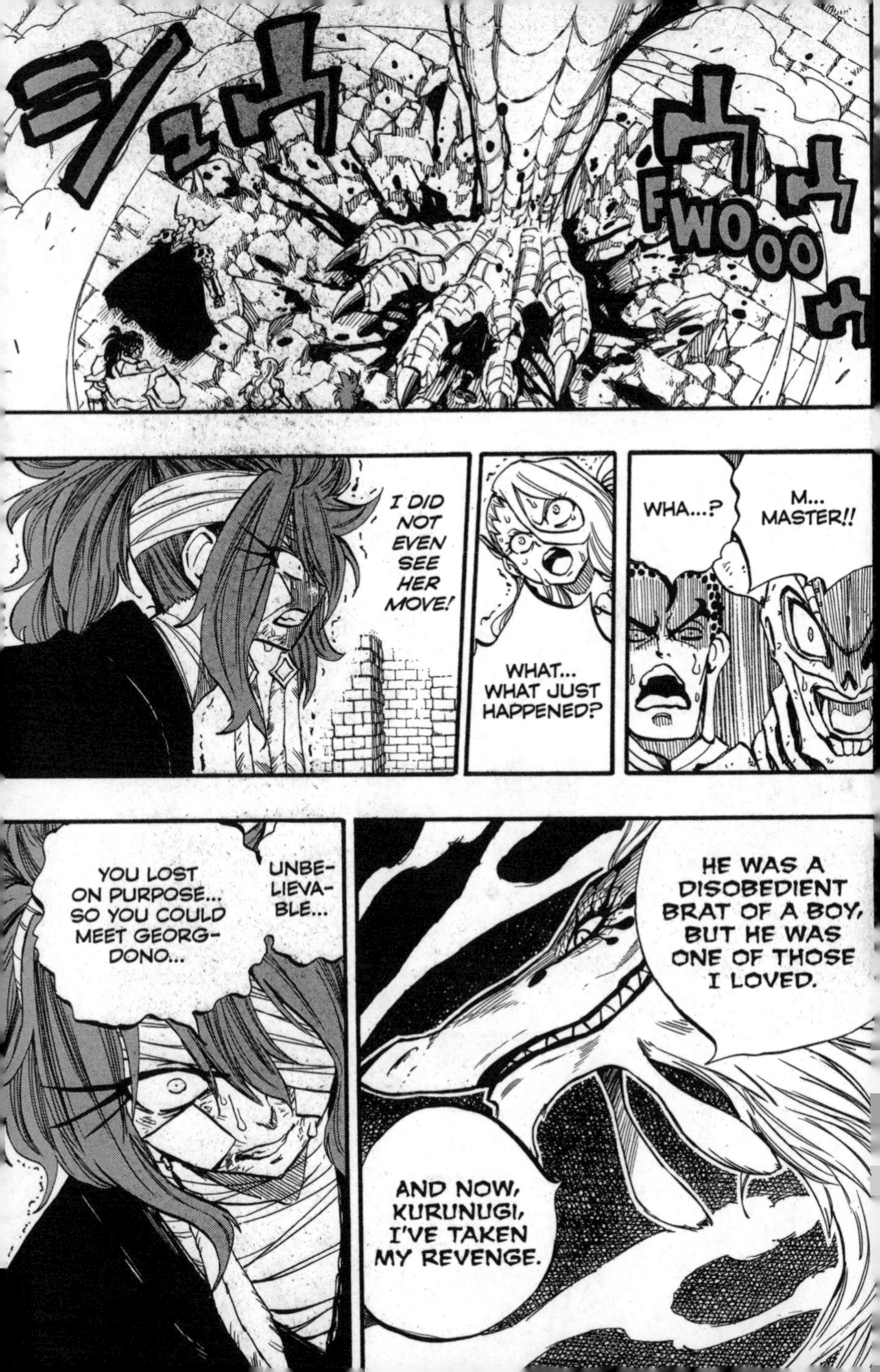
FWOOO
M... MASTER!!
WHA...?
WHAT... WHAT JUST HAPPENED?
I DID NOT EVEN SEE HER MOVE!
HE WAS A DISOBEDIENT BRAT OF A BOY, BUT HE WAS ONE OF THOSE I LOVED.
AND NOW, KURUNUGI, I'VE TAKEN MY REVENGE.
UNBE-LIEVA-BLE...
YOU LOST ON PURPOSE... SO YOU COULD MEET GEORG-DONO...

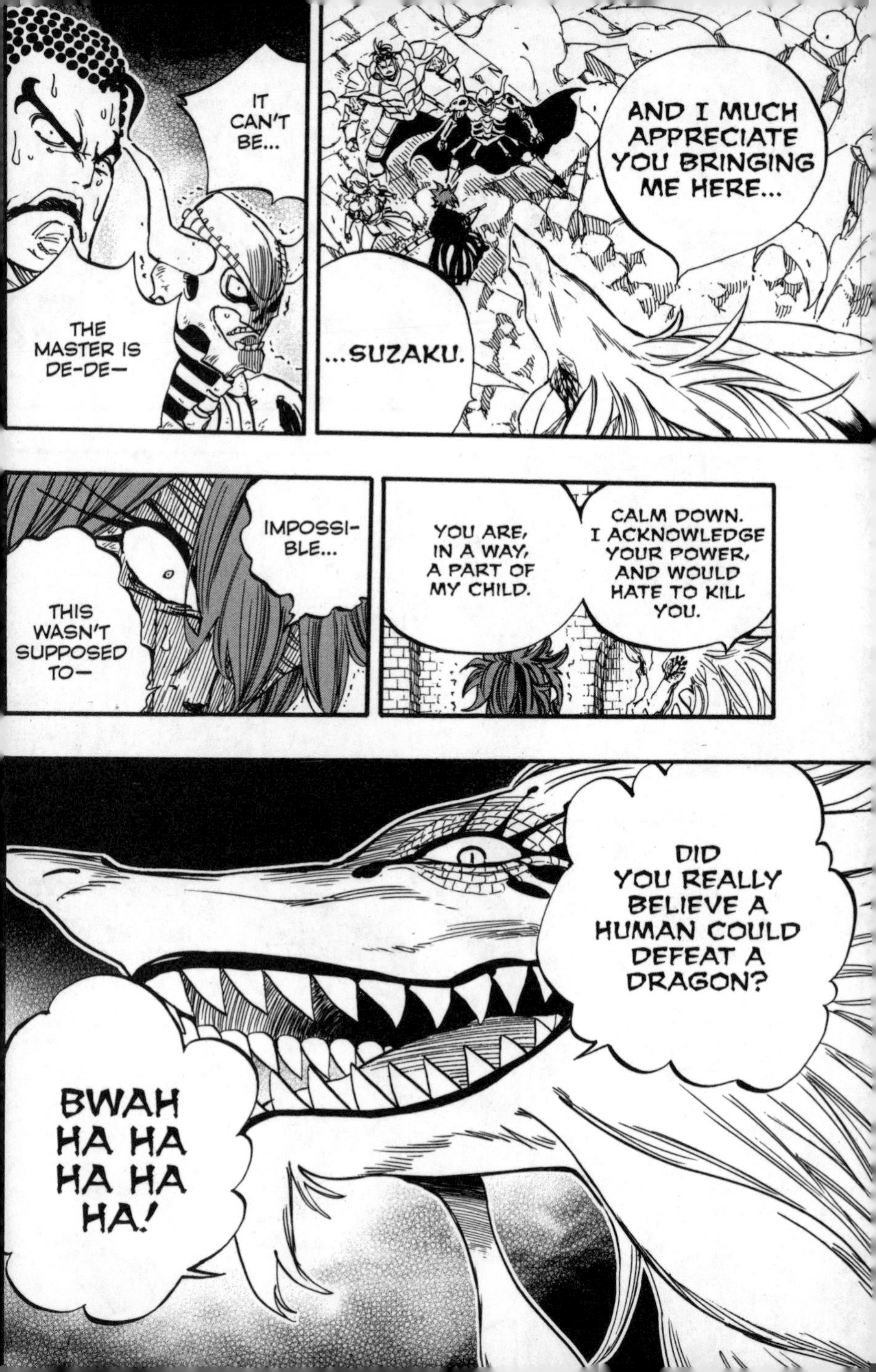
AND I MUCH APPRECIATE YOU BRINGING ME HERE...
...SUZAKU.
IT CAN'T BE...
THE MASTER IS DE-DE—
CALM DOWN. I ACKNOWLEDGE YOUR POWER, AND WOULD HATE TO KILL YOU.
YOU ARE, IN A WAY, A PART OF MY CHILD.
IMPOSSI-BLE...
THIS WASN'T SUPPOSED TO—
DID YOU REALLY BELIEVE A HUMAN COULD DEFEAT A DRAGON?
BWAH HA HA HA HA HA!

TO BE CONTINUED

ORIGINAL STORYBOARDS!!

VOL. 10 PP 10-11 (CH. 82)

REDISCOVER THE RED-HOT BATTLE BETWEEN DIABOLOS'S MASTER SWORDSMAN, THE SCARLET DRAGON SUZAKU, AND THE MOON DRAGON GOD SELENE! EVEN WHILE ABSORBING THE ENEMY'S BLOWS, SUZAKU PREPARES HIS COUNTERATTACK!!

ぐあっ
肩くらう
不可!?
はっ
ぐは
(8)
何発もくらう
踊れ人形
キイン
納刀
冥界輪廻!!!
(9)

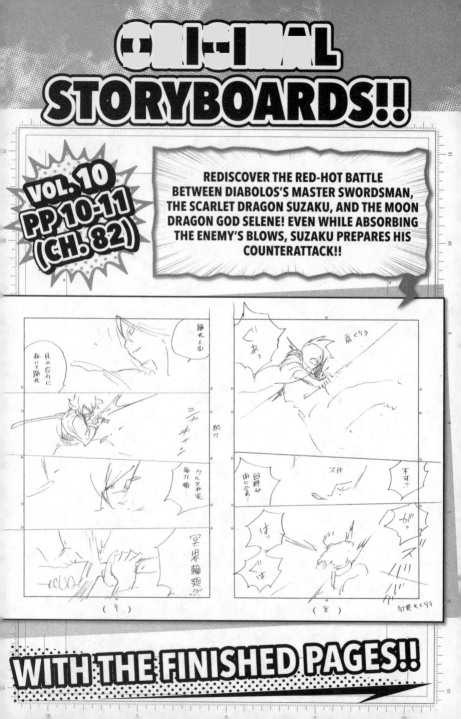

WITH THE FINISHED PAGES!!

10th VOLUME COMMEMORATIVE SPECIAL!

WE PRESENT

VOL. 10 PP 20-21 (CH. 82)

HERE, IT'S LUCY VERSUS THE MOONLIGHT BEAUTY, MIMI THE IMMOVABLE, AND HER HYPER-POWERED MUSCLES! LUCY CAN'T LEAN ON HER FRIENDS FROM FAIRY TAIL FOR THIS FIGHT. IT'S GOING TO BE LAST WOMAN STANDING!!

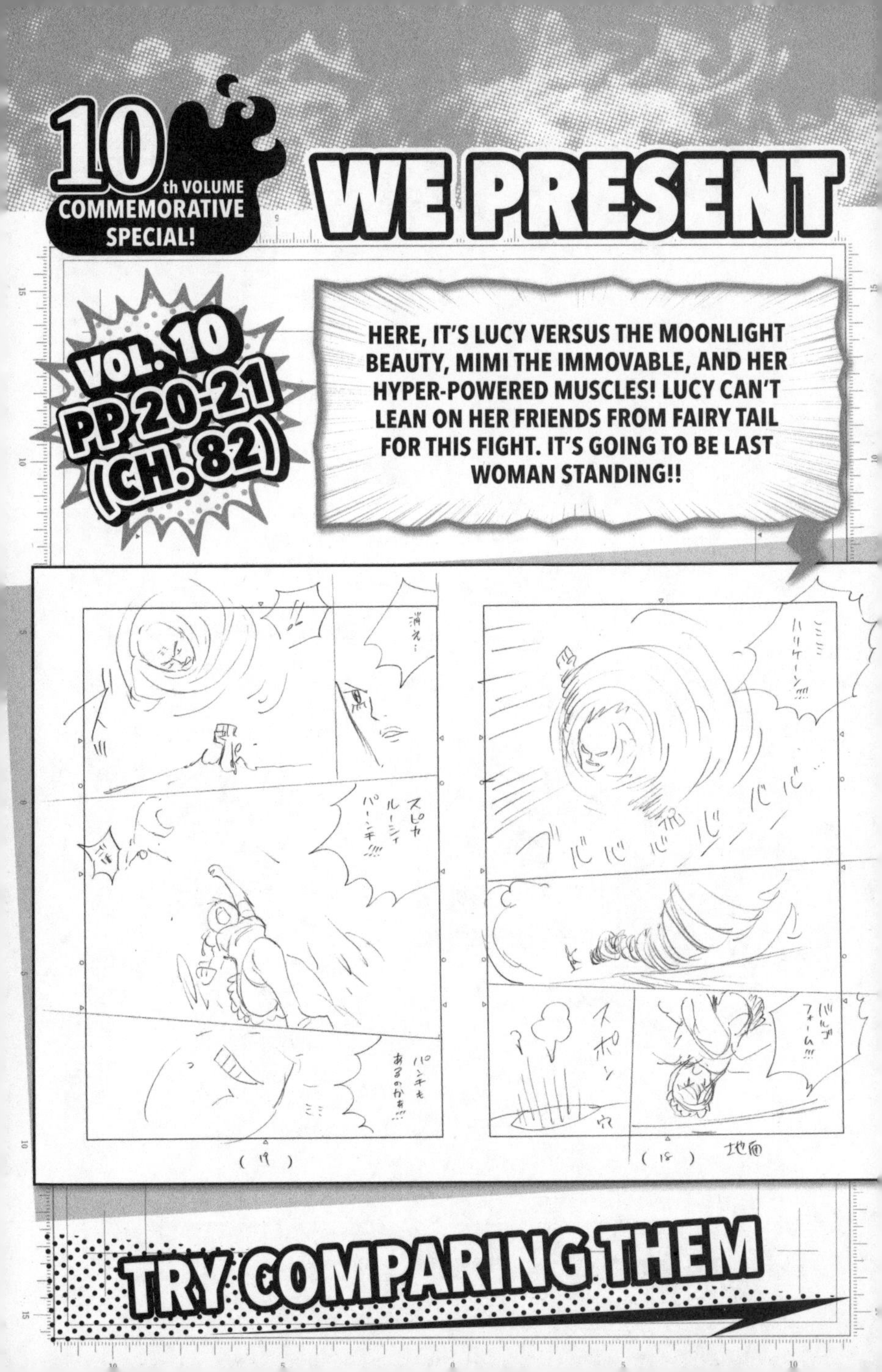

ミミミ ハリケーン!!!
ブバババババババ…
バルゴ フォーム!!!
スポン
穴
(18)
地面
消え…
スピカ ルーシィ パーンチ!!!
パンチもあるのかぁ!!!
(19)

TRY COMPARING THEM

DE ART RETURNS

(IWATE PREFECTURE KURO-NYAKO2)

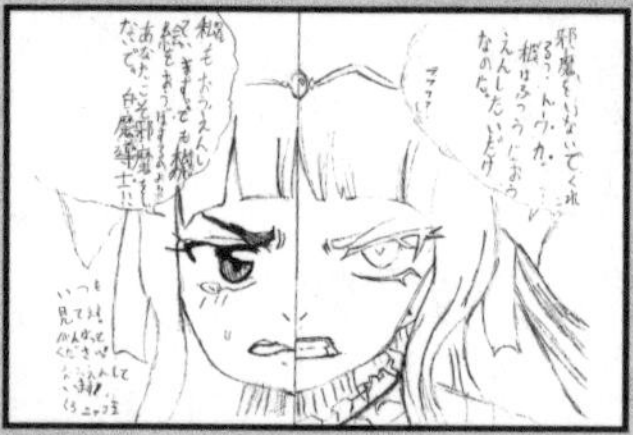

▲ I'M CHEERING FOR BOTH OF THEM, ACTUALLY (LAUGH). THANK YOU!

(CHIBA PREFECTURE KANAKO NAGAO)

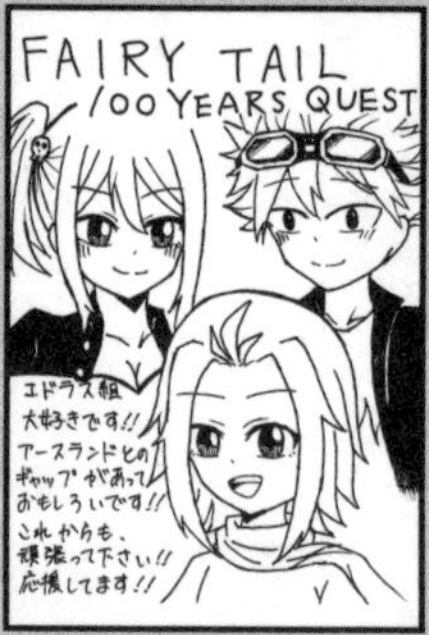
FAIRY TAIL
100 YEARS QUEST
エドラス組大好きです!!
アースランドとのギャップがあっておもしろいです!!
これからも、頑張って下さい!!
応援してます!!

▲ THE EDOLAS FAMILY. I HOPE THEY'LL BE HAPPY...

(CHIBA PREFECTURE KAZUMI SAITO)

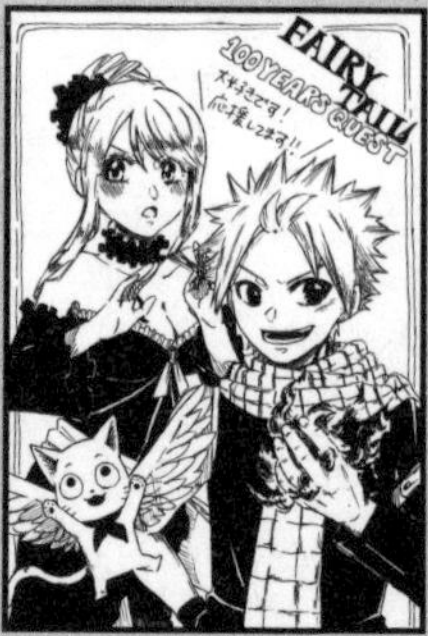
FAIRY TAIL
100 YEARS QUEST

▲ I LOVE THIS DETAILED DRAWING!

(KANAGAWA PREFECTURE RIN OHYA)

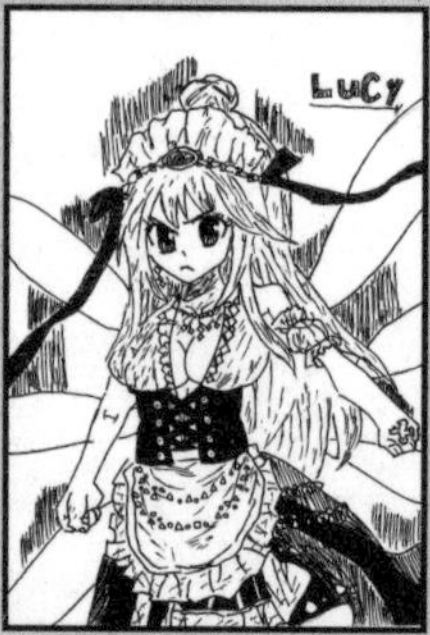
LUCY

▲ THANKS FOR THIS GORGEOUS DRESS! WONDER WHAT WILL SHOW UP NEXT!

(OKAYAMA PREFECTURE RINA SAKAMOTO)

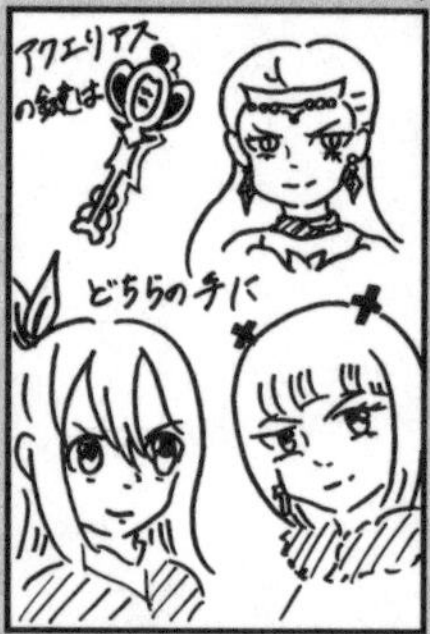
アクエリアスの鍵は
どちらの手に

▲ YOU CAN JUST FEEL THE RIVALRY!

FAIRY TAIL 100 YEARS QUEST GUILD

(TOKYO PREFECTURE YU KASATANI)

▲ THE LOOK! IT CUTS RIGHT THROUGH YOU! THANKS FOR THIS AWESOME TAKE.

(USA CRAIG CHOI)

エクシード
Craig Choi

▲ PERFECT REACTIONS FROM ALL THREE OF THEM!

(TOKYO PREFECTURE GORI-MUSCLE)

▲ A NIFTY SIDE-BY-SIDE. HOPE THEY DON'T START FIGHTING IN THIS STATE, THOUGH... (SWEAT)

(TOKUSHIMA PREFECTURE TOSHIHIRO MIKI)

100年クエスト
祝10巻
オメデトウ!

▲ THANKS SO MUCH!

(MIYAGI PREFECTURE OHYA MAH)

FAIRY TAIL
100 YEARS QUEST

▲ A SMIRKING SELENE. WONDER WHAT SHE'S PLANNING...

EDITOR'S NOTE: DRAWING SUBMISSIONS LIMITED TO JAPAN.

TRANSLATION NOTES

Rebirth, page 11

REBIRTH
IN THE
REALM OF
DEATH!!!

Each of Suzaku's techniques begins with the word *meikai;* literally meaning "the blind world," this is a traditional term for the "underworld" or the place spirits go after death. In the case of this technique, the second word (which actually occurs first in the translation because of the way the grammar works out) is *rinne,* which we rendered "rebirth." More literally, *rinne* corresponds to the Sanskrit word *samsara,* the Buddhist concept of the cycle of death and rebirth. The name of Suzaku's technique may be intended to allude to the fact that rebirth in many forms of Buddhism can encompass a wide variety of worlds – those with good karma might become gods, while those with bad karma can find themselves reincarnated in hell.

FAIRY TAIL 100 YEARS QUEST

FAIRY TAIL: 100 Years Quest 10 is a work of fiction. Names, characters, places, and incidents are the products of the author's imagination or are used fictitiously. Any resemblance to actual events, locales, or persons, living or dead, is entirely coincidental.

A Kodansha Comics Trade Paperback Original
FAIRY TAIL: 100 Years Quest 10 copyright © 2021 Hiro Mashima/Atsuo Ueda
English translation copyright © 2022 Hiro Mashima/Atsuo Ueda

Published in the United States by Kodansha Comics, an imprint of
Kodansha USA Publishing, LLC, New York.

Publication rights for this English edition arranged through
Kodansha Ltd., Tokyo.

First published in Japan in 2021 by Kodansha Ltd., Tokyo.

ISBN 978-1-64651-422-9

Original cover design by Hisao Ogawa (Blue in Green)

Printed in the United States of America.

www.kodansha.us

9 8 7 6 5 4 3 2 1
Translation: Kevin Steinbach
Lettering: Phil Christie
Editing: David Yoo
Kodansha Comics edition cover design by Phil Balsman

Publisher: Kiichiro Sugawara

Director of publishing services: Ben Applegate
Director of Publishing Operations: Dave Barrett
Associate director, publishing operations: Stephen Pakula
Publishing services managing editors: Madison Salters, Alanna Ruse
Production managers: Emi Lotto, Angela Zurlo